Climate Change and Energy Transition

This book series is a collaborative initiative between the *International Society for Energy Transition Studies (ISETS)* and *Springer*. It aims to provide a comprehensive collection of works addressing key topics on climate change and energy transition from a global perspective, with an emphasis on the interdisciplinary nature of this field. By exploring theoretical, empirical, and policy-relevant research, the series focuses on the critical challenges and opportunities in the climate-driven energy transition.

The objective of the series is to deliver diverse and accessible content to a broad audience, including policymakers, researchers, and the general public. Covering the latest advancements in the area, it seeks to offer a toolbox of vital information, a platform for knowledge sharing, and a forum for discussing pertinent issues related to the global energy transition.

Han Phoumin · Xunpeng Shi · Fukunari Kimura
Editors

Tackling the Energy Transition: Insights from ASEAN and Beyond

ERIA

ISETS
INTERNATIONAL SOCIETY FOR
ENERGY TRANSITION STUDIES

Springer

Editors
Han Phoumin
Economic Research Institute for ASEAN
and East Asia (ERIA)
Jakarta Pusat, Indonesia

Xunpeng Shi
Australia-China Relations Institute
University of Technology Sydney
Sydney, NSW, Australia

Fukunari Kimura
Institute of Developing Economies
Japan External Trade Organization
(IDE-JETRO)
Chiba, Japan

ISSN 2731-9903 ISSN 2731-9911 (electronic)
Climate Change and Energy Transition
ISBN 978-981-96-6018-6 ISBN 978-981-96-6019-3 (eBook)
https://doi.org/10.1007/978-981-96-6019-3

This Springer imprint is published by the registered company Springer Nature Singapore Pte Ltd.
The registered company address is: 152 Beach Road, #21-01/04 Gateway East, Singapore 189721, Singapore

Preface

This volume is part of the *Springer-International Society for Energy Transition Studies* (ISETS) collaborative *book series* on "Climate Change and Energy Transition". This series addresses critical topics on climate change and energy transition from a global perspective, with a particular emphasis on the interdisciplinary nature of these issues. By exploring theoretical, empirical and policy-relevant research, it highlights key challenges and opportunities presented by the climate-driven energy transition.

The objective of the series is to deliver diverse and accessible content to a broad audience, including policymakers, researchers and the general public. Covering the latest advancements in the area, it aims to offer a toolbox of vital information, a platform for knowledge sharing and a forum for discussing relevant issues related to the global energy transition.

This book, made possible through the generous funding and support of the *Economic Research Institute for ASEAN and East Asia (ERIA)*, stands as a testament to ERIA's leadership and vision in the ASEAN region's energy transition. ERIA has played a critical role by providing strategic direction and financial backing, ensuring the development of actionable, policy-driven recommendations that address the unique challenges faced by East Asian countries in their pursuit of carbon neutrality.

In collaboration with ISETS, ERIA has spearheaded research efforts aimed at offering insights into key areas such as energy security, accessibility, affordability and environmental sustainability. While ISETS has facilitated the research process, the strategic guidance and intellectual leadership from ERIA have shaped the book's content and direction. ERIA's long history of crafting regional decarbonisation roadmaps and energy policies has provided the foundation for the research presented here, ensuring its relevance and impact for key stakeholders across the region.

This book builds upon ERIA's three-stage framework for guiding countries through the decarbonisation process, addressing early-stage technologies such as coal-to-gas switching, mid-term solutions like co-combustion with biomass, and advanced strategies including carbon capture, utilisation and storage (CCUS), blue hydrogen and ammonia. The phased approach allows each country to adopt the most suitable technologies according to its energy profile and stage of development, ensuring a tailored path towards carbon neutrality.

A critical aspect of this book is the emphasis on securing financing for clean energy technologies, a challenge ERIA has long recognised. As nations transition away from fossil fuels, ERIA has been at the forefront of advocating energy finance reform and the development of de-risking mechanisms to attract investment in emerging technologies such as hydrogen and ammonia. These efforts are essential to making these technologies scalable and financially viable, particularly for countries with limited resources.

The 11 policy-driven research studies contained in this volume represent the combined expertise of ERIA and ISETS, providing strategic pathways and actionable recommendations for overcoming the technical, financial and policy barriers to decarbonisation in East Asia. While the findings are region-specific, they contribute to the broader global discourse on energy transition, offering frameworks and lessons that can be adapted by other regions striving for a sustainable, low-carbon future.

We hope that this book will serve as a valuable resource for policymakers, industry leaders, researchers and the general public, supporting efforts to advance the region's carbon neutrality while contributing to the global fight against climate change. By showcasing ERIA's leadership and commitment, this book highlights the critical steps needed to secure a more resilient, equitable and sustainable energy future for East Asia and beyond.

Jakarta Pusat, Indonesia
Sydney, Australia
Chiba, Japan
April 2025

Han Phoumin
Xunpeng Shi
Fukunari Kimura

Acknowledgements

This book is the product of a working group comprising selected research experts carrying out a study under the *Economic Research Institute for ASEAN and East Asia's (ERIA's)* energy research on low-carbon emission transitions in Asia. Through close research collaboration with the *International Society for Energy Transition Studies (ISETS)*, the research products feed into the *Springer-ISETS book series* on "Climate Change and Energy Transition", a collaborative initiative between *ISETS* and *Springer*. The outstanding researchers involved in this specific study explore ways in which countries' practices and experiences, together with low-carbon technologies, can be shared among stakeholders to ensure that countries seek appropriate and differentiated pathways to carbon neutrality, acknowledging each country's particular socio-economic and political characteristics.

We thank everyone involved for their support, including the many interviewees who provided country-specific data and other information. Special thanks to *Professor Tetsuya Watanabe*, President of *ERIA* and *Professor Xunpeng Shi*, President of *ISETS*, for facilitating collaboration between the two institutions and ensuring that this project addresses contemporary energy issues in Asia. We are also grateful to Emily Zhang of Springer Nature for managing the publishing process on the publisher's side.

Contents

Editors and Contributors

About the Editors

Dr. Han Phoumin is a senior energy economist at the Economic Research Institute for ASEAN and East Asia (ERIA) with over 20 years of experience in energy policy, market integration and sustainable development in ASEAN and East Asia. His research focuses on renewable energy, energy efficiency, carbon capture and financing energy transition technologies, contributing to high-level policy discussions at the East Asia Energy Ministerial Meeting and the East Asia Energy Forum.

Prof. Xunpeng (Roc) Shi is a distinguished expert in energy economics, sustainable development and international energy policy. He is a Research Principal and Professor at the Australia-China Relations Institute, University of Technology Sydney, and President of the International Society for Energy Transition Studies (ISETS), leading global discussions on energy transitions and sustainable resource management. Prof. Shi has authored influential research on critical minerals, clean energy policies and economic integration in the Asia-Pacific. He has also contributed to international policy dialogues through organisations such as the United Nations and the APEC Sustainable Energy Center, shaping discussions on sustainable resource governance and energy security.

Prof. Fukunari Kimura is a leading economist specialising in international production networks and economic integration in East Asia. He is the President of the Institute of Developing Economies, Japan External Trade Organization (IDE-JETRO), a Senior Research Fellow at the Economic Research Institute for ASEAN and East Asia (ERIA) and a Professor in the Faculty of Economics, Keio University.

List of Contributors

Noor Raida Abd Rahman Universiti Tenaga Nasional, Kajang, Malaysia

Nurfarhana Alyssa Ahmad Affandi Solar Energy Research Institute (SERI), Universiti Kebangsaan Malaysia (UKM), Bangi, Malaysia

Jun Arima Economic Research Institute for ASEAN and East Asia (ERIA), Jakarta Pusat, Indonesia

Alexander Bard Department of Mechanical and Aerospace Engineering, The Ohio State University, Columbus, OH, USA

Hoy-Yen Chan Invite Green Consultancy, Penang, Malaysia

Youngho Chang Singapore University of Social Sciences, Singapore, Singapore

Lam Truong Phuong Do Fulbright School of Public Policy and Management, Fulbright University Vietnam, Ho Chi Minh City, Vietnam;
Monash University, Melbourne, Australia

Felix Wisnu Handoyo Research Center for Behavioral and Circular Economics, National Research and Innovation Agency (BRIN), Jakarta, Indonesia

Mirratul Mukminah Junedi Solar Energy Research Institute (SERI), Universiti Kebangsaan Malaysia (UKM), Bangi, Malaysia

Fukunari Kimura Institute of Developing Economies, Japan External Trade Organization (IDE-JETRO), Chiba, Japan

Geoffrey Musyoki Kitetu Faculty of Economics and Business Management, National University of Laos, Vientiane, Laos;
Division of International and Area Studies, Pukyong National University, Busan, South Korea

Phouphet Kyophilavong Faculty of Economics and Business Management, National University of Laos, Vientiane, Laos

Thai-Ha Le VinUniversity & VinFuture Foundation, Hanoi, Vietnam

Norasikin Ahmad Ludin Solar Energy Research Institute (SERI), Universiti Kebangsaan Malaysia (UKM), Bangi, Malaysia

Tirthankar Mandal WRI India, New Delhi, India

Maslinawati Mohamad Universiti Teknologi MARA, Puncak Alam, Malaysia

Siti Indati Mustapa Universiti Tenaga Nasional, Kajang, Malaysia

Han Phoumin Economic Research Institute for ASEAN and East Asia (ERIA), Jakarta Pusat, Indonesia

Alloysius Joko Purwanto Economic Research Institute for ASEAN and East Asia (ERIA), Jakarta Pusat, Indonesia

Maxensius Tri Sambodo Research Center for Behavioral and Circular Economics, National Research and Innovation Agency (BRIN), Jakarta, Indonesia

Ramteen Sioshansi Department of Engineering and Public Policy, Carnegie Mellon University, Pittsburgh, PA, USA;
Carnegie Mellon Electricity Industry Center, Carnegie Mellon University, Pittsburgh, PA, USA;
Department of Electrical and Computer Engineering, Carnegie Mellon University, Pittsburgh, PA, USA;
Wilton E. Scott Institute for Energy Innovation, Carnegie Mellon University, Pittsburgh, PA, USA;
Department of Integrated Systems Engineering, The Ohio State University, Columbus, OH, USA

Sangeeta V. Sharma SIES, Indian Institute of Environment Management (SIES IIEM), Navi Mumbai, India

Vinod K. Sharma Indira Gandhi Institute of Development Research (IGIDR), Mumbai, India

Xunpeng Shi University of Technology Sydney, Sydney, NSW, Australia

Phongsili Soukchalern Faculty of Economics and Business Management, National University of Laos, Vientiane, Laos

Kei Sudo Economic Research Institute for ASEAN and East Asia (ERIA), Jakarta Pusat, Indonesia

Beni Suryadi ASEAN Centre for Energy (ACE), Jakarta, Indonesia

Tetsuya Watanabe Economic Research Institute for ASEAN and East Asia (ERIA), Jakarta Pusat, Indonesia

Tackling the Energy Transition in ASEAN and Beyond

Han Phoumin, Xunpeng Shi, and Fukunari Kimura

Abstract This chapter introduces the urgent global imperative of achieving a just energy transition, particularly in the ASEAN region. The authors highlight the complexity of this transition in the region, shaped by diverse national circumstances, socio-economic factors, and geopolitical tensions. Special attention is given to ensuring that the transition is equitable and inclusive, balancing decarbonisation with energy security and economic development. The chapter also outlines the book's structure, which spans regional policies, technological innovations, and national case studies to offer comprehensive insights into managing energy transitions effectively.

Keywords Energy transition · ASEAN · Decarbonisation

1 Background, Significance and Complexity of the Just Energy Transition

The global community stands at a critical juncture in addressing the escalating challenges posed by climate change. The Intergovernmental Panel on Climate Change (IPCC) has emphasised the urgent need for significant reductions in greenhouse gas (GHG) emissions to prevent global temperatures from rising more than 1.5 °C above pre-industrial levels (IPCC 2018). Failing to limit this rise would lead to catastrophic environmental, social and economic consequences, affecting millions

H. Phoumin
Economic Research Institute for ASEAN and East Asia (ERIA), Jakarta Pusat, Indonesia
e-mail: han.phoumin@eria.org

X. Shi (✉)
University of Technology Sydney, Sydney, NSW, Australia
e-mail: Xunpeng.shi@uts.edu.au

F. Kimura
Institute of Developing Economies, Japan External Trade Organization (IDE-JETRO), Chiba, Japan
e-mail: vzf02302@nifty.ne.jp

H. Phoumin et al. (eds.), *Tackling the Energy Transition: Insights from ASEAN and Beyond*, Climate Change and Energy Transition,
https://doi.org/10.1007/978-981-96-6019-3_1

of lives worldwide. However, global temperatures temporarily surpassed the critical 1.5 °C threshold above pre-industrial levels in 2024, emphasising the urgent need for intensified global action to limit warming and avert severe climate consequences (Borenstein 2025). Energy systems lie at the heart of this challenge, accounting for approximately 73% of global GHG emissions (IEA 2021). As such, transitioning from fossil fuels to low-carbon and renewable energy (RE) sources is not merely an option—it is an imperative for sustainable development.

The Paris Agreement (2015), adopted by 196 parties, embodies this global commitment to decarbonisation, signalling the necessity for transformative changes in energy production and consumption. Nowhere is this transformation more crucial than in East Asia, particularly within the Association of Southeast Asian Nations (ASEAN). This region is experiencing rapid economic growth, urbanisation and industrialisation, leading to surging energy demands. If current policies persist, ASEAN's energy demand could grow to 2.6 times the 2022 level by 2050, exacerbating its heavy reliance on fossil fuels like coal and natural gas (ACE 2024). This trajectory presents both significant challenges and opportunities for the region's path to decarbonisation.

Energy transition in East Asia is a complex, multi-dimensional process, shaped by technological advancements, policy development, socio-economic factors and geopolitical realities (Li et al. 2020). Each country within the region exhibits unique energy profiles, resource endowments and socio-political contexts, necessitating tailored approaches. The inherent diversity across the region makes the transition towards RE more intricate, as policies need to cater to each nation's energy needs, economic conditions and political structures. Collaborative regional efforts, such as cross-border energy trade and shared technological innovations, will play an essential role in navigating these complexities effectively.

The urgency of transitioning to RE is compounded by the need for a **just energy transition**—one that is equitable and inclusive. The "just transition" principle emphasises the importance of ensuring that the shift towards a cleaner energy future does not disproportionately affect vulnerable communities, workers in carbon-intensive industries, or regions reliant on fossil fuels for economic stability (Shen et al. 2024). For instance, **Indonesia**, the world's largest exporter of coal, must balance reducing its coal dependency while preserving employment for millions of workers in the sector. Conversely, countries like **Vietnam** have seen job creation and rural development benefits from the rapid deployment of **solar** and **wind energy**, though they face challenges related to grid integration.

Globally, the energy transition is not just about replacing coal and oil with solar and wind; it involves **deep structural changes** across entire economies, reshaping industries, labour markets and international relations. It is also a **geopolitical transformation**. Traditionally, energy geopolitics revolved around oil and gas, with countries like **Russia** and **Saudi Arabia** holding significant influence over global energy prices. However, the rise of **RE technologies**, especially in **electric vehicles (EVs)** and **battery storage**, is shifting this dynamic. China, for instance, has emerged as a leader in EV manufacturing and RE technologies, positioning itself as a dominant player in the global energy transition. This new energy landscape is creating **geopolitical tensions** and trade disputes, particularly with the **European Union (EU)** and the **United States**, over issues such as subsidies and market competitiveness.

The transition also extends to international energy trade, where renewables-rich countries, such as **Australia**, are positioning themselves as future exporters of **green hydrogen** to markets like Japan and South Korea. Traditional energy exporters are adjusting their strategies by investing in RE projects to remain relevant in a decarbonising world.

To meet the goals set by global climate agreements and to help reduce GHG emissions, **carbon pricing mechanisms** like the **European Union's Emissions Trading System (ETS)** are pivotal. In ASEAN, initiatives like the **Just Energy Transition Partnership (JETP)** are mobilising financial resources to support energy transitions in countries like **Indonesia** and **Vietnam**, ensuring that decarbonisation efforts are both effective and inclusive (IISD 2022).

The energy transition therefore represents a defining challenge of our time, especially for regions like ASEAN, where the balance between economic growth, energy security and sustainability is particularly precarious. The transition is not just a technological shift but a **holistic transformation** that touches on every aspect of society—from **job creation** and **industrial change** to **international diplomacy** and **climate justice** (UN ESCAP 2023). **ASEAN** countries, along with other emerging economies, must navigate these intertwined challenges while ensuring that the benefits of the transition are shared equitably. This book, ***Tackling the Energy Transition: Insights from ASEAN and Beyond***, delves into the intricacies of the energy transition in East Asia, offering practical strategies, policy recommendations, and insights from various regional and global perspectives to aid in the journey towards a sustainable and just future.

2 Structure of the Book

This book is divided into three sections, each offering a distinct perspective on the complex process of energy transition. The structure has been designed to guide the reader from a regional understanding of energy transition strategies to technological innovations and sectoral applications, concluding with in-depth national case studies. The overarching goal is to explore the multifaceted nature of the energy transition in ASEAN and neighbouring regions, providing insights into how global, regional and national dynamics shape the trajectory of this process.

The first part, *Regional Pathways and Policy Perspectives*, sets the foundation by examining strategies, policies and financial mechanisms at the regional level. It focuses on how ASEAN is navigating its energy transition in the context of its unique political, economic and environmental challenges. The authors in this section highlight that achieving carbon neutrality in ASEAN requires not just one approach but a range of pathways and technologies. Watanabe and colleagues, in the second chapter, emphasise the importance of promoting all clean technology options, including hydrogen, ammonia fuels, carbon capture and storage (CCUS) and renewables, to ensure energy security while reducing emissions and decarbonising ASEAN's diverse energy systems.

The regional perspective is further expanded in the third chapter, by Youngho Chang, who explores the role of cross-border power trade and integrated electricity markets in achieving net zero emissions by 2050. This chapter demonstrates that regional collaboration in power trade can lead to significant reductions in both carbon emissions and system costs. By integrating solar PV and hydropower across borders, ASEAN countries can take critical steps towards reducing their dependency on fossil fuels. This analysis reinforces the argument made in the second chapter, showing that regional cooperation is essential for optimising resources and achieving emissions targets.

Effective policy and regulatory frameworks are critical for facilitating the energy transition, but they often face significant barriers. In the fourth chapter, Chan, Suryadi and Phoumin delve into the challenges of implementing carbon pricing instruments (CPIs) in ASEAN, offering a comparative analysis of carbon taxes and emissions trading systems. The authors argue that while CPIs are strong incentives for decarbonisation, their success hinges on overcoming political feasibility issues and public misunderstandings. This chapter underscores the need for robust revenue recycling strategies and effective communication to ensure that CPIs are both effective and equitable. It connects well with the earlier discussions on regional cooperation and the importance of policy frameworks, as it highlights how regulatory measures can guide investments and reshape business landscapes in ASEAN.

In the fifth chapter, Tirthankar Mandal turns the focus to the role of public financing mechanisms in supporting RE deployment. The chapter underscores the importance of innovative financing models and policy reforms to address the risks associated with energy investments, especially in regions where the costs of RE deployment are higher than in developed economies. Public finance is presented as a crucial tool for de-risking RE investments, thus enabling ASEAN countries to overcome financial barriers to decarbonisation. This final chapter in the section ties the discussion back to the broader regional perspective, reinforcing the message that successful energy transition requires not just technological and regulatory solutions but also financial support mechanisms.

The second part, *Technological Innovations and Sectoral Strategies*, focuses on the technological advancements and sector-specific strategies that drive decarbonisation efforts in ASEAN. Integrating RE into existing power grids presents significant technical challenges, particularly due to the intermittent nature of renewable sources like solar and wind. Bard and Sioshansi, in the sixth chapter, compare the effectiveness of two solar technologies—concentrating solar power (CSP) with thermal energy storage (TES) and photovoltaic (PV) solar with battery energy storage (BES)—in meeting peak energy demand. Their findings reveal that PV with BES is more cost-effective and offers superior peaking capabilities than CSP with TES. The authors suggest that investing in modular and flexible technologies, like PV with BES, is key to enhancing grid reliability under carbon constraints. This chapter is crucial for understanding how technological innovations are shaping the future of energy systems in ASEAN.

In the seventh chapter, Ludin and colleagues tackle the growing importance of electric vehicles (EVs) and their associated charging technologies in Malaysia. This chapter provides a detailed assessment of the environmental performance of EV charging infrastructure, highlighting how integrating RE into EV charging systems can significantly reduce emissions. The authors argue that a clean energy mix is essential for maximising the environmental benefits of EV adoption. The chapter connects with the broader theme of technological innovation by emphasising the need for infrastructure development in the transport sector, particularly as ASEAN countries seek to decarbonise their economies.

Chapter "The Energy Transition in Smart Cities: Practical Insights into Environmental Performance Framework" explores the concept of smart cities and their role in the energy transition. Rahman and colleagues propose a framework for evaluating the environmental performance of firms operating within smart cities in Malaysia. The study reveals that environmental sustainability practices are still underdeveloped among many firms, and the authors call for greater collaboration between government bodies and businesses to facilitate a more effective contribution to the energy transition. This chapter broadens the scope of the section by introducing the idea that smart city initiatives can play a pivotal role in shaping energy transition efforts, particularly in urban environments.

The third part, *National Case Studies and Energy Transitions*, shifts the focus from regional strategies and sectoral approaches to individual country experiences. These national case studies provide a deeper understanding of the unique challenges, strategies and lessons learned in different countries as they navigate their energy transitions.

In chapter "The Energy Transition in Indonesia: The Impact on Women Who Switch to Using Clean Energy for Cooking", Sambodo, Handoyo and Phoumin focus on Indonesia's transition from kerosene to liquefied petroleum gas (LPG) for cooking. This chapter highlights the social and health impacts of the transition, particularly for women and children, who are disproportionately affected by air pollution from traditional cooking fuels. The authors emphasise the importance of inclusive governance and human-centred policies to ensure that the clean energy transition improves living standards while addressing the needs of vulnerable populations.

The tenth chapter shifts the focus to Laos, where Kyophilavong and colleagues analyse the impact of carbon taxation on economic growth, welfare and CO_2 emissions. The chapter demonstrates that while carbon taxes are effective in reducing emissions, they can also have adverse economic effects, particularly for low-income communities. The authors advocate revenue recycling strategies that can mitigate these impacts and ensure that the transition is both just and equitable. This chapter ties back to the broader theme of policy frameworks and regulatory mechanisms discussed in earlier sections, emphasising the need for careful policy design in advancing the energy transition.

In chapter "Energy Transition in Vietnam: Paving the Way for Sustainable Development", Le and Do examine Vietnam's rapid shift from coal to RE sources, particularly solar and wind. Vietnam's ambitious RE targets, coupled with supportive policies such as feed-in tariffs, have led to a significant increase in solar and wind capacity. The authors use dynamic principal component analysis to measure progress, revealing both the successes and challenges of Vietnam's energy transition. This chapter emphasises the role of human capital, public awareness and regulatory frameworks in shaping the transition to cleaner energy sources, thus providing a valuable case study for other countries in the region.

The final chapter, by Sharma and Sharma, provides an analysis of India's progress towards a clean and just energy transition. The world's fourth largest RE producer, India faces numerous challenges in balancing economic growth with energy justice. The authors highlight that while India has made significant progress in increasing its share of RE, the transition must address the needs of communities and workers impacted by the decline of traditional fossil fuel industries. This chapter concludes the book by reinforcing the message that achieving a clean energy transition requires not only technological and policy innovations but also a commitment to social equity and economic justice.

The progression of the chapters from broad regional pathways through technological innovations and sectoral strategies, to national case studies, allows the reader to build a comprehensive understanding of the energy transition. This structure emphasises the interconnectedness of regional cooperation, technological advancements and national experiences in shaping the trajectory of energy transitions in ASEAN and neighbouring regions.

3 A Synthesis of Insights and Takeaways

This book offers a comprehensive exploration of the complexities surrounding energy transitions in ASEAN and neighbouring regions. Key insights, grounded in technological, socio-economic and geopolitical dimensions, provide valuable guidance for policymakers, industry leaders and other stakeholders. In this section the key implications and takeaways are listed, and explicit references to the chapters are made.

3.1 A Flexible, Multi-Pathway Approach is Essential to Carbon Neutrality

Achieving carbon neutrality across ASEAN requires a flexible approach, incorporating diverse strategies suited to the specific circumstances of each country. As highlighted in chapter "Navigating Energy Complexities to Reach Carbon Neutrality in ASEAN" by Han Phoumin and colleagues, ASEAN nations face varying degrees of fossil fuel dependency, with countries like Indonesia and the Philippines still reliant on coal and gas, while Vietnam and Laos are better positioned to leverage solar and hydropower. The authors emphasise that decarbonisation efforts must include a range of clean technologies such as hydrogen, CCUS and renewables, ensuring energy security and affordability for all.

Chapter "Net Zero Transition and the Power Sector in ASEAN: Perspectives on an Integrated Electricity Market" further emphasises the importance of regional cooperation in achieving carbon neutrality. Chang's analysis of cross-border power trade in ASEAN shows how regional collaboration can optimise renewable resources, lower system costs and reduce emissions. Laos, for example, can export its abundant hydropower to countries like Thailand and Vietnam, highlighting how interconnected grids can support decarbonisation across the region. These findings illustrate that achieving carbon neutrality in ASEAN requires not just national strategies but also regional coordination and shared infrastructure investments.

3.2 Public Financing Is Critical for Scaling Renewable Energy Deployment

Chapter "Renewable Energy and Public Financing in the Asian Region: Some Reflections from Recent Trends" by Mandal underscores the crucial role of public financing in overcoming the high upfront costs and risks associated with RE projects. In countries like Cambodia and Indonesia, where financial markets are underdeveloped, public financing mechanisms such as green bonds and public-private partnerships (PPPs) are essential for mobilising private investments and scaling RE deployment. Without public financing to de-risk these projects, private investors are unlikely to commit to long-term clean energy infrastructure investments.

The importance of public finance in driving RE deployment is also applicable to other developing regions, such as Africa and Latin America, where financial barriers persist. Governments and international financial institutions must create an environment conducive to private sector investment, ensuring that the transition to RE can proceed at the scale needed to meet global climate goals.

3.3 Technological Innovations in Solar PV and Energy Storage Drive Decarbonisation

Technological advancements, particularly in solar photovoltaic (PV) systems and battery energy storage (BES), are critical to ASEAN's energy transition. In Chapter "Comparing Concentrating Solar Power and Photovoltaic Solar Plants as Extended-Duration Peaking Resources in Electricity Systems", Bard and Sioshansi compare concentrating solar power (CSP) with PV coupled with BES, demonstrating that the latter offers a more cost-effective solution for managing peak electricity demand and ensuring grid reliability. Their findings show that PV with BES is more scalable and adaptable than CSP, particularly in countries with abundant solar resources like Vietnam, Thailand and the Philippines.

Chapter "Energy Transition in Vietnam: Paving the Way for Sustainable Development", by Le and Do, reinforces the significance of these technologies by analysing Vietnam's rapid adoption of solar and wind energy. The success of Vietnam's RE sector, driven by strong policy frameworks such as feed-in tariffs, illustrates how well-designed incentives can accelerate RE deployment. Policymakers in ASEAN and beyond must prioritise long-term investments in solar PV and energy storage technologies to support the energy transition, ensuring that infrastructure investments are aligned with decarbonisation goals.

3.4 *Cross-Border Power Trading Enhances Energy Security and Reduces Emissions*

Cross-border electricity trade is a vital strategy for optimising RE resources and reducing emissions across ASEAN. Chapter "Net Zero Transition and the Power Sector in ASEAN: Perspectives on an Integrated Electricity Market", by Chang, highlights how regional cooperation, particularly through an integrated electricity market, can reduce system costs and enhance energy security. Laos, with its rich hydropower resources, can play a central role in supplying RE to neighbouring countries like Thailand, Cambodia and Vietnam, and thus help to decarbonise the entire region.

This model of cross-border energy trade has broader implications for other regions, such as Africa and Central Asia, where disparities in energy resources can be addressed through shared infrastructure. The takeaway is clear: regional electricity markets can help balance supply and demand, stabilise grids and reduce emissions, making them an essential part of the global energy transition.

3.5 *Decarbonising the Transport Sector Requires Infrastructure Investments and Policy Support*

Chapter "Comparative Environmental Evaluation of Electric Vehicle Charging Technologies, Infrastructure and Charging Stations in Malaysia: Towards a Sustainable Energy Transition", by Ludin and colleagues, examines the challenges and opportunities for decarbonising ASEAN's transport sector through electric vehicles (EVs). Malaysia's efforts to integrate RE into EV charging infrastructure show a promising pathway for reducing transport emissions, but significant barriers remain. The high cost of EV ownership, insufficient public charging infrastructure and grid limitations must be addressed to ensure the success of EV adoption strategies.

Policymakers must prioritise investments in EV infrastructure and introduce supportive policies, such as tax incentives and subsidies, to accelerate EV uptake. For the international community, this is a critical area for engagement. Regions like Latin America and Africa, where transportation remains a major source of emissions, can benefit from the lessons learned in ASEAN, especially regarding the integration of RE into charging infrastructure.

3.6 Smart Cities and Energy Efficiency Are Critical for Sustainable Urban Growth

As urbanisation accelerates across ASEAN, smart city initiatives offer a promising solution for reducing energy consumption and emissions in urban areas. Chapter "The Energy Transition in Smart Cities: Practical Insights into Environmental Performance Framework", by Rahman and colleagues, emphasises the importance of incorporating energy-efficient technologies into urban planning, such as smart grids, automated building systems, and data-driven urban management. These innovations are essential for cities like Kuala Lumpur and Jakarta, which are experiencing rapid population growth and rising energy demands.

The findings show that while smart city initiatives are progressing, businesses operating within these cities still lag in environmental performance. Policymakers must strengthen regulatory frameworks to incentivise energy efficiency and ensure that smart city projects contribute to broader decarbonisation goals. These insights are particularly relevant for other regions experiencing rapid urbanisation, such as Africa and South Asia.

3.7 Ensuring just Transitions: Addressing the Social Dimensions of Energy Transitions

Chapters "The Energy Transition in Indonesia: The Impact on Women Who Switch to Using Clean Energy for Cooking" and "The Potential Economic Impacts on the Lao PDR of CO_2Emission Reductions Achieved through the Imposition of a Carbon Tax" highlight the importance of ensuring that energy transitions are socially equitable, particularly for vulnerable populations. Chapter "The Energy Transition in Indonesia: The Impact on Women Who Switch to Using Clean Energy for Cooking" by Sambodo and colleagues examines Indonesia's transition from kerosene to LPG for cooking and finds that without proper governance, the health benefits of cleaner energy sources may not be realised, particularly for women and children who are disproportionately affected by air pollution.

In Chapter "The Potential Economic Impacts on the Lao PDR of CO_2Emission Reductions Achieved through the Imposition of a Carbon Tax", Kyophilavong and colleagues analyse the effects of carbon taxation in Laos, showing that while carbon taxes can effectively reduce emissions, they may negatively impact economic growth and welfare. To mitigate these impacts, policymakers must implement revenue recycling strategies and provide support to vulnerable communities. The broader lesson is that energy transitions must be just, ensuring that the benefits of clean energy are distributed equitably and that no community is left behind.

3.8 Public–Private Partnerships Can Bridge the Financing Gap for Renewable Energy Projects

As highlighted in Chapter "Renewable Energy and Public Financing in the Asian Region: Some Reflections from Recent Trends", PPPs are crucial for bridging the financing gap in RE projects. In countries like Cambodia and Indonesia, where access to capital remains a significant barrier, PPPs can unlock the necessary funding for clean energy infrastructure. By leveraging public funds to attract private investments, governments can reduce the risks associated with RE projects and accelerate their deployment.

The international community, particularly multilateral development banks, must support the expansion of PPPs to scale RE projects. Public financing must create the conditions for private sector engagement, ensuring that the transition to clean energy is both financially sustainable and inclusive.

4 Conclusion and Future Directions

Navigating the complexities of the energy transition in ASEAN and East Asia in general requires a multifaceted and inclusive approach, acknowledging the diverse economic, technological, and social landscapes of each country. This book offers a comprehensive examination of how regional cooperation, technological innovation and tailored national strategies can drive decarbonisation efforts. By embracing multiple pathways, as highlighted throughout the chapters, policymakers can make informed decisions that balance energy security, economic growth and environmental sustainability.

Looking forward, there are several critical areas that demand further exploration. These include in-depth studies on the deployment of emerging technologies such as carbon capture, CCUS, hydrogen fuels and advanced battery storage systems. Regional studies, particularly on subnational dynamics within countries, can provide further insight into local challenges and opportunities.

We encourage continued collaboration and engagement with stakeholders across industries, governments and civil society to implement the strategies discussed in this book. The energy transition is not only a technical challenge but a societal transformation. Engaging with the diverse perspectives presented in the following chapters will foster more inclusive, resilient and sustainable energy futures for ASEAN and beyond.

References

ACE (ASEAN Centre for Energy) (2024) 8th ASEAN Energy Outlook. https://aseanenergy.org/publications/the-8th-asean-energy-outlook/

Borenstein S (2025) Earth breaks yearly heat record and lurches past dangerous warming threshold. AP News, 10 January. Available at https://apnews.com/article/climate-change-warming-hot-record-2024-disasters-12f899f071fcdbd051ad49a872611e92. Accessed 17 Jan 2025

IEA (2021) Net Zero by 2050. Paris, France. Available at https://www.iea.org/reports/net-zero-by-2050

IISD (International Institute for Sustainable Development) (2022) Just energy transition partnerships: an opportunity to leapfrog from coal to clean energy. Winnipeg, Canada. Available at https://www.iisd.org/articles/insight/just-energy-transition-partnerships

IPCC (2018) Special Report: Global Warming of 1.5°C (ed: Masson-Delmotte V, et al). Available at https://www.ipcc.ch/site/assets/uploads/sites/2/2019/06/SR15_Full_Report_High_Res.pdf. Accessed 17 Jan 2025

Li B, et al (2020) Perspectives of energy transitions in east and southeast asia. WIREs: Energy Environ 9(1). https://doi.org/10.1002/wene.364

Shen Y, et al (2024) Quantifying energy transition vulnerability helps more just and inclusive decarbonisation. PNAS Nexus 3(10):427 [*sic*]. https://doi.org/10.1093/pnasnexus/pgae427

UN ESCAP (UN Economic and Social Commission for Asia and the Pacific) (2023) Implications of the energy transition on sustainable critical minerals development: aligning extractive industries with the sustainable development goals. Available at https://www.unescap.org/sites/default/d8files/event-documents/Implications%20of%20the%20Energy%20Transition%20on%20Sustainable%20Critical%20Minerals%20Development%20in%20the%20Asia-Pacific_ESCAP.pdf. Accessed 17 Jan 2025

Regional Pathways and Policy Perspectives

Navigating Energy Complexities to Reach Carbon Neutrality in ASEAN

Tetsuya Watanabe, Han Phoumin, Alloysius Joko Purwanto, Jun Arima, and Kei Sudo

Abstract The development of carbon neutrality pathways requires multiple approaches so that emissions in all sectors can be decarbonised effectively. This chapter investigates the maximum contribution of all clean technologies, renewables and fuels to meet carbon neutrality. It presents a variety of ERIA studies, particularly the study on "Decarbonisation of Energy Systems: Optimum Technology Selection Model Analysis up to 2060", which uses data from a linear programming model to minimise the total cost of the energy system when various constraints such as CO_2 emissions and power supply-demand balance are given, in order to check the maximum contribution of all available clean technologies and renewables in the ASEAN decarbonisation scenario. The key issues and findings provide policymakers with a recommended strategy to scale up these clean technologies and renewables in an affordable manner, necessary given all the barriers and costs associated with ASEAN's projected deep decarbonisation. This chapter also examines the policy implications of ASEAN's decarbonisation and discusses the need for each country to formulate strategies which comply with its own unique socio-economic conditions.

Keywords Carbon neutrality · Clean technologies · Smart grid · Electric vehicles (EV) · Hydrogen · Carbon capture utilisation and storage (CCUS) · Critical minerals and carbon market

1 Introduction

ASEAN faces tremendous challenges regarding its future energy landscape, the energy transition and in ensuring that a new architecture, including new policies and technologies, will provide comprehensive energy access together with affordability, energy security and energy sustainability. Given the high share of fossil fuels in the region's current energy mix (oil, coal and natural gas comprise almost 80%),

T. Watanabe · H. Phoumin (✉) · A. J. Purwanto · J. Arima · K. Sudo
Economic Research Institute for ASEAN and East Asia (ERIA), Jakarta Pusat, Indonesia
e-mail: han.phoumin@eria.org

H. Phoumin et al. (eds.), *Tackling the Energy Transition: Insights from ASEAN and Beyond*, Climate Change and Energy Transition,
https://doi.org/10.1007/978-981-96-6019-3_2

the cleaner use of fossil fuels through the deployment of clean technologies is indispensable for decarbonising ASEAN's emissions. ASEAN's future energy mix will be constructed on the basis of today's actions, policies and investments. All decisions and policy measures to be rolled out during the energy transition must be weighed against potentially higher energy costs, affordability issues and energy security risks.

COP 28, the 28th Conference of the Parties to the UN Framework Convention on Climate Change (UNFCCC), held in Dubai in 2023, steered nations across the globe towards becoming low-carbon societies in the attempt to limit global warming to well below 2 °C, preferably to 1.5 °C, compared with pre-industrial levels. Although there is consensus on the need to reduce global warming, the means adopted to achieve that end are diverse. Countries face different circumstances and many, not only in the developing world but also in the G20, are still highly dependent on fossil fuels. A key outcome of COP 28 was the high commitment from world leaders to turn the 2020s into a bold decade of climate action and support. The agreed package of decisions includes strengthened efforts to build resilience to climate change, curb greenhouse gas (GHG) emissions and provide the necessary finance for both. Although it is essential for all countries to reduce emissions, it is clearly a great challenge and risk for developing countries with high carbon intensity to achieve carbon neutrality. One of the chief issues will be the impact on energy affordability, particularly in Southeast Asia where 90% of energy demand growth since 2000 has been fuelled by coal, natural gas or oil. Among the pathways, reducing costs and increasing the deployment of renewables and clean technologies such as hydrogen fuels and carbon capture utilisation and storage (CCUS) are key to realising the transition.

Despite their decline, fossil fuels will continue to play a role in the global energy sector for many years to come. Looking into the plausible scenarios of the energy mix, even if all countries' nationally determined contributions (NDCs) agreed to in the Paris Agreement (COP 21, 2015) are implemented, coal, oil and natural gas will still occupy more than half of the total global primary energy supply. This is particularly the case in Asia, which will comprise the bulk of incremental energy demand and carbon dioxide (CO_2) emissions due to the high dependency on fossil fuels. Therefore, the developing world will need to rely on renewable energy (RE) and clean technologies such as CCUS to decarbonise emissions as many countries will still rely on fossil fuels during the energy transition. As the ten ASEAN Member States (AMS) strive to ensure energy security and to fulfil their NDCs, it is paramount to address these pressing challenges (affordability, security and environmental protection) through collaborative efforts and strategic policy discussions.

ERIA (The Economic Research Institute for ASEAN and East Asia), in close consultation with other stakeholders across the region, has published research on important carbon neutrality challenges in ASEAN. These include: the diversity of mitigation pathways towards carbon neutrality, the importance of considering all available technologies and fuels, the crucial role of natural gas and transition technologies, and underpinning finance. ERIA's *Technology List and Perspectives for Transition Finance in Asia (TLPTFA)* (ERIA 2022b) aims to support smooth energy transitions in developing Asia by foregrounding realistic approaches that can help them to embark on pathways to carbon neutrality. ERIA has classified three stages of technology development to support the shift to net zero:

1. Early decarbonisation transition technologies which involve the immediate switching from coal to natural gas power generation, waste-to-energy power plants in the power sector, and leak detection and repair (LDAR) for fugitive emissions reduction upstream. These technologies can be deployed in the early phases of a country's transition pathway and may be retired before reaching net zero emissions.
2. Partial emissions reduction transition technologies which include the co-combustion of coal-fired power generation with biomass or ammonia, and the co-combustion of gas-fired power generation with hydrogen fuel. The share of biomass, ammonia and hydrogen in the power generation mix must increase over time. For the upstream sector, we suggest introducing electrification in gas production and processing.
3. Deep decarbonisation transition technologies which include carbon CCUS combined with coal/gas power generation, blue hydrogen, blue ammonia and CCUS in gas processing. It is very important to note that CCUS has been selected on the basis of six criteria: emissions reductions, affordability, reliability and carbon lock-in prevention which highlight the emissions reduction plan, as well as do-no-significant harm, and social considerations.

To ensure successful, smooth and just energy transitions in Asia and around the world, it is very important to mobilise the needed resources to meet the growing need for clean energy and technologies while ensuring appropriate finance. Securing sufficient investment for financing sustainable energy infrastructure is a great challenge of our time. Annual investment in renewables and clean energy has grown steadily since the 2015 Paris Agreement. Globally we see a large shift in investment towards clean technologies and renewables. In 2023, an estimated USD 1.7 trillion was invested in renewables and clean technologies, while USD 1 trillion was invested in fossil fuels. This was the first time since 2016 that the investment in clean energy outpaced that of fossil fuels. This new trend of global investor sentiment towards cleaner energy systems reflects the fundamental changes in public perceptions towards climate change and the environment. However, attention still needs to be given to developing countries' ability to finance the energy transition.

2 Results Under the Carbon Neutrality Scenario

This chapter has benefited from the current data collection and analysis carried out by the joint study project between ERIA and the Institute of Energy Economics, Japan (IEEJ) on "Decarbonisation of ASEAN Energy Systems: Optimum Technology Selection Model Analysis up to 2060" (Kimura et al., eds. 2022). This study used the Optimum Technology Selection Model developed by the IEEJ adopted from the model of Otsuki et al. (2019). It covers the entire energy system of the 10

ASEAN countries with the baseline year 2017 and analysis years 2030, 2040, 2050 and 2060. It also considers energy-related CO_2 when assessing the deployment of clean technologies and renewables. Basically, the model is formulated as a linear programming model, taking the cost and performance of each energy technology as input values and yielding a single combined result of the scale and operational patterns of individual energy technologies. By such means, the model minimises the total cost of the energy system when the various constraints, such as CO_2 emissions and power supply–demand balance are given. It covers the energy conversion and end-use sectors (industry, transport, households and commercial), and incorporates more than 350 technologies. It also evaluates combinations of the technologies by inputting factors such as capital costs, fuel costs and CO_2 emissions for each one. In the transition towards carbon neutrality, ASEAN will see the huge deployment of solar PV together with battery storage, among other clean technologies. Figure 1 shows the potential of solar and wind in ASEAN (World Bank Group 2022a [*Global Solar Atlas*] and 2022b [*Global Wind Atlas*]). These data were used to make assumptions in the model about the potential resource availability of solar and wind in ASEAN.

Other assumptions about the power generation in terms of the levelised cost of energy across different types of technologies are also made, as shown in Fig. 2.

The model includes other low-carbon technologies such hydrogen (H_2)- and ammonia (NH_3)-fired power generation, and negative-emission technologies such as direct air capture with carbon storage (DACCS) and bioenergy with carbon capture and storage (BECCS). In relation to a Carbon Neutrality Scenario for ASEAN, ERIA's study considers five scenarios:

1. the Baseline Scenario without any CO_2 emissions target;

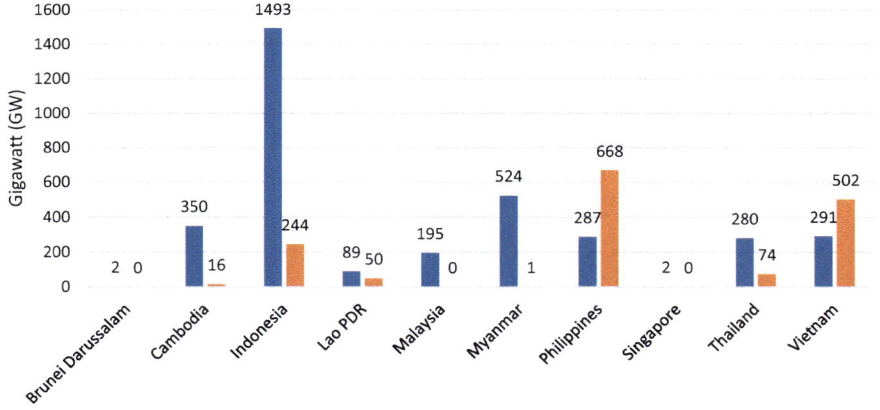

Fig. 1 Potential of solar PV and wind in the AMS, 2020. *Sources* World Bank Group (2022a [*Global Solar Atlas*] and 2022b [*Global Wind Atlas*])

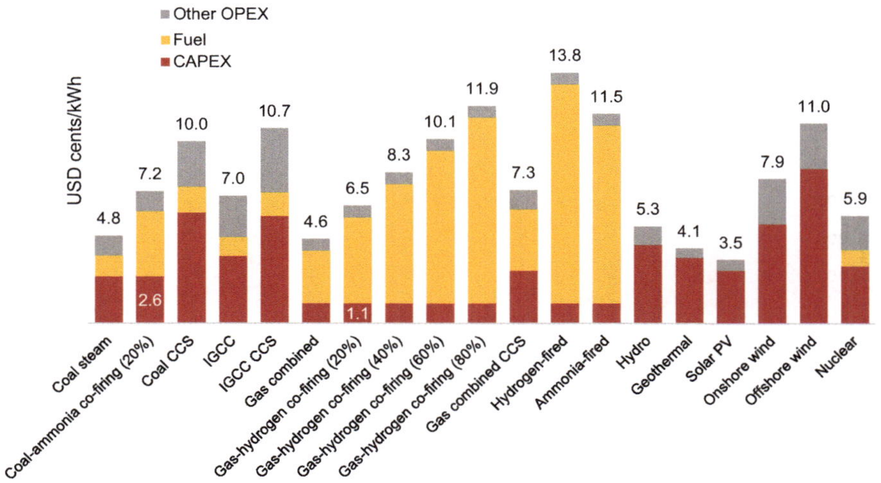

Fig. 2 LCOE assumptions according to different technology types. *Note* CAPEX: Capital Expenditures; IGCC: integrated gasification combined cycle; OPEX: Operational Expenditures. *Source* Authors' calculations, from Kimura et al. (2023)

2. the Carbon Neutrality Scenario 2050/60 (CN2050/2060) which reflects the respective nationally declared target years to reach carbon neutrality and includes carbon sinks;
3. CN2050/2060_Innovation cases, with five cases which describe the impacts of technological innovation;
4. CN2050/2060_Stringent2030 tightens emission constraints in 2030 to the same level as the International Energy Agency's (IEA's) Sustainable Development Scenario; and
5. CN2050/2060 without carbon sinks (CN2050/2060 w/o Carbon Sink) which assumes that energy-related CO_2 emissions become net zero by 2060 and does not consider carbon sinks.

For simplicity, the results of the potential solar and wind penetration into the energy mix are reported only for the Baseline and Carbon Neutrality 2050/60 (CN2050/2060) Scenarios.

2.1 ASEAN's Primary Energy Supply in the Baseline and Carbon Neutrality Scenarios

ASEAN's energy supply was 616 million tonnes of oil equivalent (Mtoe) in 2017 and is expected to grow to 2,006 Mtoe in 2060 for the Business as Usual (BAU) or Baseline Scenario (Fig. 3 and Table 1). Coal, oil and natural gas combined were about 80.06% in 2017, and their share will be 85.09% in 2060 in the Baseline Scenario.

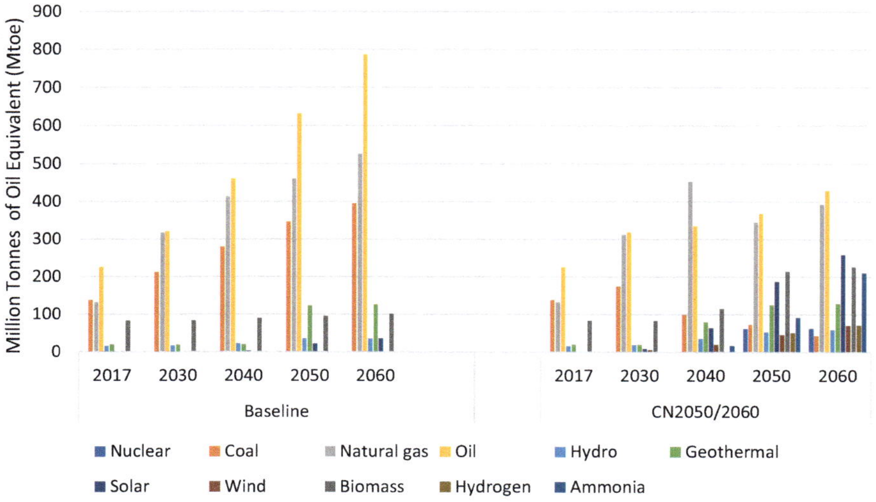

Fig. 3 Total primary energy supply (TPES) in the Baseline and CN2050/60 Scenarios. *Source* Authors' calculations

Table 1 Primary energy supply by energy sources, Baseline and Carbon Neutrality Scenarios (Mtoe)

Energy source	Baseline					CN2050/2060				
	2017	2030	2040	2050	2060	2017	2030	2040	2050	2060
Nuclear	0.0	0.0	0.0	0.0	0.0	0.0	0.0	0.0	62.4	62.7
Coal	138.8	212.5	279.8	346.8	394.9	138.8	174.3	99.2	72.8	42.8
Natural gas	132.4	317.1	413.2	460.9	526.2	132.4	312.2	453.1	345.2	393.1
Oil	225.7	322.2	460.7	631.9	785.8	225.3	318.9	335.8	368.0	429.3
Hydro	16.2	17.7	22.5	35.6	35.6	16.2	19.6	36.1	53.0	59.4
Geothermal	19.9	19.9	19.9	122.9	126.2	19.9	19.9	79.8	125.4	128.9
Solar	0.5	1.0	2.7	21.6	35.4	0.5	8.6	63.6	187.3	258.7
Wind	0.2	0.2	0.2	0.3	1.2	0.2	5.8	19.2	45.6	70.3
Biomass	82.8	82.9	88.8	94.7	100.2	82.8	82.6	114.9	214.1	226.2
Hydrogen	0.0	0.0	0.0	0.0	0.0	0.0	0.0	0.2	50.6	70.9
Ammonia	0.0	0.0	1.2	0.8	0.4	0.0	0.0	17.2	91.6	210.9
Share of imported H_2/NH_3 (%)	0%	0%	0%	0%	0%	0%	0%	1%	9%	14%
Total	616	974	1289	1716	2006	616	942	1219	1616	1953

Source Authors' calculations

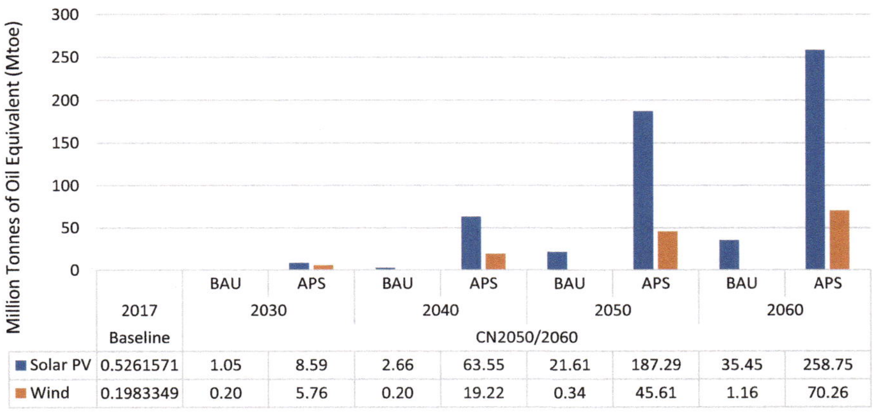

	2017 Baseline	2030 BAU	2030 APS	2040 BAU	2040 APS	2050 BAU	2050 APS	2060 BAU	2060 APS
	Baseline	CN2050/2060							
Solar PV	0.5261571	1.05	8.59	2.66	63.55	21.61	187.29	35.45	258.75
Wind	0.1983349	0.20	5.76	0.20	19.22	0.34	45.61	1.16	70.26

Fig. 4 Potential deployment of solar PV and wind in the ASEAN carbon neutrality scenario. *Note* APS: Announced Pledges Scenario (model described in IEA [2024, esp. p. 6ff]). *Source* Authors' calculations, from Kimura et al. (2023)

In the Carbon Neutrality Scenario, clean fuels and renewables are expected to increase significantly from the baseline year to 2050 and 2060. Nuclear could be an option in the Carbon Neutrality Scenario, with this source entering the primary energy mix at about 62 to 63 Mtoe by the years 2050 and 2060, respectively. Solar energy is expected to increase its capacity according to the following schedule: 8.6 Mtoe by 2030, 63.6 Mtoe by 2040, 187.3 by 2050 and 258.7 Mtoe by 2060 (Fig. 4). Likewise, wind is also expected to increase under the Carbon Neutrality Scenario: 5.8 Mtoe by 2030, 19.2 Mtoe by 2040, 45.6 Mtoe by 2050 and 70.3 Mtoe by 2060. In this scenario, other clean energy sources such as hydropower, geothermal and biomass are expected to play large roles in the primary energy supply mix. Other new types of clean fuels such as hydrogen and ammonia also enter the supply mix from 2040 onwards in the Carbon Neutrality Scenario.

Among the fossil fuels, coal is expected to decrease substantially in the Carbon Neutrality Scenario according to the following reduction schedules from peak demand: to 174.3 Mtoe by 2030, 99.2 Mtoe by 2040, 72.8 Mtoe by 2050, and 42.8 Mtoe by 2060. Oil and natural gas are, however, predicted to increase slowly in the Carbon Neutrality Scenario. Natural gas is used in the energy transition and is expected to enhance the clean energy system if combined with CCUS, and oil will remain an important fuel for transport, especially for heavy duty vehicles (e.g. buses and trucks).

It is observed that the total energy supply in the Carbon Neutrality Scenario is lower than in the Baseline Scenario. It is expected to decrease from 2006 Mtoe in the Baseline Scenario to 1953 Mtoe in the Carbon Neutrality Scenario. What significantly constitutes the difference between the Baseline and Carbon Neutrality Scenarios is the composition of the energy mix: under the latter scenario, renewables and clean fuels account for the major share.

2.2 ASEAN's Power Generation Mix in the Baseline and Carbon Neutrality Scenarios

In the Baseline Scenario, electricity demand is predicted to be 3657 TWh by 2060; in the Carbon Neutrality Scenario, electricity demand is predicted to be 6720 TWh (Fig. 5 and Table 2). This doubling of electricity demand is due to the significant introduction of intermittent renewables: solar and wind. In this case, the application of battery storage is critical to prevent electricity curtailment; storage can also be used for other purposes such as energy back-up systems or smoothing the load curve of solar or wind. In another scenario, the surplus electricity from wind and solar could be used to produce hydrogen and to power fuel cells for vehicles in the transport sector or for power generation (co-combustion of hydrogen with natural gas-fired power plants).

A proper real time simulation of the power mix is necessary to understand how much battery energy storage will be needed. However, in this study, the rule of sum is applied for the energy battery storage, which ranges from 20–25% of the installed capacity of solar and wind (Figs. 6 and 7).

In the Carbon Neutrality Scenario, it is expected that about 1,627 GW of installed capacity of wind and solar will be realised in ASEAN by 2060. Solar will account for the largest installed capacity of 1,385 GW by 2060; wind (both onshore and offshore) will be about 331 GW by that year.

Battery storage can back up the intermittent electricity production from wind and solar. However, the size of the storage depends on the composition of the energy mix and load curve. In this study, it is estimated that ASEAN's energy battery storage in the Carbon Neutrality Scenario will be about 1,365 gigawatt hours (GWh) (Fig. 7).

The deployment sequence of the energy battery storage coincides with the ramped-up installed capacity of solar and wind from 2040 onwards. In fact, ASEAN could

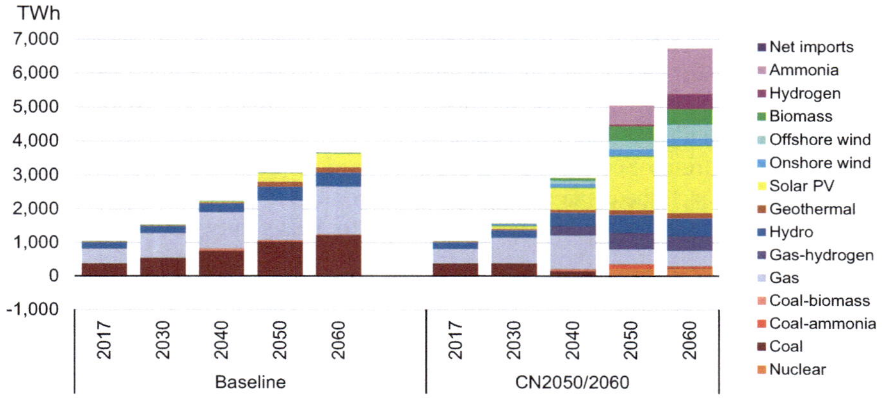

Fig. 5 ASEAN's power generation mix in the Baseline and CN2050/60 Scenarios. *Source* Authors' calculations

Table 2 Power generation mix by energy sources, Baseline and Carbon Neutrality Scenarios (TWh)

Energy source	Baseline					CN2050/2060				
	2017	2030	2040	2050	2060	2017	2030	2040	2050	2060
Nuclear	0.0	0.0	0.0	0.0	0.0	0.0	0.0	0.0	241.9	243.2
Coal	383.7	544.0	757.2	1033.6	1226.9	383.7	383.7	155.4	0.0	5.7
Coal-ammonia	0.0	0.0	24.1	15.9	8.0	0.0	0.0	24.1	100.1	44.3
Coal-biomass	0.0	0.0	48.2	31.9	15.9	0.0	0.0	48.2	31.9	15.9
Gas	437.7	741.1	1079.7	1173.3	1421.0	437.7	767.1	998.0	438.6	459.1
Gas-hydrogen	0.0	0.0	0.0	0.0	0.0	0.0	0.0	272.5	495.7	423.7
Hydro	188.0	205.9	262.2	414.5	414.5	188.0	227.4	404.1	531.0	543.4
Geothermal	23.1	23.1	23.1	142.9	146.8	23.1	23.1	92.8	145.9	149.9
Solar PV	5.9	12.2	31.0	251.4	412.3	5.9	99.9	648.9	1591.2	1985.1
Onshore wind	1.9	1.9	1.9	3.5	13.1	1.9	66.5	123.1	211.1	226.6
Offshore wind	0.4	0.4	0.4	0.4	0.4	0.4	0.4	81.0	230.5	401.0
Biomass	0.0	1.4	1.3	1.5	1.2	0.0	0.4	75.0	432.6	454.6
Hydrogen	0.0	0.0	0.0	0.0	0.0	0.0	0.0	0.0	54.5	446.7
Ammonia	0.0	0.0	0.0	0.0	0.0	0.0	0.0	0.0	554.4	1335.8
Net imports	−2.0	−2.1	−1.6	−3.5	−3.1	−2.0	−3.1	−3.2	−5.5	−5.7
Total	1,039	1,528	2,227	3,065	3,657	1,039	1,566	2,920	5,054	6,720

Source Authors' calculations

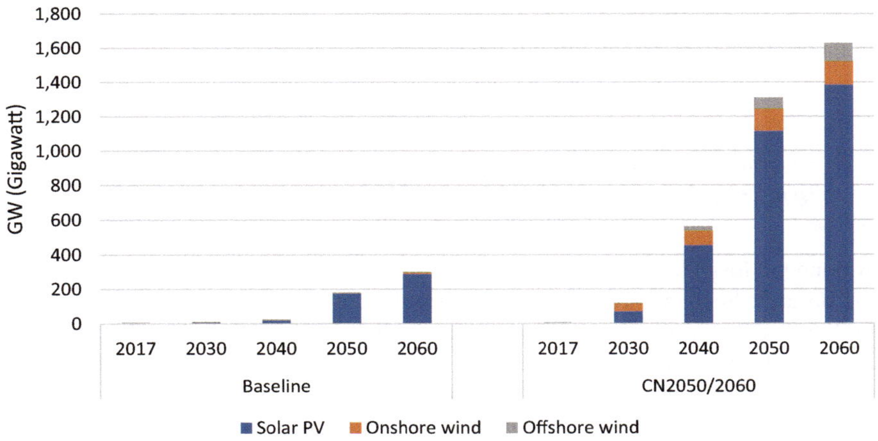

Fig. 6 Total installed capacity of solar and wind for the Baseline and Carbon Neutrality Scenarios (Gigawatts). *Source* Authors' calculations

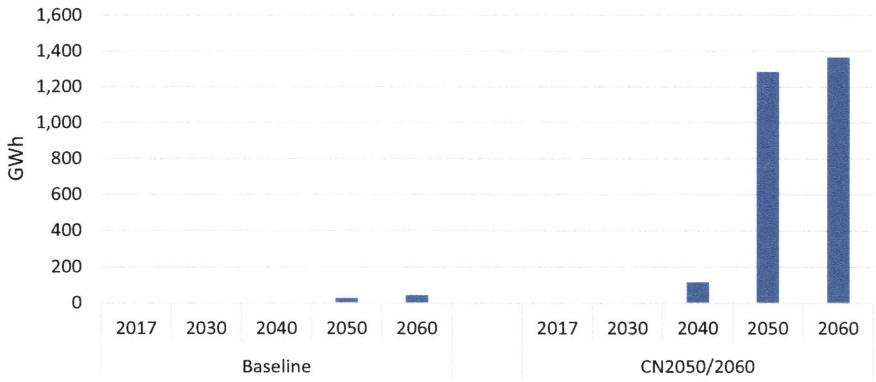

Fig. 7 Total installed energy battery storage, Baseline and Carbon Neutrality Scenarios (Gigawatt Hours [GWh]). *Source* Authors' calculations

see further large deployment of solar and wind due to their widespread availability. However, the issue of system integration and affordability could be obstacles to expanding the lead time of the introduction of these resources at large scale.

Although coal will remain in use for power generation in the Carbon Neutrality Scenario, un-abated coal is less used in the transition to cleaner power through co-combustion of coal with ammonia for the coal-fired power plants, and CCUS technologies. All clean technologies and clean fuels could be introduced in the power system according to the schedule and thus reduce the overall cost of the power system in its progress to carbon neutrality by 2050/60.

2.3 *ASEAN's Final Energy Consumption in the Baseline and Carbon Neutrality Scenarios*

Among the fossil fuels, coal consumption is predicted to decrease significantly from the Baseline Scenario (108 Mtoe in 2060) to the Carbon Neutrality Scenario (4 Mtoe in 2060). Oil is also expected to decrease by half from the Baseline Scenario (694 Mtoe in 2060) to the Carbon Neutrality Scenario (348 Mtoe in 2060). There is not much change in the use of natural gas from the Baseline to the Carbon Neutrality Scenario in 2060 as gas remains an important fuel in the energy transition and also in the future if combined with negative emission technologies such as direct air capture (DAC).

Electricity in the end-use sectors will be the largest form of energy in the Carbon Neutrality Scenario and its growth is predicted to be 127 Mtoe in 2030, 2017 Mtoe in 2040, 344 Mtoe in 2050 and 431 Mtoe by 2060 (Fig. 8 and Table 3).

The increase in the use of electricity is due to the introduction of electric vehicles (EVs) and the increased consumption in the residential and commercial sectors.

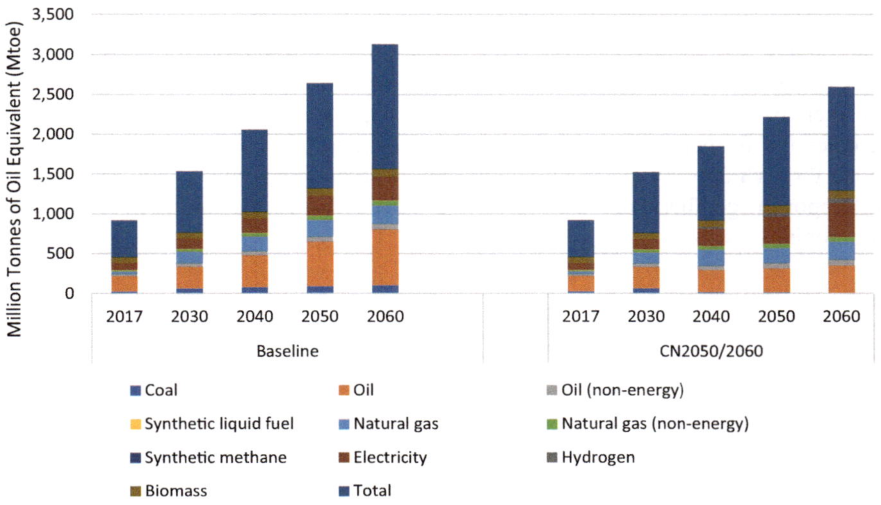

Fig. 8 Total final energy consumption in the Baseline and CN2050/60 Scenarios (Mtoe). *Source* Authors' calculations

Table 3 Final energy consumption by energy sources, Baseline and Carbon Neutrality Scenarios (Mtoe)

Energy source	Baseline					CN2050/2060				
	2017	2030	2040	2050	2060	2017	2030	2040	2050	2060
Coal	31.9	70.4	84.5	97.4	108.1	31.9	68.9	23.9	20.1	4.1
Oil	187.8	268.7	394.3	554.1	695.4	187.8	266.0	274.7	297.7	348.5
Oil (non-energy)	30.2	45.7	54.7	64.2	74.7	30.2	45.7	54.7	64.2	74.7
Synthetic liquid fuel	0.0	0.0	0.0	0.0	0.0	0.0	0.0	0.0	0.0	0.0
Natural gas	26.6	139.7	181.8	209.3	229.3	26.6	134.7	201.6	190.6	226.1
Natural gas (non-energy)	16.7	37.4	45.2	52.8	59.9	16.7	37.4	45.2	52.8	59.9
Synthetic methane	–	0.0	0.0	0.0	0.0	–	0.0	0.0	0.0	0.0
Electricity	84.8	124.8	182.0	250.3	298.7	84.8	127.8	216.9	344.0	430.6
Hydrogen	0.0	0.0	0.0	0.0	0.0	0.0	0.0	22.9	47.1	55.6
Biomass	82.2	82.5	86.0	92.7	99.1	82.2	82.5	86.0	93.4	100.3
Total	460.3	769.1	1,028.6	1,320.8	1,565.0	460.3	762.9	925.9	1,110.0	1,299.8

Source Authors' calculations

Some heavy buses and trucks will continue to use oil and hydrogen. Biomass and natural gas are expected to serve some industrial end-use sectors for heating.

In the Carbon Neutrality Scenario, decarbonisation of end-use sectors must focus on increasing the use of electricity. In fact, if possible, electricity use should be accelerated further, and the decarbonisation of the power sources will need to be done through appropriate technologies and clean energy sources such as biomass, hydropower, geothermal, wind, solar and other clean fuels such as hydrogen and ammonia.

2.4 *ASEAN's Emissions by Sector in the Baseline and Carbon Neutrality Scenarios*

Decarbonisation in each sector will be necessary for ASEAN to reach carbon neutrality by 2060. In the Baseline Scenario, ASEAN's total CO_2 emissions are expected to shoot to almost 5,000 Mt-CO_2 that year. In the Baseline Scenario, sectors such as transport, industry and the commercial and residential sectors are significant contributors of emissions towards 2060. However, in the Carbon Neutrality Scenario, electricity generated (mainly by solar, wind, biomass, hydropower and geothermal), and DACCS are expected to be introduced into the energy system. Further, the natural carbon offset through the Land Use, Land Use Change, and Forestry (LULUCF) inventory sector also helps to reduce emissions.

Carbon capture, including DACCS, plays a vital role in helping ASEAN cut emissions by about 565 Mt-CO_2 by 2060. The introduction of renewables helps cut the emissions by about 503 Mt-CO_2. Among renewable forms of energy, solar will be the largest component in the ASEAN system mix. Its role is therefore critical in helping ASEAN reach the carbon neutrality target by 2060. The emissions from transport and industry remain, but are expected to decline significantly in the Carbon Neutrality Scenario over the Baseline Scenario (Fig. 9).

2.5 *Marginal Abatement Cost of Decarbonisation in ASEAN*

The marginal CO_2 abatement cost (MAC) is the cost required for the entire energy system to reduce CO_2 by a factor (margin) of 1 (e.g. 1 ton of CO_2), as yielded by the model simulation (see Enkvist et al. 2007). Figure 10 illustrates the weighted average of MAC in ASEAN. In CN2050/2060_w/o Carbon Sink (Carbon Neutrality Scenario without Carbon Sink), the MAC rises sharply from USD 368/tCO_2 in 2050 to USD 651/tCO_2 in 2060, implying a major economic challenge to decarbonisation. Increase in the MAC is derived from more stringent constraints on CO_2 emissions from 2050 to 2060. The additional annual cost in CN2050/2060_w/o Carbon Sink compared with the Baseline Scenario is estimated at about 5.2% (USD 0.83 trillion)

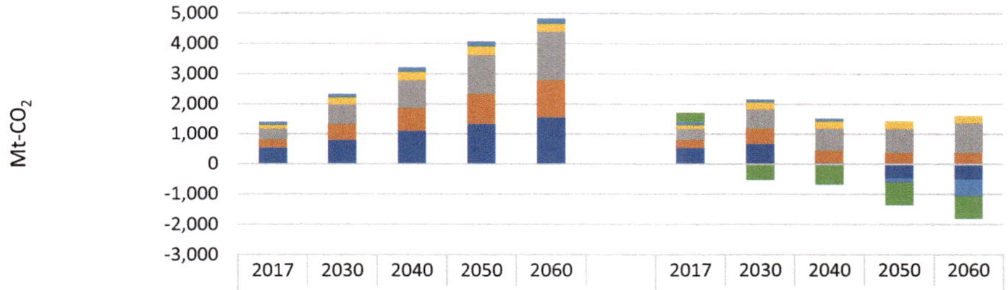

	Baseline 2017	Baseline 2030	Baseline 2040	Baseline 2050	Baseline 2060	CN2050/2060 2017	CN2050/2060 2030	CN2050/2060 2040	CN2050/2060 2050	CN2050/2060 2060
LULUCF						314.1	-519.6	-670.5	-732.8	-732.8
Other including DACCS	98.3	104.1	129.5	149.0	169.4	97.0	91.0	84.5	-148.4	-564.5
Other end-use	138.1	258.8	298.9	312.1	288.0	138.1	243.0	263.8	255.5	236.8
Transport	349.0	640.0	912.4	1266.2	1579.9	349.0	640.0	725.8	790.7	987.0
Industry	266.1	527.2	755.4	996.1	1232.0	266.1	515.1	411.7	386.8	385.7
Electricity	558.4	812.6	1119.6	1350.5	1575.9	558.4	677.7	43.1	-469.2	-502.6

Fig. 9 Emissions in ASEAN by Sector (Mt-CO_2). *Source* Authors' calculations

of ASEAN's GDP in 2060. In this regard, it is very important to reduce the MAC in order for ASEAN to afford the decarbonisation objective.

This chapter suggests the use of five technological innovations to increase the overall level of decarbonisation in ASEAN. Primarily, ASEAN needs:

1. to achieve power grid connectivity and have a fully functioning power market;
2. to have large cost reductions in battery energy storage and EVs;
3. to achieve large-scale deployment of CCUS, including DAC, with substantial cost reductions;
4. to realise other cost reductions in related technologies such as coal gasification and methane reforming and electrolysis;

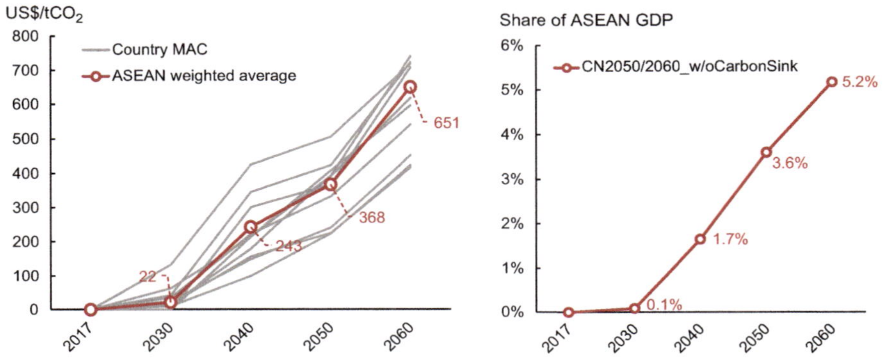

Fig. 10 Marginal carbon dioxide abatement cost (left), Additional annual cost (right) (CN2050/2060_w/o Carbon Sink). CO_2 = carbon dioxide, MAC = marginal carbon dioxide abatement cost, tCO_2 = tonnes of carbon dioxide. GDP = gross domestic product. *Source* Authors

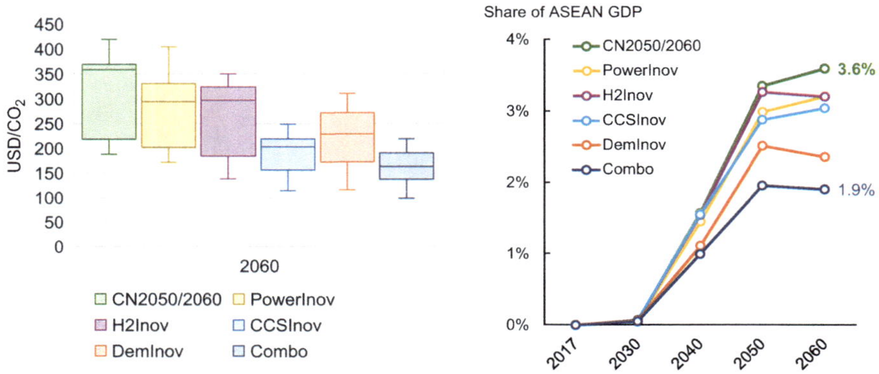

Fig. 11 Marginal abatement cost (left), additional annual cost (right). *Source* Authors

5. to achieve cost reductions in advanced end-use technologies.

If all of these innovations are achieved, it is expected that the overall cost of decarbonisation will be lower than USD 200/tCO2 by 2060 (Fig. 11). Table 4 provides assumptions about required key technological innovations.

3 Discussion

To reach carbon neutrality, the above modelling results point to the need for innovations in each technology to reduce the cost of decarbonisation. Regional and international collaborations are also necessary to ensure that appropriate and affordable technologies are deployed, and that these are consistent with the economic development in Southeast Asia. Low emission technologies such as hydrogen development, CCUS, smart grids, EVs, carbon markets, critical minerals and regional cooperation such as through the Asia Zero Emission Community (AZEC) have been mentioned. A focus on these can help the AMS formulate their technological and institutional arrangements such that the energy system can be cleaner by 2050.

3.1 Hydrogen Development in ASEAN

Hydrogen gas continues to be extensively used in industrial processes like oil refining, chemicals, fertilisers and steel production (IEA 2019). Even if it is expected to power fuel-cell electric vehicles (FCEV) in some countries, economic considerations and infrastructure limitations have constrained its use in transportation to date. This is expected to change.

Table 4 Key technology assumptions for technological innovation cases

Case	Net zero year	Key technology assumptions
CN2050/2060	2060	Reference technology cost International power grid extension constrained by planned ASEAN power grid capacity CO_2 storage up to 1.6 $GtCO_2$/year in 2060
PowerInov	2060	Cost reduction of lithium-ion batteries (−25% in 2040 and −50% after 2050, from the reference level) and international grid extension No upper limit for international power grid extension Large-scale electricity exports from Myanmar to Thailand
CCSInov	2060	Cost reduction of direct air capture (−25% in 2040 and −50% after 2050) CO_2 storage up to 2.7 $GtCO_2$/year in 2060
H_2Inov	2060	Cost reduction of coal gasification and methane reforming (−25% in 2040 and −50% after 2050), electrolyser (−22% in 2040 and 2050, −35% in 2060) Cost reduction of H_2 consumption: H_2-based DRI-EAF and fuel cell ship (−25% in 2040 and −50% after 2050) and FCEV (comparable to hybrid EV price in 2060)
DemInov	2060	Cost reduction of advanced end-use technologies (−50% in and after 2040)
Combo	2060	Combined assumptions of four innovation cases mentioned above

CO_2 = carbon dioxide, DRI-EAF = direct reduced iron–electric arc furnace, FCEV = fuel cell electric vehicle, $GtCO_2$ = gigatonnes of carbon dioxide, H_2 = hydrogen
Source Authors

On the supply side, competitively priced hydrogen continues to be sourced primarily from steam reforming of natural gas ("grey hydrogen") or coal gasification. While hydrogen from water electrolysis ("green hydrogen") has the potential to compete with transport fuels, especially when petroleum prices are high, it is much more expensive than grey hydrogen used for industry (Ball and Weeda 2015). However, recent research and pilot projects lead to the expectation that technologies like natural gas reforming combined with carbon capture ("blue hydrogen") and electrolysis of water using renewable-based electricity will gain prominence and could dominate hydrogen production in the future (APERC 2018; IEA 2021).

On the demand side, industry will continue to be the largest user of hydrogen, far exceeding use in transport. While demand for battery electric vehicles (BEV), including plug-in hybrid vehicles (PHEVs) has been rising in recent years due to increased subsidies and expanding charging station networks, the transport and logistics sectors are yet to settle on any dominant technology. Indeed, recent findings indicate a future market split between BEVs dominating the light passenger vehicle markets travelling shorter distances and FCEVs used in heavier, long distance utility vehicles such as trucks and rail (Milton 2020). Furthermore, the potential of hydrogen gas as a future energy carrier is still being developed.

Given the complex set of factors affecting the demand, supply, storage and transport of hydrogen, the search for an optimal hydrogen development strategy requires an analysis of not only technological and economic variables but also a country's geography, population structure and growth, energy demand, and supply situation and, equally importantly, their institutional setup.

The main issue is then how to contribute to the optimal hydrogen market development strategy for ASEAN. First, ASEAN had a population of 660 million and a combined gross domestic product (GDP) of more than USD 3.0 trillion in 2020 (ASEAN 2021). Second, the region's refining, chemical and steel sector output and demand for passenger and logistics transportation are concentrated in Singapore, Thailand, Indonesia, Malaysia and Vietnam, five countries that make up the region's largest industrial output and consumption market. Third, ASEAN harbours some of the world's largest natural gas reserves and resources (IEA 2021). Fourth, the existing natural gas pipeline networks in Malaysia, Indonesia, Thailand–Myanmar and Vietnam offer the potential for a future regional network of gas transport pipelines, the trans-ASEAN natural gas pipeline network, which could be crucial for the region's hydrogen market development (ACE 2022). Fifth, while the hydrogen-consuming industries and the automobile production and supply chains in Thailand and Indonesia dominate the region, they are not yet over-developed and have the potential for significant and rapid growth into the future. The proportion of RE-based electricity generation is small, and ASEAN has aimed to grow its RE capacity to 23% of primary energy consumption by 2025 (Hamdi 2020). Thus, the region still holds potential for future adaptation and transformation, to be guided by the right future development strategy and policies for its energy sector including hydrogen.

In line with the Seventh Sustainable Development Goal of the United Nations, ASEAN and East Asian Summit countries need to seriously promote the use of renewable sources, energy efficiency and measures to enhance the energy transition to cleaner fuels. The use of new energy technologies such as CCUS or carbon recycling and hydrogen should also be incorporated along with the adoption of clean technologies. Hydrogen technology should play a key role as an alternative to fossil fuels and can be applied across sectors, i.e. the industry sector in the short and medium term and the future power generation and transport sectors in the long term.

3.2 *Electric Vehicles in ASEAN*

EVs are seen to be beneficial from many different perspectives. While there are still many issues to discuss, these vehicles are increasingly believed to be one of the silver bullets to remedy many issues in ASEAN, including energy security, climate change, the environment and economic downturn.

The high purchase prices, especially of private vehicles such as electric cars and electric motorbikes, are currently among the issues that hinder private EVs' penetration in the region. Therefore, from around 2019, several AMS governments have put in place not only various incentives to reduce the total cost paid by consumers to acquire these vehicles but also various fiscal and non-fiscal measures and regulations to decrease their total operational costs.

EVs can surely help the AMS enhance energy security, save on energy import bills, mitigate climate change and improve urban air quality. Substantial EV deployment, however, may have negative side effects. Among these effects are the additional electricity demand that is met mainly by fossil-fuel based power, the inefficient and ineffective use of countries' budgets (in terms of granting subsidies and incentives), and the negative ripple effects of EV industry penetration on the production and employment structure of the country.

To avoid and minimise these possible negative effects, the transition to EVs needs to address at least three main energy and economic policy issues:

a. Decarbonising Power Generation: If the increase in power demand accompanying the distribution of EVs is covered by thermal power such as coal-fired sources, there is little effect on CO_2 reduction. ASEAN will likely become more dependent on thermal power generation, which involves large-scale power generation facilities, as demand for electricity is expected to increase rapidly for residential, commercial and industrial use. Especially in Indonesia, where coal-fired power accounts for more than 50% of the power generation mix, substantial CO_2 reductions cannot be achieved via BEV penetration. It is important to decarbonise the power supply along with the penetration of EVs. Coal is relatively inexpensive and abundant in the region, but the power companies should introduce more efficient coal-fired power generation facilities. Meanwhile, one of the options is to promote hybrid EVs, which can reduce CO_2 emissions without depending on the power supply mix, until this supply becomes clean.
b. Considering the Costs of Penetration: Currently, EV prices are high, and the extra cost compared to ICE (internal combustion engine) vehicles should be regarded as an additional cost. In general, as it is unlikely that individual consumers will be willing to pay this cost, satisfying potential customers may require economic incentives such as subsidies and tax cuts. Although battery costs, a major factor in the price of the vehicle, have been falling, EVs are still far from popular without subsidies. In the current situation, promoting vehicle electrification would require substantial subsidies. The battery cost is expected to continue to fall in the future, but the outlook, including that of international mineral prices, is still uncertain. If the cost does not drop as expected, more subsidies will be necessary to promote EVs. This should be done carefully, along with consideration of the fiscal situation. In addition, fuel price policy is an important variable impacting the spread of EVs. There is little incentive for consumers to purchase more fuel-efficient EVs if fuel prices are low. Therefore, it is necessary to provide incentives through subsidies for the vehicles themselves. Conversely, if the fuel price is relatively high, daily fuel cost savings by EVs increase, and the initial vehicle cost can be recovered earlier. In other words, subsidies can be reduced. To spread EVs, it is necessary to consider the consistency of various policies.
c. Paying Attention to Spillover Effects of EV Proliferation: It is necessary to pay attention to other economic activities affected by EV market penetration. The

production of BEVs with a small number of material parts might reduce automotive industry employment compared with the production of internal combustion engine vehicles (ICEVs) and hybrid electric vehicles (HEVs). Furthermore, as EVs become more widespread, the negative economic spillover or ripple effects will increase throughout the petroleum industry due to a massive decrease in fuel demand. However, EV penetration may create additional production and employment in the whole economy, that is, if the savings in daily fuel expenditure can be diverted into other goods and services. In general, the service industries have higher employment intensities (required number of employees per production value) than the fuel supply industry. Especially in Indonesia and Vietnam, where many motorcycles are on the road, promoting e-motorcycles may stimulate job creation in the service industries. On the other hand, in the case of passenger light duty vehicles, employment creation effects could be small or even negative, because other consumption is sacrificed to purchase the expensive EVs.

3.3 Grids and Mini-Grids Development in ASEAN

We are now in a period in which countries and companies are facing a volatile, uncertain and rapidly evolving global energy landscape. Meeting the growing demand for electricity while pursuing GHG emission reductions in ASEAN will require huge investments in power generation capacity from decarbonisation technologies such as RE and power system expansion. To address these challenges, it is necessary to implement various mechanisms and technologies; from a grid perspective, we believe that one of the keys is the development of multilateral power trading in ASEAN, known as the ASEAN Power Grid (APG). Multilateral power trading is about optimising resources on a regional basis, rather than a national one, to meet electricity demand across the region at the lowest possible cost. Some key points on the potential benefits of multilateral power trading are (ERIA 2022a, p. 494):

a. More efficient use of the region's energy resources, leading to lower overall production costs in the APG, as optimal investments can be made at the regional level rather than through sub-optimal, nation-based solutions;
b. Helping utilities in the region balance their excess supply and demand, improve access to energy services and reduce the cost of developing energy infrastructure;
c. Accelerating the development and integration of RE capacity into the regional grid;
d. Reducing the need for investment in power reserves to meet peak demand, thereby reducing operating costs, while achieving more reliable supply and reducing system losses.

There have been significant, albeit slow, developments within ASEAN to increase regional trade based on bilateral agreements and to use existing infrastructure to move electricity throughout the sub-region. However, there is still a long way to go before a fully-fledged ASEAN regional electricity market is established. One of the reasons for the slow progress is the variety of power sector structures and markets across ASEAN, which creates problems and barriers at all levels of cooperation. To address this issue, there is a need to accelerate close discussions among ASEAN-related sectoral energy bodies to establish a regional regulatory framework and technical standards, including institutional arrangements with clearly defined roles, responsibilities and coordination mechanisms (including regional institutions), a comprehensive vision for decarbonisation that highlights the multiple benefits of multilateral power trading, and an identification of minimum technical requirements.

While aiming to develop an efficient power supply system between national grids by promoting multilateral power trading, it should be noted that there are still areas with no or low electrification in the islands and remote areas of the ASEAN region. In such areas, it is often unprofitable to connect to a large grid such as a national grid due to the cost of installing trans-mountain and undersea transmission lines. As a result, small-scale diesel generation systems are generally popular, but diesel generation is also expensive and has a high environmental impact. Therefore, the introduction of RE is expected, and when the cost of batteries becomes affordable, a combined battery/RE system is expected to complement the intermittency of RE, thereby reducing reliance on diesel generation. In a future phase, replacing existing diesel generators with power generation systems fuelled by liquefied natural gas (LNG), biofuels, blue or green hydrogen would also be an effective approach. As they have a lower environmental impact than diesel generation, it is expected that their introduction will be promoted in areas where it is feasible, bearing in mind the profitability factor.

The rise of emerging technologies, including smarter grid systems, and ways in which they can be adopted are important factors here. The shift to cleaner energy requires smarter grids to manage the variability of renewables and to integrate distributed energy resources. For example, smart grid technologies such as real-time monitoring, data analytics and advanced control systems will improve grid stability and enable efficient integration of variable RE sources such as solar and wind. Artificial intelligence is also playing a crucial role in this evolution, enabling smart grids with predictive analytics for demand forecasting, fault detection and optimised grid operation. In addition, energy management systems, combined with batteries and other energy storage solutions, are becoming essential to balance supply and demand and improve grid resilience. This confluence of innovative technologies can be an enabler, paving the way for a more decentralised, intelligent and sustainable energy future.

3.4 Carbon Capture Utilisation and Storage (CCUS) Development in ASEAN

In ASEAN and East Asia, fossil fuels still play a considerable role in the energy mix. In the Business as Usual (BAU) Scenario presented in ERIA's *EAS Energy Outlook*

2023 (Kimura et al. 2023), coal and natural gas are predicted to be the dominant fuels used to generate power in 2050, with coal contributing 39.5% and gas 20.8%. Even under the Carbon Neutrality Scenario, combined coal and gas power generation will remain over 40% of the power mix with CCS. This high share of coal and gas in the energy mix by 2050 is perhaps a consequence of the relatively young age of coal-fired power plants in Southeast Asia, with an average age of 11 years. Similarly, the average of coal-fired power plants in India and China is about 13 years. In Indonesia, 58% of the coal-fired power plants are relatively young, about 10 years and below, and 22% average between 10–20 years in age. With such high dependency on fossil fuel, ASEAN and East Asia will rely on the deployment of CCS/CCUS to curb the significant emissions.

ERIA and other prominent research think tanks share the view that CCS/CCUS will become an important pathway for all countries to meet net zero emissions. CCS/CCUS is not an optional technology but a necessity for countries that need to rejuvenate their system from fossil-based dependency to a system of clean energy and renewables. ERIA is the secretariat of the Asia CCUS Network (ACN) with the vision to contribute to the decarbonisation of the region through collaboration and cooperation on development and deployment of CCUS. Three main aims of the ACN are (1) promoting knowledge sharing through holding an annual forum, conferences and workshops; (2) conducting research studies and surveys on technical, economic and legal standards especially on the common rules of CCUS in the EAS region; and (3) holding capacity building training workshops to bridge the knowledge gap on CCUS. The ACN also supports Southeast Asian countries in identifying the pilot CCUS projects into 2025 and it hopes that CCUS deployment and commercialisation can be realised by 2030. Pertinent studies have been carried out by the ACN in collaboration with knowledge partners. In 2023, the ACN commissioned the Melbourne-based Global CCS Institute (GCCSI) to do four studies and the Indonesian research institute, Badan Riset dan Inovasi Nasional (BRIN) [National Research and Innovation Agency], for one study. Collectively, these studies assess the role of CCS in Southeast Asia to support the achievement of net zero emissions targets, review the policy and legal frameworks necessary to enable CCS to play that role, estimate the need for collaboration between Southeast Asian nations including institutional networks and discuss options to facilitate the financing of CCS in the region. The five studies comprise (1) the geological storage potential of CO_2 in Southeast Asia (Global CCS Institute and ERIA 2024, chapter 1); (2) the establishment of the Asia CCS/CCUS value chain as a collective framework in the Asia Pacific region (chapter 2); (3) the legal and policy framework for deployment of CCUS in Asia, focusing on ASEAN (chapter 3); (4) A study of the financial framework for deployment of CCUS in Asia (Chapter 4); (5) the establishment of basin-scale CO_2 storage in Indonesia (Center for Technology Services, National Research and Innovation Agency [BRIN], Testing Center for Oil and Gas LEMIGAS, and Center for Geological Survey–Geological Agency, Ministry of Energy and Mineral Resources, Indonesia 2024). As presented in the GCCSI and ERIA 2024 publication, *Comprehensive CCUS Research Report: Storage, Value Chain, Policy & Regulation and Financing* (GCCSI and ERIA 2024), these studies provided the following results:

a. ***The Geological Storage Potential of CO_2 in Southeast Asia***: The Executive Summary of the *Comprehensive CCUS Research Report* (Global CCS Institute and ERIA 2024) notes that "Indonesia, Malaysia and Thailand are the most advanced, with suitable and highly suitable offshore and onshore basins, gigatonne storage resources and active CCS facilities. However, only Indonesia has a national regulatory framework to enable CCS. Brunei has a suitable offshore basin with gigatonne storage resources. However, storage development and CCS deployment have not commenced, and the nation lacks a dedicated regulatory environment for CO_2 storage exploration. Vietnam and the Philippines host potential storage basins, but there is no storage development in key areas near strategic industrial emission clusters. Lao, Myanmar and Cambodia were not assessed due to a lack of data, and the storage potential of those countries has never been reviewed. Singapore does not have a storage basin within its borders" (pp. xix–xx). With an estimated 200 gigatonnes (Gt) of storage resources, the six Southeast Asian countries assessed for storage have sufficient resources to enable CCS in the region. Around 98% of the estimated storage resources are in saline formations. The Summary notes that "this estimate is remarkable as only nine saline formations in nine basins were reviewed. However, this estimate carries a large uncertainty since the storage resources for saline formations are for theoretical storage, whereas the hydrocarbon field storage estimate uses field data" (p. xx). In Indonesia alone, the storage resources were estimated to be up to 69 Gt in the selected saline aquifers. Indonesia has significant potential of CO_2 storage in both deep saline aquifers and hydrocarbon fields and is well suited to be part of a regional CCUS hub.

b) ***The Establishment of the Asia CCS/CCUS Value Chain as a Collective Framework in the Asia Pacific Region***: In their chapter in the 2024 GCCSI and ERIA publication on this issue, Alexis Zapantis et al. describe the establishment of such a chain as follows:

"The development of CCS hubs and clusters, bringing together a number of different CO_2 emissions sources and/or storage sites in a connected network, offers participants several advantages over vertically integrated CCS projects. Benefits include reduced costs and risk, enabling more cost-effective transport and storage from small volume sources, and maintaining investment and jobs in high-emitting industrial regions. (p. 92)… Large-scale deployment of CCS in the region will require a coordinated effort between countries ... to develop frameworks and platforms for successful and timely project delivery. Integrated upstream policy and robust institutional frameworks will be key to underpin regional project implementation. In addition, coordinated institutional frameworks, including coherent decarbonisation strategies, project approval and procurement strategies, and investment plans, will reduce project risk and enable capital investment. (p. 93)… The establishment of a centralised body, such as a CCS Value Chain Centre (VCC), to coordinate and administer regional efforts, could accelerate CCS deployment in the region. (p. 113)… The VCC, as a coordinating body, could review and make recommendations on how existing national policies, legislation and regulatory frameworks could be adapted to accommodate and enable regional CCS activities, including identification of near- and mid-term activities to support national regulators and policymakers to align national CCS policies to enable collaboration in the region. In collaboration with national policymakers and regulators, the VCC could implement the Asia CCS Roadmap currently under development" by the Asia CCUS Network. "As a regional body, the VCC could act as an advisory body, tasked with monitoring national CCS legislation and regulation development in the region, in line with the Asia CCS Roadmap and make recommendations to regulators as appropriate. In addition, the VCC could develop an Asia CCS Regulatory Principles guideline, to provide guidance on the approach to developing CCS-specific regulation for the region. The VCC could also play a role in the standardisation of CCS, based on international standards and global best practice and through collaboration with other associations in the climate change space." (p. 114) (Zapantis et al. 2024).

c. ***Legal and Policy Framework for Deployment of CCUS in Asia, focusing on ASEAN***. In the Executive Summary to the aforementioned 2024 Global CCS Institute (GCCSI) and ERIA publication, the editors point out that "The approach to regulating CCS activities is an important preliminary consideration for governments seeking to develop a CCS-specific legal framework. ... Regulators and policymakers may decide to expand the focus of regulatory frameworks to include the broad suite of applications that constitute CCS technologies across the industrial and power sectors. ...Within the region, the experiences of the governments of Indonesia and Thailand offer tangible examples of the processes involved in developing regulatory frameworks for CCS. Both countries have undertaken collaborative, iterative processes, that have engaged a diverse group of stakeholders across various levels of government" (p. xxiii) ... In their chapter in the 2024 publication, Ian Havercroft et al. caution that "There is a risk of delay or a disconnect within the regulatory process, where these stakeholders take time to familiarise themselves with the technology and new regimes" (p. 154). Moreover, "activities involving the transport of CO_2 across international maritime zones and marine areas have implications under a broad range of international agreements, including those relating to the pollution of the marine environment, the safety of maritime transport, the transport of dangerous goods and the carriage of compressed gases. The London Protocol removed barriers to the technology's deployment and provided a basis under the Protocol's mechanisms for the regulation of CO_2 sequestration in sub-seabed geological formations. Recent amendments to this agreement offer an important pathway for facilitating the transboundary transportation of CO_2 for geological storage" (p. 166). Furthermore, "for many nations within the ASEAN region, existing oil and gas operations will provide a good analogue for the various regimes that may also apply to CCS activities". (p. 168) "Compliance with [such] CCS-specific legal and regulatory regimes is an important feature of many carbon crediting schemes that offer support for CCS activities" (p. 170). "The detailed reporting and accounting of stored CO_2, as part of geological storage operations, [are] an important aspect of ensuring compliance with CCS-specific legislation and for ensuring the wider integrity of CCS operations.... The 2006 IPCC Guidelines offer an important indication as to how national accounting schemes may manage the reporting of transboundary CCS operations" (p. 172) "Legal and regulatory issues will arise in the context of transboundary project models, which will trigger obligations under international, regional, and national regimes. The absence of clear legal and regulatory frameworks for these operations, within international and national law, suggests this issue is addressed in the pre-injection phase and prior to operation" (p. 196). "The responsible and safe closure of a CO_2 storage site are the focus of regulatory requirements during the closure phase. Legislation will require project operators to seek authorisation to close a CO_2 storage site upon the fulfilment of prescribed criteria and may include well decommissioning and plugging requirements" (p. 206). Finally, "regulatory obligations during the post-closure phase will include long-term monitoring and responsible site care, to ensure the safety and security of CO_2 storage sites" (Havercroft et al. 2024, p. 211).

d. ***A Study of a Financial Framework for the Deployment of CCUS in the Asian Region, including ASEAN***. CCS and other technologies addressing climate change mitigation deliver a public good. Thus, any consideration of the financing of CCS, or any related technology, necessarily requires a consideration of public policy to ensure that investment is sufficient to maximise societal benefits. All of the AMS have made commitments to achieve net zero emissions by 2050 or 2060. Having prioritised this goal as a commitment, governments need to find the lowest cost solution. This study assumes as its central scenario what it calls the Accelerated Storage Scenario. According to this, 2Gtpa CO_2 must be captured in Southeast Asia by 2060 to support net zero commitments. This will "require almost USD 880 billion to be invested in CCS between now and 2065 across Southeast Asia, peaking at over USD 40 billion per year, on average, in the 2040s. However, this investment will reduce the overall cost to the region of meeting net zero commitments by more than USD 20 trillion over the same period. Mobilising this quantum of capital for CCS will require both public and private finance. The private sector has [the] enormous financial resources, human capital, and capabilities necessary for the development and operation of CCS projects" (GCCSI and ERIA 2024, xxix). However, the sector will be willing to invest only where "there is an appropriate risk weighted return on that investment. Current experience from around the world demonstrates that significant public finance is necessary to leverage the private finance required to accelerate CCS investment. Policies are required that align private investment incentives with public good investment incentives. This can be done through any combination of: increasing the cost of emitting CO_2 (e.g. carbon taxes or emissions trading); command and control mechanisms (e.g. prohibition or mandates through regulation); reducing the cost to private sector investors of CCS (e.g. through capital grants or concessional finance); [and] increasing the revenue created through CCS (e.g. through payments per tonne of CO_2 stored or operational subsidies)" (xxix–xxx). The economic and political structures of the AMS differ significantly from those of the US and EU. ASEAN member states, perhaps apart from Singapore, have far fewer resources available to allocate to climate change mitigation. "Potential sources of external finance for CCS include multilateral development banks (World Bank Group, Asian Development Bank), international climate related funds and foreign direct investment from the governments of developed countries with climate related aid or investments in the region. ASEAN members benefit from the considerable resources, experience and expertise of national and international oil companies that are active in the region. This industry has some of the lowest cost opportunities for very significant emissions reductions in their production value chain. For example, reservoir CO_2 which is currently vented to the atmosphere, may instead be compressed ready for transport and geological storage after minimal clean up (e.g. dehydration). In some cases, existing infrastructure such as pipelines or offshore platforms may be utilised or re-tasked to support CCS operations, very significantly reducing the necessary capital investment. These first projects, being developed in the 2020s, are likely to be the lowest cost opportunities for CCS projects and may also be the anchor projects for the establishment of CCS networks that will serve the broader needs of industry in the region seeking a carbon management solution. In the absence of a material carbon price, these first CCS projects in the region will likely require capital investment support to reach Final Investment Decision[s] (FID[s])" (p. xxx).

3.5 Critical Minerals Supply Chain

To comply with the net zero emissions scenario, demand for the critical minerals related to transition technology is estimated to grow from 7.1 Mt in 2020 to 42.3 Mt in 2050, representing about a six-fold increase over the period. This jump in demand creates concerns over potential energy security in the global sourcing supply chain that China is currently dominating (Han 2023).

China currently leads mine production and reserves of rare earth elements (REE), with 44 million tons in reserves (representing about 35% of global reserves) and 140,000 tons of annual production. The United States re-commenced mining in 2018 and gradually increased production to 38,000 tons in 2021, with 1.5 million tons in reserves. Australia is ranked 3rd in the annual production of 17,000 tons with about 4.1 Mt in reserves. While Vietnam and Brazil have the second and third largest reserves of rare earth metals with 22 million tons in reserves and 21 million tons, respectively, their mine production is among the lowest at only 1,000 tons per year each (Han 2023).

Accounting for 80–85% of the global supply of rare earths, China is the dominant global supplier, and the United States relies heavily on China for about 80% of its rare earth imports. Security of supply has been an issue, underlining the need to develop new sources of rare earths in North America and elsewhere such as Australia, Vietnam and Indonesia. China demonstrated its willingness to use its rare earth elements (REE) monopoly as a diplomatic tool in 2010 when it severely limited REE exports to Japan during arguments over disputed territory. The incident heralded to the world that China had begun to see its REE monopoly as a strategic tool in foreign policy. More recently, China threatened to cut supply of REE to the United States during a trade dispute in 2019.

Thus, Australia, Indonesia, Vietnam and India could be new sources in the supply chain in the near future. Among the potential suppliers, Australia's resources sector is well positioned to develop a cost-competitive domestic processing sector that meets environmental, social and governance considerations. This includes drawing on high labour and environmental standards, reliability as a supplier, and technical expertise to drive production efficiencies. Its high standards and strong resources record give Australia an important advantage in the global critical minerals market. However, Australia, Indonesia and Vietnam will need to address barriers that miners and processors face, including skills and expertise to meet the technical challenges of production, processing and refining, and manage the sustainability of the critical minerals industry.

It is important for the Governments of Australia, Indonesia, Vietnam and India to investigate issues that can help de-risk projects at all stages of development to overcome barriers and attract private investment. This can be done through project facilitation, providing technical support and making strategic investments to scale up processing and lock in finance and offtake for production. There is a need to invest in R&D growth for this sector as China did for decades.

Finally, ERIA will conduct studies on the issue, aiming to provide a stock analysis of the critical minerals supply chain from production, processing to refining. Also of importance are the economic impacts of emerging producers in such critical minerals in the ASEAN region and beyond. It also aims to understand how countries like Indonesia, Vietnam and Australia can forge stronger relationships with key countries in terms of providing supply security of REE. External partners such as the United States, Japan, the Republic of Korea, the United Kingdom (UK), India and the European Union (EU) are key in securing off-take contracts for these critical minerals in the regional supply chains (Han 2023).

3.6 Regional Cooperation: The Asia Zero Emission Community (AZEC)

In a rapidly evolving landscape of environmental concerns, the quest for carbon neutrality in the ASEAN region has become of paramount significance. Recent research, including the 2023 *Energy Outlook and Energy-Saving Potential in East Asia* published by ERIA (Kimura et al. 2023), sheds light on the region's escalating GHG emissions. From 1990 to 2021, these emissions surged fourfold, primarily driven by robust economic growth and a mounting demand for energy. Moreover, the IEA's *World Energy Outlook 2023* indicates that, unless substantial measures are taken, the ASEAN region could potentially become the global leader in absolute growth of CO_2 emissions in the years up to 2050.

Clearly, decarbonisation in this region is pivotal for achieving global carbon neutrality. This achievement is an overarching goal shared by countries worldwide, but the pathways to attain it should be tailored to the unique circumstances of individual nations. In this perspective, decarbonisation in the AMS must be based on two imperatives.

The first imperative: the decarbonisation process must allow the AMS to preserve energy security. Considering the current global instability and the projected surge in energy consumption within the ASEAN region, it has become increasingly vital to ensure a stable energy supply.

The second imperative: decarbonisation must allow the AMS to realise economic growth. The IEA's *World Energy Outlook 2023* reveals that the ASEAN region's share of global energy consumption increased from approximately 4.2% in 2010 to around 4.5% by 2022. The AMS are expected to achieve combined real GDP growth ranging from 3 to 7% between 2005 to 2050. As economic growth continues, energy demand is poised to rise significantly and if plans for decarbonisation fail, this dynamic is estimated to lead to an increase in GHG emissions.

Diverse multilateral organisations, development banks and partner governments are encouraging ASEAN governments to decarbonise the ASEAN economies and achieve their stated policies and announced pledges. Many discussions, joint studies and pilot projects are underway now or are being planned. One of the most recent, the Asia Zero Emission Community (AZEC) launched in 2023 tries to define and implement realistic, just and affordable decarbonisation pathways for ASEAN.

AZEC is strengthening cooperation among ministers of Asian countries to work towards carbon neutrality through strategies, plans, business initiatives and technological developments. These include energy efficiency, RE, hydrogen, ammonia, energy storage, bioenergy and CCUS/carbon recycling as integral components of collaborative efforts between the public and private sectors to achieve zero emissions.

AZEC's vision can be synthesised in three objectives: first, to advance cooperation towards carbon neutrality/net zero emissions while ensuring energy security; second, to promote an energy transition while achieving economic growth, and third, to recognise the existence of various and practical pathways towards carbon neutrality/net zero emissions depending on the circumstances of each country.

In practice, aligned to the respective national policies and legislations, AZEC is expected to be a platform for information sharing, knowledge exchange and implementation of measures in decarbonisation. AZEC provides financial support to boost investment in clean energy infrastructures, including power grids, to secure interoperability of clean technologies and to strengthen human resources capacity.

At the regional level, for instance, the cooperation under AZEC is expected to accelerate the development of the APG in its various aspects, e.g., infrastructure, institutional and regulatory.

At the country level, based on the recent discussions, several topics appear to be potential areas of cooperation beyond decarbonisation, including support for a roadmap towards carbon neutrality, boosting RE penetration, capacity building and developing the potential of ammonia as a fuel source, CCS and CCUS, and green financing. They extend to energy security, especially ensuring stable supplies of LNG.

4 Conclusions, Summary and Policy Implications

Reaching carbon neutrality will require all countries to achieve large-scale GHG emissions reductions, and this involves the fundamental transformation of energy systems: the almost complete decarbonisation of the power sector, followed by the electrification or decarbonisation of energy consumption other than electricity and the offsetting of remaining CO_2 emissions using negative-emission technologies. However, the availability of power systems or low-carbon energy and the possibility of using alternative energy vary significantly across countries and regions, and the energy transition cannot be accomplished uniformly.

While numerous opportunities exist to reduce emissions in ASEAN and the East Asian region to reach carbon neutrality by 2050/60, the transition must safeguard energy supplies. Important too is the recognition that due to economic constraints and widely varying ability to pay the huge costs of decarbonisation, some countries face limitations in suddenly converting to RE. In this regard, this chapter suggests that:

i. improvements in energy efficiency and electrification in end-use sectors, combined with low-carbon power supply, are core strategies for decarbonising ASEAN energy systems;
ii. not only VRE, but also other carbon-free technologies (hydro, geothermal, biomass, nuclear, CO_2-free hydrogen and CCUS) and negative emissions technologies, as well as forest carbon sinks, should contribute to carbon neutrality;
iii. during the transition, fuel switching from coal to natural gas, deployment of more efficient turbines, and co-firing with hydrogen or ammonia, can all play important roles;
iv. while affordable technologies will be deployed in the mid-term, more niche but expensive technologies will be required in the last stage of complete carbon neutrality;
v. to ensure political, economic and social acceptance and a just and inclusive transition, mitigation costs must be reduced through technological innovation, large scale deployment and regional/international cooperation.

Thus, multiple pathways and the promotion of all clean technology and renewables options are key for the success of decarbonisation. Among other important issues of the energy transition, attention must be paid to the fact that the energy systems of most global south countries are heavily reliant on fossil fuels and any energy transformations will need to transition to cleaner systems in an affordable manner.

To pursue the pathway to carbon neutrality, we may need to consider all available technological options including hydrogen and ammonia fuels, CCUS, energy battery storage, renewables and all possible carbon off-setting mechanisms to reduce emissions, while at the same time considering energy affordability, accessibility and energy security. As many countries in ASEAN will still depend on fossil fuels for the foreseeable future, it is very important to have a stepwise and pragmatic approach which leads to a just and inclusive energy transition.

Financing clean technologies and renewables is still one of the most critical issues in the global south countries including ASEAN. Striving for a circular economy may offer environmental benefits and save resources through recirculating a larger share of materials, reducing waste in production, reducing the weight of products and structures and extending the lifetime of products. All of these activities also offer the opportunity for new business models. In addition, the role of digitalisation will offer all countries the possibility of grasping the opportunity to transform their economy in a more efficient way. All economic activities will become more energy efficient, and this will contribute to the reduction of overall emissions and also economy-wide energy intensity. Finally, the global south countries will need to adopt technological innovations that help integrate natural carbon sinks as much as possible.

References

ACE (ASEAN Centre for Energy) (2022) The 7th ASEAN energy outlook (AEO7). ACE, Jakarta. Available at https://aseanenergy.org/work/the-7th-asean-energy-outlook/. Accessed 5 Sept 2023

APERC (Asia Pacific Energy Research Centre) (2018) Perspectives on hydrogen in the APEC region. Asia Pacific Energy Research Centre, Tokyo. Available at https://aperc.or.jp/file/2018/9/12/Perspectives+on+Hydrogen+in+the+APEC+Region.pdf. Accessed 12 Dec 2025

ASEAN (Association of Southeast Asian Nations) (2021) ASEAN fuel economy roadmap for the transport sector 2018–2025: with focus on light-duty vehicles. ASEAN Secretariat, Jakarta. Available at https://asean.org/wp-content/uploads/2021/11/ASEAN-Fuel-Economy-Roadmap-FINAL.pdf. Accessed 26 Nov 2024

Ball M, Weeda M (2015) The hydrogen economy—vision or reality? In: Ball M, Basile A, Veziroğlu TN (eds) Compendium of hydrogen energy volume 4: hydrogen use, safety and the hydrogen economy. Elsevier, Amsterdam, chapter 11. Available at http://www.elsevier.com/books/compendium-of-hydrogen-energy/ball/978-1-78242-364-5. Accessed 26 Nov 2024

Center for Technology Services, National Research and Innovation Agency (BRIN), Testing Center for Oil and Gas LEMIGAS, and Center for Geological Survey–Geological Agency, Ministry of Energy and Mineral Resources, Indonesia (2024) Estimating basin scale CO_2 storage in Indonesia. ERIA, Jakarta. Available at https://www.eria.org/research/estimating-basin-scale-co2-storage-in-indonesia. Accessed 12 Dec 2025

Enkvist P-A, Nauclér T, Rosander J (2007) A cost curve for greenhouse gas reduction. McKinsey Quarterly. Available at https://www.mckinsey.com/business-functions/sustainability/our-insights/a-cost-curve-for-greenhouse-gas-reduction. Accessed 10 Jan 2025

ERIA (Economic Research Institute for ASEAN and East Asia) (2022a) The Comprehensive Asia Development Plan (CADP) 3.0: towards an integrated, innovative, inclusive, and sustainable economy. Available at https://www.eria.org/publications/the-comprehensive-asia-development-plan-cadp-30-towards-an-integrated-innovative-inclusive-and-sustainable-economy/. Accessed 12 Feb 2024

ERIA (Economic Research Institute for ASEAN and East Asia) (2022b) Technology List and Perspectives for Transition Finance in Asia (TLPTFA). Available at https://www.eria.org/research/technology-list-and-perspectives-for-transition-finance-inasia#:~:text=1st%20Version%20The%20Technology%20List,while%20considering%20energy%20security%2C%20affordability%2C. Accessed 26 Nov 2024

ERIA (Economic Research Institute for ASEAN and East Asia) (2024) Call for proposals: the carbon market in ASEAN and East Asia. Available at https://www.eria.org/news-and-views/call-for-proposals--the-carbon-market-in-asean-and-east-asia. Accessed 10 Oct 2024

Global CCS Institute (GCCSI) and ERIA (2024) Comprehensive CCUS research report: storage, value chain, policy & regulation and financing. ERIA, Jakarta. Available at https://www.eria.org/uploads/Comprehensive-CCUS-Research-Report.pdf. Accessed 9 Oct 2024

Hamdi E (2020) Racing towards 23% renewable energy. Institute for Energy Economics and Financial Analysis [Ohio, USA]. Available at https://ieefa.org/wp-content/uploads/2020/02/Racing-Towards-23-Percent-Renewable-Energy_February-2020.pdf. Accessed 26 Nov 2024

Han P (2022) Decarbonization of ASEAN energy systems: the optimum technology selection model analysis up to 2060. Presentation at the 1st Asia Green Growth Partnership Ministerial, 25 April 2022. Available at https://www.meti.go.jp/press/2022/04/20220425001/20220425001-6.pdf. Accessed 10 Oct 2024

Han P (2023) A secure and reliable rare earth mineral supply chain to meet net-zero emissions by 2050. The Asian Development Bank (ADB) Southeast Asia Development Solutions (SEADS). Available at https://seads.adb.org/solutions/secure-and-reliable-rare-earth-mineral-supply-chain-meet-net-zero-emissions-2050. Accessed 10 Oct 2024

Havercroft I et al (2024) Legal and policy framework for deployment of CCUS in Asia Region, focused on ASEAN. In: Global CCS Institute (GCCSI) and ERIA, Comprehensive CCUS research report: storage, value chain, policy & regulation and financing. ERIA, Jakarta, pp 117–211. Available at https://www.eria.org/uploads/Comprehensive-CCUS-Research-Report.pdf. Accessed 9 Oct 2024

IEA (International Energy Agency) (2019) Future of hydrogen. Seizing today's opportunities. Report prepared by the IEA for the G20, Japan. Paris. Available at https://iea.blob.core.windows.net/assets/9e3a3493-b9a6-4b7d-b499-7ca48e357561/The_Future_of_Hydrogen.pdf. Accessed 24 Nov 2024

IEA (International Energy Agency) (2021) Net zero by 2050: a road map for the global energy sector. Available at https://www.iea.org/reports/net-zero-by-2050. Accessed 10 Mar 2023

IEA (International Energy Agency) (2024) Global energy and climate model: documentation 2024. Paris. Available at https://iea.blob.core.windows.net/assets/89a1aa9a-e1bd-4803-b37b-59d6e7fba1e9/GlobalEnergyandClimateModelDocumentation2024.pdf. Accessed 12 Jan 2025

Kimura S et al (eds) (2022) Decarbonisation of ASEAN energy systems: optimum technology selection model analysis up to 2060. Available at https://www.eria.org/publications/decarbonisation-of-asean-energy-systems-optimum-technology-selection-model-analysis-up-to-2060/. Accessed 22 Nov 2022

Kimura S, Han P, Purwanto AJ (eds) (2023) Energy outlook and energy-saving potential in East Asia 2023. Economic Research Institute for ASEAN and East Asia (ERIA), Jakarta. Available at https://www.eria.org/publications/energy-outlook-and-energy-saving-potential-in-east-asia-2023. Accessed 12 Jan 2025

Milton T (2020) Hydrogen vs battery electric. Why Nikola is the leader. Reality sets in. Available at https://www.linkedin.com/pulse/hydrogen-vs-battery-electric-why-nikola-leader-reality-trevor-milton/. Accessed 27 Nov 2024

Otsuki T, Komiyama R, Fujii Y (2019) Techno-economic assessment of hydrogen energy in the electricity and transport sectors using a spatially-disaggregated global energy system model. J Japan Inst Energy 98(4):62–72. Available at https://eneken.ieej.or.jp/en/report_detail.php?article_info__id=8602. Accessed 27 Nov 2024

United Nations Framework Convention on Climate Change (UNFCCC) (2021) COP 26 Glasgow Climate Pact. Available at https://unfccc.int/process-and-meetings/the-paris-agreement/the-glasgow-climate-pact-key-outcomes-from-cop26. Accessed 11 Oct 2024

World Bank Group (2022a) Global Solar Atlas. Available at https://globalsolaratlas.info/map. Accessed 27 Nov 2024

World Bank Group (2022b) Global Wind Atlas. Available at https://globalwindatlas.info/en

Zapantis A, et al (2024) Establishment of Asia CCS/CCUS value chain as a collective framework in the Asia Pacific Region. In: Global CCS Institute (GCCSI) and ERIA, Comprehensive CCUS research report: storage, value chain, policy & regulation and financing. ERIA, Jakarta, pp 65–117. Available at https://www.eria.org/uploads/Comprehensive-CCUS-Research-Report.pdf. Accessed 9 Oct 2024

Net Zero Transition and the Power Sector in ASEAN: Perspectives from an Integrated Electricity Market

Youngho Chang

Abstract ASEAN has various electricity generation technologies available to achieve its net zero transition by 2050. This study examines the role of cross-border power trade in helping ASEAN achieve this goal. It presents the following perspectives. First, when emissions are capped at the 2030 level, emissions from cross-border power trade appear to be relatively lower than those where there is no such trade. Second, the initial phase of cross-border power trade appears to be correlated with a decrease in total capacity, but as this trade increases, total capacity increases while total system cost decreases. Third, solar PV appears to be the key driver for achieving the net zero transition by 2050; hydropower is second. Fourth, total system cost appears to decrease when more cross-border power trade is allowed. Fifth, when more cross-border power trade is allowed, solar PV and hydropower appear to replace natural gas.

1 Introduction

Countries at the meetings of the UNFCC Conference of Parties (COP) held in Paris (2015), Glasgow (2021) and Sharm el-Sheikh (2022) agreed to work towards stabilising the rise of the global mean surface temperature to 1.5 °C compared to the pre-industrial level by 2050. This in turn has led many countries to declare their pledges to achieve the net zero transition by 2050.

This transition implies that the amount of carbon dioxide (CO_2) emissions reduced or removed (sequestered) at source can offset the amount of CO_2 emitted in an economy. There are a few ways to decrease these emissions—reducing energy consumption, switching to less carbon-emitting energy sources and improving energy efficiency. Switching includes producing hydrogen from non-CO_2-emitting sources or resorting to nuclear energy. All these options come with costs and affect an economy negatively. Apart from reducing the CO_2 emissions at source, removing or

Y. Chang (✉)
Singapore University of Social Sciences, Singapore, Singapore
e-mail: yhchang@suss.edu.sg

H. Phoumin et al. (eds.), *Tackling the Energy Transition: Insights from ASEAN and Beyond*, Climate Change and Energy Transition,
https://doi.org/10.1007/978-981-96-6019-3_3

sequestering emissions incurs costs and raises another question: where is the removed CO_2 to be put?

CO_2 emissions are expected to stay in the atmosphere for about 150 or 200 years, until they completely dissipate into a natural sink such as an ocean (Nordhaus 2008; Yin and Chang 2020). This means that as long as the emissions are in the atmosphere, they contribute to radiative forcing, which is the main process by which the global mean surface temperature is increasing. Hence, achieving net zero emissions by 2050 implies that the level of CO_2 emissions must peak by 2030 at the latest (Fankhauser et al. 2022).

Through their Nationally Determined Contributions (NDCs), each ASEAN Member State (AMS) has pledged to achieve its net zero transition by 2050. A study using the Low Emissions Analysis Platform (LEAP) presents various pathways for the AMS to reach this goal. It projects greenhouse gas emissions and the costs of meeting the Paris climate goal (Handayani et al. 2022). However, this study does not consider how cross-border power trade in the ASEAN power sector affects AMS' pathways to achieve net zero emissions.

A cross-border power trade model projects the level of CO_2 emissions in the ASEAN power sector with the assumption that there are no constraints on using electricity generation technologies. The CO_2 emissions are expected to peak around 2040 as shown in Fig. 3.1.

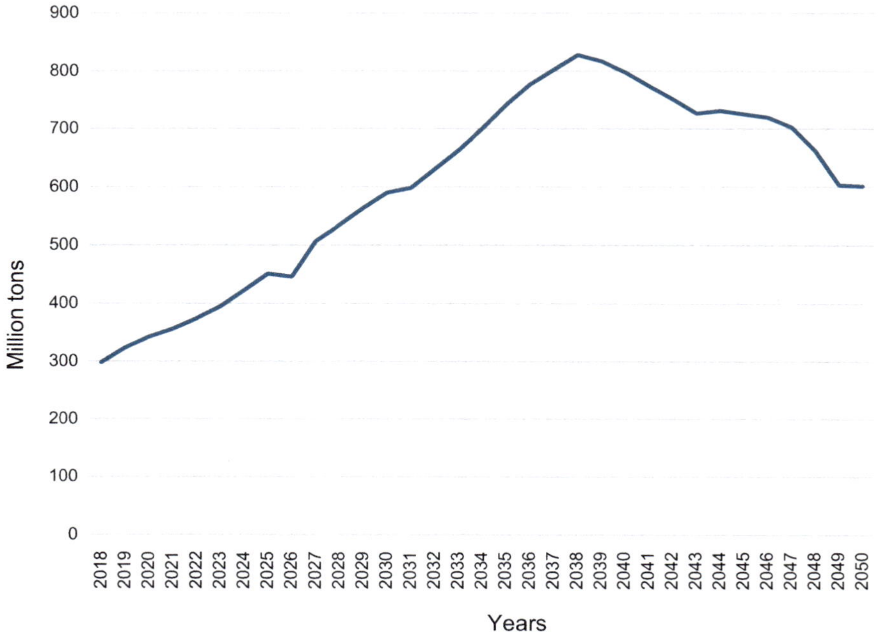

Fig. 3.1 Projected CO_2 emissions in the ASEAN power sector (million tons). *Source* Author's own calculations

This study aims to explore options for electricity generation technologies to achieve the net zero transition by 2050 in the ASEAN power sector and examine the economic and environmental implications of this transition for ASEAN. It both demonstrates how ASEAN power trading will promote renewable energy (RE) development in the region and draws policy implications. The study proceeds by collecting and evaluating information relating to electricity generation technologies in ASEAN to construct a model for simulating cross-border power trading. It then solves the model and derives solutions and policy implications, using the General Algebraic Modeling System (GAMS).

The objective of the model is to minimise the total cost of electricity generation in ASEAN from 2018 to 2050. The model considers capital and operating expenditure of generation capacities, CO_2 emissions and costs and cross-border transmission costs and losses. It also considers interconnection plans for power grids in ASEAN.

This study constructs four scenarios according to the extent of cross-border power trade of up to 50% and 80% of the domestic demand of each AMS. The reference scenario is the business-as-usual (BAU) case in which no cross-border power trade is allowed and no caps on emissions are imposed.

The simulation results of the cross-border power trade model are expected to present whether and how electricity generation technologies in ASEAN would help the AMS achieve their net zero transitions by 2050 and the economic and environmental implications of the net zero transition by 2050 for the ASEAN region as a whole.

The remainder of this chapter is structured as follows. Section 2 reviews what benefits an integrated electricity market in ASEAN will bring and how the net zero transition can be achieved in its power sector. Section 3 presents the model, four scenarios and the data. Section 4 presents results, discussions and policy implications, and Sect. 5 provides the conclusions.

2 Development of Renewable Energy Sources and Cross-Border Power Trade

Studies on the potential benefits of regional power market integration in ASEAN have noted that such an integrated power market could bring tangible benefits such as regional development and lower levels of CO_2 emissions (Yu 2003; Yu et al. 2005; Watcharejyothin and Shrestha 2009; Economic Consulting Associates [ECA] 2010). Linking resource-rich and resource-poor AMS in an integrated electricity market could reduce the overall costs of meeting the region's growing electricity demand (Chang and Li 2013; Li and Chang 2015).

Hydropower is one of the abundant RE resources in ASEAN (Energy Institute 2023). Cross-border power trade could help ASEAN as a whole make this renewable potential a reality (Chang and Han 2021). Excess electricity generated from renewable forms of energy could be wasted unless it were tapped to other uses such as producing hydrogen to replace the fossil fuels currently used to generate electricity (Chang and Han 2022). Cross-border power trade in an integrated ASEAN electricity market may well promote the development of RE sources, especially hydropower in the Greater Mekong Sub-region (GMS), which in turn reduces the amount of CO_2 emitted in the region as a whole (Chang 2024). The LEAP study mentioned above projects greenhouse gas emissions and the costs of meeting the Paris climate goal but does not consider how cross-border power trade in the ASEAN power sector affects the AMS' pathways to achieve net zero emissions.

To decarbonise the ASEAN power sector, simultaneous use of both fossil and non-fossil electricity generation technologies is suggested. For fossil fuel-fired electricity generation, switching to natural gas and adopting carbon capture and storage (CCS) are recommended. For the non-fossil fuel-fired electricity generation technologies, hydropower, biomass, geothermal energy and solar PV appear to have good potential to promote the decarbonisation of the power sector in some AMS (Lau 2023).

3 Model, Scenarios and Data

3.1 Model Descriptions

This study builds a cross-border power trade model following Turvey and Anderson (1977), Chang and Tay (2006), Chang and Li (2013) and Li and Chang (2015). The objective of this model is to minimise the total cost of electricity generation in ASEAN from 2018 to 2050 with regard to capital expenditure, operation expenditure, CO_2 emissions and costs, cross-border transmission costs and losses, and various constraint conditions. The plans for interconnecting the existing power grids in ASEAN are highlighted in the examination of the possibilities for achieving the net zero transition in the ASEAN power sector. This study provides a lower bound cost estimate by not only assuming that the planned ASEAN Power Grid operates on schedule, but also by accounting for transmission costs and losses over distances between countries in calculating the total cost of meeting the region's electricity demand.

The capital expenditure (CAPEX) of a given type of power generation capacity at a given time is expressed as follows:

$$\sum_{i=1}^{I}\sum_{v=1}^{T}\sum_{m=1}^{M} c_{miv} * x_{miv}, \qquad (1)$$

where x_{miv} is the capacity of plant type m, vintage v, in country i. Vintage indicates the date when a given type of capacity is built and made operational. c_{miv} is the corresponding capital cost per unit of capacity of the plant. In addition to the vintage dimension, a time dimension is added to the equation for simulation purposes and consistency in presentation with other cost terms, allowing capital cost amortisation using a capital recovery factor.

The operational expenditure (OPEX) of the said type of power generation capacity at a given time is expressed as follows:

$$Opex(t) = \sum_{i=1}^{I}\sum_{j}^{J}\sum_{v=-V}^{t}\sum_{p=1}^{P}\sum_{m=1}^{M} F_{mitv} * u_{mijtvp} * \theta_{jp}, \tag{2}$$

where u_{mijtvp} is the power output of plant m, vintage v, in year t, country i, block p on the load (i.e., peak and off-peak period), and exported to country j. F_{mitv} is the corresponding operating cost that varies with v, and θ_{jp} is the time interval of load block p within each year in the destination country.

The amount of CO_2 emissions from different power generation types or technologies is expressed as follows:

$$\sum_{m=1}^{M}\sum_{i=1}^{I}\sum_{j=1}^{J}\sum_{v=-V}^{T} u_{mijtvp} * \theta_{jp} * ce_m \tag{3}$$

and the carbon cost in year t is expressed as follows:

$$CC(t) = cp_t * \left(\sum_{m=1}^{M}\sum_{i=1}^{I}\sum_{j=1}^{J}\sum_{v=-V}^{T} u_{mijtvp} * \theta_{jp} * ce_m\right), \tag{4}$$

where ce_m expresses the CO_2 emissions per unit of power plant capacity of type j plant, and cp_t is the carbon price per unit of CO_2 emissions in year t.

Cross-border transmission costs comprise tariffs and transmission loss. The tariff is paid to recover grid line capital investments and operational costs. Transmission loss may be significant over long transmission distances. To model tariffs, let tp_{ijv} be the amount of new transmission capacity added between country i and j at year v. Then ct_{ijv} and co_{ijv} are the annualised CAPEX, with a 30-year contract and stipulated IRR embedded, and OPEX of the new transmission capacity, respectively. The total cost of cross-border power transmission in year t is expressed as follows:

$$TC(t) = \sum_{i=1}^{I}\sum_{j=1}^{J}\sum_{v=-V}^{T} \left(ct_{ijv} + co_{ijv}\right) * tp_{ijv}. \tag{5}$$

As mentioned above, the objective of the power trade model is to minimise the total cost of electricity during the period being studied. The objective function is written as:

$$obj = \sum_{i=1}^{I}\sum_{v=1}^{T}\sum_{m=1}^{M} c_{miv} * x_{miv} + \sum_{t=1}^{T}\{Opex(t) + CC(t) + TC(t)\} \tag{6}$$

Several constraints are required to optimise this objective function. This study makes some key assumptions about meeting domestic demand and surplus electricity trading. First, total installed regional power generation capacity should be greater than or equal to total regional electricity demand. Second, total electricity output in each country is constrained by the load factor of each installed capacity of all types of electricity generation in the country. Third, the electricity supply of every country in the region should be greater than or equal to said country's electricity demand. Fourth, total electricity supply from one country to all countries in the region, including the country itself, must be less than or equal to the country's total available supply capacity at a given time.

Equation (7) shows a first set of constraints, which requires total power capacity to meet total power demand in the region. Q_{itp} is the power demand of country i in year t for load block p:

$$\sum_{i=1}^{I}\sum_{j=1}^{J}\sum_{m=1}^{M}\sum_{v=-V}^{t} u_{mijtvp} \geq \sum_{i=1}^{I} Q_{itp} \tag{7}$$

The second constraint, shown in Eq. (8), states that the constraint of load factor lf_{mi} of each installed capacity of power generation. kit_{mi} is the initial vintage capacity of type m power plant in country i:

$$u_{mijtvp} \leq lf_{mi} * (kit_{mi} + x_{miv}) \tag{8}$$

The third constraint, shown in Eq. (9), states that all countries' power supply to a given country must be greater than the country's demand. $tl_{i,j}$ is the ratio of transmission loss in cross-border electricity trade between country i and country j:

$$\sum_{j=1}^{J}\sum_{m=1}^{M}\sum_{v=-V}^{t} u_{mijtvp} \cdot tl_{ij} \geq Q_{itp} \tag{9}$$

The fourth constraint, shown in Eq. (10), states that the total power supply of one country to all countries, including itself, must be less than the aggregate of the country's.

available power capacity at the time:

$$\sum_{j=1}^{J} u_{mijtvp} \leq \sum_{m=1}^{M}\sum_{v=-V}^{t} lf_{mi} * (kit_{mi} + x_{miv}) \tag{10}$$

The fifth constraint, shown in Eq. (11), is the capacity reserve constraint. pr is the rate of reserve capacity as required by regulation. $p = 1$ represents the peak load block:

$$\sum_{i}^{I}\sum_{m=1}^{M}\sum_{v=-V}^{t} lf_{mi} * (kit_{mi} + x_{miv}) \geq (1 + pr) * \sum_{i}^{I} Q_{it,p=1} \tag{11}$$

Hydroelectric facilities have a so-called energy factor constraint, as shown in Eq. (12). ef_{mi} is the energy factor of plant type m in country i. Other facilities have $ef = 1$:

$$\sum_{p=1}^{P}\sum_{j=1}^{J} u_{mijtvp} \leq ef_{mi} * (kit_{mi} + x_{miv}) \tag{12}$$

Last, the development of power generation capacity faces the resource availability constraint, per Eq. (13). $XMAX_{mi}$ is the type of resource constraint of plant type m in country i:

$$\sum_{v=1}^{T} x_{miv} \leq XMAX_{mi} \tag{13}$$

3.2 Scenarios

As shown in Fig. 3.1, achieving the net zero transition by 2050 means that emissions must peak by 2030. Using a cross-border power trade model developed by Chang and Li (2013), Li and Chang (2015) and Chang (2024), this study takes the peak level of emissions at 2030 from the BAU case of the cross-border power trade model. There are four scenarios: Business-As-Usual (NZT NT BAU), No cross-border power trade with emissions capped at the level of 2030 (NZT NT 2030), Cross-border power trade up to 50% of domestic demand for each AMS with emissions capped at the level of 2030 (NZT T50 2030), and Cross-border power trade up to 80% of domestic demand for each AMS with emissions capped at the level of 2030 (NZT T80 2030). The reference scenario is constructed by replicating the current cross-border transmission network in which no cross-border power trade takes place. This scenario replicates current GMS system-to-system interconnections where no third-party or open access is allowed, to reflect current GMS cross-border interconnections. The model is solved using GAMS. Table 3.1 provides a summary of these scenarios.

Of the two scenarios of cross-border power trade, NZT T50 2030 imposes a minimum level of electricity supplied from domestic sources at 50%: up to 50% of a country's electricity demand can be met by imports. NZT T80 2030 imposes the

Table 3.1 Scenarios

Scenarios	Maximum import %	Remarks
NZT NT BAU	No cross-border imports	Reference case
NZT NT 2030	No cross-border imports	Emissions peak in 2030
NZT T50 2030	Up to 50% imports	Emissions peak in 2030
NZT T80 2030	Up to 80% imports	Emissions peak in 2030

Source Author's compilation

Table 3.2 Ongoing and planned cross-border power transmission line projects in the ASEAN Power Grid (APG)

Country A	Country B	To be completed in (according to 2018 data)	Capacity (MW)
Cambodia	Vietnam	2019	465
Cambodia	Thailand	2025	1800
Indonesia	Malaysia	2020	200
Brunei	Malaysia	2020	100
Laos	Thailand	2018	1169
Laos	Thailand	2019	1535
Laos	Thailand	2020	630
Laos	Thailand	2023	1040
Laos	Vietnam	2020	100
Singapore	Malaysia	2018	600
Singapore	Indonesia	2020	600
Philippines	Malaysia	2020	500
Myanmar	Thailand	2022	1190
Myanmar	Thailand	2025	10,150

Sources Chimklai (2013), Zhai (2010), ADB (2013), APERC (2004), and Bunthoeun (2012)

level of minimum electricity supplied from domestic sources at 20%: up to 80% of a country's electricity demand can be met by imports.

Table 3.2 presents planned interconnections with completion dates and capacities as of 2018.

3.3 Data

This study covers all ten AMS: Brunei, Cambodia, Indonesia, Lao PDR, Malaysia, Myanmar, the Philippines, Singapore, Thailand and Vietnam. Technologies for power generation discussed in the study are coal, coal CCS, diesel, natural gas, natural gas CCS, hydro, small hydro, geothermal, wind, solar PV and biomass. The period studied by this optimisation simulation model is 2018–2050.

Key data are existing capacities of power generation types, their CAPEX and OPEX, the load factor and life expectancy of each vintage, resources available for power generation in each country, peak and non-peak demand and duration of demand in each country, projected demand growth rates, and cross-border power trade transmission cost and loss. This study takes data used in Chang and Li (2013) and Li and Chang (2015) and updates initial capacities given in Chang and Li (2013) based on data taken from ACE (the ASEAN Centre for Energy) (2022), IRENA (the International Renewable Energy Agency) and ACE (2019), the Energy Information Administration [U.S.] (EIA) (2020) and Handayani et al. (2022). Figure 3.2 shows ASEAN's initial installed capacity by plant type as of 2018. Relevant data for this figure are collected from various sources such as ACE, the International Energy Agency (IEA) and the statistical offices of the respective AMS.

The load factors of various generation technologies are as shown in Table 3.3. (The Appendix gives input data and sources.)

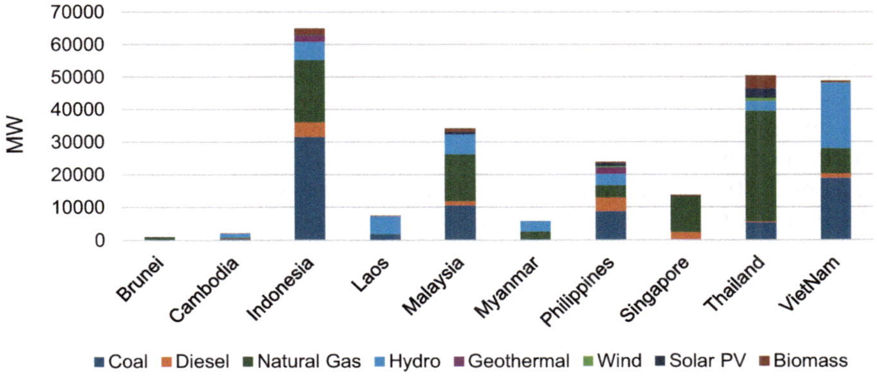

Fig. 3.2 Installed capacity by plant type in ASEAN, 2018 (MW). *Sources* ACE (2022) and IRENA and ACE (2019)

Table 3.3 Load factors of generation technologies

Type of generation technologies	Load factor
Fossil fuel-fired	0.80–0.95
Hydro	0.90
Geothermal	0.90
Wind	0.28
Solar PV	0.177
Biofuel	0.80

Sources Chang and Li (2013) and Handayani et al. (2022)

4 Results, Discussion and Policy Implications

This study presents power generation technologies and the level of power trade among the AMS required to meet the transition to net zero in the ASEAN power sector by 2050. The key results are as follows. First, in two scenarios of cross-border power trade (NZT T50 2030 and NZT T80 2030), CO_2 emissions appear to be lower than in the scenario of no cross-border power trade with emissions capped at the 2030 level (NZT NT 2030). Second, when cross-border power trade is allowed, the total capacity appears to decrease initially. However, as more cross-border power trade is allowed, the total capacity increases but the total system cost decreases. Third, solar PV appears to be the key driver for achieving the net zero transition by 2050, followed by hydropower. Fourth, total system cost or objective value appears to decrease when more cross-border power trade is allowed. NZT T80 2030 appears to be the least costly case while NZT NT BAU appears to be the costliest. Fifth, when more cross-border power trade is allowed, solar PV and hydropower appear to replace natural gas.

4.1 Carbon Emissions

As shown in Fig. 3.3, in the BAU scenario, CO_2 emissions appear to peak around 2040 and decrease afterwards. When the level of these emissions is capped at the level of 2030 from that year onwards, the other three scenarios show an apparent decrease in CO_2 emissions. However, when cross-border power trade is allowed as shown in the two scenarios of NZT T50 2030 and NZT T80 2030, the level of CO_2 emissions is lower over the entire period. In the NZT T50 2030 scenario, hydropower appears to be the key driver of reduced CO_2 emissions while for the NZT T80 2030, solar PV appears to be the key driver.

4.2 Total Capacity

Figure 3.4 shows that total capacity appears to increase when the level of CO_2 emissions is capped at the level of 2030 from 2030 onwards and no cross-border power trade is allowed. But it appears to decrease when cross-border power trade is allowed. When the allowed level of cross-border power trade increases, total capacity increases but the level of CO_2 emissions appears to be lower when the level of cross-border power trade is lower. Total system cost also appears to be lower when the allowed level of cross-border power trade increases.

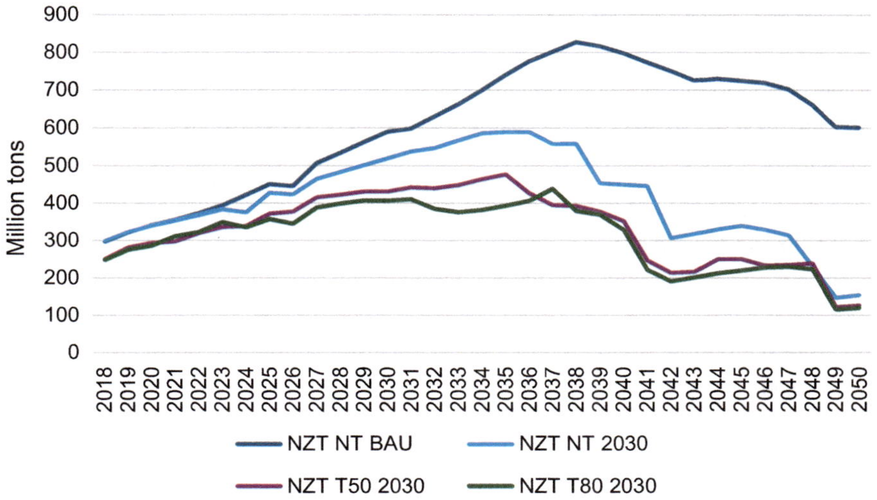

Fig. 3.3 CO_2 emissions: No Trade, 50% and 80% Trade (million tons). *Source* Author's calculations

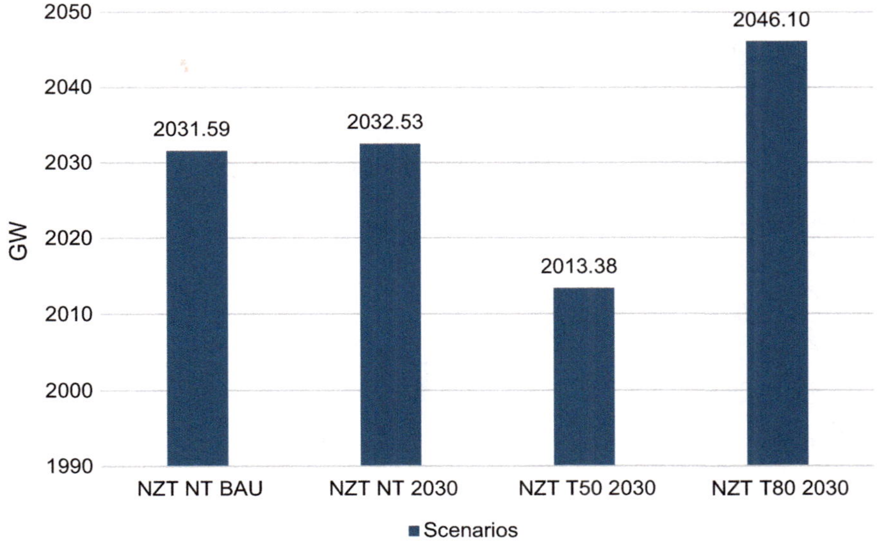

Fig. 3.4 Total capacity (Unit: GW). *Source* Author's calculations

4.3 Total Capacity by Fuel

Figure 3.5 presents the total capacity by fuel in 2050 including solar PV; Fig. 3.6 presents the total capacity by fuel excluding solar PV. As shown in Figs. 3.5 and 3.7, solar PV appears to be the main fuel for electricity generation from 2040 onwards. Indeed, it appears to dwarf the other fuels. Hydropower appears to be an earlier driver of the net zero transition as shown in Figs. 3.6 and 3.8. It appears to be extensively used from 2025 to 2037 by which time solar PV is used.

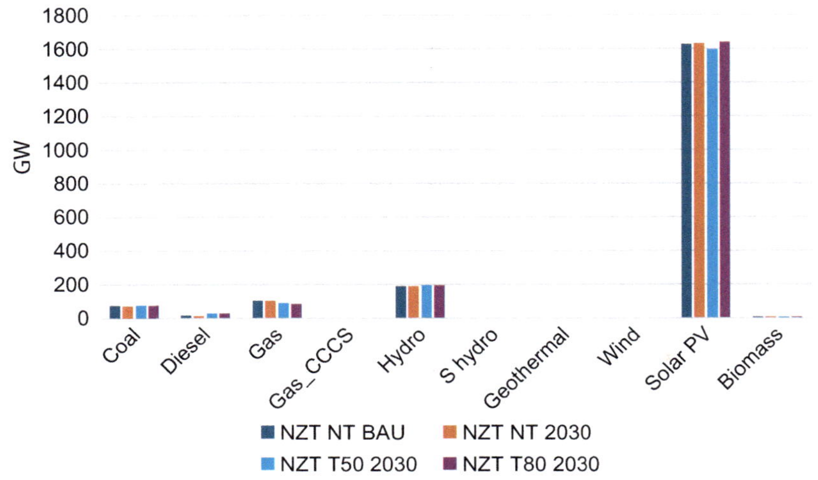

Fig. 3.5 Total capacity by fuel (Unit: GW). *Source* Author's calculations

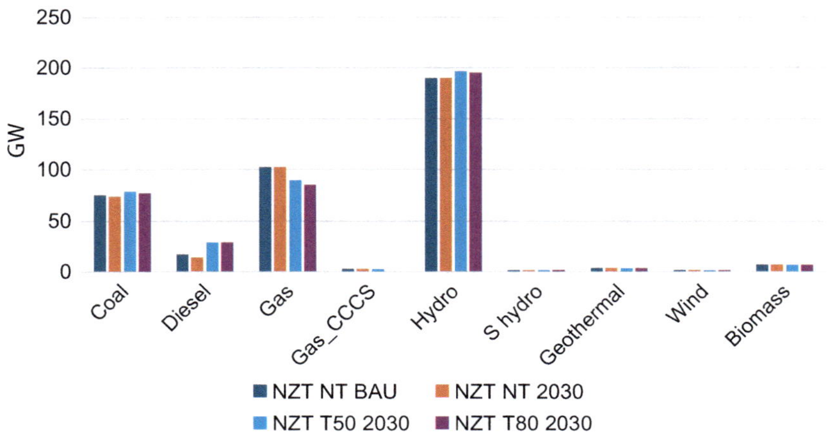

Fig. 3.6 Total capacity by fuel excluding solar PV (Unit: GW). *Source* Author's calculations

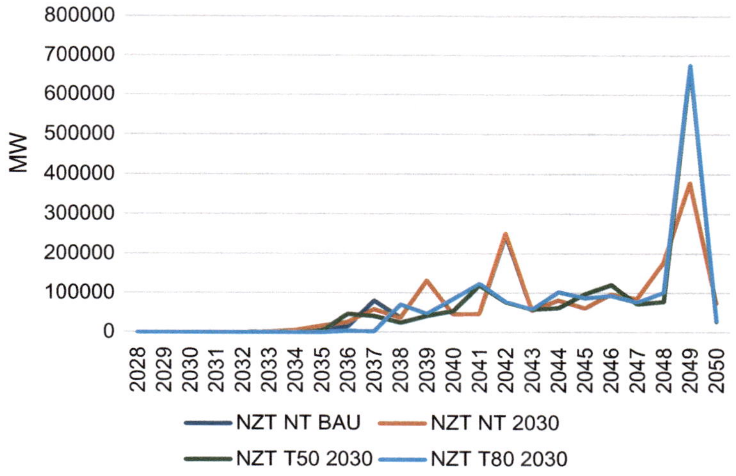

Fig. 3.7 Added capacity by solar PV (Unit: MW). *Source* Author's calculations

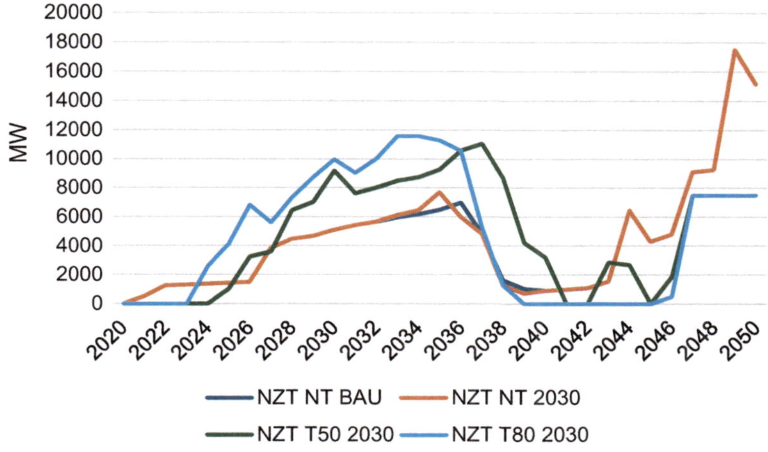

Fig. 3.8 Added capacity by hydropower (Unit: MW). *Source* Author's calculations

4.4 Added Capacity by Fuel

Figures 3.7 and 3.8 present added capacity by solar PV and hydropower, respectively. Solar PV appears to be extensively used from 2037 onwards and to peak in 2049, mainly due to its cost-competitiveness.

As shown in Fig. 3.8, hydropower appears to be extensively used from around 2026 to 2037 and to be extensively used again from 2046 onwards. As shown in Fig. 3.4, however, the magnitude of hydropower use is about 15% of solar PV use.

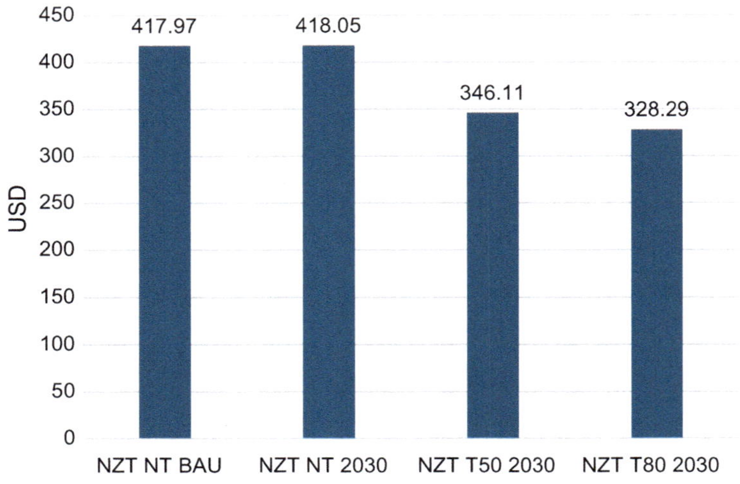

Fig. 3.9 Objective values (million USD). *Source* Author's calculations

4.5 Total System Cost

Figure 3.9 presents total system cost or objective value. When the level of CO_2 emissions is capped at the level of 2030 from 2030 onwards, total system cost appears to increase. However, total system cost appears to decrease when cross-border power trade is allowed. The higher the level of cross-border power trade, the lower the total system cost will be.

5 Conclusions

Reaching the goal of net zero emissions by 2050 would require, as mentioned above, that the level of CO_2 emissions in the ASEAN power sector peaks around 2030. Even if the level of CO_2 emissions in this sector appears to increase until 2040, the region is endowed with huge quantities of RE resources such as hydropower, wind and solar. It also has the applicable power technologies to achieve the goal. Among various renewable sources, solar PV and hydropower will likely be the key drivers of this transition.

The following policy implications are drawn from the key findings. First, it would be beneficial to complete the planned cross-border interconnections across ASEAN. As shown in Fig. 3.9, the total discounted system cost is the lowest under the scenario in which up to 80% of the domestic demand of each country is allowed to be imported. This is the net benefit after taking into account transmission costs and losses. This could justify why the planned cross-border interconnections should be completed sooner rather than later. Second, it would also be good to accelerate the integration of solar PV and hydropower into the ASEAN power system. As shown in Figs. 3.5 and 3.6, solar PV and hydropower appear to be the key electricity generation technologies that could help ASEAN achieve the transition by 2050. However, addressing possible environmental repercussions of hydropower development should be considered. Third, it is imperative to develop transparent, fair and efficient frameworks for cross-border power trade in the sector. The outcomes of the cross-border power trade model clearly show how cross-border power trade could help the AMS achieve their transitions when acting collectively. However, the current framework for cross-border power trade is not ready to realise its possible benefits in ASEAN.

Appendix: Input Data of the Model and Sources of Data

See Tables 4, 5, 6, 7, 8, and 9.

Table 4 CAPEX, OPEX, lifespan and availability of power generation assets

	Coal*	Diesel	Natural Gas	Hydro**	Geothermal	Wind	Solar PV	Biomass
CAPEX (million USD/MW)	1.710	0.800	0.945	2.125	3.249	2.025	1.195	2.150
OPEX (USD/MWh)	18.42	66.43	37.36	12.60	6.59	24.46	9.29	17.98
Lifespan (years)	30	30	30	50	30	27	25	25
Load factor (percentage of year)	0.80	0.95	0.85	0.36	0.90	0.28	0.177	0.80
CO_2 emissions (ton/MWh)	1.0	0.8	0.5	0.001	0.05	0.01	0.05	0.05

*Due to their abundance of coal resources, Indonesia, Malaysia, Thailand and Vietnam are assumed to have 30% lower CAPEX and OPEX in coal-fired power generation

**Due to their abundance of hydropower resources, Cambodia, Indonesia, Laos, Malaysia, Myanmar and the Philippines are assumed to have 30% lower CAPEX and OPEX in hydropower generation

Sources IEA (2010), EU Commission (2008), Energy Information Administration [U.S.] (2020), and Handayani et al. (2022)

Table 5 Power generation resources in the AMS (MW)

	Brunei	Cambodia	Indonesia	Laos	Malaysia	Myanmar	Philippines	Singapore	Thailand	Vietnam
Coal	15,000	15,000	50,000	15,000	50,000	30,000	30,000	0	50,000	50,000
Diesel	15,000	15,000	15,000	15,000	15,000	15,000	15,000	0	15,000	15,000
Natural Gas	15,000	15,000	50,000	15,000	50,000	30,000	30,000	30,000	50,000	50,000
Hydro	700	10,000	75,000	26,000	29,000	40,400	10,500	0	15,000	35,000
Geothermal	0	0	29,500	50	0	0	4,000	0	0	340
Wind	20	69,000	50,000	13,000	2,000	482,000	217,000	20	239,000	311,000
Solar PV (GW)	16	3,198	1,052	1278	1965	7717	1910	2	10,538	2847
Biomass	0	700	49,810	0	29,000	4,098	200	50	7,000	400

Sources Lidula et al. (2007), World Energy Council, *Survey of Energy Resources 2010*, and Handayani et al. (2022)

Table 6 AMS' electricity demand and duration

	Brunei	Cambodia	Indonesia	Laos	Malaysia	Myanmar	Philippines	Singapore	Thailand	Vietnam
Peak demand (MW)	454.7	291	23,438	350	12,990	1,140	8,766	5,711	22,586	11,605
Peak duration (hours)	4,681.7	4,925.2	4,681.7	4745	4681.7	2,428	4,015	5,840	4,015	2,428
Non-peak demand (MW)	257	85	5,338	60	8,388	162	3,394	1,324	8,692	6,862
Non-peak duration (hours)	4,078.3	3,834.8	4,078.3	4015	4,078.3	6,332	4,745	2,920	4,745	6,332

Sources HAPUA website; Ministry of Energy and Mineral Resources, Indonesia (2011), Electricité du Laos (2010), and Zhai (2008, 2010)

Table 7 AMS' electricity demand growth, 2018–2050

	Growth rate (%)
Brunei	1.2
Cambodia	9.9
Indonesia	3.9
Laos	7.7
Malaysia	4.5
Myanmar	9.0
Philippines	4.5
Singapore	4.2
Thailand	4.9
Vietnam	6.7

Source Institute of Energy Economics, Japan (2011)

Table 8 Change in OPEX and CAPEX

	Rate of change (%)
Coal	2.1
Diesel	1.26
Natural Gas	1.36
Hydro	−0.5
Geothermal	−0.5
Wind	−1.4
Solar PV	−4.6
Biomass	0.3

Source EU Commission (2008)

Table 9 AMS' transmission loss and cost

		Transmission Loss (%)	Transmission Cost (USD/MWh)
Estimated distance	0–1,600 km	0.01	3
	>1,600 km	0.087	5
	>3,200 km	0.174	7.5

Source Claverton Energy Research Group, http://www.claverton-energy.com/

References

ACE (ASEAN Centre for Energy) (2022) Available at https://aseanenergy.org/aeds/statistics/. Accessed 2 Jan 2025

ADB (Asian Development Bank) (2013) Assessment of the Greater Mekong subregion energy sector development progress, prospects, and regional investment priorities. Manila

APERC (Asia Pacific Energy Research Centre) (2004) Electric power grid interconnections in the APEC region. Institute of Energy Economics, Japan

Bunthoeun P (2012) Country report for the group training course in energy policy (B). Training and Dialogue Programs, presentation slides, Institute of Energy Economics, Japan, August. Available at eneken.ieej.or.jp/data/4470.pdf. Accessed 20 Nov 2013

Chang Y (2024) Power trade and hydroelectricity development in the Greater Mekong Subregion: perspectives on economic and environmental implications. In: Han P et al (eds) Large-scale development of renewables in the ASEAN: economics, technology and policy. Springer, Singapore, pp 55–77

Chang Y, Han P (2021) Harnessing wind energy potential in ASEAN: modelling and policy implications. Sustainability 13:4279

Chang Y, Han P (2022) Curtailed electricity and hydrogen in association of southeast Asian nations and east Asia summit: perspectives from an economic and environmental analysis. Int J Hydrogen Energy 47:24548–24557

Chang Y, Li Y (2013) Power generation and cross-border grid planning for the integrated ASEAN electricity market: a dynamic linear programming model. Energ Strat Rev 2:153–160

Chang Y, Tay TH (2006) Efficiency and deregulation of the electricity market in Singapore. Energy Policy 34:2498–2508

Chimklai S (2013) Briefing on ASEAN power grid: interconnectivity and cross border trade. Available at http://portal.erc.or.th/aern/images/Panel%201-1%20Briefing%20on%20ASEAN%20Power%20Grid.pdf. Accessed 20 Nov 2013

Claverton Energy Research Group. Available at http://www.claverton-energy.com/. Accessed 20 Nov 2013

Economic Consulting Associates (ECA) (2010) Greater Mekong Subregion (GMS) transmission & trading case study

Electricité du Laos (2010) Electricité du Laos Annual Report 2010

Energy Information Administration (U.S.) (EIA) (2020) Capital cost and performance characteristic estimates for utility scale electric power generating technologies. U.S. Department of Energy, Washington, DC

Energy Institute, London (2023). 72nd Statistical Review of World Energy

EU Commission (2008) Energy sources, production costs and performance of technologies for power generation, heating and transport. Commission staff working document accompanying the communication on a second strategic energy review. Brussels: SEC (2008) 2872 final, 13 November 2008

Fankhauser S et al (2022) The meaning of Net zero and how to get it right. Nat Clim Chang 12(January):15–21

Handayani K et al (2022) Moving beyond the NDCs: ASEAN pathways to a net-zero emissions power sector in 2050. Appl Energy 311:118580

HAPUA (Heads of ASEAN Power Utilities/Authorities) (No date) Available at https://hapua.org/main/. Accessed 20 Nov 2024

IEA (International Energy Agency) and NEA (Nuclear Energy Agency) (2010) Projected cost of generating electricity: 2010 edition

Institute of Energy Economics, Japan (2011) The 3rd ASEAN energy outlook. Available at https://asean.org/wp-content/uploads/2021/08/3rd-ASEAN-Energy-Outlook-AEO3.pdf. Accessed 2 Jan 2025

IRENA (International Renewable Energy Agency) and ACE (2019) Renewable Energy Outlook for ASEAN

Lau HC (2023) Decarbonization of asean's power sector: a holistic approach. Energy Rep 9:676–702

Li Y, Chang Y (2015) Infrastructure investments for power trade and transmission in ASEAN+2: Costs, benefits, long-term contracts and prioritized developments. Energy Econ 51:484–492

Lidula NWA et al (2007) ASEAN towards clean and sustainable energy: potentials, utilization, and barriers. Renew Energy 32:1441–1452

Ministry of Energy and Mineral Resources, Indonesia (2011) Handbook of energy & economic statistics of Indonesia 2011. Center for Data and Information on Energy and Mineral Resources, Ministry of Energy and Mineral Resources

Nordhaus WD (2008) A question of balance: weighing the options on global warming policies. Yale University Press, New Haven, CT

Turvey R, Anderson D (1977) Electricity economics: essays and case studies. The Johns Hopkins University Press, Baltimore and London

Watcharejyothin M, Shrestha RM (2009) Effects of cross-border power trade between Laos and Thailand: energy security and environmental implications. Energy Policy 37:1782–1792

World Energy Council (2010) 2010 Survey of Energy Resources. Available at https://www.worldenergy.org/assets/downloads/ser_2010_report_1.pdf. Accessed 2 Jan 2025

Yin D, Chang Y (2020) Energy R&D investments and emissions abatement policy. Energy J 41(6):133–156

Yu X (2003) Regional cooperation and energy development in the Greater Mekong sub-region. Energy Policy 31:1221–1234

Yu Z et al (2005) Integrated energy resources planning for the ASEAN countries and Southern China. Oil Gas Energy Law Intell 3(4):1–12

Zhai Y (2008) ADB's role in supporting power sector restructuring in the Philippines—electricity market development project. Presentation slides for the Orientation Program for DMC officials, ADB, October

Zhai Y (2010) Energy sector integration for low-carbon development in greater Mekong subregion: towards a model of south-south cooperation. Available at www.worldenergy.org/documents/congresspapers/52.pdf. Accessed 20 Nov 2013

Carbon Pricing in ASEAN Countries: Incentivising Decarbonisation and Addressing the EU's Carbon Border Adjustment Mechanism

Hoy-Yen Chan, Beni Suryadi, and Han Phoumin

Abstract Carbon pricing instruments (CPIs) are crucial in the climate policy framework as they provide a solution to the energy–climate nexus and address climate change while ensuring energy security. Well-designed CPIs guide countries towards decarbonisation, acting as a defence against negative events like the economic impacts of the European Union's Carbon Border Adjustment Mechanism (CBAM). Despite their importance, however, CPIs face challenges such as political feasibility and public misunderstanding. A deeper understanding is therefore required to encourage adoption, facilitate more ambitious Nationally Determined Contribution (NDC) targets and motivate progressive actions for urgent decarbonisation. This chapter aims to present fundamental insights into CPIs. We conduct a comparative analysis between carbon taxes and cap-and-trade (CAT) programmes, using Brunei Darussalam as a case study. Subsequently, we provide a comprehensive review of the current carbon pricing status in ASEAN countries, analysing CPI implementation readiness based on monitoring, reporting and verification (MRV) infrastructure and the related legal framework. We introduce the EU's CBAM and analyse CBAM-regulated goods from ASEAN countries exported to the EU, thereby indicating the importance of addressing CBAM. Our review found that while Singapore and Indonesia adopted a carbon tax and CAT programme, respectively, Vietnam is the most prepared for CPI implementation among the other eight ASEAN countries.

H.-Y. Chan (✉)
Invite Green Consultancy, Penang, Malaysia
e-mail: hyen23@gmail.com

B. Suryadi
ASEAN Centre for Energy (ACE), Jakarta, Indonesia
e-mail: benisuryadi@aseanenergy.org

H. Phoumin
Economic Research Institute for ASEAN and East Asia (ERIA), Jakarta Pusat, Indonesia
e-mail: han.phoumin@eria.org

H. Phoumin et al. (eds.), *Tackling the Energy Transition: Insights from ASEAN and Beyond*, Climate Change and Energy Transition,
https://doi.org/10.1007/978-981-96-6019-3_4

Singapore is the most resilient to the impacts of the CBAM, and Malaysia, a significant exporter to the EU, is relatively more vulnerable, lacking robust CPI infrastructure and legal framework. We recommend that the ASEAN countries consider CPIs to incentivise decarbonisation, mitigate CBAM's economic impacts and address carbon leakage. However, for a just transition, carbon pricing must be coupled with a robust revenue recycling strategy.

1 Introduction

The rapid economic growth anticipated across ASEAN is set to triple the region's energy demand by 2050 compared to 2020 levels (Asian Development Bank [ADB] 2020). Despite high economic growth and a relatively low contribution to global emissions, ASEAN faces the challenge of implementing more ambitious actions to mitigate climate threats. In addition to their Nationally Determined Contributions (NDCs), nearly all of the ASEAN Member States (AMS) have pledged to reach net zero emissions or carbon neutrality (ADB 2020). This highlights the urgent need to move energy transition strategies beyond simply adopting low-carbon technologies and compensating for the current business-as-usual (BAU) approach. New decarbonisation policies are needed, and the existing ones need strengthening.

In this context, carbon pricing instruments (CPIs) emerge as pivotal components within the broader climate policy framework, offering an energy–climate nexus solution to address climate change and ensure energy security. Their efficacy lies in their ability to cost-effectively fulfil climate commitments and create opportunities for increased financing in energy-related investments from both the public and private sectors. This, in turn, can leverage capital to stimulate both domestic and foreign investments (ADB 2022). Well-structured carbon pricing serves as an economical policy instrument, offering a range of benefits in the environmental, economic, social and political domains. Recognising this potential, various international organisations, including the World Bank (2017), ADB (2022), International Monetary Fund (IMF) (2020), International Energy Agency (IEA) (2020) and United Nations Framework Convention on Climate Change (UNFCCC) (2023), as well as economists and academia more widely (Hongo 2018; Alvarez 2019; Andersson and Atkinson 2020; Bloomberg L.P. 2023), consistently regard carbon pricing as a powerful tool for decarbonising the energy sector.

Carbon pricing empowers regulated entities with the flexibility to choose the most efficient approach to emissions reduction in response to the carbon price (World Bank 2021b). Command-and-control regulations such as rigid technology mandates or direct regulations that set uniform standards according to technical or engineering criteria are likely to impose higher costs on the economy. In contrast, carbon pricing allows entities to opt for cost-effective methods to find the least-cost solutions to achieve emission reductions (Baranzini et al. 2016; Doshi 2018). For instance, unlike traditional regulations that may limit energy or emissions intensity only per unit of output, carbon pricing goes further by creating incentives to reduce overall demand

(Hafstead 2022). Carbon pricing promotes investments in climate-friendly alternatives by raising the costs of technologies and activities associated with high greenhouse gas (GHG) emissions. This motivation prompts entities to go beyond the limitations of conventional regulations and thus fosters a more substantial reduction in GHG emissions.

Moreover, carbon pricing plays a critical role in driving economic diversification, particularly for countries heavily dependent on the fossil fuel industry. The ASEAN Centre for Energy (ACE) acknowledges that the implementation of carbon pricing would promote the utilisation of carbon capture and storage (CCS) technologies, further enhancing the appeal of modern electrified technologies and electric solutions (ASEAN Centre for Energy [ACE] 2022). In the long run, such pricing not only stimulates continuous improvement and innovation in low-carbon technologies, preventing the existence of stranded assets, but also yields various development benefits. These include improved air quality, the creation of green jobs, and enhanced energy security and behavioural change (Partnership for Market Readiness/ International Carbon Action Partnership 2021). These collective outcomes enable developing countries to transition towards a low-carbon economy while simultaneously addressing their sustainability priorities.

Carbon pricing can function as a revenue generator for governments. The primary revenue sources encompass receipts from carbon taxes and payments for emission trading allowances, typically conducted through auctions. In 2022, global initiatives collectively generated USD 95 billion in revenue, covering nearly 23% of worldwide GHG emissions (World Bank 2023b). This significant increase in revenue collection from carbon pricing highlights its potential role as a fiscal policy instrument, redirecting funds towards policy objectives. Beyond merely creating a direct incentive for low-carbon investments, this revenue can play a crucial role in supporting broader initiatives. For instance, it can contribute to a just transition, aid in pandemic recovery, and protect vulnerable communities from climate impacts and energy price fluctuations (Asian Development Bank 2022). Moreover, these funds support a range of initiatives, including low-carbon investments, environmental projects, research and development, and poverty alleviation. Nonetheless, ensuring effective revenue distribution, guided by principles of fairness, is crucial to ensuring an equitable transition to a low-carbon economy that leaves no one marginalised (World Bank 2017).

Carbon pricing acts as a dual-purpose instrument, guiding countries towards achieving decarbonisation goals while also providing a shield against potential negative events. For instance, it prevents countries from becoming targeted destinations for businesses looking to transfer production from their home countries to locations with less stringent emissions regulations, a phenomenon known as carbon leakage. In response to this concern, the European Union (EU) has recently introduced a Carbon Border Adjustment Mechanism (CBAM) (Council of the European Union 2022). CBAM entails a carbon tariff on products with high carbon intensity imported into the EU. EU importers are required to purchase carbon certificates, and if non-EU producers can demonstrate that they have already paid a price in a third country for the carbon used in the production of imported goods, the corresponding cost can be fully deducted for the EU importer. Therefore, implementing domestic carbon pricing in ASEAN countries not only aligns with global decarbonisation efforts but also serves as a strategic measure to mitigate the economic impact of the CBAM, ensuring continued competitiveness in trade with the EU.

Nonetheless, CPIs, particularly carbon taxes, encounter challenges such as political feasibility and public misunderstanding (Andersson 2019; Metcalf 2022). For instance, inadequate communication can lead opponents to discredit carbon pricing as a punitive tax. In Australia, the carbon pricing implemented in the three years 2012–2014 saw a substantial reduction of approximately 17 million tonnes of GHG emissions in the electricity sector (O'Gorman and Jotzo 2014). However, it was abolished due, in part, to the government's failure to clarify how carbon pricing revenue benefited low- and middle-income earners (Jotzo 2013). The interpretation of policy effectiveness using economic models requires caution, as assumptions and oversimplifications may not accurately reflect real-world effects (Asuka 2017). In Sweden, Andersson (2019) observed an almost 11% decline in CO_2 emissions from transport, with 6% attributed to the carbon tax alone; these figures contrast with earlier studies. The improved simulation was relatable because it used a better-constructed control unit and empirical data. The European Union's Emissions Trading System (ETS), however, faced debates and confusion in its first decade, attributed to insufficient stakeholder understanding (Jotzo 2013).

We anticipate that a better understanding of carbon pricing will encourage its adoption, subsequently facilitating more ambitious NDC targets and motivating more progressive actions in addressing its urgency. Therefore, the objective of this chapter is to present fundamental knowledge about carbon pricing, covering various CPIs—including mandatory carbon tax, Cap-and-Trade (CAT) programmes and voluntary carbon crediting mechanisms. We conduct a comparative analysis between carbon tax and CAT programmes, utilising a case study to elaborate on CPI options. Subsequently, we provide a comprehensive review of the current status of carbon pricing in ASEAN countries, analysing the readiness of CPI implementation based on the developments of the Monitoring, Reporting, and Verification (MRV) infrastructure and legal framework for CPIs. We also introduce the EU's CBAM and analyse CBAM-regulated goods from ASEAN countries exported to the EU. The intention is to underscore the importance of CPIs as a tool to mitigate the economic impact of the CBAM, as well as the consequences of carbon leakage. Finally, we conclude the chapter with recommendations.

2 Carbon Pricing Instruments (CPIs)

According to the World Bank (2023c), carbon pricing is any policy that places an explicit price on GHG emissions. The concept aims to address climate change by incentivising polluters to reduce emissions through the use of pricing signals. Governments typically enforce carbon pricing policies, and these policies commonly manifest in two ways: (1) through carbon taxes, or (2) via CAT programmes or ETSs.

2.1 Carbon Tax

The carbon tax establishes a monetary value on GHG emissions through the taxation of products or activities according to their emission levels. Typically, this involves imposing a tax on fossil fuels per their carbon content or on other goods according to the emissions generated during their production processes. Consequently, a consistent cost is assigned to each tonne of carbon dioxide equivalent (tCO_2e) or to each unit of fuel based on its carbon content. Entities subject to regulation are required to remit this fee for every tonne they emit. Although the carbon tax ensures price predictability, the degree of emissions reduction achievable at a specific tax rate remains uncertain. Determining a tax rate does not necessarily guarantee a particular level of emissions reduction (World Bank 2021b). Thus, aligning the necessary tax rate with an emissions reduction objective proves challenging. In essence, a carbon tax manages the cost of emissions but not the actual quantity emitted.

2.2 Cap-and-Trade Programme (Emissions Trading System)

A CAT programme establishes a restriction (cap) on the total volume of GHG emissions within one or multiple sectors of the economy. The government issues a limited quantity of emissions allowances based on specific criteria (also referred to as permits), and each allowance authorises the holder to emit a single unit of emissions. These allowances can be allocated directly to the regulated entities (at no cost from the regulator) or sold through auction markets. Regulated emitters with lower emissions are permitted to sell their unused (surplus) allowances to larger emitters whose emissions surpass the prescribed limit. Changes in the supply and demand of these tradable allowances lead to a market value for such allowances. Hence, a CAT programme operates through a market-driven mechanism; in essence, the carbon price is determined by the market. Unlike the carbon tax, a CAT programme manages the total volume of emissions rather than the price (World Bank 2021b).

Banking and Borrowing

Some CAT programmes allow regulated entities to bank surplus allowances for later use and, in some cases, to borrow allowances from future compliance periods. These provisions for banking and borrowing bestow upon regulated entities added flexibility in determining their compliance approaches and the optimal timing for making investments based on their individual requirements. As a result, this flexibility could lead to a reduction in the expenses associated with achieving a cumulative emissions objective. The practice of banking allowances might encourage earlier reductions in emissions due to the anticipation of elevated carbon prices in the future. Nonetheless, the implementation of borrowing mechanisms must be carefully devised, considering that borrowing entails the risk of challenges in enforcing repayment (World Bank 2021b), potentially resulting in delays in mitigation actions.

2.3 Carbon Crediting Mechanism

The carbon crediting mechanism is an initiative that issues tradable credits to entities voluntarily undertaking emissions reduction activities alongside their regular operations. There are three approaches to managing this crediting mechanism (World Bank 2021a):

i. Domestic (or regional) Crediting Mechanisms: Credits are issued through mechanisms established by the government(s), which set regulations and criteria for credit generation.
ii. International Crediting Mechanisms: Governed by international institutions; examples include the Clean Development Mechanism (CDM) and Joint Implementation under the Kyoto Protocol, or Article 6 under the Paris Agreement.
iii. Independent Crediting Mechanism: Administered by private and independent third-party organisations, such as the Gold Standard and the Verified Carbon Standard (VCS).

In some instances, a carbon tax or CAT programme allows regulated entities to utilise "carbon credits" from voluntary market programmes to meet a share of (or "offset") their compliance requirements. However, it is essential to ensure that the crediting mechanism's scope excludes entities, gases or activities covered by carbon pricing instruments (or other mandatory GHG emissions reduction regulations) to prevent overlaps and potential double counting of emissions reductions (World Bank 2021a).

Furthermore, Article 6 of the Paris Agreement sets the stage for international collaboration to assist governments in meeting their NDCs. Article 6.4 outlines the international mechanisms governing credit issuance. As a result, regulated entities or businesses can utilise these credits to meet their compliance obligations or commitments to a net zero approach, extending beyond the purview of the domestic voluntary carbon market.

However, the World Bank (2021a) views mandatory carbon pricing instruments (carbon tax or CAT programmes) as more effective tools for driving reductions across the entire economy than voluntary carbon crediting. Nevertheless, carbon crediting does offer its own set of benefits. For instance, credits can be used by regulated entities to fulfil compliance requirements within a carbon tax or CAT programme, thereby adding flexibility in compliance. Additionally, a crediting mechanism can serve as an alternative to carbon pricing instruments in cases of legal barriers or political resistance.

3 Assessing Carbon Pricing Options

Despite the growing use of carbon-pricing tools, the political challenge of implementing carbon pricing persists, especially in the context of increasing inflation and unpredictable energy prices. While carbon taxes have encountered substantial public resistance due to the apparent additional costs, CAT programmes are also facing challenges. Both carbon tax and CAT models have distinct strengths and limitations, with their efficiency and effectiveness closely tied to the unique circumstances of a jurisdiction. The question is not whether one model is superior to the other but rather about selecting the most suitable model for the specific local context.

Table 1 presents a simplified comparison of the key features of carbon taxes and CAT programmes. Although there are differences between the two CPIs, both instruments exhibit relatively flexible design features. However, the preference for one instrument over the other is likely to depend on the jurisdictional context and policy priorities. Moreover, it is not the "choice of instrument that primarily determines effectiveness, but rather the design choices and trade-offs made" (World Bank 2021b, p. 7).

3.1 Carbon Tax vs. CAT Programme: Brunei Darussalam

In this section, we draw insights from our previous study (ASEAN Centre for Energy and Brunei Climate Change Secretariat 2023) focusing on Brunei Darussalam as a case study for exploring carbon pricing options. Figure 1 illustrates the carbon pricing assessment process in the country. The study began by prioritising the objectives of carbon pricing, integrating the country's economic, policy and emission profiles into assessments of the carbon tax and CAT models. This process involved identifying the potential and challenges of each model and ultimately recommending the most appropriate carbon pricing model for Brunei Darussalam.

Our findings revealed that Brunei Darussalam has emissions concentrated from a small number of large emitters, with only 12 entities in total (4 auto-producers and 8 utility power producers). The primary challenge anticipated for the CAT programme lies in the expected poor market liquidity in carbon trading, a consequence of this concentration. Implementing a carbon tax, in contrast, presents fewer complexities than a CAT programme does. A carbon tax can seamlessly leverage existing tax infrastructure, while a CAT programme would necessitate the establishment of a new institutional framework, including the creation of a secondary market for trading allowances. This inherent simplicity positions the implementation of a carbon tax as a more feasible option under conditions of limited institutional capacity such as in Brunei Darussalam. Consequently, our recommendation leans towards the adoption of a carbon tax over a CAT programme.

Our proposal involves implementing a carbon tax to regulate direct emissions from fuel combustion activities at industrial facilities, covering the emissions of three GHGs (CO_2, CH_4 and N_2O) at the initial stage. Setting a threshold is crucial to include all major industrial emitters while excluding smaller ones. We further recommend introducing the carbon tax at an initial lower rate, coupled with a transparent plan for progressive rate increases in the future. Given the hypothetical timeline for implementing carbon pricing—applicable to identified sectors emitting beyond the threshold limit around 2025 (Brunei Climate Change Secretariat 2020)—coupled

Table 1 Comparison of the key features of carbon taxes and CAT programmes

Elements	Carbon tax	Cap-and-trade (CAT) Programme
Certainty of emissions levels	A tax rate (USD/tCO_2e) would not ensure a specific level (quantity) of emissions reduction (tCO_2e). Hence it is hard to align the tax rate with targets such as the NDC and the goal of net zero emissions	A "cap" can be set and aligned with the NDC or net zero targets, whereby it defines the emissions budget (maximum allowances) of the covered sectors under a CAT programme. Therefore, the quantity of emissions reduction (tCO_2e) is certain
Cost-effectiveness	Regulated entities are incentivised to abate emissions when the tax rate is higher than the abatement costs. However, there is no economic gain. Instead, regulated entities are obligated to pay for every tCO_2e of emissions that they have produced; the lower the emissions, the lower the tax bill	Regulated entities are incentivised to abate more when the allowance price is higher than the abatement costs. Abating emissions reduces the cost of purchasing allowances for compliance, and in case of excess allowances, they can be traded and generate revenues. However, a lack of liquidity in the secondary market (trading) reduces the cost effectiveness
Timeline of implementation and ease of administration	As the carbon tax can be built on the existing tax infrastructure, it is relatively simpler and quicker to be implemented compared to a CAT programme (World Bank 2021b). For example, Singapore established the Carbon Pricing Act in 2018 and it came into force in 2019 (Government of Singapore 2018a; National Climate Change Secretariat Singapore [NCCS] 2022)	A CAT programme needs to develop a secondary market for trading the allowances, and also an auction if the government-issued allowances are to be sold through this means. Therefore, a CAT programme requires a relatively longer process. For example, in Korea, the legal basis of the Framework Act on Low Carbon and Green Growth was established in 2010 and was followed by the Emissions Trading Act and its Enforcement Decree in 2012. Phase 1 of the emissions trading was launched in 2015 (Asian Development Bank [ADB] 2018)
Price predictability	A carbon tax controls the price of emissions but not the quantity. "The carbon price is set by predefined tax rates. This provides a stable price signal to inform investment decisions" (World Bank 2021b, p. 7)	A CAT programme controls the quantity of emissions, but not the price. The carbon price is determined by the market. However, regulators may apply a "price or supply adjustment measure (PSAM)" to set the floor and ceiling prices to avoid the volatility of the allowance prices

Source World Bank (2021b) and authors

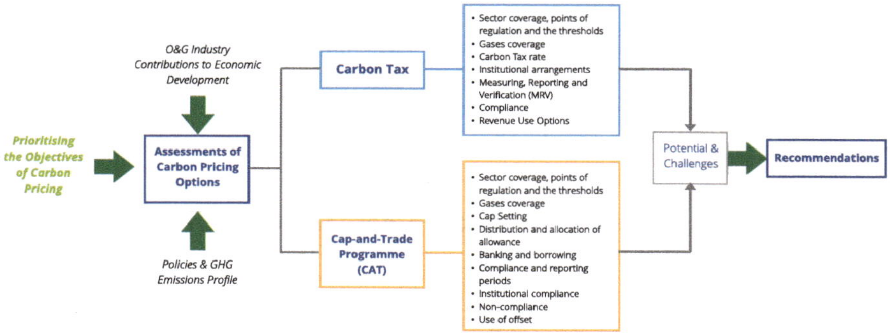

Fig. 1 The process of carbon pricing assessment in Brunei Darussalam. *Source* ASEAN Centre for Energy and Brunei Climate Change Secretariat (2023)

with limited institutional capacity and a lack of experience in carbon crediting, our recommendation emphasises the importance of maintaining simplicity in the initial stages of carbon taxation, without incorporating an offset mechanism.

However, a significant challenge for the successful implementation of a carbon tax in Brunei Darussalam is the issue of cost pass-through, particularly given that more than 50% of the products from large emitters, which are in the oil and gas industry, are exported (ASEAN Centre for Energy and Brunei Climate Change Secretariat 2023). Cost pass-through is challenging under the existing political landscape. Furthermore, energy prices, including electricity tariffs, are regulated by the government, indicating a non-liberalised electricity market. The challenge becomes more pronounced as the Department of Electrical Services (DES), a government authority under the Department of Energy in the Prime Minister's Office, also functions as the electric utility of Brunei Darussalam (Brunei Darussalam Department of Energy, 2022). Without cost pass-through, the price signal may not effectively reach consumers and may thus provide only minimal encouragement for changes in consumption behaviour. Therefore, the government may consider either liberalising the electricity market or introducing new business models in the energy sector. Additionally, we recommend revisiting existing fiscal measures, including fuel subsidies and tax exemptions, to prevent adverse economic consequences for regulated entities and government finances.

Another challenge stems from the interaction between policies. For instance, the government aims to boost the use of renewable energy (RE) in the industrial and power sectors through the Renewable Portfolio Standard (RPS). The overlapping policies of carbon pricing and RPS encourage entities to take steps to mitigate their environmental impact. While this policy mix has the potential to increase the deployment of RE, it poses a political challenge that might undermine the effectiveness of the carbon tax (MIT Energy Initiative [MITEI] 2019).

In summary, the decision between a carbon tax and a CAT model should carefully weigh economic and emission profiles, policy objectives and the political environment. Certain jurisdictions might devise a hybrid approach, incorporating elements of both systems, in order to strike a balance between their respective strengths and limitations. Ultimately, the success of either model hinges on careful planning, effective implementation and robust enforcement within a specific context that embraces the principles of a just transition.

4 Current Development and Readiness for Carbon Pricing Implementation in the AMS

This section provides an overview of the latest developments in carbon pricing across the AMS. The covered CPIs include mandatory measures, such as carbon taxes and CAT programmes. Mandating facility-level GHG reporting sets the stage for integration with other climate initiatives, such as disclosure mechanisms and voluntary carbon markets. In the context of carbon pricing, MRV represents the initial step (Hongo 2018). Emissions data from facilities are crucial references for regulators, aiding in shaping coverage, setting emissions thresholds, and distributing caps and allowances. Regardless of CPI types, the MRV system serves as fundamental infrastructure, while the regulatory framework acts as the legal basis for CPI implementation. Consequently, the development of MRV infrastructure and legal frameworks becomes foundational in assessing countries' readiness for CPI implementation.

Table 2 summarises the findings, and the subsequent discussions revolve around the development of CPIs, including conclusions regarding the readiness for the implementation of CPIs in each AMS.

Brunei Darussalam

As part of the Brunei National Climate Change Policy (BNCCP) (Brunei Climate Change Secretariat 2020), the country stated its aim to introduce carbon pricing applicable to identified sectors emitting beyond a carbon emissions threshold by 2025. A collaborative effort between the ASEAN Centre for Energy (ACE) and Brunei Climate Change Secretariat (BCCS) in 2022, resulting in the study mentioned above on carbon pricing options (ASEAN Centre for Energy and Brunei Climate Change Secretariat 2023), indicated the efficiency of a carbon tax over a CAT programme. The challenges and recommendations from this study are factored into the regular reviews of the BNCCP. Consequently, updates to targets and timelines, including the implementation of carbon pricing, may be anticipated.

In addition, Brunei Darussalam took a significant step towards this goal by launching the Directive on Mandatory Reporting on GHG Emissions in April 2023, which applies to all facilities (Brunei Climate Change Secretariat [BCCS] 2023). This move aligns with the Enhanced Transparency Framework (ETF) under the UNFCCC, reinforcing the country's consideration of the implementation of carbon pricing.

Therefore, Brunei Darussalam has established the basic infrastructure for CPIs; however, no legal framework is currently in place.

Table 2 Summary of the current development of carbon pricing in the AMS, as of November 2023

	BRN	KHM	IDN	LAO	MYS	MMR	PHL	SGP	THA	VNM
Type(s)	Undecided	–	Hybrid	–	Undecided (CAT and carbon tax are under consideration)	–	Undecided (CAT and carbon tax are under consideration)	Carbon tax; with offset mechanism starting from 2024	Hybrid	CAT or hybrid
Year of implementation	2025	–	2023: CAT (power sector) 2025: Tax	–	–	–	–	2019	–	2026–2027: Pilot voluntary CAT 2028: Mandatory CAT

(continued)

Table 2 (continued)

	BRN	KHM	IDN	LAO	MYS	MMR	PHL	SGP	THA	VNM
Legal framework	2023: Directive on Mandatory Reporting on Greenhouse Gases (Brunei Climate Change Secretariat [BCCS] 2023)	–	2017: Legal basis for CAT implementation Government of Indonesia 2017) 2021: Framework for regulating the carbon pricing in meeting NDC (Government of Indonesia 2021b) 2021: Framework for carbon tax (Government of Indonesia 2021a) 2022: Framework for emissions trading implementation (Government of Indonesia 2022b) 2022: Framework for emissions trading implementation of power generation sub-sector (Government of Indonesia 2022a) 2023: Regulations on carbon trading through carbon exchanges (Otoritas Jasa Keuangan [OJK] 2023)	–	–	–	Low Carbon Economy Investment Act of 2023 (House Bill No. 7705, 19th Congress) (Eco-Business 2024)	2018: Carbon Pricing Act (Government of Singapore 2018a) 2022: Carbon Pricing (Amendment) Bill (Government of Singapore 2022) 2018: Carbon Pricing (Measurement, Reporting and Verification) Regulations Government of Singapore 2018b) 2023: International Carbon Credits (ICC) Framework (National Environment Agency [NEA] 2023)	Climate Change Act: Pending at the cabinet (International Carbon Action Partnership [ICAP] 2023b)	2022: Decision No. 01/2022/ QD-TTg on mandatory GHG emissions inventory (Prime Minister of Vietnam 2022) 2022: Decree 06/ 2022/ND-CP provided clear regulations for the development of Vietnam's carbon market with a roadmap for the implementation of the National Crediting Mechanism (NCM) and the domestic CAT programme (Government of Vietnam 2022)

(continued)

Table 2 (continued)

	BRN	KHM	IDN	LAO	MYS	MMR	PHL	SGP	THA	VNM
Implementing authority	–	–	Ministry of Environment and Forestry (MoEF): Implementation of emissions trading Ministry of Energy and Mineral Resources (MEMR): Coordinates CAT implementation in the power sector Ministry of Finance: Implementation of carbon tax	–	Ministry of Finance leads the study on carbon pricing mechanism; NRECC as a coordinating agency for the emissions trading component	–	Climate Change Commission (CCC): Philippine Greenhouse Gas Inventory Management and Reporting System (as proposed under Low Carbon Investment Economy Act) (Chatto 2023)	National Environment Agency (NEA)	Office for Natural Resources and Policy (ONEP): Cap-And-Trade (International Carbon Action Partnership [ICAP] 2023b); Excise Department: Carbon tax (The Nation 2023)	Ministry of Natural Resources and Environment: CAT and NCM (Government of Vietnam 2022) Ministry of Finance: Tax (Vietnam Chamber of Commerce and Industry [VCCI] 2023)
Facility-level MRV infrastructure	Mandatory; ready	–	In progress	–	Voluntary	-	In progress	Mandatory; ready	Voluntary	Mandatory; ready

'–': Information was not mentioned in national plan or policy as of October 2023
"Undecided": Carbon pricing was mentioned in national plan or policy; however, the government has yet to announce which types of CPIs to implement
NRECC: Malaysian Ministry of Natural Resources, Environment and Climate Change

Cambodia

Cambodia has yet to adopt a carbon pricing instrument. However, experts and reports published by different institutions have recognised carbon pricing as a potential fiscal policy instrument for the country. In 2019, the UNFCCC RCC (Regional Collaboration Centre for Asia and the Pacific) recommended a carbon tax in the transport and power sectors (UNFCCC RCC Asia-Pacific 2019a); a 2021 ADB study recommended carbon pricing to abate emissions from coal generation and to reduce businesses' carbon footprints (Durrani-Jamal and Byers 2021); and the World Bank rated carbon pricing instruments incorporated with revenue recycling as medium cost and high urgency policy actions that can fill the financial gap for the country's low-carbon transition (World Bank 2023a).

Despite such findings by the UNFCCC, ADB and the World Bank, our review exercise uncovered no official information about the development of CPIs. Consequently, we conclude that Cambodia is not currently prepared for the implementation of carbon pricing. Support through regional or wider international cooperation could help bridge knowledge gaps and pave the way for considering carbon pricing as an option for decarbonisation strategies.

Indonesia

The Indonesian Cap-and-Trade (CAT) programme is scheduled for rollout in three phases. The initial phase, spanning 2023–2024, exclusively covered coal-fired power plants. Subsequently, the second phase (2025–2027) and third phase (2028–2030) aim to expand the programme's scope to include oil and gas-fired power plants, as well as additional coal-fired power facilities. On 22 February 2023, Indonesia initiated the first phase of its emissions trading system, which focuses on the power generation sector. The CAT programme applies to facilities with a production capacity exceeding 100 megawatts (MW), although smaller coal and fossil fuel plants may be included in the programme at a later stage. This phase covers 99 coal-fired power plants, accounting for 81.4% of the nation's total power generation capacity. The government establishes intensity targets, which determine the number of allowances allocated to each facility for every megawatt-hour (MWh) of electricity generated (International Carbon Action Partnership [ICAP] 2023a; World Bank 2023b). The carbon trading is anticipated to generate a yearly transaction volume of approximately USD 9 million, facilitating an annual exchange of carbon credits equivalent to 500,000 tCO_2e, with a projected carbon credit price ranging from USD 2 to USD 18 per tonne of CO_2e (Hidranto 2023).

Additionally, the CAT programme will evolve into a hybrid system encompassing "cap-tax-and-trade" elements, running alongside a carbon tax that was initially announced in 2021. Facilities failing to meet their obligations within this system will face taxation, with tax rates eventually linked to the domestic carbon market's pricing (ICAP 2023a). Nonetheless, the introduction of the carbon tax, originally scheduled for April 2022, has been postponed to 2025. This delay is attributed to the Russia–Ukraine conflict, which has contributed to a rise in domestic inflation (Reyes 2022).

The legal basis has been well established, and Indonesia has successfully implemented the initial phase of the CAT programme. However, a mandatory facility-level MRV system is not yet in place. In the initial phase, carbon trading occurs directly between companies, with prices determined by market mechanisms once a carbon exchange is established by the Financial Services Authority. Indonesia is not yet ready for the second phase of the CAT programme, which extends to a broader scope of regulated entities and is scheduled for 2025–2027.

Lao PDR

As of this writing, there is no policy or regulation pertaining to carbon pricing in Lao PDR. Nonetheless, Khamphilavanh and Masui (2021) found that policies mixed with carbon pricing in the transport sector can avoid GDP loss in the long-term. Lao PDR set conditional mitigation targets under its NDC in renewables, transport, energy efficiency and waste sectors. Of these, the transport sector would contribute the largest emissions reduction among these sectors. The targets for 2030 are (1) 30% electric vehicle (EV) penetration for 2-wheelers and passenger cars in the national vehicles mix, and (2) biofuels to account for 10% of fuels in the transport sector. If these targets are achieved, the Lao PDR would reduce GHG emissions by a total of 320 $ktCO_2e$ per year equivalent to USD 730 million (Government of Lao People's Democratic Republic 2021). Furthermore, the study found that implementing mitigation actions through EV and biofuel measures would cause a gradual decline in GDP growth in the long term. If these measures are combined with a carbon tax and EV subsidy, GHG emissions would drop by 57% (approximately 800 $ktCO_2e$) in the transport sector by 2050 (Khamphilavanh and Masui 2021).

We were not able to find any official information regarding the development of CPIs in the Lao PDR. Consequently, we concluded that the country is not currently prepared for the implementation of carbon pricing. Support from regional or international cooperation could help fill the knowledge gaps and provide an avenue for considering carbon pricing as an option for decarbonisation strategies.

Malaysia

Carbon pricing is recognised as a financing and investment enabler under the National Energy Transition Roadmap that was launched in August 2023 (Ministry of Economy in Malaysia 2023b). Led by the Ministry of Finance, Malaysia is currently conducting a study to develop a carbon pricing mechanism under the Partnership for Market Implementation (PMI). This study is expected to be completed by 2025 (Ministry of Natural Resources, Environment and Climate Change [NRECC] Malaysia 2023). The Government of Malaysia commenced preliminary work in 2023 to investigate the potential for a carbon tax and plans to develop a policy and design framework for a domestic CAT programme. Therefore, Malaysia may introduce a hybrid type of carbon pricing instrument. In addition, climate change legislation that takes into account recent developments at the domestic and international levels will be formulated to regulate the implementation of national climate change policies and obligations (Ministry of Economy in Malaysia 2023a).

Yahoo and Othman (2017) employed a computable general equilibrium model to assess the effects of carbon and energy tax policies in Malaysia. The findings revealed that implementing a carbon tax would result in minimal negative macroeconomic impacts while achieving significant reductions in CO_2 emissions. Notably, the study highlighted the effectiveness of coupling carbon taxation with revenue recycling, particularly through household consumption subsidies. Carbon taxes were found to outperform energy taxes in terms of achieving emission reductions, and the adoption of RE witnessed substantial growth under carbon tax policies.

Significantly, although the federal government has not yet implemented regulations pertaining to GHG emissions reduction, the Sarawak Legislative Assembly took a notable step by passing the Environment (Reduction of Greenhouse Gases Emission) Bill on 20 November 2023 (Ling 2023). This landmark move makes Sarawak the first state in Malaysia to enact legislation addressing climate change. The bill mandates registered businesses in specific economic sectors to submit annual reports on carbon emissions, with specified carbon emission thresholds. Entities failing to reduce emissions below the prescribed thresholds will be subject to a carbon levy.

At the national level, Malaysia lacks developed MRV infrastructure. However, Sarawak is poised to establish a mandatory facility-level MRV system. The Central Bank of Malaysia stresses the importance of a mandated GHG emissions inventory for a low-carbon economy (Bank Negara Malaysia 2023). Establishing regulatory systems and infrastructure is crucial for enforcement. Therefore, implementing a mandatory MRV system is a top priority. As of this writing, Malaysia is not yet ready for carbon pricing, lacking a legal basis and practical preparedness despite official plans and ongoing studies.

Myanmar

At the time of writing, there was no specific policy plan for carbon pricing in Myanmar. Nonetheless, through the assistance of the Global Green Growth Institute (GGGI) and Australian Volunteers Programme, a MRV system was being established to enable Myanmar to meet its obligations within the enhanced transparency framework of the Paris Agreement (ASEAN Working Group on Climate Change [AWGCC] 2022a).

According to the UNFCCC's study in 2019 (UNFCCC RCC Asia-Pacific 2019b), low awareness about the need and benefits of putting a price on negative externalities was the potential reason that carbon pricing was not under consideration. The IMF conducted a study on the impact of a carbon tax on households and found that the tax would be mildly progressive for consumers in Myanmar at a tax rate of USD 50 per tonne of CO_2e. It would also raise fiscal revenues by about 1.3% of GDP which would be distributed back as a cash grant per person to 40% of the poorest households, thereby reducing economic inequality in terms of income distribution (Alonso and Kilpatrick 2022). Therefore, wise use of carbon revenues may add to economic development even in a developing country like Myanmar.

Our review uncovered no official information regarding the development of CPIs in Myanmar. Consequently, we conclude that Myanmar is not currently prepared for the implementation of carbon pricing. Regional or international cooperation could provide support to bridge knowledge gaps and pave the way for considering carbon pricing as an option for decarbonisation strategies.

The Philippines

The Philippines established the National Integrated Climate Change Database Information and Exchange System (NICCDIES) (ASEAN Working Group on Climate Change [AWGCC] 2022b) in 2021. Serving as the integrated climate information portal of the Climate Change Commission (CCC), NICCDIES acts as a platform for decision-makers to access, distribute and exchange data for use in policymaking, development planning and investment decision making (Chatto 2023). One crucial component of NICCDIES is the GHG inventory, which outlines an MRV system—the Philippine Greenhouse Gas Inventory Management and Reporting System (PGHGIMRS)—proposed under the House Bill 7705 Low Carbon Economy Investment Act of 2023, which was approved by the House Committee on Climate Change on 6 August 2024 (Eco-Business 2024). The bill will mandate large enterprises across various sectors to develop decarbonisation plans aligned with the Paris Agreement. Additionally, the Philippines will develop a CAT programme, as recommended by the NDC steering committee (Chatto 2023).

Although a World Bank study (2022a) highlights the benefits of implementing a carbon tax in the Philippines, political sensitivity has thus far impeded its adoption as the primary option. Nevertheless, under Bongbong Marcos's administration, the Department of Finance is contemplating a carbon tax as an alternative approach to address climate challenges in the country (Caraballo 2022). Ongoing research focuses on the taxation of carbon emissions, with 2025 implementation, subject to approval. Furthermore, the fully liberalised electricity market in the Philippines favours the cost pass-through mechanism of carbon pricing. This model seamlessly incorporates carbon costs into electricity prices, facilitating a price signal that encourages the adoption of low-carbon sources, energy efficiency and consequential long-term behavioural change.

While the potential benefits of carbon pricing, such as generating additional fiscal revenues to fund climate actions and alleviating the fiscal burden on the government, are evident, concerns about negative impacts on economic activities persist, posing challenges to political feasibility. Contrary to these concerns, the World Bank's perspective differs. According to the World Bank (2022a), the adoption of a moderate carbon price, reaching up to USD 5 per tonne of CO_2e in the Philippines, could be a signal to both firms and individuals that they should embrace low-carbon technologies. This move could concurrently generate revenues equivalent to 0.4% of GDP annually. To address short-term concerns, the negative impacts could be mitigated by recycling carbon tax revenues, directing them towards income support or reskilling programmes for affected workers, steering them towards "green jobs". Moreover, the combined effect of increased investment in low-carbon energy generation and using carbon tax revenues for growth-focused public expenditures is projected to boost GDP by 0.5% and create approximately 80,000 jobs by 2030. The study also highlights that even relatively high carbon prices would have minimal macroeconomic impacts on the Philippines, emphasising the importance of a well-calibrated carbon pricing mechanism to ensure equity.

Under the Low Carbon Economy Investment Bill, the Philippines is at the initial stage of developing both infrastructure and a legal framework for carbon trading.

Singapore

In 2018, Singapore enacted the Carbon Pricing Act (Government of Singapore 2018a), followed by the implementation of a carbon tax in 2019, thereby pioneering the carbon pricing policy among the AMS. The revenues generated from the carbon tax are allocated to support decarbonisation initiatives and the shift towards a green economy and to mitigate the impact on businesses and households. Aligned with heightened climate ambitions aiming for net zero emissions by 2050, the government conducted a review of the tax rate. In 2022, a progressive increase in the tax rate was announced, later set at SGD 5 per tonne of CO_2e. The plan announced a rate of SGD 25 (USD 18) in 2024 and 2025, followed by SGD 45 (USD 33) in 2026 and 2027, with a strategy of reaching SGD 50–80 (USD 37–59) per tonne by 2030 (National Climate Change Secretariat Singapore [NCCS] 2023). This forward-looking announcement not only provides businesses with greater planning certainty but also strengthens the business case for investing in low-carbon technologies and participating in carbon markets. Starting in 2024, taxable facilities have the option to utilise high-quality international carbon credits (ICC) to offset up to 5% of their taxable emissions. The ICC Framework is aligned with Article 6 of the Paris Agreement, enabling Singapore to cooperate with other countries to support respective climate targets. Moreover, eligibility criteria have been established to ensure the high integrity of the ICCs (National Environment Agency [NEA] 2023). Additionally, a framework is in the pipeline to facilitate a smooth transition for existing emissions-intensive trade-exposed (EITE) companies. This framework allows for the distribution of allowances to EITE companies based on efficiency standards and decarbonisation targets, providing them with more time to adjust to a low-carbon economy and preventing carbon leakage (National Climate Change Secretariat Singapore [NCCS] 2023).

When planning for CPIs, the dynamics of business models within the energy sector become pivotal. Carbon pricing, typically encompassing the power sector, gains greater importance in an era in which the global landscape is transitioning to modern electrified technologies and electric solutions. Until 2018, Singapore's electricity market operated under a non-liberalised framework (Singapore, Energy Market Authority [EMA] 2023). In such "regulated electricity markets", utilities wield substantial control over electricity, from generation to the consumer's meter. Here, electricity tariffs are often regulated by public utility commissions. The absence of competitive forces and the regulation of tariff-setting in non-liberalised markets, especially with state-owned power entities, can result in the lack of pass-through for carbon costs into electricity prices (Asian Development Bank [ADB] 2022). Consequently, there is a lack of incentives for energy efficiency or reduced energy consumption. Recognising this limitation, Singapore took a strategic step by liberalising and restructuring its electricity industry in 2018, a precursor to the introduction of its carbon tax in 2019. By including electricity generators in the carbon tax framework with a fully liberalised electricity market, Singapore aimed to make its power grid more climate-friendly while maintaining competitive electricity prices. Moreover, empowering consumers to choose their electricity providers added an extra layer of influence. This shift has the potential to encourage the adoption of low-carbon energy sources as consumers transition to providers with a greater focus on RE generation. Hence, the carbon tax development process in Singapore, including this pre-introductory step, offers valuable insights for other ASEAN countries, with the exception of the Philippines (Aris et al. 2020), which operates within a fully liberalised electricity market.

Singapore is the first ASEAN country to adopt carbon pricing, providing valuable insights for the other AMS on how this approach can accelerate decarbonisation.

Thailand

At the time of writing, the Thai government is in the process of revising the Climate Change Act, contemplating the introduction of an economic mechanism such as carbon pricing instruments, to effectively reduce GHG emissions (International Carbon Action Partnership [ICAP] 2023b). This revision aims to establish a regulatory framework empowering relevant government and private sector agencies to collect essential data for the national GHG inventory, particularly data currently unavailable (Thailand, Office of Natural Resources and Environmental Policy and Planning [ONEP] 2023).

Thailand is exploring various carbon pricing initiatives. Notably, a voluntary cap-and-trade programme has been in operation for a decade. In 2013, the Thailand Greenhouse Gas Management Organization (TGO) initiated the development of an MRV system and fundamental trading infrastructures for the Thailand Voluntary Emissions Trading Scheme (Thailand V-ETS). This voluntary pilot project focuses on refining MRV systems, cap-setting and allocation procedures, and trading infrastructure for 12 GHG-intensive sectors. Sector-specific targets, based on average emissions intensity in the base years of 2012–2013, cover both direct and indirect emissions. Allowances are granted for free, based on MRV reporting, with the option to use offsets from the domestic crediting mechanism, Thailand Voluntary Emission Reduction (T-VER), to meet targets. Complementing these initiatives, the TGO consistently conducts capacity-building activities to engage key stakeholders nationwide. In 2022, the Thailand V-ETS pilot project was extended to the Eastern Economic Corridor, one of the country's pivotal industrial regions (International Carbon Action Partnership [ICAP] 2023b; World Bank 2023b).

In April 2023, the Thai Excise Department announced plans to impose a carbon tax on the energy, transport and industrial sectors (The Nation 2023). This carbon tax not only aligns with the country's objectives of achieving carbon neutrality by 2050 and net zero GHG emissions by 2063 but also addresses increasing fuel import costs and the impending implementation of the CBAM by the EU in 2026. The carbon tax is anticipated to stimulate greater adoption of cleaner and RE, potentially reducing CO_2 emissions by up to 30%. However, specific details about the tax, including the implementation timeline, are yet to be provided by the Department.

Two studies have examined the impact of carbon pricing on income inequality and poverty reduction in Thailand. In Wattanakuljarus's simulation (2019), a carbon tax which aimed at achieving a 20% reduction in GHG emissions by 2030, aligning with Thailand's NDC, demonstrated effectiveness. With a rate of approximately USD 1.40 per tonne of CO_2e, emissions saw a significant reduction of 6.4 MtCO_2e, predominantly in coal and lignite. This initiative generated approximately USD 300 million in carbon revenues. The findings suggest that the impacts of a carbon tax would not be severe and tend to be progressive. Moreover, when coupled with a revenue recycling mechanism, the strategy adequately compensates for the burdens placed on the poorest households.

Saelim (2019), on the other hand, utilised a microsimulation model with a carbon tax set at the social cost of carbon (SCC), representing a potential worst-case scenario at USD 37 per tonne of CO_2e. Results from this study also indicated a progressive impact on income inequality and poverty reduction in Thailand. Particularly noteworthy were the positive outcomes when carbon tax revenues were directed towards social transfer programmes, such as pensions for the elderly. While higher carbon tax rates could potentially impact the poorest groups, both studies underscore that a well-designed carbon tax with a revenue recycling mechanism can effectively mitigate possible negative socio-economic impacts.

While Thailand has not yet enacted mandatory MRV reporting, the MRV infrastructure was developed a decade ago under the V-ETS programme. The pending Climate Change Act will serve as a crucial legal basis, enabling a compliance framework for CPIs.

Vietnam

In 2022, Vietnam implemented two crucial mandates. The Prime Minister issued Decision 01/2022/QD-TTg (Prime Minister of Vietnam 2022), outlining sectors and facilities with emissions inventory obligations. Concurrently, Decree 06/2022/ND-CP (Government of Vietnam 2022) established clear regulations for the development of Vietnam's carbon market and outlined the roadmap for the National Crediting Mechanism (NCM) and the CAT programmes. These programmes are anticipated to commence in 2024 and 2026, respectively, reaching full operational status by 2026 and 2028 (International Carbon Action Partnership [ICAP] 2023c). According to the Decree, the mandatory CAT programme will encompass the steel, cement and thermal power sectors, developing a declining cap aligned with Vietnam's NDC. Meanwhile, the NCM will establish a legal framework and technical foundations, encompassing the solid waste and transport sectors.

Moreover, according to a research study utilising multi-criteria analysis, a carbon tax would be highly suitable in Vietnam, provided it is politically viable (Do and Burke 2021). This contrasts with a CAT programme, which is considered an attractive option due to the higher perceived political viability in the national context. The study indicates that even with a relatively low initial carbon price ranging from USD 1.85 to USD 3.86 per tonne of CO_2e, starting in 2022 with a real annual increase of 10%, emissions in the energy sector could be reduced by up to 11.2% relative to the BAU scenario. It is estimated that the carbon tax will generate a cumulative revenue of about

USD 21.9 billion by 2030. Furthermore, the study highlights that carbon pricing has the potential to improve local air quality, potentially reducing cumulative emissions of non-CO_2 air pollutants by about 2.9% over the period 2022–2030. Importantly, the research suggests that significant negative economic and social impacts are unlikely, as the effects of the low initial carbon price on final energy prices would mostly be minimal. This study offers insights for policymakers exploring a hybrid CPI, in which the carbon tax serves as a mechanism to effectively and promptly address the EU's CBAM (Vietnam News 2023b), set to be in full operation by 2026.

Vietnam has established the fundamental requirements for a CAT programme in terms of both the MRV infrastructure and the legal basis. Currently, the country is making progress in developing a fully operational system.

5 Carbon Pricing: Mitigating Carbon Leakage and Addressing the EU's CBAM

Carbon leakage occurs when GHG emissions shift across jurisdictions due to differing carbon regulation stringency (Partnership for Market Readiness 2015). Countries lacking or with less stringent carbon regulations become attractive for emissions-intensive industries, posing a risk of industries relocating to avoid high carbon costs elsewhere.

In March 2022, the EU introduced CBAM regulations to combat carbon leakage and encourage global adoption of carbon pricing policies. CBAM entered into effect on 1 October 2023, with a transitional phase until the end of 2025 before full operation in 2026 (European Commission 2024). Initially covering imports of carbon-intensive products (cement, iron and steel, aluminium, fertilisers, electricity and hydrogen production), CBAM aims to prevent carbon leakage, extending its scope to more sectors in the future. CBAM operates in tandem with the EU ETS, where EU producers cover CO_2 emissions with EU ETS allowances, increasing production costs. Importantly, CBAM ensures equal treatment by requiring importers to pay the same carbon price as domestic producers, averting carbon leakage.

Under CBAM, EU importers of products from outside the EU must purchase CBAM certificates to cover the price difference under the EU ETS. Importers surrender certificates based on embedded GHG emissions; if a carbon price was paid during production by third-country producers, the corresponding amount can be deducted from their final bill (European Commission 2024; European Parliament and Council of the European Union 2023). Consequently, EU importers are likely to prefer goods from partners whose countries have implemented a carbon price to mitigate or reduce the obligation cost.

Figure 2 illustrates the CBAM-regulated goods from ASEAN countries exported to the EU in 2022, with a total export value exceeding USD 5.8 billion. Vietnam emerges as the largest import partner, followed by Malaysia, Indonesia, Thailand and Singapore. Currently, only Singapore enforces a carbon tax on the production

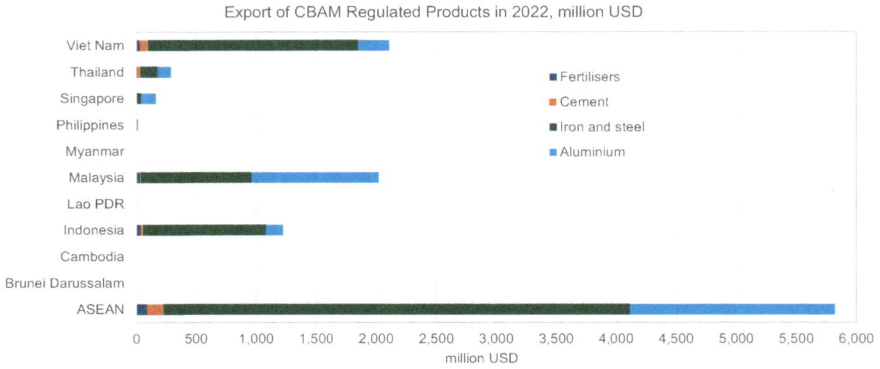

Fig. 2 CBAM-regulated goods from the AMS exported to the EU in 2022. *Source* Constructed by the authors; data obtained from ASEANstats (2022)

of these goods, while Indonesia's CAT programme covers only the power sector. Consequently, goods from Indonesia will be subject to compliance costs. These ASEAN countries are potentially at risk of losing trading partners for these goods once CBAM is fully operational by 2026. While the export values represent less than 1% of ASEAN's total GDP (ASEANstats 2023), the annual income losses could exceed USD 1.2 billion for Indonesia and USD 2 billion for Malaysia and Vietnam. Thus, carbon pricing can be a fiscal policy instrument in preparing industrial producers for international trade and incentivising the low-carbon transition in the corporate sector.

For example, the Southeast Asia Energy Transition Partnership (ETP) estimates that CBAM will directly impact these four regulated industrial sectors (fertilisers, cement, iron and steel, and aluminium) in Vietnam, potentially causing a decline of USD 100 million in export turnover from these sectors to the EU (Vietnamnet Global 2023). Hence, in addition to preparing a CAT programme, the government is also considering a carbon tax to mitigate the impacts of CBAM (Vietnam Chamber of Commerce and Industry [VCCI] 2023; Vietnam News 2023b). Presently, Vietnam indirectly imposes a tax on carbon through the environmental protection tax on fossil fuel producers and importers, but this tax rate does not truly reflect the nature of carbon pricing (Vietnam News 2022; World Bank 2022b). The government could consider amending the draft Decree by the Ministry of Finance on new environmental protection fees for emissions to include GHG emissions among the regulated pollutants (Vietnam News 2023a). Alternatively, the government could consider including a carbon tax in the amendment of the environmental protection tax, expected around 2026 by the Ministry of Finance (Vietnam Chamber of Commerce and Industry [VCCI] 2023). This will align with strategies aimed at mitigating the risk of economic impacts posed by the EU's CBAM.

Moreover, CBAM is expected to expand, gradually incorporating new products (European Commission 2023). This suggests that the impact of CBAM on ASEAN economies may increase in the future, affecting countries that were not initially impacted during its first phase. Presently, except for Singapore, none of the AMS can evade CBAM obligations. As cost competition is a key factor in profitability, without implementing a carbon price, these nations risk losing their trading competitiveness in the EU market.

While a consensus can be reached through trading negotiations between importers and exporters, the CBAM obligation, either fully or partially shouldered by exporters, could serve as a motivation for exporters to invest in emissions reduction through environmentally responsible production. However, this endeavour may come at the expense of reducing profit margins for emissions-intensive exporters, subsequently leading to a decline in GDP. For instance, "it is estimated that 57% of Malaysia's total exports will be affected by the implementation of CBAM" (Ministry of Economy in Malaysia 2023b). Concerning CBAM, "Malaysia may lose trade worth over USD 24 billion to the European countries" if its "exporters fail to produce goods with greater GHG efficiency" (Muhammad 2021).

Li and Su (2017) sought to compare the consequences of imposing a domestic carbon tax in Singapore versus paying the cross-border adjustment (CBA) on exports, both set at a price of SGD 10/t-CO_2 and incorporating a revenue recycling mechanism. In terms of GDP, the study found that a domestic carbon tax generally results in more modest declines, with total exports only marginally more affected if the tax revenue is not recycled. The emissions reduction potential in the carbon tax scenario, encompassing all sectors, is also higher than that of the CBA. Furthermore, paying the CBA emerges as the more expensive option, with the highest average abatement cost at SGD 399 per tonne of CO_2e compared to carbon tax scenarios ranging from SGD 111 to SGD 184 per tonne of emissions reduction. With an increasing number of countries adopting carbon pricing policies and potential pressure from paying CBA, the simulation results suggest that a domestic carbon tax may not prompt the relocation of these sectors away from Singapore. Although this study primarily focused on Singapore, the findings offer insights into the effectiveness of carbon pricing with revenue recycling as the most cost-effective tool in emissions abatement.

With the adoption of a mechanism similar to CBAM by the United States (Smith 2023), carbon pricing emerged as a crucial fiscal policy tool for ASEAN countries. This strategic approach aims to mitigate risks and enhance resilience against potential economic impacts in international trade. Additionally, countries with carbon regulations can effectively lower the risk of carbon leakage, preventing the ASEAN region from becoming a dumping ground for carbon emissions.

6 Conclusions and Recommendations

In this chapter we introduce fundamental concepts related to carbon pricing and present a real case study assessing CPI options based on national circumstances. We are optimistic that this knowledge will encourage greater consideration of the adoption of CPIs among ASEAN countries, facilitating the formulation of more ambitious future NDC targets. Three key messages arise regarding the implementation of CPIs:

1. Carbon pricing serves as a powerful incentive for decarbonisation

Carbon pricing plays a crucial role in expediting the necessary financial investments for the energy transition. The introduction of a carbon price acts as a guiding force in decision-making processes related to climate change impacts, risks and opportunities, particularly within corporate organisations. As the compliance cost of carbon pricing increases, it reshapes the business landscape, encouraging companies to assess and adopt sustainable practices. Beyond providing a strong incentive, the adoption of carbon pricing also has the potential to generate substantial fiscal revenues. A portion of this revenue influx can be directed towards financing climate actions, alleviating the fiscal burden on governments and propelling the global movement towards a sustainable and decarbonised future. However, it is essential for jurisdictions to take into account the potential countervailing policies associated with CPIs. For example, subsidies for fossil fuels and electricity often run counter to the incentives created by carbon pricing (World Bank 2021b). These subsidies encourage the domestic consumption of fossil fuels, whereas the primary objective of carbon pricing is to reduce GHG emissions by minimising reliance on such fuels. As a result, this contradiction undermines the effectiveness of carbon pricing in driving the transition towards a low-carbon economy. Therefore, reforming subsidies is crucial to ensure the effectiveness of CPIs.

2. Carbon pricing with robust revenue recycling facilitates a just energy transition

Ideally, regulating carbon pricing at the upstream (importers and producers) or midstream (distributors or electricity generators) levels of the supply chain allows the price signal to permeate downstream to consumers if cost pass-through is permitted. However, without cost pass-through, the price signal may struggle to reach consumers, providing minimal incentive for changes in consumption behaviour. Despite potential benefits, concerns persist regarding adverse distributional impacts on household welfare, income inequality and poverty. These concerns can be effectively addressed through the recycling of carbon pricing revenue—whether through direct transfers to poor and vulnerable consumers or compensatory schemes involving tax swaps or cuts. Additionally, separating carbon pricing revenues from the general budget enhances transparency in revenue use. A well-designed carbon pricing mechanism with a robust revenue recycling strategy is pivotal in ensuring a just transition.

3. Clearing the decks through effective communication

A well-thought-out communication strategy is essential to convey the benefits of carbon pricing to the public, especially in the relatively new context of the ASEAN region. Given the potential limited engagement with the terms associated with climate change among the general public, emphasising other national concerns or aspirations for the future should be central to narratives, with climate change arguments playing a complementary rather than central role in the communication strategy. The success story of Costa Rica, framing its carbon pricing policy around air pollution, illustrates the effectiveness of this approach (Partnership for Market Readiness [PMR] and Carbon Pricing Leadership Coalition [CPLC] 2018). Conversely, poor communication by the former Australian government on revenue recycling contributed to the repeal of the carbon tax there (Jotzo 2013; Asian Development Bank (ADB) 2022), despite studies showing its effectiveness in emissions reduction (O'Gorman and Jotzo 2014). Hence, early dialogue and broad stakeholder involvement can help avert political opposition. Researchers and policymakers must enhance their communication effectiveness to avoid political conflicts that might result in less effective policy outcomes. Reframing the role of carbon pricing instruments within the broader development and climate agendas can address cost concerns and bolster stakeholder buy-in.

Presently, only Singapore and Indonesia have embraced mandatory CPIs, positioning themselves as potential role models for other ASEAN nations. Notably, Cambodia, Lao PDR and Myanmar, classified as the least developed countries in Southeast Asia, have yet to express interest in CPIs. Conversely, the majority of other AMS are contemplating CPI implementation, with a notable preference for a hybrid approach, combining both taxation and CAT. This trend indicates a collective interest in adopting diverse strategies for carbon pricing across the region.

After reviewing the progress of CPI implementation in ASEAN countries, our assessment is based on fundamental requirements—the readiness of MRV infrastructure and legal frameworks. Apart from Singapore, facility-level MRV infrastructures have been developed under a mandate in Brunei Darussalam and Vietnam, and on a voluntary basis in Thailand for a decade. Although Indonesia adopted a CAT programme, its initial phase involves direct carbon trading between regulated entities in the power sector. The MRV infrastructure needs further development for broader scope and coverage under the next phases of the CAT programme. Regarding the legal basis for carbon pricing implementation, besides Indonesia and Singapore, Vietnam has enacted regulations for its CAT programmes, scheduled to be fully operational by 2028, while the Philippines and Thailand have drafted laws currently pending cabinet approval. Among the eight AMS yet to implement a CPI, Vietnam is the most advanced with both MRV infrastructure and a legal basis in place.

Countries must carefully consider the timeframe when planning the implementation of CPIs. While many nations are exploring the potential of CPIs, introducing a new legal framework can be a comprehensive undertaking, especially for a complex CAT programme. In contrast to a carbon tax, which can leverage existing tax systems, CAT infrastructure is more intricate and demands substantial resources. For instance, both Indonesia (Government of Indonesia 2017; Hidranto 2023) and the Republic of Korea (Hidranto 2023) took approximately five years to develop and implement CAT programmes, whereas Singapore's implementation of a carbon tax (Government of Singapore 2018a; National Climate Change Secretariat Singapore (NCCS) 2023) required only about a year from establishing a legal basis to initial application. Therefore, when deciding on the type of CPI to adopt, individual AMS may need to consider the urgency of meeting their NDC targets in addressing the global effects of climate change.

In addition, we strongly encourage the AMS to use carbon pricing as a tool to mitigate the risk of carbon leakage and economic impacts associated with the EU's

CBAM. Our findings reveal that Vietnam is the largest exporter to the EU, followed by Malaysia, Indonesia, Thailand and Singapore. With the full operation of CBAM expected by 2026, currently, only Singapore appears resilient to the economic impact of CBAM. Despite Indonesia's initiation of a CAT programme, it currently regulates only the power sector, which does not export electricity to the EU. Unless the second phase of Indonesia's CAT covers goods regulated under CBAM and is implemented by 2026, the country will still be affected under the existing CAT programme. Similarly, although Vietnam is prepared for the fundamental requirements of carbon pricing implementation, the full operation of the CAT programme is scheduled for 2028. Consequently, Vietnam will be unable to avoid the impact of the first two years of CBAM. Carbon taxes require relatively simpler infrastructure and legal frameworks. To address the impact of CBAM by 2026, the Philippines, Thailand and Vietnam have expressed the possibility of adopting carbon taxes, changing their plans from CAT programmes to hybrid CPIs. The countries in ASEAN that have yet to develop a robust MRV infrastructure and legal framework for CPIs, like Malaysia, are relatively more vulnerable compared to other neighbouring nations, given that the EU is one of their crucial trading partners. Furthermore, the AMS with carbon regulations, such as carbon pricing, will reduce the risk of becoming an emissions dumpsite, mitigating consequences from carbon leakage.

Acknowledgements This study is an outcome of the ASEAN Climate and Energy Project II (ACCEPT II), which is managed by the ASEAN Centre for Energy (ACE) in cooperation with the Norwegian Institute of International Affairs.

References

Alonso C, Kilpatrick J (2022) The distributional impact of a carbon tax in Asia and the Pacific. International Monetary Fund. Available at: https://doi.org/10.5089/9798400212383.001. Accessed 27 Nov 2024

Alvarez M (2019) Distributional effects of environmental taxation: an approximation with a meta-regression analysis. Econ Anal Policy 62:382–401. Available at: https://www.sciencedirect.com/science/article/abs/pii/S0313592618302133?via%3Dihub. Accessed 27 Nov 2024

Andersson JJ (2019) Carbon Taxes and CO_2 emissions: Sweden as a case study. Am Econ J Econ Policy 11(4):1–30. Available at: https://doi.org/10.1257/pol.20170144. Accessed 26 Nov 2024

Andersson J, Atkinson G (2020) The distributional effects of a carbon tax: the role of income inequality. Centre for Climate Change Economics and Policy Working Paper 378/Grantham Research Institute on Climate Change and the Environment Working Paper 349. London School of Economics and Political Science, London

Aris H, Mohd Zawawi IS, Jørgensen, BN (2020) The Philippines' and Singapore's journeys towards liberalised electricity supply industries—takeaways for Malaysia. Energies 13(14). Available at: https://doi.org/10.3390/en13143514. Accessed 27 Nov 2024

ASEAN Centre for Energy (ACE) (2022) The 7th ASEAN Energy Outlook (AEO7). Jakarta

ASEAN Centre for Energy and Brunei Climate Change Secretariat (2023) Assessment of carbon pricing options in Brunei Darussalam. Jakarta

ASEAN Working Group on Climate Change (AWGCC) (2022a) MRV information platform for ASEAN region: Myanmar. Available at: https://www.mrv-info.com/ams/myanmar.html. Accessed 4 Nov 2022

ASEAN Working Group on Climate Change (AWGCC) (2022b) MRV information platform for ASEAN region: Philippines. Available at: https://www.mrv-info.com/ams/philippines.html. Accessed 9 Nov 2023

ASEANstats (2022) Trade in Goods (IMTS), annually, HS 2-digit up to 8-digit (AHTN), in US$, ASEANstats Data Portal. Available at: https://data.aseanstats.org/trade-annually. Accessed 1 Dec 2023

ASEANstats (2023) ASEAN member states: selected basic indicators. Available at: https://cdn.aseanstats.org/public/data/statics/2023/10/table1_2022.xls. Accessed 1 Dec 2023

Asian Development Bank (ADB) (2018) The Korea emissions trading scheme: challenges and emerging opportunities. Manila

Asian Development Bank (ADB) (2020) Asian Development Outlook (ADO) 2020: what drives innovation in Asia? Manila. Available at: https://www.adb.org/publications/asian-development-outlook-2020-innovation-asia. Accessed 27 Dec 2024

Asian Development Bank (ADB) (2022) Carbon Pricing for Energy Transition and Decarbonization. Manila

Asuka J (2017) INDC costs and experiences in removing low-carbon technology barriers: Japan. In Anbumozhi V Kalirajan K (eds) Globalization of low-carbon technologies: the impact of the Paris agreement. Springer Nature, Singapore

Bank Negara Malaysia (2023) Towards a Greener Financial System

Baranzini A et al (2016) Seven reasons to use carbon pricing in climate policy. Centre for Climate Change Economics and Policy Working Paper No. 253/Grantham Research Institute on Climate Change and the Environment Working Paper No. 224, London. Available at: https://www.lse.ac.uk/granthaminstitute/wp-content/uploads/2016/02/Working-Paper-224-Baranzini-et-al.pdf. Accessed 25 Dec 2024

Bloomberg L.P. [Limited Partnership] (2023) Carbon Pricing, NetZero Pathfinders. Available at: https://www.netzeropathfinders.com/. Accessed 27 Dec 2024

Brunei Climate Change Secretariat (BCCS) (2020) Brunei Darussalam National Climate Change Policy

Brunei Climate Change Secretariat (BCCS) (2023) Directive on Mandatory Reporting on Greenhouse Gases

Brunei Darussalam Department of Energy (2022) Department of Electrical Services. Available at: https://www.energy.gov.bn/SitePages/index.aspx. Accessed 11 Dec 2023

Caraballo MU (2022) Diokno open to carbon tax. Manila Times, 8 July. Available at: https://www.pids.gov.ph/details/news/in-the-news/diokno-open-to-carbon-tax. Accessed 26 Dec 2024

Chatto EM (2023) An act promoting a low carbon economy, establishing for this purpose and emission trading system and implementation mechanism to achieve national climate targets. Philippines: 19th Congress. Available at: https://docs.congress.hrep.online/legisdocs/basic_19/HB07705.pdf. Accessed 3 Dec 2024

Council of the European Union (2022) Infographic—fit for 55: how does the EU intend to address the emissions outside of the EU? Available at: https://www.consilium.europa.eu/en/infographics/fit-for-55-cbam-carbon-border-adjustment-mechanism/. Accessed 20 Aug 2022

Do TN, Burke PJ (2021) Carbon pricing in Vietnam: options for adoption. Energy Climate Change 2:100058. Available at: https://doi.org/10.1016/j.egycc.2021.100058. Accessed 27 Nov 2024

Doshi TK (2018) Costs and benefits of market-based instruments in accelerating low-carbon energy transition. In: Anbumozhi V, Kalirajan K, Kimura F (eds) Financing for low-carbon energy transition: unlocking the potential of private capital. Springer Nature, Singapore

Durrani-Jamal S, Byers D (2021) Cambodia is making strides on the long road to low-carbon economic growth. Asian Development Blog. Available at: https://blogs.adb.org/blog/cambodia-making-strides-long-road-low-carbon-economic-growth. Accessed 31 Oct 2023

Eco-Business (2024) Landmark low carbon economy bill to bridge climate investment gap in Philippines' decarbonisation plans. Philippines Climate Change Commission (CCC)—News Roundup, 16 August. Available at: https://www.climate.gov.ph/public/ckfinder/userfiles/files/News%20Roundup/08_16_2024.pdf. Accessed 3 Dec 2024

European Commission (2023) Questions and answers: Carbon Border Adjustment Mechanism (CBAM)

European Commission (2024) Carbon Border Adjustment Mechanism. Available at: https://taxation-customs.ec.europa.eu/carbon-border-adjustment-mechanism_en. Accessed 27 Dec 2024

European Parliament and Council of the European Union (2023) Regulation (EU) 2023/956 of the European Parliament and of the Council of 10 May 2023 Establishing a Carbon Border Adjustment Mechanism, pp 52–104

Government of Indonesia (2017) Peraturan Pemerintah (PP) Nomor 46 Tahun 2017 tentang Instrumen Ekonomi Lingkungan Hidup. Indonesia: LN.2017/No. 228, TLN NO.6134, LL Setneg : 38 hlm

Government of Indonesia (2021a) Undang-undang (UU) Nomor 7 Tahun 2021 tentang Harmonisasi Peraturan Perpajakan. Available at: https://peraturan.bpk.go.id/Details/185162/uu-no-7-tahun-2021?a=4JDQYKRG. Accessed 27 Dec 2024

Government of Indonesia (2021b) Peraturan Presiden (PERPRES) Nomor 98 Tahun 2021 tentang Penyelenggaraan Nilai Ekonomi Karbon untuk Pencapaian Target Kontribusi yang Ditetapkan Secara Nasional dan Pengendalian Emisi Gas Rumah Kaca dalam Pembangunan Nasional. LN.2021/No.249, jdih.setneg.go.id: 68 hlm

Government of Indonesia (2022a) Peraturan Menteri Energi dan Sumber Daya Mineral Nomor 16 Tahun 2022 tentang Tata Cara Penyelenggaraan Nilai Ekonomi Karbon Subsektor Pembangkit Tenaga Listrik. BN.2022 (1323) : 18 hlm.; peraturan.go.id

Government of Indonesia (2022b) Peraturan Menteri Lingkungan Hidup Dan Kehutanan Nomor 21 Tahun 2022 tentang Tata Laksana Penerapan Nilai Ekonomi Karbon. BN 2022/No 1064; peraturan.go.id: 79 hlm

Government of Lao People's Democratic Republic (2021) Nationally Determined Contribution (NDC)

Government of Singapore (2018a) Carbon Pricing Act 2018

Government of Singapore (2018b) Carbon Pricing (Measurement, Reporting and Verification) Regulations 2018

Government of Singapore (2022) Carbon Pricing (Amendment) Bill

Government of Vietnam (2022) Decree No. 06/2022/ND-CP on mitigation of greenhouse gas emissions and protection of ozone layer

Hafstead M (2022) Carbon pricing 101, carbon pricing explainer series. Available at: https://www.rff.org/publications/explainers/carbon-pricing-101/. Accessed 15 May 2022

Hidranto F (2023) Jualan Baru Bernama Perdagangan Karbon. Portal Informasi Indonesia, 14 March

Hongo T (2018) Prospects of quality infrastructure program and private sector MRV for accelerating the transition towards low-carbon energy system. In: Anbumozhi V, Kalirajan K, Kimura F (eds) Financing for low-carbon energy transition: unlocking the potential of private capital. Springer Nature Singapore, Singapore

International Carbon Action Partnership (ICAP) (2023a) ICAP ETS Map: Indonesia

International Carbon Action Partnership (ICAP) (2023b) ICAP ETS map: Thailand. Available at: https://icapcarbonaction.com/en/ets/thailand. Accessed 16 Nov 2023

International Carbon Action Partnership (ICAP) (2023c) ICAP ETS map: Vietnam

International Energy Agency (IEA) (2020) Implementing effective emissions trading systems. Paris

International Monetary Fund (IMF) (2020) Mitigating climate change—Growth- and distribution-friendly strategies. World Economic Outlook, October 2020: A Long and Difficult Ascent

Jotzo F (2013) Keep Australia's carbon pricing. Nature 502(7469):38. Available at: https://doi.org/10.1038/502038a. Accessed 28 Nov 2024

Khamphilavanh BE, Masui T (2021) Assessing the impacts of introducing of carbon tax and technologies for road transportation in Laos. Chem Eng Trans 89:103–108 SE-Research Articles. Available at: https://doi.org/10.3303/CET2189018. Accessed 28 Nov 2024

Li Y, Su B (2017) The impacts of carbon pricing on coastal megacities: a CGE analysis of Singapore. J Cleaner Prod 165:1239–1248. Available at: https://doi.org/10.1016/j.jclepro.2017.07.206. Accessed 16 Jan 2025

Ling S (2023) Sarawak first in the country to enact anti-climate change law. The Star, 20 November

Metcalf GE (2022) Five myths about carbon pricing. National Bureau of Economic Research, Cambridge, MA. Available at: https://www.nber.org/system/files/working_papers/w31104/w31104.pdf. Accessed 28 Nov 2024

Ministry of Economy in Malaysia (2023a) Advancing sustainability. In: Mid-Term Review of the Twelfth Malaysia Plan. Putrajaya

Ministry of Economy in Malaysia (2023b) National Energy Transition Roadmap (NETR). Putrajaya

Ministry of Natural Resources, Environment and Climate Change (NRECC) Malaysia (2023) Malaysia's plan for implementation of carbon pricing. In the Accept II Workshop on Carbon Pricing Implementation in ASEAN, Nusa Dua, Bali, Indonesia, 24–26 July

MIT [Massachusetts Institute of Technology] Energy Initiative (MITEI) (2019) Renewable Energy and Carbon Pricing Policies. Available at: https://energy.mit.edu/research/renewable-energy-and-carbon-pricing-policies/. Accessed 13 July 2023

Muhammad I (2021) Challenges in implementing carbon pricing policy in Malaysia. The Bartlett. University College London: The Bartlett Faculty of the Built Environment. Available at: https://www.ucl.ac.uk/bartlett/news/2021/nov/challenges-implementing-carbon-pricing-policy-malaysia. Accessed 26 Dec 2024

National Climate Change Secretariat (NCCS) Singapore (2022) Carbon Tax. Available at: https://www.nccs.gov.sg/singapores-climate-action/mitigation-efforts/carbontax/. Accessed 26 Dec 2024

National Climate Change Secretariat Singapore (NCCS) (2023) Carbon Tax. Available at: https://www.nccs.gov.sg/singapores-climate-action/mitigation-efforts/carbontax/#:~:text=Singapore implemented a carbon tax,period for emitters to adjust. (Accessed: 10 November 2023)

National Environment Agency (NEA) Singapore (2023) Singapore sets out eligibility criteria for international carbon credits under the carbon tax regime. Available at: https://www.nea.gov.sg/media/news/news/index/singapore-sets-out-eligibility-criteria-for-international-carbon-credits-under-the-carbon-tax-regime. Accessed 10 Nov 2023

O'Gorman M, Jotzo F (2014) Impact of the carbon price on Australia's electricity demand, supply and emissions. ANU Crawford School of Public Policy CCEP Working Paper 1411, Canberra. Available at: https://crawford.anu.edu.au/publication/crawford-school-working-papers/9816/impact-carbon-price-australias-electricity-demand#:~:text=Over%20this%20period%2C%20electricity%20demand,period%20before%20the%20carbon%20price. Accessed 28 Nov 2024

Otoritas Jasa Keuangan (OJK) (2023) Carbon Trading on Carbon Exchange

Partnership for Market Readiness (2015) *Carbon leakage: theory, evidence and policy design.* Washington, DC

Partnership for Market Readiness/International Carbon Action Partnership (2021) Emissions trading in practice, second edition: a handbook on design and implementation. Washington, DC

Partnership for Market Readiness (PMR) and Carbon Pricing Leadership Coalition (CPLC) (2018) Guide to communicating carbon pricing. Washington, DC. Available at: https://openknowledge.worldbank.org/server/api/core/bitstreams/448db6f0-1b31-51d3-aac4-2566d8b12f23/content

Philippines, Climate Change Commission (CCC) (2023) National Integrated Climate Change Database Information and Exchange System (NICCDIES). Available at: https://niccdies.climate.gov.ph/niccdies. Accessed 9 Nov 2023

Prime Minister of Vietnam (2022) Decision No. 01/2022/QD-TTg: promulgating the lists of sectors and establishments emitting greenhouse gases subject to greenhouse gas inventory

Reyes Ad (2022) Indonesia delays carbon tax scheme again on global risk. Argus Media, 28 June

Saelim S (2019) Carbon tax incidence on household demand: effects on welfare, income inequality and poverty incidence in Thailand. J Cleaner Prod 234:521–533. Available at: https://doi.org/10.1016/j.jclepro.2019.06.218. Accessed 28 Nov 2024
Senate of the Philippines (2023) Senate Bill No. 1992, 19th Congress, Legislative Digital Resources. Available at: https://issuances-library.senate.gov.ph/bills/senate-bill-no-1992-19th-congress. Accessed 8 Nov 2023
Singapore, Energy Market Authority (EMA) (2023) Today, Singapore has a liberalised electricity industry that promotes effective market competition, electricity market. Available at: https://www.ema.gov.sg/our-energy-story/energy-market-landscape/electricity. Accessed 12 Dec 2023
Smith T (2023) U.S. carbon border adjustment proposals and world trade organization compliance. American Action Forum Insight. Available at: https://www.americanactionforum.org/insight/u-s-carbon-border-adjustment-proposals-and-world-trade-organization-compliance/. Accessed 27 Dec 2024
Thailand, Office of Natural Resources and Environmental Policy and Planning (ONEP) (2023) Thailand's Fourth Biennial Update Report (BUR4). Bangkok
The Nation (Bangkok) (2023) Excise department to impose a carbon tax on 3 sectors, 9 April
United Nations Framework Convention on Climate Change (UNFCCC) (2023) About Carbon Pricing. Available at: https://unfccc.int/about-us/regional-collaboration-centres/the-ciaca/about-carbon-pricing#What-are-the-benefits-of-carbon-pricing?-. Accessed 9 Dec 2023
UNFCCC RCC Asia-Pacific (United Nations Framework Convention on Climate Change Regional Collaboration Centre for Asia and the Pacific) (2019a) Cambodia country report. Bangkok
UNFCCC RCC Asia-Pacific (2019b) Myanmar country report. Bangkok
Vietnam Chamber of Commerce and Industry (VCCI) (2023) Carbon tax helps 'decarbonize' the economy. News, 1 September
Vietnam News (2022) Carbon market to help achieve net zero emissions. Economy, 29 September
Vietnam News (2023a) Environment protection fee proposed for emissions. Environment, 29 December
Vietnam News (2023b) Proposal to apply carbon tax to mitigate CBAM for exported goods. Economy, 31 August
Vietnamnet Global (2023) Vietnam to benefit from EU's new carbon border tax. Available at: https://vietnamnet.vn/en/vietnam-to-benefit-from-eu-s-new-carbon-border-tax-2133101.html. Accessed 17 Nov 2023
Wattanakuljarus A (2019) Effects and burdens of a carbon tax scheme in Thailand. Eurasian Econ Rev 9(2): 173–219. Available at: https://doi.org/10.1007/s40822-018-0100-x. Accessed 29 Nov 2024
World Bank (2017) Carbon tax guide: a handbook for policy makers. International Bank for Reconstruction and Development/The World Bank, Washington, DC. Available at: https://documents.worldbank.org/en/publication/documents-reports/documentdetail/728421535605566659/carbon-tax-guide-a-handbook-for-policy-makers. Accessed 24 Dec 2024
World Bank (2021a) A guide to developing domestic carbon crediting mechanisms. Washington, DC
World Bank (2021b) Carbon pricing assessment and decision making: a guide to adopting a carbon price. Washington, DC. Available at: https://documents.worldbank.org/en/publication/documents-reports/documentdetail/443321617707561042/carbon-pricing-assessment-and-decision-making-a-guide-to-adopting-a-carbon-price. Accessed 4 Nov 2024
World Bank (2022a) Philippines country climate and development report. Washington, DC
World Bank (2022b) Vietnam country climate and development report. Washington, DC
World Bank (2023a) Cambodia: country climate and development report. Washington, DC
World Bank (2023b) State and trends of carbon pricing 2023. Washington, DC. Available at: https://doi.org/10.1596/978-1-4648-2006-9
World Bank (2023c) What is carbon pricing?, Carbon pricing dashboard. Available at: https://carbonpricingdashboard.worldbank.org/what-carbon-pricing. Accessed 1 June 2023

Yahoo M, Othman J (2017) Carbon and energy taxation for CO_2 mitigation: a CGE model of the [sic] Malaysia. Environ Dev Sustain 19(1):239–262. Available at: https://doi.org/10.1007/s10668-015-9725-z. Accessed 29 Nov 2024

Renewable Energy and Public Financing in the Asian Region: Some Reflections from Recent Trends

Tirthankar Mandal

Abstract Deploying clean energy through renewable forms of energy is key to mitigating greenhouse gas emissions across the world. While Asian economies are no different in this respect, the challenge for the deployment of renewable energy arises from the fact that the infrastructure required for renewable forms of energy is fundamentally different from that needed for traditional forms. As the cost of deploying renewable energy in Asia is higher than in developed economies, public finance plays an especially important role. In this chapter a review is made of the specific roles that public finance mechanisms can play going forward to increase the deployment of renewable energy in Asian economies. It identifies how public finance can be effective in enhancing the deployment of renewable resources and examines four key Asian economies that are trying to rapidly increase the share of electricity generated from renewable energy in their total power generation.

1 Introduction

In 2023, the decisions of the 28th Conference of the Parties (COP28) to the United Nations Framework Convention on Climate Change (UNFCCC) highlighted the urgent need for faster, futuristic, formidable actions to reduce greenhouse gas (GHG) emissions (UNFCCC 2023). As global energy systems are the largest contributors of GHG emissions (Clarke et al. 2022), they must be the focus of attention (Dubash 2001). While there is a growing thrust centred around replacing traditional fossil fuel-based energy systems with new modes of cleaner and novel energy systems, there is still substantial variation in their efficacies (IEA 2022a).

In the global south, policymakers focus particularly on the reliability and affordability factors of electricity options as they are the foundation of achieving basic development outcomes (World Bank 2023). Due to the imperatives of affordability and reliability, the Asian economies have relied heavily on security and centralised

T. Mandal (✉)
WRI India, New Delhi, India
e-mail: tirthankar.mandal@wri.org

H. Phoumin et al. (eds.), *Tackling the Energy Transition: Insights from ASEAN and Beyond*, Climate Change and Energy Transition,
https://doi.org/10.1007/978-981-96-6019-3_5

planning over the last few decades to ensure fully integrated power supplies (Dubash and Singh 2005). This approach soon proved to be a source of vulnerabilities and real consequences. It is not just about technical capacities—the energy sector in developing Asian countries currently faces the burden of extensive government budgetary support through various financial mechanisms (Bhattacharya 2022). In addition to the fiscal strain on governments, many Asian countries have also grappled with the instability of the coal industry over the past decade. Thus, Asian countries face three key challenges: (a) overcoming the growing issues of traditional energy systems, (b) managing the transition towards reliable and resilient sources of clean energy for the future, and (c) carrying out all such activities in a cost-effective manner that benefits the people. Tackling these challenges will require unprecedented cooperation between the public and private sectors in Asia to fundamentally transform energy infrastructure and markets across the region.

2 Key Issues for the Asian Energy Transition

In developing countries, the energy transition is more complex than in the developed world because in addition to reducing emissions, these countries are striving to achieve basic development outcomes and attain economic prosperity through their use of energy (World Bank 2023; Chawla 2023). The transition narrative in Asian economies has three major objectives. First are the economy-centric objectives, which ensure that industries remain competitive even after the transition to cleaner alternatives (Anderson 2009). Second are the people-centric objectives, which ensure that the new forms of energy create employment opportunities for the workers who had been employed in the fossil fuel sector. Third, the available energy must be affordable and completely reliable (IEA 2022a). Achieving these three objectives simultaneously is fundamental to the Asian economies' energy transitions (Fruman and Gupta 2023) and requires large-scale technocratic changes in the energy sectors of all Asian economies. These changes can be possible only if an enabling environment is provided to the key stakeholders of the energy sector (Taghizadeh-Hesary and Rasoulinezhad 2020).

To achieve the successful implementation of new sources of energy, the key is to make them highly affordable. While policies and regulations support this goal, a substantial part of achieving it lies in ensuring that public finance facilitates the adoption of cleaner technologies quickly and economically. Moreover, public financing must attract cooperation with the private sector.

This chapter explores potential ways to facilitate the shift from fossil fuels to cleaner forms of energy and discusses the role of public finance in four Asian economies (Indonesia, India, Thailand and the Philippines) in which the energy systems are more geared to providing support to fossil-fuel technologies than to renewable energy (RE) technologies.

2.1 Analytical Approach

The next section is a literature review which focuses on (a) energy sector developments and the issues that developing countries, including Asian economies, face in adopting RE, (b) financing issues and (c) examples of best practices and initiatives that other countries have taken to overcome these issues. This is followed by a secondary analysis of the relevant data, to clarify the overall ecosystem of investments, notably the differences between the developed and developing world in terms of building the necessary infrastructure for RE. The third section discusses the relevant policies and measures that support the transition in the four developing countries of Asia studied. The final section provides some recommendations for the way forward.

3 Contribution to Existing Research

The investment needed to generate electricity from RE is very different than what is needed for fossil fuel-fired power generation because (a) RE systems are different from traditional energy systems (Dubash 2011), (b) the risk perception is different due to the intermittency issues associated with RE which makes it difficult to operate 24×7 systems on their own without supplementary technologies like battery energy storage systems and other storage technologies (IEA 2023a), and (c) RE systems also require networks which are much more flexible and which can respond to the variabilities quickly.

The role of public finance will be very specific in the deployment of RE in Asia. Public finance needs to address the current bottlenecks or risks perceived by investors. It must also be able to provide adequate system level changes through tariff support and other means to facilitate the uptake of RE. Public financing should also render the RE projects bankable in terms of global investment standards.

4 Significance

It is important to review the current policies through the lens of RE financing, as they are different from traditional energy sector financing. The energy transition has to occur without negatively impacting the development and economic prosperity-related goals of the governments.

5 Background

Asia is going to be the powerhouse of the global energy transition over the next few decades in terms of exploiting opportunities in renewables and providing low-cost, cleaner energy systems. When undergoing their energy transitions, the Asian countries must address the trilemma of climate change, growing income inequalities amongst people and accessing the solutions affordably (Zhang and Zhu 2020; WCED 1987; WEC 2020). The three dimensions of energy transitions—energy security, energy equality and environmental sustainability (Khan et al. 2021)—are interconnected and must be handled simultaneously. Matching the fiscal and monetary mechanisms needed to support and maintain the speed of the transitions is key (Sethi et al. 2020). It is also important to make informed trade-offs between environmental activism and developmental choices (Ang 2008). One of the basic tenets of the trade-offs has been based on the Environment Kuznets Curve (EKC) which portrays a U-shaped relationship between environment and development. However, the rising greenhouse gas (GHG) emissions over the past few decades have meant that the relationship no longer holds for many countries because the emissions flow across country borders (Frankel 2009).

The EKC was the basis of policy frameworks in many countries around the world for environment and development related trade-offs. But in the case of GHG emissions, specifically, the inconclusiveness of the relationship has resulted in a chaotic situation because the externalities are not limited to one country. The UNFCCC notes that the emissions from the world's emerging economies are increasing as they pursue development goals, while the emissions from the developed world are starting to decrease (Meng et al. 2023). While emission reductions are a top priority for all countries, the debates over the share of responsibilities between the developed and developing world have been contentious. A support framework and fair burden sharing agreement was formulated for the developing world. However, the inability of the United States and other developed countries, who are part of the Kyoto Protocol of 1997, to cut their emissions as required by the agreed Protocol caused the developing world to mistrust the developed world (Dubash 2019; IISD 2022). The development of RE solutions at lower and lower costs has made it possible for the world to adopt them to fight climate change. However, the unhappiness over unequal burden sharing of mitigation actions remains, especially as the emerging economies are now regarded as the main centres of GHG emissions (WEF 2022).

While Meng and others (2023) observed that a global agreement on burden sharing was becoming increasingly impossible, individual emerging economies were amassing formidable RE capacities. Most of these countries at the forefront of the RE revolution are in Asia. This was made possible through the substantial drop in the costs of RE technologies and the enabling ecosystem created by the governments in many different countries. Indeed, between 2000 and 2021, more and more countries in Asia became world leaders in solar installed capacity. In 2000, only China (Fig. 1 [a]) was in the list of the top ten countries in terms of solar installed capacity. However, by 2021, there were five Asian countries which made this list (Fig. 1 [b]), reflecting the favourable ecosystem of policies, enabling investment regimes and supporting regulatory frameworks which facilitated solar business in these countries.

Without a supportive ecosystem of governmental support, the solar capacity would not have grown in these countries (TMF Group 2023). Technical parameters have also favoured the development of solar power in ASEAN, as well as the adoption by ASEAN ministers in 2015 of the aspirational target to achieve a 23% share of renewables by 2025 in the power generation mix across the region (IRENA 2017).

6 Energy Sector Reforms in Asia and Renewable Energy Growth

Starting in 2010, several ASEAN economies and other countries in Asia undertook policies and regulations to assist the deployment of RE. However, the pace and growth of RE deployment have varied across the region. While many ASEAN economies have experienced slow capacity additions in RE, there has been huge deployment in countries like India, which were almost at the same level as in the ASEAN Member States around the beginning of the decade. This is due to the relatively unequal pace in creating favourable ecosystem-level reforms that could have attracted the necessary investments. These reforms are meant to ensure a well-functioning electricity market, stable political environment and effective institutional mechanisms (Sen et al. 2016).

In Asia, the most complicated issue has been the need to change the fundamental organisation of the power sector. The uptake of RE-related reforms has been brought about through a series of push and pull factors (Nepal and Jamasb 2012). Among the push factors, the most important has been the structural adjustment programmes of the economy (Sen et al. 2016). The second set of push factors has emanated from endemic issues that were crippling the power sector in many countries (Gratwick and Eberhard 2008). The power sector often had vertically integrated monopolistic structures where generation, transmission and distribution were undertaken mostly by state-owned entities in order to achieve economies of scale (Williams and Ghanadan 2006; Dubash and Singh 2005). The main goal behind the restructuring was to increase competitiveness and provide more choices to the consumers. To achieve this, most of the countries introduced other associated reforms (Dubash 2011): "Unbundling of existing utilities is the means by which separate and competing entities are created. Management and/or ownership changes, potentially including full privatisation, prepare the unbundled entities for competition. Liberalisation removes barriers to entry and increases the effectiveness of competition. And not least, new forms of regulation are necessary to ensure an effective and competitive market" (Dubash and Singh 2005). Of these initiatives, the most important driving force has been the introduction of competition. During the early and mid-2000s, when the Asian economies were undergoing various degrees of restructuring, the power sector became a potential segment for foreign investment. Overall, the sector

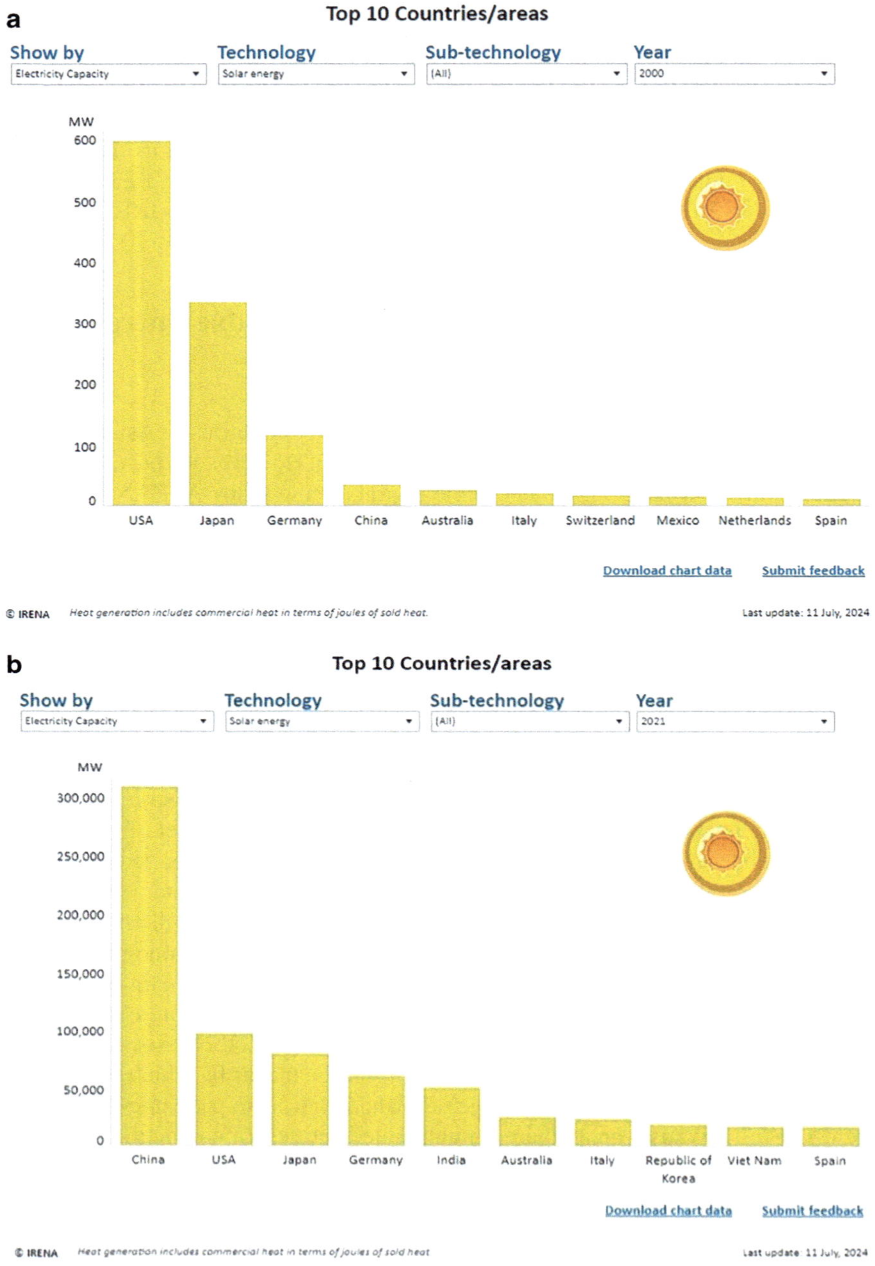

Fig. 1 Comparison of the world's top 10 countries in solar capacity, 2000 and 2021. (**a**) Top 10 countries in 2000. (**b**) Top 10 countries in 2021. *Source* IRENA (2023)

was attractive but the risks were high during this time because the structure of Asian power sectors did not meet the "standard'" global guidelines (Foster and Rana 2020).

The main thrust of the reforms has been to increase competition and efficiency (Dubash 2011; Foster and Rana 2020) as in other sectors that were undergoing structural changes, such as the airlines, telecommunications and natural gas industry (Malloy 2005). However, the power sector has certain characteristics[1] that make it different from other sectors in which the reforms aimed at increasing competition and efficiency were relatively effective (Dubash and Singh 2005). It was subsequently observed that the efforts to increase efficiency were not followed in all three segments of the power sector. Rather, they were limited to the distribution and generation of electricity (Foster and Rana 2020). The transmission segment was regarded as a natural monopoly that required high degrees of system coordination. Hence it was left to the public sector for its management (Foster and Rana 2020). During the early and mid-2000s, the market for competition in the power sector had few players. In the UK, the power sector became a duopoly and regulators had to intervene to ensure benefits for consumers (Thomas 2005). In Latin America, three generating firms captured over 50% of the market share. Since electricity by its nature cannot be stored, the concentration of the market gives generators undue advantage, i.e. a "pivotal supplier" problem—which becomes severe if there are fewer large firms (Blumsack et al. 2005).

Even if there were few big players in the power markets, privatisation efforts continued in the developing economies. This was despite the failure of privatisation efforts in countries such as the United States, where the California energy crisis occurred despite privatisation, as it did in European markets (Anderson 2009). It was expected that electricity prices would fall due to these imperfect competitive power markets in Europe and the U.S. However, this did not happen even after almost a decade of privatisation since the 1990s (Anderson 2009). In developing economies as well, the expected fall in electricity prices did not occur (Sen et al. 2016; IEA 2015).

Despite these outcomes, the countries followed specific systemic routes which were mainly pushed by the multilateral development banks during that time. For example, in Malaysia, Indonesia, Thailand, the Philippines and India, the integrated structure gave way to unbundling at the interventions of the Asian Development Bank, and in some cases International Monetary Fund recommendations in order to correct the balance of payments problems of the economy (Nikomborirak and Manachotphong 2007). The same fate also met the Indian power sector (Dubash 2019). The reforms were resulting in mixed to low impacts in Asia. The dominant role of the state in the power sector was reduced but not greatly changed (Hall and Nguyen 2017). Most of the Asian economies that we examined have offered (a) counter-guarantees to default by state purchasers, (b) a high rate of return on

[1] As Dubash and Singh (2005) observed, electricity cannot be stored and at any point of time supply and demand must match in order to keep the voltage frequency intact. Also, the vast transmission network acts as a gigantic commons. As consumers are not price responsive, there is an overall low elasticity of demand.

investment by private players and (c) fiscal benefits in the form of tax sops (Dubash 2011; Hall and Nguyen 2017; Foster and Rana 2020). These efforts have paved the way for private investments in the sector, despite unsustainable incentives to the long run (Dubash 2011). This has resulted in not addressing the main issue facing the power sector in these countries, namely, their financial health. Due to the forced introduction of reforms and subsequent creation of incentives to attract private sector players, the power sectors in India, Indonesia, Thailand and the Philippines were never able to become financially independent.

7 Renewable Energy Financing in Selected Asian Economies

It was recognised in a report recently published by the International Energy Agency (IEA 2023a) that for the world to shift towards net zero emissions, there has to be enhanced investment in the clean energy sectors of the developing world. This essentially means that most of the investment must be made in the Asian economies. Our focus is on the four Asian economies which have been at the forefront of the RE policies in recent years, and which have designed commendable RE policies (Table 1). However, we see that the costs at which the emerging and developing world has been receiving clean energy investments have been quite high compared to the cost in the developed world (Fig. 2).

The demand for RE investments in the Asian economies poses new challenges (IEA 2023a). In the fossil fuel-based energy sector, the investments were in dollarised values of globally traded commodities like oil and coal. But, in the RE energy sector, the investments are driven by capital intensive energy investments and higher risks emerge from local currency-led pricing, demand and "less developed risk management approaches" (IEA 2023b). In the 2023 IEA regional report on renewables (IEA

Table 1 Major RE-related targets and goals in selected Asian countries

Country	Published target(s)	Reference
Indonesia	• To increase the share of new and RE in TPES • To reach at least 23% by 2025 and at least 31% by 2050	Republic of Indonesia (2023)
Philippines	• To aim for RE to comprise 35% of total power generation by 2030 and 50% by 2040	DOE (2022)
Thailand	• To increase the share of renewables to 30% in TFEC by 2037 • To increase the share of RE power to 35% in capacity and 29% in generation by 2037	MOE (2023)
India	• Net Zero by 2070 • Non-Fossil fuel capacity target by 2030: 500GW • At least 50% generation from non-fossil fuel by 2030	MoEFCC (2023)

Source Compiled by author from different sources like MOE (2023), Republic of Indonesia (2023), PIB (2023), and DOE (2022)

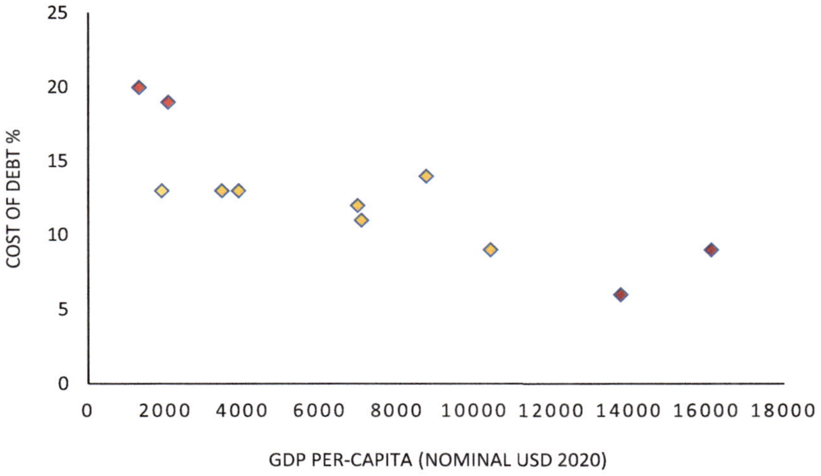

Fig. 2 Emerging economies pay higher costs on debt than developed countries in RE.[2] *Source* IEA (2021) Indicators of economy-wide cost of capital for equity (Government bond + Equity risk premium), Nominal values, 2016 and 2020. IEA, Paris. Available at https://www.iea.org/data-and-statistics/charts/indicators-of-economy-wide-cost-of-capital-for-equity-government-bond-equity-risk-premium-nominal-values-2016-and-2020, Licence: CC BY 4.0

2023a), it was observed that between 2016 and 2020, the countries of Southeast Asia received the lowest capital investment in renewables. Vietnam drew the highest amount of that investment despite not having a very stable power sector. Moreover, the country's power sector was less stable than that in other Southeast Asian countries.

Various sources (IEA 2023a; Fruman and Gupta 2023; Dubash and Singh 2005; Foster and Rana 2020) suggest that the investment climate in Indonesia, Thailand and the Philippines was not as conducive as it was in India which attracted substantial amounts of RE investments over the same period. Despite having power sectors dominated by fossil fuels, one factor that stood out in these countries was their ambition in undertaking RE. Between 2014 and 2023, India's RE targets increased substantially. This sent a positive signal across the world given the fact that the country has relied heavily on fossil fuels for decades. In recent years, a change in outlook has been observed in Thailand, Indonesia and the Philippines. The Indonesian government introduced the Just Energy Transition Partnership (JETP), which is a framework for an economy-wide energy transition including substantial RE growth. This coincided with the G20 declaration in 2022 regarding clean energy outcomes which sent a signal to the community of investors about the changes underway.

[2] This is a work derived by Tirthankar Mandal from IEA material and Tirthankar Mandal is solely liable and responsible for this derived work. The derived work is not endorsed by the IEA in any manner.

In the four countries examined here, even if they set ambitious carbon neutral targets commensurate with the developed world's ambitions, their fossil fuel subsidies emanating from oil imports remain a source of concern (see Table 2). This suggests: (a) the energy sectors in these countries are locked in fossil-fuel based ecosystems, and (b) the investment perception of the financing world is increasingly dominated by measures that do not match the developments happening in the region.

Various recent regional studies suggest that ecosystem-level changes may help change the situation, but one important thing that must be understood in this regard is that RE projects are fundamentally different from fossil-fuel based systems. One of the main concerns is that the Asian economies are very much integrated with their traditional electricity systems. Specifically, this means that the old systems cannot cope with much intermittency. With the introduction of more RE, the grids will face challenges in balancing and overall planning to maintain the frequency and harmonics. Secondly, the RE projects in Asia are costlier than the fossil fuel projects despite the drastically falling prices of popular clean energy technologies (Iyer 2023). Thirdly, the energy tariffs which are the main source of revenue for RE projects in Asia are built on a traditional model which is driven by fossil fuels. Intermittent sources play little or no role at all. Regulators fail to understand the need to design innovative tariff models which would give attractive returns on renewable generation through optimisation of the low cost of their production. In many countries, such as India, the low-cost RE is bundled with high-cost thermal power at the procurement level so that the average cost of procurement for distribution companies becomes low. This sub-optimises the benefits to the RE sector and to the investments.

One of the main reasons for such a bias against investment in RE has been observed in various recent studies. First, most of the distribution companies in the region are state-owned and function as "primary counterpart[-ies] to private generators" (Waldron and Sarazola 2019). With the intermittency of renewables on one hand and the stability of thermal and fossil-fuel based generation on another, the distribution companies tend to favour an energy mix that optimises the cost recovery calculations and which does not greatly jeopardise financial health. The distribution companies of the region must cross-subsidise the agricultural and residential consumers and typically charge them less than the supply cost of the electricity (Dubash 2019; Dubash and Singh 2005; Foster and Rana 2020). This has resulted in financial pressure on the distribution companies in Asia. The government of India used to give bailouts

Table 2 Oil imports in three Southeast Asian Countries and their commitments to energy transition

Country	Oil imports in 2022 (billion USD)	Energy transition commitment
Indonesia	16.3	Net zero by 2060 Net GHG reduction: 43% (with support) by 2030
Philippines	14.5	72.29% GHG reduction with support by 2030
Thailand	31.5	Net zero by 2035

Source IEA (2023a)

to the sector every five years to cover the losses of the distribution companies. In Indonesia, the government kept the retail tariffs frozen and gave a 3% subsidy to the electricity sector on an annual basis to meet the rising power purchase and fuel cost (Waldron and Sarazola 2019).

The second factor biasing against renewables is that the way RE is promoted in Asia. Instruments used in this promotion have not effectively bolstered investors' confidence. Studies by Lehmann (2013), Guan et al. (2019), and Sappington and Weisman (2016) have found that the feed-in-tariff mechanism, tax subsidies on RE projects and special treatments of other cleaner technologies have had limited effects because the fossil-fuel subsidies were quite high in the Asian countries. There were high fossil-fuel import bills which were subsidised in the four countries under consideration here (see Table 2). Instruments like transparency in auction, reverse bidding and competitive bidding processes have helped the sector to grow, but at the same time they have not been fully effective because the energy markets in these countries were not fully reformed. In India, the electricity reforms began in 2003 and are still underway. Even though substantial changes have been made in favour of RE, fundamental issues like the separation of agricultural from non-agricultural demand, which is not subsidised, is a concern. This is a result of the vertically integrated system. In the Philippines and Indonesia, there have been no auctions in RE in recent years. The projects were either determined on the basis of post feed-in-tariff mechanisms or direct selections (IEA 2023a).

These points indicate that private capital does not flow automatically despite the fact that some of the countries have shown ambition in their climate and net zero declarations. Public funding of RE projects is key to the growth of the Asian economies. Public money has played a facilitative role. The IEA's analysis (Fig. 3) portrays the sources of public money in RE projects.

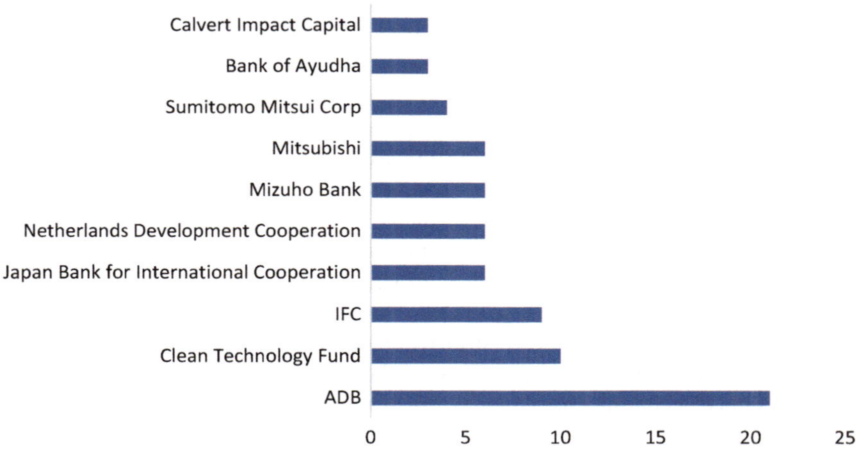

Fig. 3 Major blended finance players in the asian region supporting renewable energy. *Note* Calculated by number of commitments. *Source* IEA (2023a)

8 Role of Public Finance in Renewable Energy

As the IEA (2023d) observes, if the world is to achieve a successful energy transition, the emerging developing countries need to increase their foreign investments in clean energy substantially. However, the latest data on energy sector investments suggest that foreign investments in clean energy are declining. Since 2016, the emerging economies have been attracting less investment in clean sources of energy, despite the falling prices of RE systems and improved ecosystems in countries like India and other emerging economies (IEA 2023a).

At present, the emerging economies account for only 10% of global investment in clean energy (IEA 2023d). In Asia, most of this goes to China. Only 10% goes to other emerging economies in Asia. Due to regulatory issues in the energy sector and investment regimes, the share of private finance is less than public finance in the Asian economies. However, according to the IEA, this will be reversed by 2040 for all emerging economies of the world, including the Asian ones, with private investments averaging almost 60% of the clean energy sector (IEA 2023c; Foster and Rana 2020). This will be possible through reduced debt costs in the Asian economies.

9 De-Risking the Investment

The role that public finance has been playing in recent years has been increasingly characterised as being of a de-risking nature. As we have seen, the RE sector receives investments from sources such as commercial banks, pension funds, insurance funds, endowments and sovereign wealth funds, and foundations. Of these, the largest players are commercial banks and the pension funds. The two big issues these typical investors face are: (a) a mismatch in liquidity requirements and risk profile of the energy projects and (b) a mismatch between institutional investor capacity and project investor profile (Tonkonogy et al. 2018). Public finance is being used in the RE sector for large scale projects to address the perception of risk emanating from the two types of mismatches. In category "a", the majority of private sources belong to pension funds which intend to invest in RE. For them, the investment is through liquid assets. As the pension fund investors are highly flexible in terms of moving in and out of the sector, they do it in the form of equity. This is typically done in the development stage of a renewable project, where the return on investment is comparatively low, as compared to its later stages. This makes the risk perceptions high. Thus, only 1% of private investment is in the development phase of a project. Therefore, the governments need to provide support to build investor confidence and give stability to the ecosystem. This can be done in a multiplicity of ways. The easiest way is to undertake non-financial means through policy certainty that instils confidence in the sector.

From the commercial banks' perspective, the Basel norms which have undergone changes in recent years necessitate that the loan periods be shorter for energy projects

(Tonkonogy et al. 2018). This means that a typical solar project, which is the main type of renewables project in Asian countries, needs to be refinanced. As this increases the financing risk at the evaluation stage, public finance can be a game changer. It serves as a guarantor of sorts.

Specific public finance instruments are being used to attract private financing. For example, the early-stage risks which are identified in the mismatch between liquidity requirements and risk profile of the energy projects (category "a" above) were being addressed through grants, mostly bilateral flows. These are government to government flows, often made from the official development advances from countries in the developed world. For the liquidity risks, there are public finance instruments like securitisation and first loss support. These are primarily made for large-scale renewable projects. Most help reduce the cost of private financing. In effect these financial instruments are used to play the role of blended finances with the private financial instruments. At best they play the role of facilitator. A successful example in recent years is the Indonesian case where these multitudes of arrangements have helped to substantially increase private investments in the RE sector. Figure 4 reflects the various blended financing arrangements with private and public investment.

While blended finance has been effective to some extent in addressing the risk to investment in utility-scale RE, instruments that can address the issues in the distributed RE sector are needed. The issue is that the risk perception of the private sector is much higher than that of the utility scale sector. This primarily originates from inadequate policy and regulation support. Specifically, it does not allow sufficient scales of operation which enable developers to provide the RE at lower prices. Moreover, the cyclic nature of the challenges arises because the perception of high risks leads to high costs for distributed RE. This makes for high per unit generation costs and hinders the transition of the sector. The role of public finance must be to create ecosystems of certainty whereby economies of scale can be achieved through

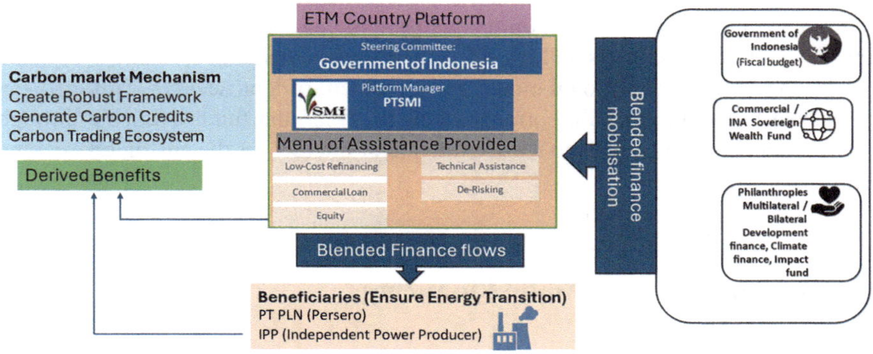

Fig. 4 Country level blending of public and private finance. *Source* MOF (Indonesia) (2023) PMK 103 Tahun 2023: Pemberian Dukungan Fiskal Melalui Kerangka Pendanaan dan. Pembiayaan dalam Rangka Percepatan Transisi Energi di Sektor Ketenagalistrikan. Available at https://peraturan.bpk.go.id/Details/270988/pmk-no-103-tahun-2023. Accessed Feb 2025

aggregation. These can be brought in through non-financial intervention and fiscal policy measures. Governments can also introduce performance-based support to the developers which can be achieved through special arrangements which assist the whole sector.

10 Increasing End-Users' Access to Finance

Mere de-risking of investment solves one part of the financial arrangement that facilitates the flow of money. Substantial RE deployment occurs through the ownership of electricity generating systems, mainly in the form of decentralised renewable generating systems. Asian countries have devised mechanisms which allow for ownership of the RE producing systems for consumers of clean energy. This involves a sunk cost when establishing these systems. Acknowledging the substantial upfront capex requirements, public finance mechanisms either provide capex support, or provide business models through which a third party owns the systems on a rental arrangement with the consumers. However, these have not facilitated the scaling up of deployment, mainly because the end-consumers seeking clean energy can access funds only when they put up substantial collateral. This is an issue for both residential consumers and small industries or commercial entities. For them, putting up collateral for renewable financing would mean putting up assets with the financing organisations which are disproportionate in value terms with the RE projects. For example, banks and non-banking financial organisations ask for homes to be used as collateral against solar rooftop systems in India. Small commercial entities face the additional challenge of not owning the premises. Hence, they are not able to obtain the requisite permissions to access loans. In this situation, public finance mechanisms can be devised whereby they become the guarantor of the loans and financing modes. This reduces the cost of lending for both the residential and small commercial and industrial entities. In addition to this, the banks and lending organisations can also devise alternative mechanisms to rate the customers seeking RE loans based on their ability to pay indicators, rather than by using traditional modes of assessment of loan seekers. This also can be backed by public financing arrangements in which the funds available through public financing can be used to reduce the rate of interest for the customers seeking loans.

11 Bankability and Public Financing

As shown in the four countries examined here, the RE sector faces a number of issues. First, apart from India, they have not reached the hoped pace of renewables growth. Even with the recent growth, the main issue has been the inability to meet the international standards of detailed project reports (DPRs) that are required to assess the bankability of an RE project. Two things are observed in this regard.

First and foremost is the fact that most of these bankability assessments are done on the basis of traditional infrastructure-based criteria, which are not applicable to RE projects. The main issue is the inability to monetise the environmental benefits that accrue from the RE projects. Secondly, due to the sector's immaturity, the various systems and due diligence that are required to be followed at different levels of project ideation have not been followed in the developing countries. This leads to uncertainty whether the projects will pass the environmental impact assessment. However, this is generally regarded as being addressable, with regulators' intervention. Thirdly, the international norms of bankability undergo frequent changes, while at the project level, things tend to move slowly. Furthermore, there is a multiplicity of paradigms which interact. For example, the environment, social and governance (ESG) framework, taskforce on climate-related financial disclosures (TCFD) and country specific frameworks tend to impose as stringent-as-possible clearances, causing delays or even the discarding of projects.

This is where public financing can be helpful. In recent years, bankability has been increased for projects in India due to public guarantees. This could be explored as a standard norm for other Asian countries. In the post Covid-19 world, governments are increasingly shifting away from a subsidy- and tax-based model of financing renewables. What can be done is to use the non-financial arm of government to secure bankability. This instrument is to give confidence for the investor that the project will run its full term and meet the criteria already set by the different standards.

The real challenge for bankability comes with the decentralised sector. Here, public finance can play a bigger role than at any other segment. The positive impacts that public finance can make are: (a) to create a cushion against risks perceived, like unattractive business models, uncertainty over policies, absence of instruments to mitigate project specific risks, and (b) to reduce the high cost of borrowing for private players caused by the lack of economies of scale. It has been observed that both these factors are of high importance for financing a distributed RE project in Asian developing economies, especially in India and Indonesia (ckinetics 2018; Wijaya et al. 2020).

12 Addressing Issues Around Pricing Renewable Generation

In most countries, energy pricing is calculated on an average pooled cost basis at the distribution companies' end. However, this pooled cost is based on the subsidised cost of fossil fuel which is paid at different levels outside the purview of the power sector. In India, for example, the fossil fuel subsidy is paid directly to the coal company or oil imports. In Indonesia the same is true. Unlike the fossil fuel sector, the RE sector does not receive any direct subsidy. The tariffs are therefore also somewhat higher. This is being balanced through feed-in-tariffs, net-metering and other mechanisms where public finance is being used. But this does not directly address the risks associated with the RE projects. Increasingly, governments are moving towards mechanisms in which the performance of the RE systems is being used to pay for these kinds of arrangements. In recent years, the Indian government undertook performance-linked incentives for manufacturing of solar panels, batteries etc. and at the same time, provided generation-based tariffs on rooftop solar. This was done along with the discarding of the age-old feed-in tariff models that used to be the main instrument for the solar and other RE segments.

13 Way Forward

Renewable energy is the mainstay of the Asian economies' energy transition. The technologies are mature, not hugely expensive and can be optimised for Asian conditions. However, there are several issues relating to the financing of RE projects which require a closer focus from policymakers and stakeholders alike.

The governments of the Asian economies are necessarily focused on providing cleaner electricity which is both reliable and affordable. While large-scale RE systems provide opportunities for investments at lower cost, the decentralised ones face challenges but have the maximum potential opportunities to innovate.

Public finance should address the risks associated with energy financing. Rather than continuing with the existing models of subsidy-based plans and programmes, specific designs could be developed targeting a specific risk component. Public finance could also serve as an additional guarantee for re-financing projects. Exploring these various mechanisms using public financing can help in the creation of innovative business models for the RE sector.

The Asian governments' concern to provide affordable electricity is paramount. Because RE has substantial capex requirements at the installation phase, it is a challenge for governments to recover the costs. The system requirements of the grid also involve costs. Putting together these costs, the ways and means to keep RE cheap should focus on monetising the opportunities arising from the carbon market mechanisms where the cleaner electricity sector accrues credits. Furthermore, there are opportunities to restructure the tariffs in countries which can help the consumers pay according to the time of use during the day, thereby minimising the total systems cost and increasing efficiency in totality. These measures, which involve some reforming of the existing energy sector within and between countries, could make the transition fruitful.

References

Anderson JA (2009) Electricity restructuring: a review of efforts around the world and consumer response. Electr J 22(3):70–86

Ang JB (2008) Economic development, pollutant emissions and energy consumption in Malaysia. J Policy Model 30(2):271–278

Bhattacharya S (2022) Clean energy financing: sources, instruments, risks, and mitigation options. In: Susantono Y, Zhai ShreshthaYRM, Mo L (eds) Financing clean energy in developing Asia. ADB, Manilla.

Blumsack S, Jay A, Lester LB (2005) A cautionary tale: US electricity sector reforms. Econ Pol Wkly 40(50):5279–5290

Chawla K (2023) Navigating the dual concerns of energy affordability and security in the global south. IEEFA, Valley City, OH

ckinetics (2018) India initiative for dre financing: capital landscape summary for discussion. New Delhi

Clarke L et al (2022) Mitigation of climate change. Contribution of Working Group III to the Sixth Assessment Report of the Intergovernmental Panel on Climate Change, IPCC, Cambridge, UK

CPI (Climate Policy Initiative) (2023) Landscape of climate-aligned investment in Indonesia's financial sector. Available at: https://www.climatepolicyinitiative.org/wp-content/uploads/2023/12/Landscape-of-Climate-Aligned-Investment-in-Indonesias-Financial-Sector-CPI-December-2023.pdf

DOE, Philippines (2022) Department of Energy. [Online] Available at: https://www.doe.gov.ph/sites/default/files/pdf/announcements/nrep_2020-2040.pdf?withshield=1. Accessed Feb 2024

Dubash N (2011) From norm taker to norm maker? Indian energy governance in global context. Global Pol 2(1):66–79

Dubash N (2019) Integrating climate change and development. India in a warming world. Oxford University Press, New Delhi

Dubash NK (2001) The public benefits agenda in power sector reform. Energy Sustain Dev 5(2):5–14https://doi.org/10.1016/S0973-0826(08)60265-3

Dubash N, Singh D (2005) Of rocks and hard places: a critical overview of recent global experience with electricity restructuring. Econ Pol Wkly 40(50):5249–5259

Foster V, Rana A (2020) Rethinking power sector reforms in a developing world. World Bank, Washington DC

Frankel J (2009) Global environmental policy and global trade policy. Discussion Paper 2009-09. Harvard Environmental Economics Program, Cambridge, MA

Fruman C, Gupta P (2023) World Bank Blogs. [Online] Available at: https://blogs.worldbank.org/en/endpovertyinsouthasia/south-asia-navigating-green-energy-transitions-together. Accessed 16 Mar 2024

Gratwick NK, Eberhard A (2008) Demise of the standard model for power sector reform and the emergence of hybrid power markets. Energy Policy 36(10):3948–3960

Guan P et al (2019) Analysis of emission taxes levying on regional electric power structure adjustment with an inexact optimization model—a case study of Zibo, China. Energy Econ 84(October):104485

Hall D, Nguyen TA (2017) Electricity liberalisation in developing countries. Prog Dev Stud 7(2):1–17

IEA (2015) Energy and Climate Change. Paris

IEA (2021) Indicators of economy-wide cost of capital for equity (Government Bond + Equity Risk Premium), Nominal Values, 2016 and 2020. Paris. Available at https://www.iea.org/data-and-statistics/charts/indicators-of-economy-wide-cost-of-capital-for-equity-government-bond-equity-risk-premium-nominal-values-2016-and-2020

IEA (2022a) Renewables 2022: analysis and forecast to 2027. Paris

IEA (2022b) World Energy Employment. Paris

IEA (2023a) ASEAN renewable investment: opportunities and challenges. Paris

IEA (2023b) Financing clean energy transition in emerging and developing economies. Paris

IEA (2023c) Scaling up private finance for clean energy in emerging and developing economies. Paris

IEA (2023d) World Energy Investment. Paris

IISD (International Institute for Sustainable Development). 2022. Summary of the Sharm el-sheikh Climate Change Conference: 6–20 November 2022. Winnipeg, Canada
IRENA (International Renewable Energy Agency) (2017) ASEAN countries Rally behind energy transition. IRENA Quarterly, September-December, pp 2–5
IRENA (2023) Workbook: renewable energy country rankings. Available at: https://public.tableau.com/views/IRENAREsourceRenewableEnergyRankings/Rankings?:showVizHome=no. Accessed 28 Jan 2025
Iyer R (2023) Renewables are having a good year but challenges loom ahead. IEEFA (Institute for Energy Economics and Financial Aanalysis), Valley City, OH
Khan I et al (2021) Does energy trilemma a driver of economic growth [sic]? The roles of energy use, population growth, and financial development. Renew Sustain Energy Rev 146(August):111157
Lehmann P (2013) Supplementing an emissions tax by a feed-in tariff for renewable electricity to address learning spillovers. Energy Policy 61(October):635–641
Malloy K (2005) Clash of world views over electric competition. Nat Gas Electr J 21(7):1–31
Meng J et al (2023) The narrowing gap in developed and developing country emission intensities reduces global rrade's carbon leakage. Nat Commun 14. Available at: https://www.nature.com/articles/s41467-023-39449-7
MOE (Thailand) (2023) Ministry of Environment. [Online] Available at: https://policy.asiapacificenergy.org/node/4351. Accessed Feb 2024
MoEFCC (India) (2023) Ministry of Environment, Forest and Climate Change. Zero emissions target (Press release). Available at: https://pib.gov.in/PressReleaseIframePage.aspx?PRID=1945472#:~:text=India%2C%20at%20the%2026th%20session,achieve%20net%20zero%20by%202070. Accessed Feb 2024
MOF (Indonesia) (2023) Ministry of finance. PMK 103 Tahun 2023: Pemberian dukungan fiskal melalui kerangka pendanaan dan pembiayaan dalam rangka percepatan transisi energi di sektor ketenagalistrik*an*. Available at: https://peraturan.bpk.go.id/Details/270988/pmk-no-103-tahun-2023. Accessed Feb 2025
Nepal R, Jamasb T (2012) Reforming the power sector in transition: do institutions matter? Energy Econ 34(5):1675–1682
Nikomborirak D, Manachotphong W (2007) Electricity reforms in practice: case of Thailand, Malaysia, Indonesia and the Phillippines. Intergov Group Compet Law Policy:17–19. Available at: https://www.researchgate.net/publication/242168806_Electricity_Reform_in_Practice_The_Case_of_Thailand_Malaysia_Indonesia_and_the_Philippines
PIB (2023) Press Information Buerau. [Online] Available at: https://pib.gov.in/PressReleaseIframePage.aspx?PRID=1945472#:~:text=India%2C%20at%20the%202
Republic of Indonesia (2023) Enhanced nationally determined contribution 2023. Available at: https://unfccc.int/sites/default/files/NDC/2022-09/23.09.2022_Enhanced%20NDC%20Indonesia.pdf. Accessed Feb 2024
Sappington DE, Weisman DL (2016) The price cap regulation paradox in the electricity sector. Electr J 29(3):1–5
Sen A, Nepal R, Jamasb T (2016) Rethinking electricity sector reform in developing Asia: balancing economic and environmental objectives, also in the Routledge handbook of energy in Asia, Bhattacharyya SC (ed). Abingdon, Routledge, pp 221–240
Sethi P, Chakrabarti D, Bhattacharjee S (2020) Globalization, financial development and economic growth: perils on the environmental sustainability of an emerging economy. J Policy Model 42(3):520–535
Taghizadeh-Hesary F, Rasoulinezhad E (2020) Analyzing energy transition patterns in Asia: evidence from countries with different income levels. Front Energy Res 8:162. https://doi.org/10.3389/fenrg.2020.00162
Thomas S (2005) British experience of electricity liberalisation: a model for India? Econ Pol Wkly 40(50):5260–5268
TMF Group (2023) TMF Group. Available at: https://www.tmf-group.com/en/news-insights/articles/esg/renewable-energy-in-asia-policy-and-potential/. Accessed 24 Jan 2024

Tonkonogy B et al (2018) Blended finance in clean energy: experiences and opportunities. Climate Policy Initiative (San Francisco, USA). Available at: https://climatepolicyinitiative.org/wp-content/uploads/2018/01/Blended-Finance-in-Clean-Energy-Experiences-and-Opportunities.pdf. Accessed 29 Nov 2024

UNFCCC (2009) Conference of the Parties Fifteenth Session (COP15); Draft Decision. Available at: https://unfccc.int/resource/docs/2009/cop15/eng/l07.pdf. Accessed 18 Jan 2024

UNFCCC (2015) The Paris Agreement. Available at: https://unfccc.int/sites/default/files/english_paris_agreement.pdf. Accessed 18 Jan 2024

UNFCCC (2023) Matters relating to the globalsstocktake under the Paris Agreement. Dubai, Bonn

Waldron M, Sarazola LA (2019) Energy investment in emerging economies: transforming Southeast Asia's power sector. IEA, Paris

WCED (World Commission on Environment and Development) (1987) Our common future. World Commission On Environment And Development (the Brundtland Report). Oxford University Press, Oxford, New York

WEC (World Energy Council) (2020) World energy trilemma index. World Energy Council, London

WEF (World Economic Forum) (2022) 3 actions to accelerate emerging market climate transition. Geneva

Wijaya ME, Haesra A, Mecca BM (2020) Enhancing decentralized renewable energy investment to achieve Indonesia's nationally determined contribution. Climate Policy Initiative. Available at: https://www.climatepolicyinitiative.org/publication/enhancing-decentralized-renewable-energy-investment-to-achieve-indonesias-nationally-determined-contribution/#:~:text=Decentralized%20renewable%20energy%20(DRE)%20is,National%20Determined%20Contribution%20(NDC). Accessed 29 Nov 2024

Williams JH, Ghanadan R (2006) Electricity reform in developing and transition economies: a reprisal. Energy 31:815–844

World Bank (2023) Breaking down barriers to clean energy transition. Available at: https://www.worldbank.org/en/news/feature/2023/05/16/breaking-down-barriers-to-clean-energy-transition. Accessed 26 Mar 2024

Zhang S, Zhu D (2020) Have countries moved towards sustainable development or not? Definition, criteria, indicators and empirical analysis. J Clean Prod 267(September):121929

Technological Innovations and Sectoral Strategies

Comparing Concentrating-Solar-Power and Photovoltaic-Solar Plants as Extended-Duration Peaking Resources in Electricity Systems

Alexander Bard and Ramteen Sioshansi

Abstract This chapter compares the performance of two solar electricity-generation technologies with complementary energy-storage technologies—concentrating solar power (CSP) with thermal energy storage (TES) and photovoltaic (PV) solar with battery energy storage (BES)—in providing capacity during time periods with high electricity demand. We develop optimisation models, which determine the configuration and hourly operation of the two technologies, and apply the models to a case study that is based on the southwestern United States of America, which is a region that has excellent solar availability. Our models and case study demonstrate that PV with BES is superior to CSP with TES in terms of capital cost and peaking capability. Altogether, our results suggest that solar technologies can help to maintain reliable electricity supply under carbon constraints in regions of the world, such as east Asia, with relatively good solar resource. We conclude this chapter with a discussion of policy and regulatory changes that can help to achieve such an end.

Keywords Solar generation · Concentrating solar power · Thermal energy storage · Photovoltaic solar · Battery energy storage · Peaking generation · Capacity value

---

A. Bard
Department of Mechanical and Aerospace Engineering, The Ohio State University, Columbus, OH, USA
e-mail: bard.41@buckeyemail.osu.edu

R. Sioshansi (✉)
Department of Engineering and Public Policy, Carnegie Mellon University, Pittsburgh, PA, USA
e-mail: rsioshan@andrew.cmu.edu

Carnegie Mellon Electricity Industry Center, Carnegie Mellon University, Pittsburgh, PA, USA

Department of Electrical and Computer Engineering, Carnegie Mellon University, Pittsburgh, PA, USA

Wilton E. Scott Institute for Energy Innovation, Carnegie Mellon University, Pittsburgh, PA, USA

Department of Integrated Systems Engineering, The Ohio State University, Columbus, OH, USA

H. Phoumin et al. (eds.), *Tackling the Energy Transition: Insights from ASEAN and Beyond*, Climate Change and Energy Transition,
https://doi.org/10.1007/978-981-96-6019-3_6

1 Introduction

Solar generation can be enhanced significantly by integrating it with energy storage, which can help to manage variable solar availability, thereby making the generator partially dispatchable. Concentrating-solar-power (CSP) plants can benefit from thermal energy storage (TES), which is a relatively low-cost and efficient energy-storage technology that uses a constructed tank as the energy-storage medium (Peinado Gonzalo et al. 2019; Sun et al. 2021). Similarly, photovoltaic (PV) solar can be coupled with energy storage—for instance lithium-ion batteries, which is the technology that we consider in this study. Gami et al. (2017), Yagi et al. (2019), and Varghese and Sioshansi (2020) provide foundational studies of CSP, PV, and energy-storage technologies, and our current work builds upon these.

Integrating TES into CSP can enable the delivery of electricity during periods of low or zero solar availability (*e.g.*, during nights and cloudy time periods) or to desirable time periods (*e.g.*, of high energy prices or electricity demand). This benefit mirrors the capabilities of PV solar that is coupled with battery energy storage (BES). Historically, solar availability, wholesale energy prices, and electricity demand are fairly correlated in many electricity systems. These correlations are driven by air-conditioning demand during the summer, when solar availability tends to peak. The increasing penetration of solar energy is reducing these correlations (Ueckerdt et al. 2015). Thus, the ability of energy storage to align solar generation with peaks in energy prices and electricity demand will be of increasing value as the electricity-generation mix and demand patterns change.

This chapter investigates the potential of solar generation with energy storage to supply energy during peak-demand periods, considering future electricity systems that may have very different demand and supply patterns compared to today's systems. The ability of a resource to serve on-peak demand reliably often underlies a reliability or resource-adequacy assessment of an electricity system (Singh and Billinton 1977; Billinton and Allan 1984; Kim et al. 2022). A variety of metrics, including effective load-carrying capability (ELCC), can be used to determine the contribution of an individual resource to meeting an electricity system's reliability criteria (Garver 1966). These assessments involve applying reliability and statistical modeling to resource-availability and demand data. In some instances, approximations or heuristics are applied to avoid the computational cost of reliability modeling (Madaeni et al. 2013a).

Madaeni et al. (2012, 2013b) conduct ELCC analyses of CSP with and without TES. Their analyses make several assumptions, which we cannot apply, given our desire to understand solar technologies in future electricity systems. First, they analyze a well defined electricity system, with assumed known capacities and failure probabilities of each generator that is in the system. Second, they assume a known historical electricity-demand pattern. Their ELCC calculations are sensitive to the assumed demand pattern, due to the aforementioned historical correlation between solar availability and electricity demand. Consequently, their analysis is unlikely to reflect accurately the contribution of solar generation to the reliability of future electricity systems (Yagi et al. 2019, 2021).

Unlike other electricity-generation technologies, solar resources exhibit declining marginal reliability benefit as their penetration levels increase (Awara et al. 2018). This decline arises from the real-time production of solar plants being highly correlated (energy production is driven by the same fundamental diurnal pattern). As such, each incremental solar generator that is added produces energy contemporaneously with the output of existing solar generators. This decline can be addressed through the use of energy storage, which is the focus of our analysis.

We overcome the complexities in assessing the reliability benefit to future electricity systems of solar generation, including its declining marginal benefit, by eschewing a formal reliability analysis. Rather, we use a less formal approach, whereby we examine whether the solar generator has sufficient energy available to operate at its nameplate capacity during a prescribed set of target hours of the modelled year (Yagi et al. 2019, 2021). By varying the target hours, we examine the performance of the solar generator *vis-à-vis* a varying reliability standard. Our primary performance metric of the solar generator is what we term its energy deficit, which is defined as the amount of additional energy that is needed for the generator to meet the prescribed performance target.

We evaluate and compare CSP with TES and PV solar with BES based on their energy deficits and estimated capital costs. Our findings suggest that attaining a given reliability level from CSP with TES is more expensive compared to doing so from PV solar with BES. This finding is reflective of significant recent decreases in the costs of PV-solar plants and BES systems. Although our analysis does not carry the rigor of a formal reliability analysis, it provides insights into the reliability benefits to future electricity systems of these technologies, a reliability analysis of which is exceedingly difficult to conduct.

The remainder of this chapter is organised as follows. Section 2 describes briefly the technologies that we study and their design and sizing characteristics. Section 3 details the models that are used in our analysis and defines formally the energy-deficit performance metric. Section 4 summarises our case-study data and results. Section 5 concludes, contextualises our results for decarbonising electricity systems globally and within east Asia, and discusses some policy, regulatory, and market-design considerations.

2 Technical Overview of CSP with TES and PV Solar with BES

Our analysis considers power-tower CSP plants. He et al. (2020) survey different CSP technologies, including power-tower, parabolic-trough, and linear-Fresnel systems. Power-tower CSP plants consist of three major components—a powerblock, a solar field, and a TES system. The powerblock converts thermal energy into electricity. Its size is characterised normally by its nameplate input or output capacity, which are measured in MW-t and MW-e, respectively. The solar field is a collection of mirrors, known as heliostats. These are mounted onto double-axis solar-tracking systems and concentrate sunlight onto the plant's power tower, which collects the thermal energy. This thermal energy can be fed into the powerblock (to produce electricity) or into the TES system (to be stored for later use). The typical unit of measure for the solar field is its solar multiple, which gives the ratio between the nameplate thermal capacity of the powerblock and the thermal power that is collected by the solar field under reference conditions. The TES system can store thermal energy that is collected by the power tower but not used by the powerblock. The capacity of the TES system can be measured by its rated thermal-energy capacity (MWh-t). However, it is common to measure this capacity by the number of consecutive hours that the powerblock can operate at its nameplate capacity, solely using energy from a fully charged TES system. This latter measure is called the number of hours of storage.

These three components can be sized independently of one another. However, when considering plant configurations, it is common to hold the powerblock size fixed, because solar multiple and hours of storage are measured relative to this capacity. Moreover, it is common for each of solar-field and TES-system size to be chosen considering the size of the other component. For instance, increasing a plant's solar multiple allows the power tower to collect more thermal energy during periods with less-than-ideal weather conditions. However, the power tower collects excess thermal energy that must be rejected by the powerblock during peak-solar conditions. Increasing the size of the TES system allows this excess thermal energy to be stored for use during subsequent low-solar time periods. As such, optimising the design of a CSP plant requires considering weather conditions and solar-field and TES-system size holistically.

We model the PV solar and BES system as consisting of two key components—an array of PV panels and a set of batteries. The PV array is characterised by its nameplate capacity, measured either as MW-dc or MW-ac. The BES system is characterised by its power and energy capacities. The power capacity is the maximum charging and discharging rate of the BES system, measured in MW. The energy capacity can be measured in MWh. As with a TES system, it is common to measure the energy capacity of the BES system by the number of hours of storage, which gives the number of consecutive hours that the fully charged BES system can discharge at its power capacity.

3 Modelling Approach

This section provides detailed formulations of the models that we use to compare the cost and performance of the two solar electricity-generation technologies. The CSP-plant model assumes a fixed plant configuration and determines how to operate the plant to minimise its energy deficit. We use two model variants to study PV solar. Both variants of the model determine the sizes of the PV array and BES system and how to operate the plant. The first variant minimises the plant's energy deficit subject to a constraint that limits the cost of the plant configuration. The second variant minimises the plant's cost with a constraint that limits the plant's energy deficit.

We take this modelling approach because it is reasonable to assume that the cost and performance of a PV array and BES system scale linearly with component sizes. Conversely, the performance and cost of a CSP plant's solar field scale non-linearly. This non-linearity stems from the field's physical properties, *i.e.*, its circular layout and the resultant changing marginal thermal-energy collection by each concentric ring of heliostats as the field size changes. As such, our modelling approach determines the cost and energy deficit of a given CSP-plant configuration and determines how the PV plant must be configured to achieve the same cost and energy deficit.

3.1 CSP-Plant Model

The CSP-plant model is patterned around the work of Sioshansi and Denholm (2010, 2013). The model takes as an input the hourly thermal energy that is collected by the plant's power tower, which depends upon a fixed plant configuration and assumed weather data. The model determines how to use the collected thermal energy—what amount is fed into the powerblock to produce electricity as opposed to being stored using the TES system. As needed, collected thermal energy can be supplemented with previously stored energy that is extracted from the TES system.

3.1.1 Model Notation

We begin by defining model notation. Because CSP plants convert thermal energy into electricity, we use the suffix '-t' to denote thermal power and energy. First, we define the following indices and parameters:

E_t^{R}	thermal power that is needed to start up the powerblock from an offline state (MW-t);
E_t^{W}	thermal power that is collected by the power tower during hour t (MW-t);
H	energy-storage capacity of the TES system (h);
K_t^{P}	hour-t energy-deficit penalty ($/MW);
l_0	ending hour-0 state of energy (SOE) of the TES system (MWh-t);
t	time index;
T	number of hours in optimisation horizon;
u_0	binary parameter that equals 1 if the powerblock is online during hour 0 and equals 0 otherwise;
$\theta^{\max}$	maximum input to the powerblock when it is online (MW-t);

$\theta^{\min}$ minimum input to the powerblock when it is online (MW-t); and

Υ self-discharge rate of the TES system (p.u.).

Next, we define the following decision variables:

l_t ending hour-t SOE of the TES system (MWh-t);

r_t binary variable that equals 1 if the powerblock is started up during hour t and equals 0 otherwise;

u_t binary variable that equals 1 if the powerblock is online during hour t and equals 0 otherwise; and

θ_t thermal power that is input to the powerblock during hour t (MW-t).

3.1.2 Model Formulation

The model is formulated as:

$$\min \sum_{t=1}^{T} K_t^{\mathrm{P}} \cdot (\theta^{\max} - \theta_t) \tag{1}$$

$$\text{s.t.}\ \theta^{\min} u_t \le \theta_t \le \theta^{\max} u_t - E_t^{\mathrm{R}} r_t, \forall t = 1, \dots, T \tag{2}$$

$$r_t \ge u_t - u_{t-1}, \forall t = 1, \dots, T \tag{3}$$

$$l_t \le \Upsilon l_{t-1} + E_t^{\mathrm{W}} - E_t^{\mathrm{R}} r_t - \theta_t, \forall t = 1, \dots, T \tag{4}$$

$$0 \le l_t \le H\theta^{\max}, \forall t = 1, \dots, T \tag{5}$$

$$r_t, u_t \in \{0, 1\}, \forall t = 1, \dots, T. \tag{6}$$

Objective function (1) minimises the plant's energy deficit over the T-hour optimisation horizon. For each $t = 1, \dots, T$, the hour-t energy deficit is defined as the difference between the nameplate capacity of the powerblock, $\theta^{\max}$, and θ_t, which is the thermal power that is fed into the powerblock during hour t. Thus, the hour-t energy deficit measures the amount by which the plant operates below its nameplate capacity. The hourly energy deficits are multiplied by coefficients, $K_1^{\mathrm{P}}, \dots, K_T^{\mathrm{P}}$, which reflect that depending upon how the performance requirement is set, plant operations may consider energy deficits only during a subset of what we term target hours that are within the optimization horizon. We set $K_t^{\mathrm{P}} = 1000$ for all $t = 1, \dots, T$ that are target hours and $K_t^{\mathrm{P}} = 1$ for other hours. Setting K_t^{P} equal to a small strictly positive value during non-target hours provides an incentive for the CSP plant not to curtail energy needlessly during these hours.

Constraint set (2) imposes bounds on the powerblock while it is online. Thermal power that is input to the powerblock is reduced during any $t = 1, \ldots, T$when the powerblock is started up from an offline state, which is represented by having $r_t = 1$. On the other hand, if the powerblock is offline during a given $t = 1, \ldots, T$, this is denoted by $u_t = 0$. Constraint (2) for such $t = 1, \ldots, T$ forces $\theta_t = 0$. Constraint set (3) defines, $\forall t = 1, \ldots, T$, the value of r_t in terms of the values of u_{t-1} and u_t. Specifically, if $u_{t-1} = 0$ and $u_t = 1$, which means that the powerblock is offline during hour $(t-1)$ and online during hour t, r_t is forced to equal 1. Constraint set (4) imposes a standard energy-balance restriction to give the evolution of the SOE of the TES system from one hour to the next. Specifically, $\forall t = 1, \ldots, T$, the hour-t SOE is limited to be no greater than the sum of the previous hour's SOE (accounting for energy that is lost due to temperature loss of the storage medium) and power that is collected by the power tower during hour t, less the sum of power that is fed to the powerblock and to start up the powerblock during hour t. Constraints (4) are inequalities to allow excess thermal energy that cannot be stored to be curtailed. Constraint set (5) imposes SOE limits on the TES system and (6) imposes integrality restrictions on the two sets of binary variables.

3.2 *PV Model*

The PV model is built upon the work of Varghese and Sioshansi (2020). The model co-optimises the size of the PV array and BES system, as well as their operations. It takes as an input hourly weather-dependent factors, which specify the per-unit electricity output of the PV array.

3.2.1 Model Notation

Below, we define notation for the PV model, without repeating notation that is shared with the CSP-plant model. Because a PV plant does not convert thermal energy into electricity, all energy and power in the PV model are electric and no '-e' suffix is included in any definitions. Moreover, all energy and power quantities are assumed to be ac (as opposed to dc), using standard inverter performance characteristics in this conversion. The following parameters are model inputs:

$C^{\mathrm{B,E}}$ cost of BES-system energy capacity (\$/MWh);

$C^{\mathrm{B,P}}$ cost of BES-system power capacity (\$/MW);

$C^{\max}$ maximum allowable cost of the PV plant (\$);

C^{PV} cost of PV capacity (\$/MW);

E_t^{A} hour-t capacity factor of the PV array (p.u.);

$\Delta^{\max}$ maximum allowable energy deficit of the PV plant (MWh);
η round-trip efficiency of the BES system (p.u.);
λ_0 ending hour-0 SOE of the BES system (MWh); and
τ target PV-plant output (MW).

Next, we define the following decision variables:

B_t^{C} hour-t BES-system charging (MW);
B_t^{D} hour-t BES-system discharging (MW);
δ_t hour-t PV-plant energy deficit (MWh);
$\kappa^{\mathrm{B,E}}$ energy capacity of the BES system (MWh);
$\kappa^{\mathrm{B,P}}$ power capacity of the BES system (MW);
κ^{PV} capacity of the PV array (MW);
λ_t ending hour-t SOE of the BES (MWh); and
ξ_t hour-t PV-array electricity production that is supplied to the electricity system during hour t (MW).

3.2.2 Formulation of Energy-Deficit-Minimisation Model

The model is formulated as:

$$\min \sum_{t=1}^{T} K_t^{\mathrm{P}} \delta_t \tag{7}$$

$$\text{s.t.} \delta_t \geq \tau - \xi_t - B_t^{\mathrm{D}}, \forall t = 1, \ldots, T \tag{8}$$

$$0 \leq \xi_t + B_t^{\mathrm{C}} \leq E_t^{\mathrm{A}} \kappa^{\mathrm{PV}}, \forall t = 1, \ldots, T \tag{9}$$

$$\lambda_t = \lambda_{t-1} + \eta B_t^{\mathrm{C}} - B_t^{\mathrm{D}}, \forall t = 1, \ldots, T \tag{10}$$

$$0 \leq \lambda_t \leq \kappa^{\mathrm{B,E}}, \forall t = 1, \ldots, T \tag{11}$$

$$0 \leq B_t^{\mathrm{C}}, B_t^{\mathrm{D}} \leq \kappa^{\mathrm{B,P}}, \forall t = 1, \ldots, T \tag{12}$$

$$C^{\mathrm{B,E}} \kappa^{\mathrm{B,E}} + C^{\mathrm{B,P}} \kappa^{\mathrm{B,P}} + C^{\mathrm{PV}} \kappa^{\mathrm{PV}} \leq C^{\max} \tag{13}$$

$$\delta_t \geq 0, \forall t = 1, \ldots, T. \tag{14}$$

Objective function (7) minimises the plant's energy deficit and includes the coefficients, $K_1^{\mathrm{P}}, \ldots, K_T^{\mathrm{P}}$, to capture that the plant may seek to minimise its energy deficit during a subset of target hours during the optimisation horizon. For all $t = 1, \ldots, T$, (8) defines the hour-t energy deficit as the difference between the plant's target output level, τ, and its hour-t production, which is given by the sum of PV-array production, ξ_t, and BES output, B_t^{D}.

Constraint set (9) restricts the total energy that is used by the plant during each hour to be no greater than what the PV array provides. For each $t = 1, \ldots, T$, total energy that is used by the plant during hour t is defined as the sum of ξ_t and energy that is stored into the BES system, B_t^{C}. This sum is constrained to be no greater than the PV array's capacity, κ^{PV}, which is scaled by the array's hour-t capacity factor, E_t^{A}. Constraint set (9) does not allow the BES system to be charged using excess energy from the electricity system. Instead, we assume that the plant must rely upon excess energy from the PV array for any BES-system charging. We make this assumption because we do not want the PV plant to rely upon an external energy source to meet its reliability criterion. Constraint set (10) is the energy-balance constraint for the BES system and has an interpretation that is akin directly to (4). Constraint set (11) restricts the SOE of the BES system, based on the chosen capacity, and is akin directly to (5). Constraint set (12) restricts charging and discharging of the BES system based on its chosen power capacity. Budget constraint (13) ensures that the total cost of the PV array and BES system does not exceed the prescribed limit. Constraint set (14) ensures that the hourly energy deficits are non-negative.

3.2.3 Formulation of Cost-Minimisation Model

The model is formulated as:

$$\min C^{\mathrm{B,E}}\kappa^{\mathrm{B,E}} + C^{\mathrm{B,P}}\kappa^{\mathrm{B,P}} + C^{\mathrm{PV}}\kappa^{\mathrm{PV}} \tag{15}$$

$$\text{s.t.}\,\delta_t \geq \tau - \xi_t - B_t^{\mathrm{D}}, \forall t = 1, \ldots, T \tag{16}$$

$$0 \leq \xi_t + B_t^{\mathrm{C}} \leq E_t^{\mathrm{A}}\kappa^{\mathrm{PV}}, \forall t = 1, \ldots, T \tag{17}$$

$$\lambda_t = \lambda_{t-1} + \eta B_t^{\mathrm{C}} - B_t^{\mathrm{D}}, \forall t = 1, \ldots, T \tag{18}$$

$$0 \leq \lambda_t \leq \kappa^{\mathrm{B,E}}, \forall t = 1, \ldots, T \tag{19}$$

$$0 \leq B_t^{\mathrm{C}}, B_t^{\mathrm{D}} \leq \kappa^{\mathrm{B,P}}, \forall t = 1, \ldots, T \tag{20}$$

$$\sum_{t=1:K_t^{\mathrm{P}}>1}^{T} \delta_t \le \Delta^{\max} \tag{21}$$

$$\delta_t \ge 0, \forall t = 1, \ldots, T. \tag{22}$$

Model (15)–(22) is identical to (7)–(14), with two differences. First, (15) minimises the cost of the combined PV array and BES system; (7) minimises its energy deficit. Second, (21) imposes an upper limit on the energy deficit of the PV array and BES system. Constraint (21) uses the aforementioned convention regarding the values of $K_1^{\mathrm{P}}, \ldots, K_T^{\mathrm{P}}$ by considering energy deficits only during hours $t = 1, \ldots, T$ with $K_t^{\mathrm{P}} > 1$. Models (7)–(14) and (15)–(22) can be thought of as having a dual relationship. Model (7)–(14) determines the minimal energy deficit that can be achieved with a given budget limit whereas (15)–(22) determines the cost-minimising design that achieves a given energy-deficit limit.

4 Case Study

4.1 Overview

We conduct a three-step analysis to compare the cost and technical characteristics of CSP and PV-solar plants. First, we solve (1)–(6) with a fixed configuration to determine the energy deficit of the CSP plant. Next, we use (7)–(14) to determine the minimal energy deficit that can be achieved by PV solar with BES that costs no more than the CSP plant that we model costs. Finally, we use (15)–(22) to determine the cost of designing a PV-solar plant with BES that has an energy deficit no greater than that of the CSP plant.

We examine first a base case, in which the eight highest-load hours of each day of the modelled year (using historical load data) are target hours. Then we conduct a parametric analysis in which we vary the number of target hours during each day between the one and the 24 highest-load hours of each day of the modeled year. The case in which the 24 highest-load hours of each day are target hours means that the objective is to have the plant operate at its target output continuously during every hour of the year.

All three of (1)–(6), (7)–(14), and (15)–(22) are formulated using version 3.6.10 of the AMPL mathematical-programming software package. The models are solved using version 22.1.1 of IBM ILOG CPLEX on a system with an eight-core Apple Silicon M2 processor and 8 GB of memory. Default AMPL and CPLEX settings are used.

4.2 Data

We assume a typical CSP-plant design with a powerblock with nameplate thermal-input and electric-output capacities of 538 MW-t and 222 MW-e, respectively, a solar multiple of 3.0, and 12 hours of TES. This plant configuration has a cost of \$1.5 billion, based on data that are obtained from version 2021.12.02 of System Advisor Model (SAM) (Blair et al. 2014, 2018). Using SAM data, we estimate a PV-array cost of \$960 000 per MW of rated dc capacity and energy- and power-capacity costs for BES of \$282 790 MWh and \$233 170 MW, respectively.

We model solar plants at a location near Boulder City, Nevada (at coordinates 35.80° N, 114.98° W), which has 7.60 kWh/m^2 of average daily direct normal irradiance (DNI). We use historical weather and load data for the year 2014. Specifically, we use modelled weather data, which are obtained from version 2.0.1 of National Solar Radiation Database (NSRDB) (Wilcox 2012; Sengupta et al. 2014a, b, 2018). The NSRDB data are processed using SAM to determine the hourly thermal energy that is collected by the CSP plant's power tower, *i.e.*, the values of $E_1^{\mathrm{W}}, \ldots, E_T^{\mathrm{W}}$. Similarly, SAM is used to determine from the NSRDB data the capacity factors of the PV array, *i.e.*, the values of $E_1^{\mathrm{A}}, \ldots, E_T^{\mathrm{A}}$.

Hourly year-2014 electricity-demand data for NV Energy, which is the utility that has Boulder City, Nevada within its geographical footprint, are obtained from Federal Energy Commission Form 714. Form-714 data are used to determine target hours.

When solving (1)–(6), we use the powerblock's nameplate thermal-input capacity, $\theta^{\max} = 538$, as the target operating level. After solving the model, the CSP plant's energy deficit is given by:

$$\sum_{t=1:K_t^P>1}^{T} (\theta^{\max} - \theta_t). \tag{23}$$

The energy deficit can be reported in absolute terms or as a percentage of the total energy that is needed to operate the CSP plant at its target level during all target hours. This total energy need is:

$$\sum_{t=1:K_t^{\mathrm{P}}>1}^{T} \theta^{\max}.$$

To model the PV plant, we set its target output level as $\tau = 222$, which is the nameplate electric-output capacity of the CSP plant. Constraint (13) requires a budget limit for the PV array and BES system, which we set as $C^{\max} = 1\,500\,000\,000$, which is the modeled CSP-plant cost. Constraint (21) requires setting an energy-deficit limit, $\Delta^{\max}$, for the PV plant. We set this as:

$$\Delta^{\max} = \sum_{t=1:K_t^{\mathrm{P}}>1}^{T} [\tau - F_t(\theta_t)]; \tag{24}$$

where $F_t(\cdot)$ is the hour-t heat-rate function of the CSP plant and is obtained from SAM. Equation (23) computes the energy deficit of the CSP plant in terms of additional thermal energy that is needed to operate the plant at is nameplate thermal-input capacity during all target hours. Equation (24) converts the thermal-energy deficit into an equivalent electrical-energy deficit. This is done by computing, $\forall t = 1, \ldots, T$ such that $K_t^{\mathrm{P}} > 1$, the difference between the CSP plant's nameplate electric-output capacity, which is $\tau = 222$, and its actual electric output, which is given by $F_t(\theta_t)$. The conversion of the CSP plant's energy deficit from thermal energy, as is given by (23), to electrical energy is necessary, because the PV plant does not use thermal energy as an input as a CSP plant does.

4.3 Results

4.3.1 Single-Day Results

Figure 1 illustrates the general framework for analysing our results. It shows the hourly operation of the modelled CSP plant during 1 August, 2014, which is a typical hot summer day with high solar availability. The bars that are labelled 'Solar-Field Energy' show hourly energy that is collected by the plant's solar field. The bars that are labelled 'TES SOE' show the beginning hourly SOE of the TES system. Thus, the sums of these two bars indicate the total energy that is available for use by the CSP plant during each hour. The bars that are labelled 'Powerblock Energy Input' indicate (the negative of) hourly energy (from the solar field or TES) that is input to the powerblock. These bars are negative to indicate that they represent a use of thermal energy. The blue horizontal line that is across a portion of the horizontal axis that is at the bottom of the figure indicates the eight highest-load hours of the day, which are the eight target hours. During this day (which is common of the summer) the eight highest-load hours are consecutive and occur during the afternoon (due to air-conditioning demand). It is common during the winter for there to be two load peaks, which correspond to morning and evening lighting and heating demands. The bars that are labelled 'Energy Deficit' (of which there are none, because the CSP plant experiences no energy deficits during the eight target hours of this day) indicate hourly energy deficits.

Figure 1 shows that the CSP plant operates at its nameplate capacity during 12 hours of the day that is shown, and meets its performance requirement during all eight target hours. This is typical of hot sunny days during the spring, summer, and autumn. The TES system does not reach its maximum energy-storage capacity. Indeed, the plant operates continuously beginning as of 25 July, 2014 until hour 20 of 1 August, 2014, due to an abundance of thermal energy that is gathered during these

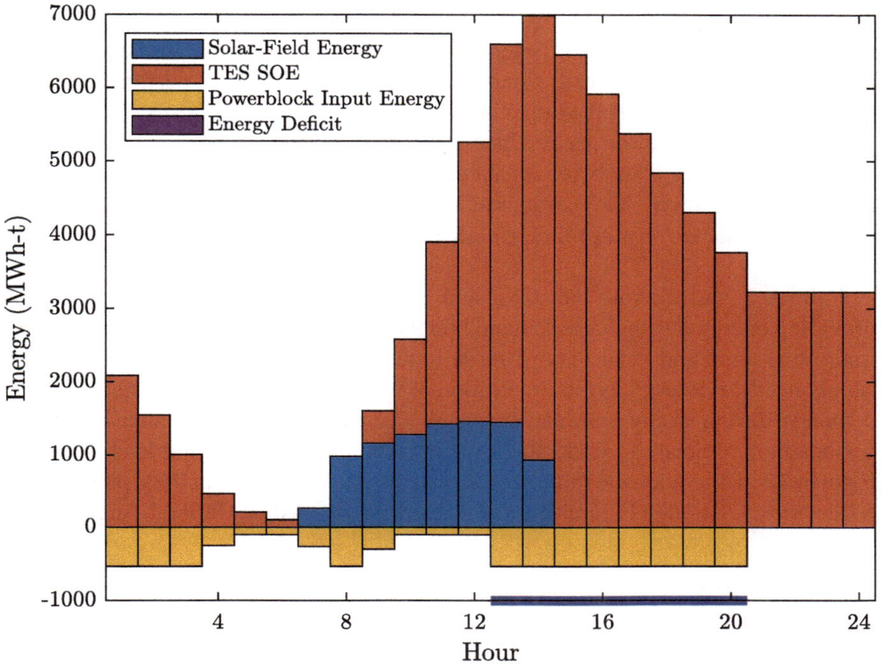

Fig. 1 Hourly thermal energy that is collected by the solar field, beginning TES-system SOE, powerblock input energy, and energy deficit for the modelled CSP plant during 1 August, 2014. The horizontal line that is across a portion of the horizontal axis indicates the eight highest-load target hours of the day

eight days. Excess thermal energy does not need to be stored for the plant to meet its performance requirement during the target hours of 1 August, 2014. Additionally, the CSP plant having sufficient energy to operate continuously during these eight days saves thermal energy that would be needed to start up a powerblock that is cycled to and from an offline state. Despite the abundance of solar energy, the TES system is valuable, in that it allows shifting solar energy to produce electricity during the load peak. Thermal energy that is collected by the solar field during 1 August, 2014 peaks between hours 9 and 13, but the load peaks between hours 13 and 20. The TES system allows the CSP plant to produce energy during the day's peak-demand hours.

Figure 2 summarises for the cost-minimising PV plant similar operational data to that which is presented for the CSP plant by Figure 1. Specifically, the bars that are labelled 'PV-Array Energy' and 'BES SOE' give the hourly amounts of electrical energy that is produced by the plant's PV array and the beginning hourly SOE of the plant's BES system. Thus, the sums of these bars indicate total electrical energy that is available to the plant during each hour. The bars that are labelled 'PV-Plant Output' indicate (the negative of) hourly electrical output of the PV plant to the electricity system. Electrical output can be from the PV array or by discharging the BES system.

The bars that are labeled 'Energy Deficit' and the blue horizontal line that is across a portion of the horizontal axis that is at the bottom of Figure 2 have the same interpretation as with Figure 1. Figure 2 shows that the PV plant performs similarly to the CSP plant *vis-à-vis* the target hours. A notable difference between the PV and CSP plants is that the former produces electricity during a longer window of time. This is due to a CSP plant being reliant upon DNI, which is reflected by the heliostats upon the power tower. A PV array is able to produce electricity using diffuse energy, which is available for more time (relative to DNI) during early mornings and late afternoons.

Figures 1 and 2 show that CSP and PV plants perform well with respect to providing energy during high-demand hours of sunny summer days. With low penetrations of wind and solar energy, these remain time periods with high electricity-supply needs. However, as the penetration of wind and solar increases, net electricity demands during sunny summer days will decrease, which will make other time periods more crucial. To understand the impacts of these changing load dynamics, Figures 3 and 4 provide the same operational results for the CSP and PV plants during 5 December, 2014 that Figures 1 and 2 do for 1 August, 2014. Unlike 1 August, 2014,

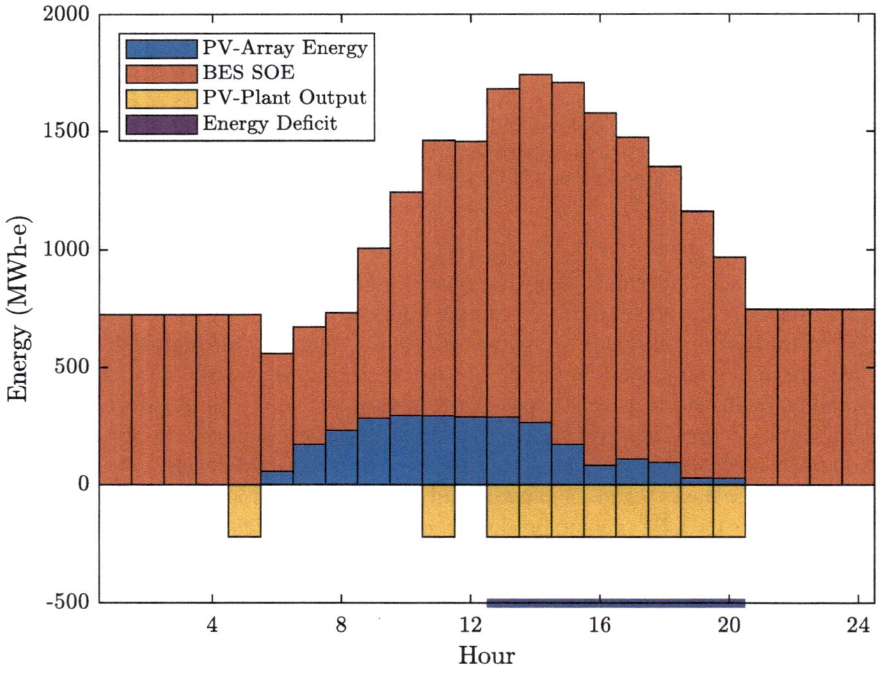

Fig. 2 Hourly electrical energy that is collected by the PV array, beginning BES-system SOE, PV-plant output, and energy deficit for the modelled cost-minimising PV plant during 1 August, 2014. The horizontal line that is across a portion of the horizontal axis indicates the eight highest-load target hours of the day

5 December, 2014 is a winter day with very limited solar availability. As such, both the CSP and PV plants experience energy deficits. Indeed, the CSP plant does not produce energy during any target hours between 2 December, 2014 and 4 December, 2014, due to the solar field not being able to collect any thermal energy during these days. As such, the CSP plant retains the stored energy in the TES system and uses it during 5 December, 2014 to meet the performance criterion partially. This is an optimal operational profile, because using the stored energy between 2 December, 2014 and 4 December, 2014 requires an additional powerblock start up, with associated energy losses. Because the PV plant uses diffuse solar radiation to produce electricity, it is able to meet partially the performance criteria between 2 December, 2014 and 4 December, 2014, due to some limited electricity output from the PV array during these days.

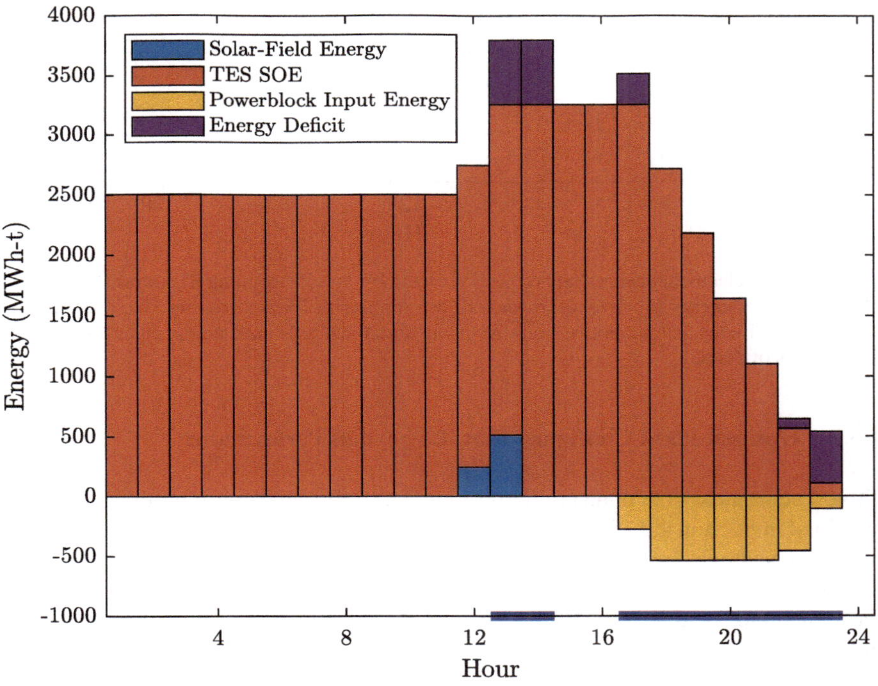

Fig. 3 Hourly thermal energy that is collected by the solar field, beginning TES-system SOE, powerblock input energy, and energy deficit for the modelled CSP plant during 5 December, 2014. The horizontal lines that are across portions of the horizontal axis indicate the eight highest-load target hours of the day

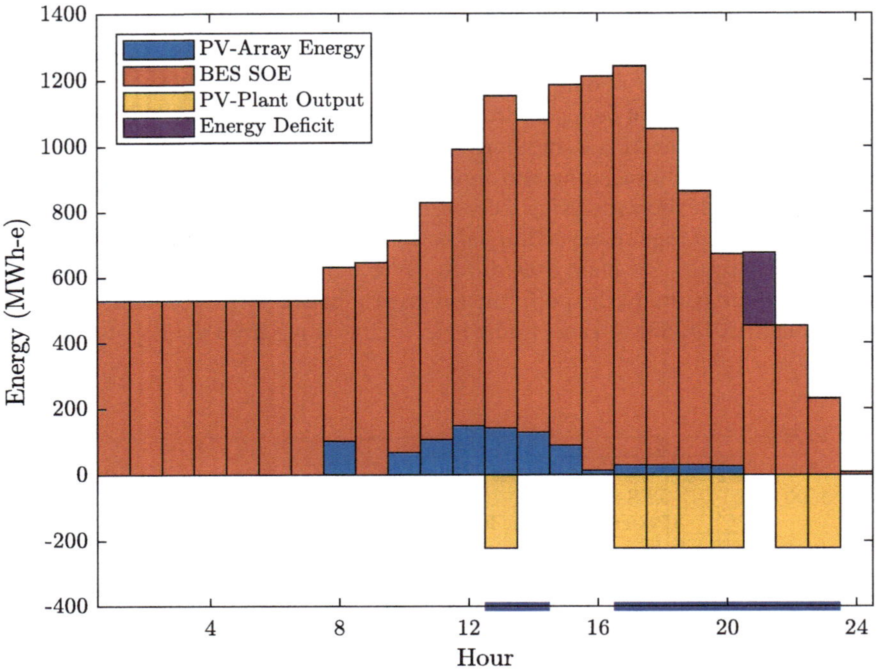

Fig. 4 Hourly electrical energy that is collected by the PV array, beginning BES-system SOE, PV-plant output, and energy deficit for the modelled cost-minimising PV plant during 5 December, 2014. The horizontal lines that are across portions of the horizontal axis indicate the eight highest-load target hours of the day

4.3.2 Optimal Plant Configurations, Costs, and Performance

Table 1 summarises the plant configurations. The CSP-plant configuration is fixed, as specified in Section 4.2. The two PV-plant configurations that are reported in Table 1 are optimised by solving (7)–(14) and (15)–(22), respectively. The table reports also each plant's total energy deficit during the year and its corresponding cost. Overall, the CSP plant is able to deliver 95.6% of the energy that is needed to meet the performance requirement, when it is applied to the eight highest-load hours of each day of the year. PV solar with BES can achieve the same overall performance, at a lower cost of $820 million, as opposed to $1.5 billion for the CSP plant. If a PV plant with BES can be built at the same $1.5 billion cost of the CSP plant, it delivers 99.66% of the energy that is needed to meet the performance requirement during the eight highest-load hours of each day of the year.

Although the PV plants have target electricity outputs of $\tau = 222$ MW-e, both the energy-deficit- and cost-minimising designs have oversized PV arrays with name-plate capacities of 703 MW-e and 338 MW-e, respectively. These design choices are akin to having a CSP plant with a solar multiple that is greater than 1.0. By oversizing

Table 1 Selected CSP-plant configuration, cost, and performance and optimised configuration, cost, and performance of PV plants

	CSP	Energy-Deficit-Minimising PV	Cost-Minimising PV
Nameplate Output Capacity (MW-e)	222	703	338
Hours of Energy Storage	12.0	10.2	6.3
Energy-Storage Power Capacity	538 MW-t	262 MW-e	222 MW-e
Energy Deficit (%)	4.4	0.34	4.4
Cost ($ million)	1 500	1 500	820

the PV array, the plant is able to produce 222 MW-e during a greater number of hours with less-than-ideal weather conditions. The cost-minimising PV-plant design has a BES system with a power capacity of 222 MW-e, meaning that the BES system is sized so that the PV plant operates at its target capacity entirely from stored energy. Conversely, the energy-deficit-minimising design has a BES system with a power capacity of 262 MW-e. This is because the BES is sized to charge a greater amount of excess PV output (from the significantly oversized PV array) to improve the plant's performance *vis-à-vis* the target hours.

Table 2 summarises the monthly energy deficits of the three plant configurations. The table provides insights regarding the relative performance of CSP and PV solar. Performance differences stem from fundamental differences between the physical properties of the two technologies. CSP requires high DNI and makes minimal use of diffuse solar radiation. This property of CSP is apparent in the energy deficits of the technologies during the cloudy (relative to other summer months) months of July and August. As a result, the CSP plant's energy deficit is one or two orders of magnitude greater than those of the two PV-plant configurations during these months. PV solar's improved performance is due to it being able to produce more energy during hours with low DNI (due to cloud cover) but with diffuse solar radiation being available. Conversely, the CSP plant outperforms the cost-minimising PV-plant design during the winter months of January and February, due to the CSP plant's larger energy-storage capacity. The energy-deficit-minimising PV plant is able to overcome this performance deficiency during the winter by increasing the size of the BES system from six to 10 hours of energy-storage capacity. Among the months of the year, December has a notably higher energy deficit that is one to six orders of magnitude larger compared to other months. This is expected, given weather patterns and limited daylight hours during December. Indeed, most of the energy deficit during December is accrued during the first two days of the month, which have particularly poor solar availability. Overall, the CSP plant has energy deficits during 128 hours of the year, as opposed to only 10 hours of energy deficits for the energy-deficit-minimising PV plant.

Table 2 Monthly energy deficits (%) of CSP and PV plants

	CSP	Energy-Deficit-Minimising PV	Cost-Minimising PV
January	0.068	0.009	0.096
February	0.045	0.001	0.060
March	0.013	0.000	0.004
April	0.001	0.000	0.001
May	0.000	0.000	0.001
June	0.000	0.000	0.001
July	0.013	0.000	0.001
August	0.026	0.000	0.001
September	0.009	0.000	0.001
October	0.007	0.000	0.009
November	0.016	0.001	0.036
December	0.320	0.032	0.317

4.3.3 Varying Target Hours

We conclude our case study by conducting a parametric analysis in which we vary the number of target hours during each day between the one and the 24 highest-load hours of the day. Table 3 summarises energy-deficit information for the CSP and energy-deficit-minimising PV plants with each number of target hours. Specifically, for each plant it reports the annual energy deficit as well as the deficit-weighted number of hours with energy deficits. The deficit-weighted number of hours with energy deficits for the CSP plant is computed as:

$$\sum_{t=1:K_t^{\mathrm{P}}>1,\theta_t<\theta^{\max}}^{T} \frac{\theta^{\max}-\theta_t}{\theta^{\max}};$$

whereas this value is computed as:

$$\sum_{t=1:K_t^{\mathrm{P}}>1,\delta_t>0}^{T} \frac{\delta_t}{\tau};$$

for the PV plant.

In most cases energy deficits are increasing in the number of target hours. However, CSP-plant performance improves slightly when the number of daily target hours increases from 15 to 16, from 17 to 18, and from 23 to 24. These improvements occur because increasing the number of target hours can change the target hours from occurring during two blocks of time during the day (*e.g.*, a morning and evening demand peak) to having a consecutive block of target hours. This change can be beneficial because of the energy that is consumed to shut down and start up the CSP

Table 3 Total energy deficits (%) and energy-deficit-weighted number of hours with energy deficits for CSP and energy-deficit-minimising PV plants with varying number of daily target hours

Number of Target Hours per day	CSP		Energy-Deficit-Minimising PV	
	Energy deficit	Deficit hours	Energy deficit	Deficit hours
1	0.00	0.00	0.27	0.97
2	0.03	0.22	0.14	0.99
3	0.53	5.82	0.09	0.99
4	1.30	18.97	0.07	0.99
5	2.00	36.43	0.05	0.99
6	2.84	62.29	0.10	2.25
7	4.12	105.35	0.27	6.79
8	4.39	128.21	0.34	9.90
9	6.48	212.75	0.55	18.18
10	7.60	277.22	0.86	31.21
11	8.61	345.66	1.06	42.68
12	9.94	435.51	1.36	59.36
13	11.10	526.75	1.79	84.96
14	12.56	641.96	2.21	112.97
15	13.93	762.76	2.63	144.11
16	12.85	750.65	3.07	179.19
17	16.83	1044.48	3.55	220.24
18	15.82	1039.45	4.12	270.53
19	20.46	1418.71	4.74	328.93
20	22.50	1642.50	5.62	410.35
21	24.64	1888.93	6.63	508.56
22	26.87	2157.70	8.16	651.71 lePara>
23	28.86	2423.14	9.59	805.11
24	27.23	2385.05	11.38	997.19

plant's powerblock if it must be cycled between two non-consecutive blocks of target hours. This phenomenon is notable when the number of daily target hours increases from 15 to 16, as the added target hour creates consecutive blocks of target hours during 21 days, which reduces by 12 the number of hours with energy deficits. If there are 24 daily target hours, then all 8,760 hours of the year are target hours and the CSP plant maximises energy production while it is online before exhausting stored energy and having to shut down the powerblock.

Figure 5 summarises the costs of the cost-minimising designs of PV plants with varying number of daily target hours. The costs of the PV-plant designs are not monotone in the number of daily target hours, which is to be expected, given the energy-deficit results that are reported in Table 3. For instance, increasing the number

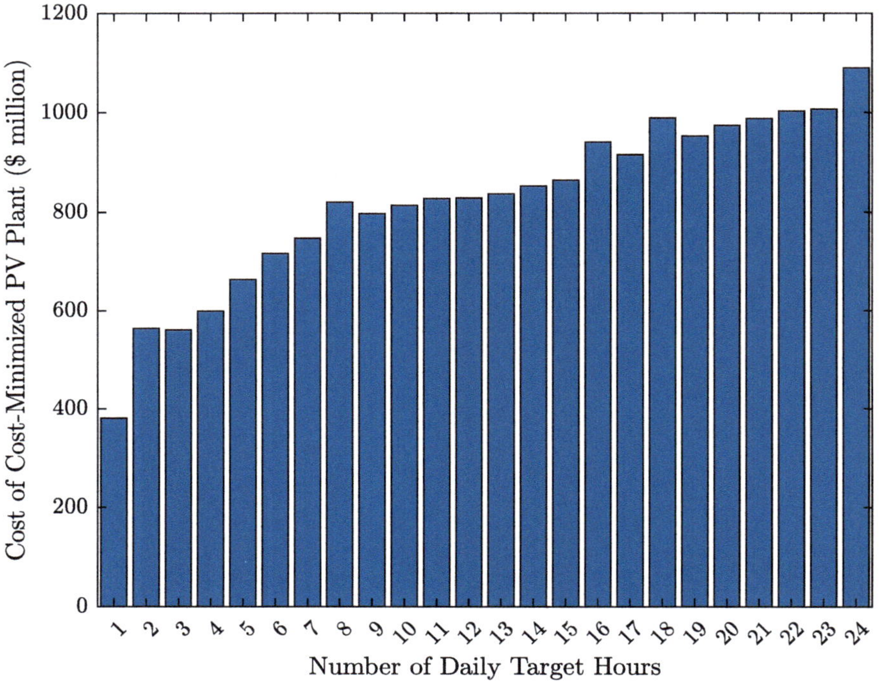

Fig. 5 Costs of cost-minimising PV plants with varying number of daily target hours

of daily target hours from 1 to 2 doubles the number of target hours. Yet, there is a negligible change in the energy deficit of the CSP plant. As such, the PV plant's design must be changed to meet the same performance criterion during twice as many hours. On the other hand, increasing the number of target hours from 18 to 19 yields a significant energy-deficit increase for the CSP plant. Because the PV plant is being designed to minimise cost while meeting the CSP plant's performance level, a less expensive plant design can be adopted with 19 target hours. Overall, Figure 5 shows that PV with BES can match the energy-deficit performance of CSP with TES at a much lower cost. This result is reflective of the significant decreases in the costs of PV modules and BES systems during the past several years (Fu et al. 2018; Cole et al. 2021).

5 Conclusions and Discussion

This chapter investigates the relative performance of two solar-electricity and energy-storage technologies—CSP with TES and PV solar with BES—as capacity resources. This focus is motivated by the fact that maintaining low-cost and reliable electricity supply is a grand challenge of decarbonising electricity systems. Recent studies show that resource adequacy (*i.e.*, the ability to serve electricity demand reliably) will be a major challenge in planning and operating future electricity systems that cannot rely upon dispatchable fossil-fuelled generation (Cochran et al. 2021; Denholm et al. 2022). Moreover, these resource-adequacy challenges are known to become more acute during periods of limited wind and solar availability. This is because as wind and solar are added to an electricity system, peaks in the residual demand will be concentrated during periods of low wind and solar availability (*e.g.*, during the evening when electricity demand is high but solar availability is limited). Thus, the ability to serve these demands without using fossil fuels is critical. One may be tempted to dismiss these concerns as pertaining to future electricity systems. However, a series of rotating outages in California during 2020 is attributed to electricity-system planners not paying due attention to this phenomenon (CAISO, CPUC, and CEC 2021). In the same vein, these issues are important to efforts to decarbonise east-Asian electricity systems as that region of the world electrifies further.

We develop optimisation models to determine the operation and design of the CSP and PV plants and use energy deficit as our primary metric to measure the plants' abilities to serve electricity demand. Despite CSP being coupled with low-cost and efficient TES, we find that PV solar that is coupled with BES is a more cost-effective source of reliable electricity-system capacity. The poor cost performance of CSP is due, in part, to the cost of building its solar field, meaning that efforts to reduce these costs could improve CSP economics. PV solar benefits, also, from its modular design and deployment flexibility. CSP plants must be large to exploit economies of scale, whereas PV arrays can be deployed on greenfield or brownfield sites or on existing structures. Another possibility to improve CSP economics is to couple the technology with geological thermal energy storage (GeoTES) (Sharan et al. 2021; McTigue et al. 2023). As opposed to using constructed storage tanks (as is the case for TES), GeoTES uses existing abundant aquifers as the energy-storage medium. As such, the technology scales (*e.g.*, theoretically to thousands of hours of energy-storage capacity) much more cost-effectively compared to conventional TES. In addition, GeoTES has the potential to use geothermal energy to supplement solar-field energy. Calderón et al. (2018) survey other TES technologies that could improve CSP-plant economics further.

Decarbonising electricity systems while maintaining resource adequacy is not solely a technology challenge. Regulatory, policy, and market-design choices will impinge upon these outcomes (Conejo and Sioshansi 2019). Our work highlights the need for policies that incentivise the adoption of these technologies and address their integration into energy systems. Financial incentives, such as tax credits, subsidies, and feed-in tariffs, have proven effective in accelerating the deployment of renewable-energy technologies (Sioshansi 2016). These incentives should be structured to encourage innovation in energy-storage integration and efficiency improvements (Sioshansi 2011). The variable nature of solar availability necessitates policies that support electricity-system flexibility and stability (Mansouri and Sioshansi 2022). This includes investment in electricity-system infrastructure that is capable of handling the variable output from solar plants and integrating them with existing and future energy sources (Yang et al. 2022).

Acknowledgements The authors thank A. Sorooshian and the editorial team for helpful discussions, comments, and suggestions. Any errors, opinions, and conclusions that are expressed in this paper are solely those of the authors.

Declarations

- Funding: This work was supported by The Ohio State University, National Science Foundation grants 1463492, 1808169, and 1922666, and Carnegie Mellon Electricity Industry Center.

References

Awara S, Zareipour H, Knight A (2018) Solar power capacity value evaluation—a review. In: 2018 IEEE Canadian Conference on Electrical & Computer Engineering, Institute of Electrical and Electronics Engineers, Quebec City, Quebec, Canada

Billinton R, Allan RN (1984) Reliability evaluation of power systems. Pitman Advanced Publishing Program, Boston, Massachusetts

Blair N, Dobos AP, Freeman J et al (2014) System Advisor Model, SAM 2014.1.14: General Description. Tech. Rep. NREL/TP-6A20-61019, National Renewable Energy Laboratory, Golden, CO

Blair N, DiOrio N, Freeman J et al (2018) System Advisor Model (SAM) General Description (Version 2017.9.5). Tech. Rep. NREL/TP-6A20-70414, National Renewable Energy Laboratory, Golden, CO

CAISO, CPUC, and CEC (2021) Root cause analysis: mid-August 2020 extreme heat wave. California Independent System Operator, California Public Utilities Commission, and California Energy Commission

Calderón A, Palacios A, Barreneche C et al (2018) High temperature systems using solid particles as TES and HTF material: a review. Appl Energy 213:100–111

Cochran J, Denholm P, Mooney M, et al (2021) The Los Angeles 100% Renewable Energy Study (LA100): executive summary. Tech. Rep. NREL/TP-6A20-79444-ES, National Renewable Energy Laboratory, Golden, CO

Cole W, Frazier AW, Augustine C (2021) Cost projections for utility-scale battery storage: 2021 update. Tech. Rep. NREL/TP-6A20-79236, National Renewable Energy Laboratory, Golden, CO

Conejo AJ, Sioshansi R (2019) Electricity market: a conversation on future designs. IEEE Power Energy Mag 17:18–19

Denholm P, Brown P, Cole W, et al (2022) Examining supply-side options to achieve 100% clean electricity by 2035. Tech. Rep. NREL/TP-6A40-81644, National Renewable Energy Laboratory, Golden, CO

Fu R, Feldman D, Margolis R (2018) U.S. solar photovoltaic system cost benchmark: Q1 2018. Tech. Rep. NREL/PR-6A20-72133, National Renewable Energy Laboratory, Golden, CO

Gami D, Sioshansi R, Denholm P (2017) Data challenges in estimating the capacity value of solar photovoltaics. IEEE J Photovoltaics 7:1065–1073

Garver LL (1966) Effective load carrying capability of generating units. IEEE Trans Power Apparatus Syst PAS-85:910–919

He YL, Qiu Y, Wang K et al (2020) Perspective of concentrating solar power. Energy 198:117373

Kim H, Sioshansi R, Lannoye E et al (2022) A stochastic-dynamic-optimization approach to estimating the capacity value of energy storage. IEEE Trans Power Syst 37:1809–1819

Madaeni SH, Sioshansi R, Denholm P (2012) Estimating the capacity value of concentrating solar power plants: a case study of the Southwestern United States. IEEE Trans Power Syst 27:1116–1124

Madaeni SH, Sioshansi R, Denholm P (2013a) Comparing capacity value estimation techniques for photovoltaic solar power. IEEE J Photovoltaics 3:407–415

Madaeni SH, Sioshansi R, Denholm P (2013b) Estimating the capacity value of concentrating solar power plants with thermal energy storage: a case study of the Southwestern United States. IEEE Trans Power Syst 28:1205–1215

Mansouri MA, Sioshansi R (2022) Using interim recommitment to reduce the operational-cost impact of wind uncertainty. J Mod Power Syst Clean Energy 10:839–849

McTigue JD, Zhu G, Akindipe D, et al (2023) Geological thermal energy storage using solar thermal and Carnot batteries: techno-economic analysis. Tech. Rep. NREL/CP-5700-87000, National Renewable Energy Laboratory, Golden, CO

Peinado Gonzalo A, Pliego Marugán A, García Márquez FP (2019) A review of the application performances of concentrated solar power systems. Appl Energy 255:113893

Sengupta M, Habte A, Gotseff P et al (2014a) A physics-based GOES product for use in NREL's National Solar Radiation Database. Tech. Rep. NREL/CP-5D00-62776, National Renewable Energy Laboratory, Golden, CO

Sengupta M, Habte A, Gotseff P et al (2014b) A physics-based GOES satellite product for use in NREL's National Solar Radiation Database. Tech. Rep. NREL/CP-5D00-62237, National Renewable Energy Laboratory, Golden, CO

Sengupta M, Xie Y, Lopez A et al (2018) The National Solar Radiation Data Base (NSRDB). Renew Sustain Energy Rev 89:51–60

Sharan P, Kitz K, Wendt D et al (2021) Using concentrating solar power to create a geological thermal energy reservoir for seasonal storage and flexible power plant operation. J Energy Resour Technol 143:010902

Singh C, Billinton R (1977) System reliability modelling and evaluation. Hutchinson Educational Publishers, London, UK

Sioshansi R (2011) Emissions impacts of wind and energy storage in a market environment. Environm Sci Technol 45:10728–10735

Sioshansi R (2016) Retail electricity tariff and mechanism design to incentivize distributed renewable generation. Energy Policy 95:498–508

Sioshansi R, Denholm P (2010) The value of concentrating solar power and thermal energy storage. IEEE Trans Sustain Energy 1:173–183

Sioshansi R, Denholm P (2013) Benefits of colocating concentrating solar power and wind. IEEE Trans Sustain Energy 4:877–885

Sun Z, Su L, Gao X et al (2021) Influences of impurity Cl^- on the thermal performance of solar salt for thermal energy storage. Solar Energy 216:90–95

Ueckerdt F, Brecha R, Luderer G (2015) Analyzing major challenges of wind and solar variability in power systems. Renew Energy 81:1–10

Varghese S, Sioshansi R (2020) The price is right? How pricing and incentive mechanisms in California incentivize building distributed hybrid solar and energy-storage systems. Energy Policy 138:111242

Wilcox SM (2012) National solar radiation database 1991–2010 update: user's manual. Tech. Rep. NREL/TP-5500-54824, National Renewable Energy Laboratory, Golden, CO

Yagi K, Sioshansi R, Denholm P (2019) Evaluating a concentrating solar power plant as an extended-duration peaking resource solar energy. Solar Energy 191:686–696

Yagi K, Sioshansi R, Denholm P (2021) Using concentrating-solar-power plants as economic carbon-free capacity resources. Energy Convers Manag: X 12:100112

Yang J, Dong ZY, Wen F et al (2022) Enhancing hosting capability for renewable energy generation in active distribution networks. IET Renew Power Gener 16:651–654

Comparative Environmental Evaluation of Electric Vehicle Charging Technologies, Infrastructure and Charging Stations in Malaysia: Towards a Sustainable Energy Transition

Norasikin Ahmad Ludin, Han Phoumin, Mirratul Mukminah Junedi, and Nurfarhana Alyssa Ahmad Affandi

Abstract Increasing the speed of the adoption of electric vehicles (EVs) is expected not only to help decarbonise the transport sector but also to attract investments. The commitment to these goals is also envisaged by the ASEAN Leaders' Declaration on developing a regional EV ecosystem (ASEAN Secretariat Indonesia 2023a). However, ASEAN countries like Malaysia face several challenges that stand in the way of EV adoption. This chapter discusses EVs, the charging technologies available and their pros and cons, particularly in regard to charging infrastructure, and the charging power and power transfer between the EV and the grid. A comparison of various energy sources found that in average monthly emissions per km travelled there is a 20% difference between an internal combustion engine vehicle (ICEV) and a charged EV charged with energy from Malaysia's current electricity mix. Hydrogen and solar PV energy sources supplied for EV charging are a better option. Based on the amount of monthly fuel sales, if Malaysia were to replace about 50% of the ICEVs with EVs, emissions could drop significantly, but higher adoption rates may yield greater reductions. However, this shift could strain the grid without upgrades, and a fossil fuel-heavy energy mix might offset the benefits.

N. A. Ludin (✉) · M. M. Junedi · N. A. A. Affandi
Solar Energy Research Institute (SERI), Universiti Kebangsaan Malaysia (UKM), Bangi, Malaysia
e-mail: sheekeen@ukm.edu.my

H. Phoumin
Economic Research Institute for ASEAN and East Asia (ERIA), Jakarta Pusat, Indonesia

H. Phoumin et al. (eds.), *Tackling the Energy Transition: Insights from ASEAN and Beyond*, Climate Change and Energy Transition,
https://doi.org/10.1007/978-981-96-6019-3_7

1 Introduction

In the context of ASEAN's energy transition, there is a potential to implement an energy transition by increasing its renewable energy (RE) share from just a 19% in final energy consumption in 2018 to 65% by 2050, and to reduce energy-related carbon dioxide (CO_2) emissions by 75% compared to current policies (IRENA 2022). At a global level, transportation is known to be one of the main contributors of emissions, and power generation (including international bunkers) increased CO_2 emissions by 261 Mt and 254 Mt in 2021 and 2022, respectively, more than offsetting reductions from industry and buildings of 156 Mt and 37 Mt, respectively, in the same years.

Accelerating electric vehicle (EV) adoption is expected to help decarbonise the transport sector as well as attract investments. It is also envisaged by the ASEAN Leaders' Declaration on developing a regional EV ecosystem (ASEAN Secretariat Indonesia 2023a). The region is emerging as a potential market and manufacturing hub for EVs, with EV sales increasing from 1.6% of total car sales (approximately 35,000 vehicles) in 2022 to 6.2% (141,095 vehicles) in 2023 across the six key markets, driven by favourable regulations, local brands and the introduction of low-cost EV models (Maybank Investment Bank 2024). Meanwhile, the market size has been projected to grow from USD 500 million in 2021 to USD 2.7 billion by 2027 (Malaysian Investment Development Authority 2023). However, the countries face several challenges that stand in the way of EV adoption: among others, the lack of public charging infrastructure, high cost of ownership, safety considerations, driving range, operation and maintenance of EVs, and energy sources and reliability of power supply. Malaysia too faces these difficulties in promoting and implementing EV consumption and infrastructure.

This chapter focuses on reviewing the current development of EV technology and infrastructure. It discusses the pros and cons of EV charging technologies, particularly of charging infrastructure, charging power and power transfer between EVs and the grid.

2 State-of-the Art EV Technology

2.1 The Development of EVs in Malaysia: Financing and Market Growth

Malaysia is one of the ASEAN countries that have embraced EV technology. The EV evolution in Malaysia (Fig. 7.1) began in the late 90 s, in which the *Perusahaan Otomobil Elektrik Malaysia* (Electric Automobile Company (Malaysia)) (POEM) introduced Eleksuria, a fully electric buggy-type vehicle that was proclaimed as Malaysia's first electric vehicle (Bernama 1997). POEM was founded by Tenaga Nasional Berhad (TNB) in 1997 and there were later plans to produce the third

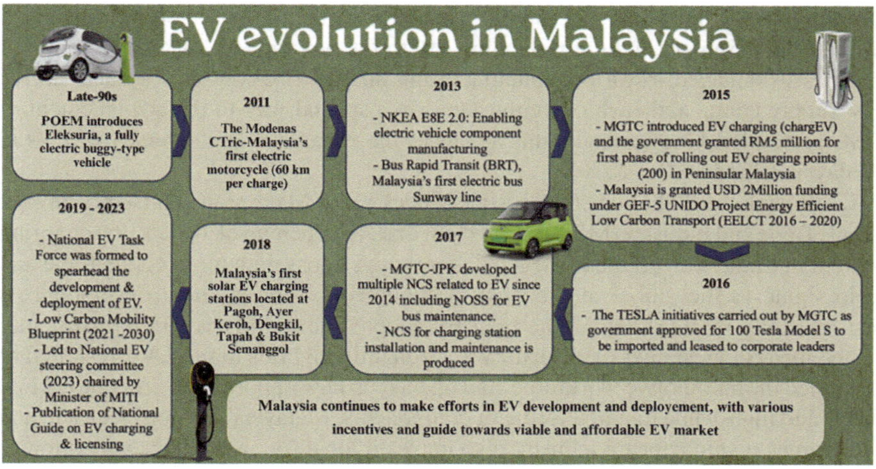

Fig. 7.1 EV evolution in Malaysia

national car, with ownership shared between Tenaga Nasional and Frazer-Nash Research Limited (Bernama 1998). During the Kuala Lumpur 1998 Commonwealth Games, Eleksuria, were widely used, with 300 units deployed for transport at the venues, marking a significant step towards the forecasted development of EVs in the country. The establishment of POEM and its effort was a stepping stone for the energy industry in Malaysia in gaining attention for the viability of EVs.

The biggest breakthrough that truly caught the investment flow began in 2011, when the energy transition enveloped the transportation industry. Launched on 21 September 2010, the economic transformation programme, a comprehensive plan to propel Malaysia's economy into a high-income economy, was organised by the Performance and Delivery Unit (PEMANDU) to identify the twelve National Key Economic Areas (NKEA). The programme's aim was set out as follows: It was forecasted that Malaysia's gross national income (GNI) per capita would increase from USD 6,700 (RM 23,700) in 2009 to over USD 15,000 (RM 48,000) by 2020, bringing the country to the level of other high-income nations. This growth was expected to be 6% annually (PEMANDU 2010). As of 2023, Malaysia's GNI per capita was approximately USD 11,710, according to the World Bank (World Bank Group n.d.), still below the target of USD 15,000, showing that the goals set for 2020 were not fully met. Even though progress towards the original targets was slower than expected, Malaysia is still working towards becoming a high-income nation.

The private sector was heavily involved in the programme as it was targeted to provide 92% of all investments. Within the first eight months of implementation, approximately RM 170 billion in committed investments were achieved, representing about 12% of the ten-year target (Daly and Singham 2011).The government will give priority to economic operations that fall under the NKEA category when allocating finances and planning. With the aim of revitalising Malaysia's private sector, the programme allocated 60% of its investment to that sector, 32% to enterprises affiliated with the government and the remaining 8% to the government. A diverse range of businesses engaged in various manufacturing and distribution phases make up the EV supply chain, and each one contributes in a special way to the advancement of ESG principles. Consequently, this advances the expansion and diversity of EVs in Malaysia (PEMANDU 2010).

Following the 2023 launch of Tesla's Model Y, the Malaysian Minister of Investment, Trade and Industry (MITI) pointed out that "the opening of Tesla's first charging station in Malaysia will make the local automotive ecosystem more competitive and help signal to the global market that the country is serious about developing its EV industry" (MIDA 2023). The industry adopted new skillsets and infrastructure suited to varying degrees of electrification from mild hybrids to full EVs, reskilled or upskilled the automotive workforce, and opened up new opportunities for innovation, R&D and high-value manufacturing of components. Malaysia's strong electrical and electronics manufacturing industry also makes it ideal for automakers and automotive investors to seamlessly secure their supply chains for growing their production of next-generation vehicles.

Malaysia's budget 2024 has allocated the following measures related to EV implementation (Malaysian Ministry of Finance 2024):

- Investment worth RM 170 million (USD 3.5 million) from established companies, namely Tenaga Nasional Bhd (TNB), Gentari and Tesla Malaysia, to build 180 EV charging stations.
- For individuals whose annual income is RM 120,000 (USD 25,000) and below, the government introduced the Encourage Electric Bike Usage Scheme. Buyers will be given rebates of up to RM 2,400 (~ USD 500).
- Prasarana Malaysia Bhd also agreed to build three bus depots valued at RM 600 million (USD 126 million) and obtain 150 electric buses to support the LRT 3 project.
- Extending the individual income tax relief up to RM 2,500 (~500 500) on EV charging facility expenses for a period of four years and tax deductions for EV rental costs for another two years.

2.2 EV Charging Technology

According to recent information, Malaysia has been making progress in the development of EV charging technology. In 2023, the country increased the number of electric vehicle charging bays (EVCB) to 1,434, consisting of 317 DCFC and 1,117 AC chargers (Lim 2023). This shows an increase from the 700 EVCB at the beginning of the year. To achieve the goal of 10,000 EVCBs by the end of 2025 (MIDA 2024), a monthly establishment of 554 EVCBs starting from January 2024 has been necessary (Technode Global Staff 2024). As of October 2024, there are 3,354 existing EVCB's, which represents 33.54% of the goal for 2025 (PLANMalaysia and MGTC 2025). Out of the 1,113 available stations, 2,398 are of the AC variety, while 956 are

DC fast EVCB. Out of the total, 1,501 are indoor EVCB, while 1,855 are outdoor. This demonstrates a commitment to expanding and enhancing the electric vehicle charging infrastructure in Malaysia.

Additionally, the Malaysian Green Technology and Climate Change Corporation (MGTC) has been actively involved in the development and planning of electric vehicle infrastructure across the country. Their efforts include the formulation of a strategic framework for the development and planning of EV infrastructure (MGTC 2023). The focus on electric vehicle technology development in Malaysia is exemplified by events such as Malaysia EV Tech 2023, which "underscores the nation's commitment to advancing its electric vehicle sector" (MTE 2023). Overall, Malaysia is dedicated to the development of electric vehicle charging technology and infrastructure and, in 2023, demonstrated progress and commitment towards a sustainable transportation future.

In general, the ratio of charging stations to BEVs falls as the market's share of battery-electric LDVs increases. The IEA (2023) notes that even in countries with a large number of private charging alternatives, public charging infrastructure is becoming more important as the market penetration of EVs continues to rise. The global adoption of EVs is largely dependent on the development of EV charging infrastructure, as the automotive industry moves ever faster towards a greener future.

2.3 Environmental Impact of the EV Ecosystem

Examining the environmental impact of charging stations throughout their entire life cycle, from material extraction and production to operation and disposal, is crucial. Studies by Wohlschlager, Haas and Neitz-Regett (2022) and Zhang et al. (2019) highlight the importance of this approach. Their research reveals that unidirectional (V1G) technology and direct current (DC) charging generally generate lower carbon emissions compared to their counterparts. Zhang et al. (2019) also identified home chargers as having the lowest environmental impact, followed by public AC and DC chargers, with public mixed chargers having the highest impact due to differences in materials and technology.

In addition, minimising carbon emissions from EV charging requires utilising smart charging strategies. Research by Tang et al. (2021) and Meinrenken, Shou and Di (2020) emphasises the crucial role of this technology, which adjusts charging times based on grid emissions, leading to significant reductions, especially during periods of low demand. Integrating smart charging can significantly reduce the environmental impact of EVs, particularly when considering the emissions associated with electricity generation. Tang et al. (2021) found that smart charging could achieve a 6% reduction in carbon emissions, particularly during common tasks like overnight charging. Additionally, countries with higher emissions factors benefit more from smart charging implementation.

While life cycle assessment and charging technologies provide insights into the environmental impact of different charging options, the type of energy used for charging also plays a significant role. Exploring and implementing alternative energy sources like hydrogen *and* solid oxide fuel cell (SOFC) technology can further contribute to the sustainability of EV charging infrastructure. Pourrahmani, Xu and Van herle (2022) explored the use of SOFC in charging stations, finding it to have lower carbon emissions, higher efficiency and lower costs compared to traditional grid-based charging. Gauto et al. (2023) and Lubecki, Szczurowski and Zarębska (2023) suggest hydrogen as a promising alternative energy source for both charging stations and electric buses, highlighting its potential for lower environmental impact and cost compared to conventional options.

In Malaysia, the potential for hydrogen to power EV charging stations is gaining attention as the country moves towards a more sustainable energy future. The government's plan to introduce hydrogen-powered cars by Q1 2025 (Yusry 2024) is aligned with the exploration of hydrogen as a clean energy alternative (Ministry of Economy 2023). This move could offer benefits such as lower carbon emissions and increased efficiency compared to traditional grid-based charging. Upgrading Malaysia's infrastructure to include hydrogen refuelling stations alongside EV charging stations offers a promising path for sustainable transportation. Policy intervention is essential to address the challenge of the high costs, such as providing subsidies for the clean energy i.e., hydrogen. While green hydrogen is more expensive to produce, with costs ranging from USD 10–15 per kg, targeted subsidies can help make it more competitive and accelerate its adoption (Ravimalar 2024). The Malaysian government is actively supporting hydrogen development through initiatives like the NETR and HETR, with regions such as Sarawak leveraging hydropower. Although the transition requires investment in infrastructure, both hydrogen and EV technologies can complement each other, and with strong public–private partnerships and supportive policies (Jumaat and Khalid 2024), Malaysia can make significant achievement in this matter.

Next, the location and design of charging infrastructure significantly impact its environmental footprint. Integrating solar PV panels into charging station canopies, as demonstrated by Fakour et al. (2023), can significantly reduce carbon emissions compared to relying solely on the grid. This approach utilises cleaner energy and maximises land use efficiency. Strategically locating charging infrastructure also promotes electric vehicle adoption and its environmental benefits. Horesh, Zhou and Quinn (2023) highlight the economic and environmental benefits of installing charging infrastructure in multi-unit dwellings (MUDs), addressing the limited access faced by residents in such buildings and contributing to GHG emissions reduction. While emphasising the importance of considering the embodied emissions associated with building charging infrastructure, Mulrow and Grubert (2023) find that the cumulative emissions from charging infrastructure and EV charging activities are relatively small compared to total emissions from light-duty vehicles. Therefore, focusing efforts on reducing emissions from other aspects of the transportation system remains crucial.

Furthermore, expanding charging infrastructure offers not only environmental but also economic benefits. Roxana J. Javid, M. Salari and Ramina J. Javid (2019) demonstrated the economic and environmental co-benefits, finding that increased charging stations led to significant reductions in petroleum use, air pollutants and greenhouse gas emissions. Additionally, expanding charging infrastructure promotes economic growth and job creation (MPC 2024). Expanding charging infrastructure can create jobs in construction, maintenance, and service sectors as new stations are built and existing ones upgraded. Increased demand for electric vehicles (EVs) may boost manufacturing jobs, particularly in vehicle and component production. Furthermore, implementing sustainable solutions like PV-based charging stations, as reported by Faisal et al. (2024), can reduce both the carbon and ecological footprints compared to conventional stations. This is attributed to the use of cleaner energy sources and efficient energy management strategies, providing environmental benefits while contributing to cost savings in the long run.

Developing and implementing EV charging infrastructure should take into consideration a thorough understanding of its environmental footprint. By employing life cycle assessments, using smart charging and alternative energy sources, designing efficient and strategically located infrastructure, and maximising resource sustainability, we can minimise the environmental impact of charging stations while maximising their benefits in promoting the transition towards cleaner transportation. Table 7.1 gives a summary of the main points of the research reviewed here.

3 Methodology

Using the life cycle assessment (LCA) approach integrated with the hourly marginal emissions factor (HMEF) (Zhong, Yu and Zhao, 2023), for evaluating the GHG implications of EV growth, a comparison of environmental benefits was conducted for various sources of energy, especially solar, at selected charging stations. The barriers, policy implications and strategies were discussed and highlighted. Environmental evaluations were carried out at selected EV charging stations in Malaysia using a LCA and SimaPro Simulation. The assessment was then conducted for various RE sources with focus on the LCA. Three analytical steps were applied to this study:

- Step 1: LCA analysis of energy sources and charging system.
- Step 2: Integration with hourly HMEF, for evaluating the GHG implications of EV growth.
- Step 3: Sensitivity analysis for various EV charging technologies and costs.

3.1 Life Cycle Impact Assessment (LCIA)

This method does not specifically focus on a product but instead provides a framework for assessing environmental impacts. In the context of this study, the analysis centres on the energy and material inputs required to produce a product, such as an EV. For instance, while the drivetrain of an EV produces little or no tailpipe GHG emissions

Table 7.1 Summary of reviewed studies on EVs

Author(s)	Study focus	Highlights
Bothe and Steinfort 2020 (Doluweera et al. 2020)	Assessment of emissions from charging infrastructure expansion, impact on electricity generation and EV recharging	• Carbon equivalent emissions of 1.03 tons CO_2eq/life
Faisal et al. (2024)	Ecological footprints of the charging station that uses electricity generated from the PV system to charge the batteries	• 89% reduction in ecological footprints with PV-generated electricity • A decrease in ecological footprint from 3.1 × 10–4 gha/kWh to 3.15 × 10–5 gha/kWh
Fakour et al. (2023)	Environmental impact of EV charging infrastructure; focuses on carport canopy configuration in urban areas in Taiwan	• Solar PV integration results in 94% lower carbon emissions than the standard grid
Horesh et al. (2023)	Comparison of home-charging and solar-powered carports	• PV-powered carports offer better benefits with carbon pricing • Highlights economic advantage and 86% GHG reduction in multi-unit dwellings
Javid et al. (2019)	Quantification of economic and environmental benefits of expanding charging stations	• Benefits depend on buyer percentages and travel patterns • Expansion scenario reduces California-wide GHG emissions by approximately 87,000 metric tons and air pollutant emissions by approximately 996 metric tons over 15 years
Krim et al. (2022)	30-year lifespan of PV-powered charging stations, pinpointing the manufacturing phase's impact	• The use of recycled PV systems potentially reduces up to 32.1% of carbon emissions
Meinrenken et al. (2020)	Optimisation of All-Electric Ranges (AERs) for electric vehicles based on trip distance distributions	• Adjusting All-Electric Ranges (AERs) based on drivers' trip distance distributions, charging technology and drivetrain architecture is crucial

(continued)

Table 7.1 (continued)

Author(s)	Study focus	Highlights
Mulrow and Grubert (2023)	Emphasises environmental impact assessment of charging infrastructure build-out	• Developed methodology suggests negligible cumulative GHG emissions of this build-out: < 1% of light-duty travel emissions
Pourrahmani, Xu and Van herle (2022)	Proposals for EV charging stations using LiMn2O4 lithium-ion batteries, solid oxide fuel cell (SOFC), and absorption refrigeration cycle (ARC) technology	• SOFC exhibited better performance with lower carbon emissions (1.48 kg CO_2 eq/Wh), a cost of 0.247 (USD/kWh), an energy efficiency of 75%, and an exergy efficiency of 51.68%
Tang et al. (2021)	Greenhouse gas emissions from charging EVs in the UK and other European countries	• Smart charging reduces emissions by 6%, crucial for overnight charging • Charging behaviour influences emissions
Zhang et al. (2019)	Life-cycle assessment of the environmental impact of different types of chargers in China	• Home chargers exhibited the lowest energy consumption and greenhouse gas emissions. Public AC and DC chargers followed, with public mix chargers showing the highest impact

during operation, the production of its battery pack presents a significant environmental consideration. The manufacturing process of EV batteries involves energy-intensive steps, including the extraction and processing of materials like lithium and cobalt. Outputs assessed in LCIA can encompass various environmental impact indicators, including GHG emissions, cumulative energy demand (CED), particulate matter emissions, land transformation, eutrophication and global warming potential (GWP).

A 2023 study at Imperial College London highlights that tyre wear particles contribute significantly to environmental pollution, accounting for approximately 52% of small particle emissions from road transport (Brogan 2023). These particles, composed of a complex mix of chemicals, microplastics and heavy metals, pose potential risks to both human health and ecosystems (Robbins 2023). The environmental impact of tyre wear is a concern for all vehicle types, including EVs, as they are not exempt from generating tyre wear particles. In fact, the heavier weight of some EVs, due to their batteries, can lead to increased tyre wear compared to internal combustion engine vehicles (ICEVs). This underscores the need for comprehensive strategies to mitigate pollution from such wear across all vehicle categories. Addressing the issue of tyre wear pollution requires a multifaceted approach, including the development of more durable tyre materials, advancements in vehicle design to reduce tyre abrasion, and the implementation of policies aimed at monitoring and controlling non-exhaust emissions. Such measures are essential to fully realise the environmental benefits of transitioning to electric mobility. This being said, the present analysis focuses solely on GHG emissions to evaluate the life cycle impact.

3.2 *Life Cycle Inventory (LCI)*

To evaluate the greenhouse gas emissions saved in a switch from ICEVs to electric vehicles (EVs), the life cycle inventory (LCI) (pump to wheel) assesses average fuel emissions in relation to average electricity charging (various energy sources). The projected emissions value is based on goods (freight) vehicle technology using conventional petrol and fuel. About 6×10^5 L of petrol and diesel are sold per month on average. The predicted yearly CO_2 emissions from petrol and diesel are 8.5 and 9.5×10^6 metric tonnes, respectively; the total annual fuel emissions are 18×10^6 metric tonnes of CO_2. For petrol, the monthly fuel carbon emissions distribution falls between 600 and 750 million g CO_2, while for diesel, it falls between 600 and 900 million g CO_2 (Ahmad Affandi et al. 2022).

In addition to reducing emissions through the use of the electrical grid, carbon emissions from the trade and sale of fuel at petrol stations can be offset by the adoption of RE technologies and the growth of electric vehicle (EV) production (Bi et al. 2019). However, the expectation that EVs alone can significantly reduce emissions may be overly optimistic in contexts where RE is not the dominant source in the energy mix. This is particularly relevant for nations like Malaysia, where coal still plays a significant role in electricity generation. While the shift from internal combustion engine vehicles to EVs reduces tailpipe emissions, the increased demand for electricity means power plants—often powered by fossil fuels—will produce additional emissions during the charging process. This highlights the reality that transitioning from fossil fuels cannot happen entirely or immediately, especially in regions where the energy infrastructure relies heavily on coal and other non-renewable sources. While clean technologies can help mitigate emissions, their effectiveness depends on an energy system that prioritises renewables. For nations in Southeast Asia, like Malaysia and Indonesia, what is feasible in western cities such as Paris or Sydney may not be directly applicable due to differing energy mixes and development stages. Therefore, adopting cleaner technologies must also include raising awareness and promoting gradual divestment from fossil fuels, recognising the complex realities of regional energy systems.

3.3 *Hourly Marginal Emissions Factor (HMEF)*

A marginal generator determines the change in GHG emissions that results from adding 1 MWh of electricity load at a specific period, which is represented by the HMEF. There are differences in magnitudes and orientations between the EV life cycle GHG estimations derived from the annual average emissions factor (AAEF) and HMEF. As Zhong, Yu and Zhao (2023) assert, "this difference varies between electricity systems and requires specific analysis". Through HMEF-based estimates, two factors may be seen to influence EV life cycle GHG emissions: the electricity dispatching rule and the EV charging energy source:

1. The electricity dispatching rule—Electricity dispatching rules affect the HMEF, which in turn influences the EV life cycle GHG. In Malaysia, the single buyer model is the authorised entity by the government under the Electricity Supply Act (ESA) 1990. "The single buyer buys electricity from generators based on a least-cost approach, such that the lowest marginal cost generating unit is dispatched first, followed by the next-lowest marginal cost generating unit until all the demand is met". This approach also aligns with the Single Buyer Market Rules and New Enhanced Dispatch Arrangement (NEDA) (Kumar et al. 2021).
2. EV charging energy source—This affects the whole life cycle of the EV, which in turn alters the quantity of GHG emissions. The present study includes the energy sources available in Malaysia which are highly likely to be used as EV charging sources: solar PV, hydrogen and electricity mix.

4 Life Cycle Assessment (LCA) of EV Charging in Malaysia

Before discussing the LCA of EV charging, it may be helpful to give a short overview of energy supply in Malaysia to provide a basis for our comparative environmental evaluation. Malaysia is highly dependent on coal and natural gas and is one of the largest natural gas exporters in the world. RE resources account for only 1—3% of the country's energy mix (Fig. 7.2).

In 2022, Malaysia's total energy supply was predominantly derived from fossil fuels, with natural gas accounting for 47% and oil contributing 25% of the energy mix (IEA 2024). This reliance on fossil fuels underscores the country's significant reserves, particularly in natural gas, positioning Malaysia as one of the largest oil and gas producers in the Asia–Pacific region. Despite this, Malaysia has been increasingly importing coal to meet its energy demands, with coal accounting for more than 43% of electricity generation in 2023. RE sources, including hydropower and solar, remain underutilised, with clean electricity constituting only 19% of the total generation, and solar and wind making up a mere 1.5%. This energy profile highlights the challenges Malaysia faces in diversifying its energy mix and reducing its carbon footprint.

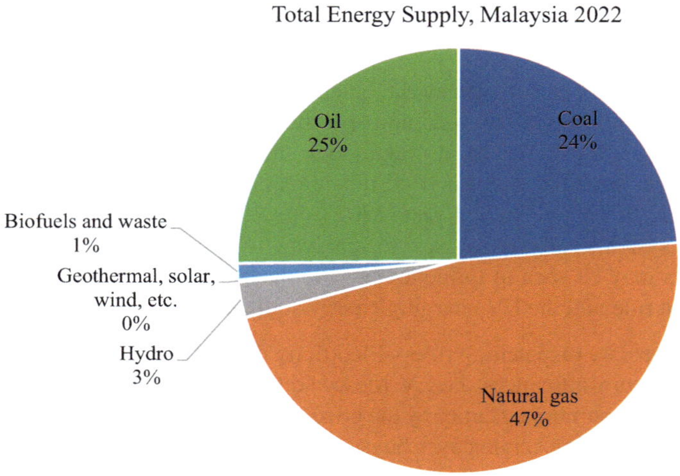

Fig. 7.2 Total energy supply, Malaysia 2022 (IEA 2024)

Urban emission displacement refers to the reduction in emissions achieved through the integration of clean energy technologies (CET) and energy efficiency measures in response to changes in energy demand and supply. As defined by the U.S. Environmental Protection Agency (EPA), displaced emissions are realised through the response of power markets to changes in demand and/or supply caused by the penetration of CET and energy efficiency. This concept is typically assessed using statistical techniques and case study data to estimate the reduction in emissions relative to a business-as-usual (BAU) scenario. Importantly, this approach focuses on the broader context of how GHG emissions are mitigated across an entire energy system rather than in a localised manner.

A comprehensive understanding of the GHG life cycle, including emissions from production, operation and decommissioning, is essential to evaluate its ecosystem-wide economic impacts. For example, while photovoltaic (PV) systems produce no emissions during operation, their life cycle emissions, including manufacturing and disposal, must also be accounted for (Schmidt and Crawford 2018). The emissions rate can be calculated according to Eq. 1 below:

$$CO2eqemissionsrate(\frac{\mathrm{gCO2eq}}{kWh}) = \frac{Total\mathrm{CO2eq}emissionsduringlifecycle}{E_{gen}xL} \tag{1}$$

E_{gen} is the annual power generation (kWh/ year) and L is the lifetime (year).

As mentioned by Ahmad Affandi et al. (2022), "Different fuels emit a different amount of CO_2 related to the energy content they produce when carbon (C) and oxygen (O) are burned". In the example of petroleum retail, and the two types of fuel considered in the case study (diesel and gasoline), the emissions can be calculated according to Eq. 2.

$$qCO_2 = \frac{c_f}{h_f}\left(\frac{M_{CO_2}}{M_C}\right) \tag{2}$$

where qCO_2 is the specific CO_2 emission ($kgCO_2$/ kWh), c_f is the particular carbon content of the fuel (kg_C/kg_{fuel}), h_f is the specific energy content of the fuel (kWh/ kg_{fuel}), M_C is the molecular weight of carbon (kg/kmol carbon) and MCO_2 is the molecular weight of carbon dioxide (kg/kmol CO_2). As in Ahmad Affandi et al. (2022) (p. 6), the number of grams of CO_2 emitted is computed per gallon of gasoline combusted: 8.887×10^{-3} metric tons of CO_2 per gallon of gasoline. For diesel, the number of grams of CO_2 emitted per gallon is found to be 10.180×10^{-3} metric tons CO_2. The ratio of CO_2 emissions to total GHG emissions (including CO_2, N_2O and CH_4) for a passenger vehicle is 0.993 (US EPA 2024). Thus, the annual GHG emissions per mile are: (8.89×10^{-3} metric tons CO_2/ gallon gasoline) *(1/22.2 miles/gallon car/truck average) *(1CO_2, CH_4 and N_2O/ 0.994 CO_2) = 4.03×10^{-4} metric tons CO_2 eq/mile. The CO_2 emissions from the combustion of 1 L of diesel are 2,640 g CO_2/litre diesel. This is calculated by the chemical composition of diesel fuel, which comprises 720 g of carbon and 1920 g of oxygen needed to combust the fuel completely. In contrast, 1 L of petrol is 2,392 g CO_2/litre. This is also calculated by its respective chemical component, which comprises 652 g of carbon and 1,740 g of oxygen required for the combustion (US EPA 2024). Furthermore, CO_2 emissions from a vehicle, in which the average consumption is 5 L for every 100 km travelled, shows average emissions of 132 g CO_2 eq/km for diesel and 120 g CO_2 eq/km for petrol without heat loss.

Generally, the fuel most EVs use does not produce emissions on the road. EVs encompass various types, each with distinct propulsion systems and environmental impacts. Battery electric vehicles (BEVs) operate solely on electric power; plug-in hybrid electric vehicles (PHEVs) combine an electric motor with an internal combustion engine and rechargeable batteries; hybrid electric vehicles (HEVs) utilise both an electric motor and a gasoline engine without external charging capabilities; and fuel cell electric vehicles (FCEVs) are powered by hydrogen fuel cells that produce electricity.

EVs consume energy when charging and emissions vary based on the source of energy used to produce one kilowatt of electricity. The average emissions factor from three different energy sources is as shown in Fig. 7.3: the average emissions factor from Malaysia's energy mix in 2023 was about 422 gCO_2e/ kWh; from PV it was 50 gCO_2e/ kWh (Ludin et al. 2021) and from hydrogen 12 $kgCO_2e$/ kg H_2 (Hydrogen Europe Intelligence Department 2020). The carbon footprint of the electric versions of identical vehicle models, but with a different power supply, is already lower than that of the corresponding variants with internal combustion engines. Additionally, EVs have a greater possibility for CO_2 reduction in all stages of the product's life cycle.

While it is true that photovoltaics (PV) and hydrogen (H_2) generally have lower emissions than gasoline during operation, the broader life cycle emissions of these energy systems warrant a detailed examination, particularly when comparing them to

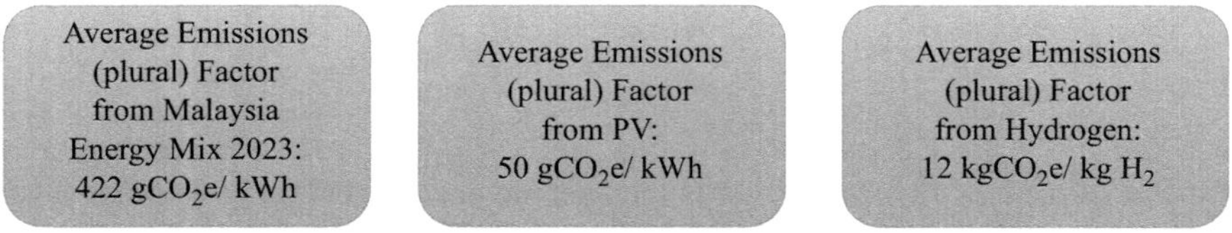

Fig. 7.3 Average emissions from different fuel sources (Karib 2023)

fossil fuel infrastructure. One key consideration is the existing infrastructure for gasoline production and distribution, such as oil refineries and petrol stations, which are already operational. This existing infrastructure represents a sunk environmental cost, meaning additional emissions are not incurred to establish new systems. In contrast, transitioning to RE sources like PV and H_2 requires substantial upfront investments in infrastructure, including solar panel manufacturing facilities, hydrogen electrolysis plants, and distribution networks, all of which carry significant emissions associated with construction and raw material extraction.

Hydropower, often cited as a low-emission energy source, highlights this dilemma. Building large dams involves massive amounts of concrete and steel, both of which have large amounts of embodied carbon emissions. Similarly, battery giga factories, such as Tesla's facilities, are massive operations that rely on energy-intensive processes for producing batteries and extracting metals like lithium and cobalt. These emissions must be accounted for when evaluating the net environmental benefits of transitioning to EVs or other renewable-powered vehicles.

On the other hand, fossil fuel operations like oil drilling and refining also involve continuous emissions and environmental impacts, including methane leaks, oil spills and land degradation. While the infrastructure is established, its ongoing use perpetuates carbon emissions and resource depletion. The transition to renewables, despite its initial carbon footprint, offers the potential for substantial long-term reductions in emissions, particularly as technologies evolve to reduce the environmental impacts of production and construction. This underscores the importance of considering the full life cycle of energy systems when assessing their sustainability.

In a comparison of the CO_2 emissions of several vehicle models with either an internal combustion engine or an electric motor, an LCA of the Volkswagen Golf by *Electric Motor Engineering* Magazine (2022) certified this finding, (IEA 2023). The magazine found:

> In short, the current Golf TDI (Diesel) emits on average 140 g of CO_2/km along the entire lifecycle whereas e-Golf1 just 119 g of CO_2/km. It is clear that, for a vehicle with an internal combustion engine, most of emissions come from the use phase, i.e., from the fossil fuel provisioning chain and from combustion: in these cases, the Diesel version reaches 111 g of CO_2/km, whereas, in this phase, a corresponding electrically powered vehicle emits only 62 g of CO_2/km, deriving from the energy generation and supply. On the contrary, most of emissions for an electric car are generated during the production phase. According to the LCA, the datum referred to the diesel version is 29 g of CO_2/km; whereas the one of a corresponding electrically driven car is 57 g of CO_2/km. The battery production and the complex mining of raw materials weigh significantly, and this number corresponds to almost

half of CO_2 emissions for the entire lifecycle that, during the use phase, depend on energy production sources—their decrease depends on the availability of renewable energies.

The emissions data recorded here underscore the importance of transitioning to RE sources, as the carbon footprint of EV usage is directly linked to the energy mix powering the grid (Table 7.2).

While EVs produce emissions throughout their life cycle, these are significantly lower than gasoline vehicles. The U.S. Environmental Protection Agency (EPA) estimates that a typical gasoline vehicle emits about 400 g of CO_2 per mile, or roughly 250 g per kilometre (US EPA 2024). The UK, with a carbon intensity of 182 gCO_2/kWh in 2022 (Edenseven 2025), reported that emissions from EVs reached 47 gCO_2/km (Lee et al. 2023). This value serves as a benchmark, highlighting the potential for significant emissions reduction with a favourable energy mix. Considering the advancements in EV technology and the global push for RE integration into grids, current lifecycle emissions are expected to be even lower. From our case study in Malaysia, the average emissions per kilometre travelled by an EV are estimated to be around 63.3 gCO_2/km with the country's carbon intensity of 422 gCO_2/kWh (World Benchmarking Alliance 2019). This indicates that a cleaner energy mix and lower carbon intensity in Malaysia would further reduce these emissions.

An increase in the proportion of RE in the electricity mix from 3 to 6% would have a meaningful impact on the emissions associated with EVs across their entire life cycle. EV life cycle emissions are largely influenced by the carbon intensity of electricity used during vehicle operation and manufacturing. A doubling of the RE share reduces reliance on fossil fuels such as coal, lowering average emissions per kilowatt-hour of electricity generated. While the precise reduction would depend on the energy sources being displaced, studies suggest that life cycle emissions for EVs could decrease by 5–10% with such an increase in RE, depending on the baseline carbon intensity of the grid.

If coal usage is reduced by 10% by 2030, the emissions intensity of the electricity mix would decrease proportionally, provided that coal is replaced with lower-emission sources such as natural gas or renewables. For a coal-dominated grid, this shift could result in a reduction of 5–15% in the overall carbon footprint of EV charging and operation. This change would further enhance the emissions advantage of EVs over ICEVs, particularly in regions where coal currently dominates the energy mix.

Hydrogen (H_2) as a fuel has negligible emissions at the point of use; however, the full life cycle emissions must account for the production of hydrogen, construction of infrastructure (such as electrolysis plants and refuelling stations), and retrofitting or manufacturing hydrogen vehicles. For green hydrogen produced using RE, emissions

Table 7.2 Average emissions of conventional, electric and plug-in hybrid vehicles (gCO_2/ km)

Type of vehicles	ICEVs	EVs	PHEVs
Average emissions (gCO_2/ km)	250	70—370	50—120

are relatively low, but the embedded emissions from building the necessary infrastructure and manufacturing vehicles could add approximately 10–20% to the life cycle carbon footprint of hydrogen-powered vehicles. This figure could increase if fossil fuels are used in hydrogen production or in the manufacturing process. Retrofitting vehicles and constructing new assembly lines would further add to emissions, though advancements in sustainable construction and manufacturing practices could mitigate some of these impacts over time. In sum, reducing coal use, increasing RE, and adopting hydrogen fuel all contribute to lowering emissions, but infrastructure and life cycle considerations must be factored into any calculation of net environmental benefit.

The average monthly emissions per vehicle km travelled by various energy sources Table 7.3 shows a difference of 20% between an ICEV and a Malaysia's Electricity Mix charged EV. Hydrogen and solar PV energy sources supplied for EV charging are a better option. Based on the amount of monthly fuel sales, if Malaysia were to replace about 50% of ICEV with EVs, the country's GHG emissions could see a significant reduction (Fig. 7.4). However, the choice of 50% is not an absolute target; higher adoption rates could lead to even greater emissions reductions. Nevertheless, this transition is not without challenges. A large-scale shift to EVs would place additional demands on Malaysia's electricity grid, potentially leading to over-extension and reliability issues if infrastructure is not scaled up in tandem (Energy Commission 2022). Furthermore, if the energy mix continues to rely heavily on fossil fuels, increased electricity consumption for EV charging could offset some of the emissions reductions, undermining the environmental benefits of EV adoption.

The construction of charging infrastructure also raises concerns about its environmental impact, as the materials and processes used may contribute to emissions unless sourced sustainably (Ministry of Transport Malaysia 2023). Addressing these challenges requires strategic planning, including integrating RE into the grid, enhancing grid resilience and ensuring that charging stations are built with sustainability in mind. While a 50% replacement offers a tangible goal, achieving a higher percentage in the long term will depend on Malaysia's ability to address these systemic issues holistically.

Table 7.3 Average emissions per Vehicle km travelled by energy source (IEA 2024)

	ICEV (gCO_2/km)	Solar PV (gCO_2/km)	Hydrogen (gCO_2/km)	Electricity Mix (gCO_2/km)
Average	157.4	36.0	9.0	307.0

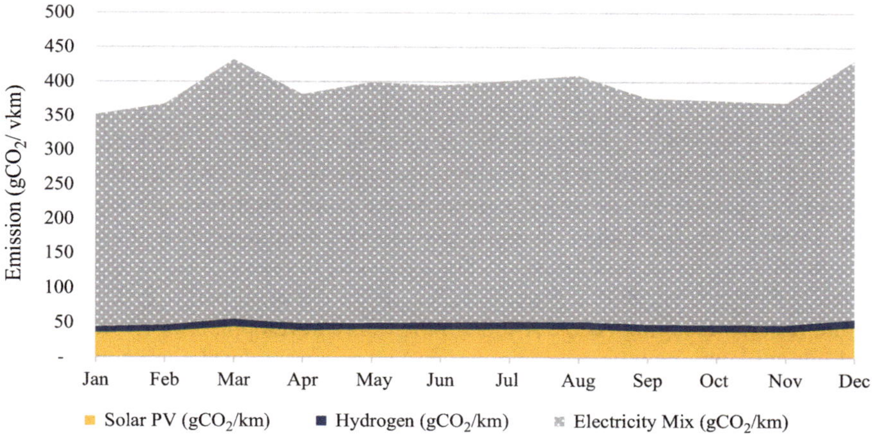

Fig. 7.4 Average monthly EV emissions per km travelled

5 EV Policy Implications and Barriers

Currently, one of the main reasons why Malaysians are reluctant to adopt EVs is the hefty road tax. The Transport Ministry is ready to introduce a new road tax system for EVs based on the wattage of the vehicle. With this modification, prospective purchasers who are considering purchasing an EV will know exactly how much road tax they will be paying. Such a measure has shown results in the past: significant fiscal incentives spurred the initial uptake of electric light-duty vehicles (LDVs) and underpinned the scale-up in EV manufacturing and battery industries.

In Malaysia, the adoption of EVs has been hindered by limited charging infrastructure, a significant barrier to widespread use. While the government has taken steps to encourage EV uptake, such as exempting import and excise duties on EVs, the deployment of charging infrastructure remains underdeveloped compared to other countries. Efforts have been made to install publicly accessible chargers in urban areas and along major highways, but coverage is insufficient for comprehensive national use. Barriers to deployment include high installation costs, regulatory hurdles and low EV penetration, which discourage private sector investment. Unlike the more aggressive measures seen in other countries, such as the establishment of low-emission zones or extensive networks of fast chargers, Malaysia's progress has been slower, partly due to budgetary constraints and the lack of a unified national EV strategy. Addressing these barriers will require coordinated policies, incentives for private investment and a clearer roadmap for EV infrastructure expansion.

End-of-life or waste management issues are significant barriers to EV adoption, particularly due to challenges in handling and recycling used batteries. In Malaysia, efforts are being made to develop policies and infrastructure for proper EV battery disposal and recycling. These initiatives include pilot programmes for battery collection, partnerships with private recycling firms, and the exploration of second-life applications for retired EV batteries. Across East Asia, the rapid growth of the EV market has exacerbated battery waste issues. Although many EV batteries (12% according to the IEA 2024) are exported for reuse or recycling, significant volumes remain, posing environmental challenges. A strong emphasis on waste management policies will be critical to ensuring the sustainable growth of the EV industry.

Policymakers supporting EV development may want to consider offering more incentive programmes for improvements in the connection between EVs and the grid. In ten years, local and provincial governments should create and implement a programme to support landlords and strata councils in their efforts to upgrade their buildings' power distribution systems and create retrofit plans that will accommodate future resident charging needs. Although the future development of EV technology and infrastructure may be a game changer, Malaysia as a developing country must focus on working to stabilise the medium to excel in EV deployment policy before upgrades.

6 Implications

A review of research on EV charging technology highlights the environmental impact. Unidirectional (V1G) charging significantly reduces emissions, while smart charging, especially overnight, lowers the carbon footprint. Prioritising home and public AC chargers is crucial for minimising environmental effects. Optimising all-Electric ranges and utilising innovative battery designs contribute to greenhouse gas reductions. Additionally, strategic EV charging, paired with cleaner electricity, minimises peak demand and overall emissions.

In terms of charging infrastructure, solar PV systems in carport canopies reduce carbon emissions by 94%, emphasising clean energy potential. EV charging shared at multi-unit dwellings shows an 86% reduction in greenhouse gas emissions. Such infrastructure expansion should take into account carbon emission equivalencies of various energy sources and related embodied emissions through life cycle assessments. For example, exploring biofuels for EVs offers possibilities through incorporation in existing fuel networks. Quantitative evaluations of station expansion reveal the intricate interplay between growth, regional air quality and greenhouse gas reduction.

Moreover, cleaner alternatives to traditional grid-tapped stations should be urged. The integration of photovoltaic (PV) systems stands out, offering significant reductions in carbon footprint and ecological impact. Advancements in battery technologies, particularly second-life batteries, show superior environmental performance. While strategies like smart charging hold promise in emissions reduction, careful consideration of potential marginal increases is crucial. Overall, these collective findings stress the critical importance of holistic approaches in designing, locating and operating EV charging stations for a more sustainable future in electric transportation.

Finally, based on the case study presented, the comparison between the Golf TDI (Diesel) and e-Golf indicates that EVs are more environmentally friendly over their entire life cycle. However, while diesel vehicles emit more during usage, the manufacturing phase of EVs contributes to their emissions. However, EVs, when charged with a cleaner energy mix, demonstrate significantly lower emissions per kilometre compared to traditional vehicles. Transitioning to EVs, especially with RE sources, offers a promising solution to reduce overall greenhouse gas emissions and contribute to a more sustainable future for Malaysia. Developing and implementing EV charging infrastructure should take into consideration a thorough understanding of its environmental footprint. By employing life cycle assessments, utilising smart charging and alternative energy sources, designing efficient and strategically located infrastructure, and maximising resource sustainability, we can minimise the environmental impact of charging stations while maximising their benefits in promoting the transition towards cleaner transportation. A holistic approach that considers the various aspects discussed in this chapter is crucial for ensuring the long-term sustainability of EV charging infrastructure and its role in mitigating the environmental impact of the transportation sector.

References

Ahmad Affandi NA et al (2022) The resiliency of photovoltaic applied fuelling station in Malaysia : a dynamic Urban emission displacement assessment. Clean Eng Technol 11(November):100584. https://doi.org/10.1016/j.clet.2022.100584

ASEAN Secretariat Indonesia (2023) Asean leaders' declaration on asean as an epicentrum of growth. ASEAN Indonesia 2023.

Bernama (1997) Dr Mahathir Launches 'Eleksuria', Country's First Electric Vehicle. http://lib.perdana.org.my/PLF/Digital_Content/Prominent_Leaders/Mahathir/News_1968-2004/1996-1998/1997aj/dr%20mahathir%20laectric%20vehicle.pdf [accessed 15 January 2025]

Bernama (1998) 300 electric cars for commonwealth games

Bi Z et al (2019) Life cycle assessment and tempo-spatial optimization of deploying dynamic wireless charging technology for electric cars. Transp Res Part C Emerg Technol 100(January):53–67. https://doi.org/10.1016/j.trc.2019.01.002

Bothe D, Steinfort T (2020) Cradle-to-Grave life-cycle assessment in the mobility sector a meta-analysis of LCA studies on alternative powertrain technologies. Forschungsvereinigung Verbrennungskraftmaschinen e.V, Frankfurt am Main

Brogan C (2025) Prioritise tackling toxic emissions from tyres, Urge Imperial Experts. *Imperial News*. https://www.imperial.ac.uk/news/243333/prioritise-tackling-toxic-emissions-from-tyres/ [accessed 16 January 2025].

Daly E, Singham S (2011) Jump-starting Malaysia's growth: an interview with Idris Jala. *McKinsey Quarterly* (October): 1–7. https://www.mckinsey.com/~/media/McKinsey/Industries/Public%20Sector/Our%20Insights/Jump%20starting%20Malaysias%20growth%20An%20interview%20with%20Idris%20Jala/Jump%20starting%20Malaysias%20growth%20An%20interview%20with%20Idris%20Jala.pdf [accessed 15 January 2025]

Doluweera G et al (2020) A scenario-based study on the impacts of electric vehicles on energy consumption and sustainability in Alberta. Appl Energy 268(January):114961. https://doi.org/10.1016/j.apenergy.2020.114961

Edenseven (2025) Britain's electricity generation—annual review. Edenseven.co.uk, 16 January 2025. https://www.edenseven.co.uk/national-grid-eso-analysis-annual-review-24 [accessed 6 February 2025]

Electric Motor Engineering (2022) Life cycle assessment, electric car wins. https://www.electricmotorengineering.com/life-cycle-assessment-electric-car-wins/ [accessed 12 December, 2024]

Energy Commission (2022) Energy Malaysia. Suruhanjaya Tenaga (Energy Commission), vol 22. https://www.st.gov.my/contents/files/download/112/Energy_Malaysia_Vol_22.pdf [accessed 12 February 2025]

Faisal S et al. (2024) Reducing the ecological footprint and charging cost of electric vehicle charging station using renewable energy based power system. E-Prime Adv Elect Eng Electr Energy 7(March):100398. https://doi.org/10.1016/j.prime.2023.100398

Fakour H et al (2023) Evaluation of solar photovoltaic carport canopy with electric vehicle charging potential. Sci Rep 13(1):1–13. https://doi.org/10.1038/s41598-023-29223-6

Gauto MA et al. (2023) Hybrid vigor: why hybrids with sustainable biofuels are better than pure electric vehicles. Energy Sust Devel 76(June). https://doi.org/10.1016/j.esd.2023.101261

Horesh N, Zhou Y, Quinn J (2023) Home charging for all: techno-economic and life cycle assessment of multi-unit dwelling electric vehicle charging hubs. J Clean Product 383(July 2022):135551. https://doi.org/10.1016/j.jclepro.2022.135551

Hydrogen Europe Intelligence Department (2020) Hydrogen demand and supply in the EU, *Hydrogen Europe Clean Hydrogen Monitor*, pp 6–22. https://hydrogeneurope.eu/wp-content/uploads/2021/11/Clean-Hydrogen-Monitor-2020.pdf [accessed 12 December 2024]

IEA (International Energy Agency) (2021) Global EV Outlook 2021 Accelerating Ambitions Despite the Pandemic, Paris. https://iea.blob.core.windows.net/assets/ed5f4484-f556-4110-8c5c-4ede8bcba637/GlobalEVOutlook2021.pdf [accessed 12 December, 2024].

IEA (International Energy Agency) (2023) Global EV Outlook 2023, Paris. https://iea.blob.core.windows.net/assets/dacf14d2-eabc-498a-8263-9f97fd5dc327/GEVO2023.pdf [accessed 12 December 2024]

IEA (International Energy Agency) (2024) Energy System of Malaysia, Paris. https://www.iea.org/countries/malaysia [accessed 15 January 2025]

IRENA (International Renewable Energy Agency) (2022) World Energy Transitions Outlook 2022. https://www.irena.org/Digital-Report/World-Energy-Transitions-Outlook-2022 [accessed 12 December, 2024]

IRENA (International Renewable Energy Agency) (2023) Renewable energy statistics 2023. https://www.irena.org/-/media/Files/IRENA/Agency/Publication/2023/Jul/IRENA_Renewable_energy_statistics_2023.pdf [accessed 12 December, 2024]

Javid RJ, Salari M, Javid RJ (2019) Environmental and economic impacts of expanding electric vehicle public charging infrastructure in California′s counties. Transp Res Part d: Transp Environ 77:320–334. https://doi.org/10.1016/j.trd.2019.10.017

Jumaat NAS, Halip Khalid AA (2024) A comprehensive review of challenges, prospects, and future perspectives for hydrogen energy development in Malaysia. Intern J Hydr Energy 55(August 2023):65–77. https://doi.org/10.1016/j.ijhydene.2023.11.058

Karib SA (2023) Malaysia country report. *17th Asia Construct Conference*, New Delhi, India. Business Environment Development Sector Construction Industry Development Board (CIDB) Malaysia. https://asiaconst.com/asiacwp/wp-content/uploads/2024/08/17th_Malaysia_Country-Report.pdf [accessed 13 Jan 2024]

Krim Y et al (2022) Global cost and carbon impact assessment methodology for electric vehicles' PV-powered charging station. Appl Sci (Switzerland) 12:9. https://doi.org/10.3390/app12094115

Kumar M, Poudineh R, Shamsuddin A (2021) Electricity supply industry reform and design of competitive electricity market in Malaysia, Oxford Institute for Energy Studies. https://www.oxfordenergy.org/wpcms/wp-content/uploads/2021/01/Electricity-Supply-Industry-Reform-and-Design-of-Competitive-Electricity-Market-in-Malaysia.pdf [accessd 15 January 2025]

Lee DS et al. (2023) Which form of transport has the smallest carbon footprint? Our World in Data 244(August). https://doi.org/10.1016/j.atmosenv.2020.117834

Lim A (2023) Development of EV charging infrastructure in malaysia led by private sector. The Star Online. https://paultan.org/2023/11/24/development-of-ev-charging-infrastructure-in-malaysia-led-by-private-sector-govt-not-involved-minister/ [accessed 12 December 2024]
Lubecki A, Szczurowski J, Zarębska K (2023) A comparative environmental life cycle assessment study of hydrogen fuel, electricity and diesel fuel for public buses. Appl Energy 350(June) https://www.sciencedirect.com/science/article/pii/S0306261923011303 [accessed 12 December, 2024]. https://doi.org/10.1016/j.apenergy.2023.121766
Ludin NA et al. (2021) Sustainability and life-cycle cost analysis of solar photovoltaic-generation systems in ASEAN countries, in *Energy Sustainability and Climate Change in ASEAN*, ed. Han Phoumin et al., pp 277–302. Singapore: Springer. https://doi.org/10.1007/978-981-16-2000-3_12
Malaysian Investment Development Authority (2023) Tengku Zafrul Says Govt Eyes a 'Good Slice' of Projected US$2.7b Asean EV Market. https://www.mida.gov.my/mida-news/tengku-zafrul-says-govt-eyes-a-good-slice-of-projected-us2-7b-asean-ev-market/
Malaysian Ministry of Economy (2023) *National Energy Transition Roadmap*
Malaysian Ministry of Finance (2024) Budget 2024 highlights. https://www.mof.gov.my/portal/en/news/press-citations/budget-2024-highlights [accessed 12 December 2024]
Maybank Investment Bank (2024) "Maybank: ASEAN EV adoption will continue to increase due to favourable regulations, Technode.Global. https://technode.global/2024/04/12/maybank-asean-ev-adoption-will-continue-to-increase-due-to-favourable-regulations/?utm_source=chatgpt.com [accessed 15 January 2025]
Meinrenken CJ, Shou Z, Di X (2020) Using GPS-data to determine optimum electric vehicle ranges: a michigan case study. Transp Res Part d: Transp Environ 78:102203. https://doi.org/10.1016/j.trd.2019.102203
MGTC (Malaysian Green Technology And Climate Change Corporation) (2023) MGTC drafting strategic framework to develop EV charging infrastructure. https://www.mgtc.gov.my/2023/02/malaysian-government-drafting-strategic-framework-to-develop-ev-charging-infrastructure-report/ [accessed 12 December 2024]
MIDA (Malaysian Investment Development Authority) (2023) Shifting the EV Sector to the Next Gear. https://www.mida.gov.my/mida-news/shifting-the-ev-sector-to-the-next-gear/#:~:text=In%20its%20retabled%20Budget%202023%2C%20the%20government,of%20Budget%202023%20to%20December%2031%2C%202024 [accessed 12 December, 2024]
MIDA (Malaysian Investment Development Authority) (2024) MITI Working with Selangor, Johor Governments to Expand EV Charging Infrastructure. https://www.mida.gov.my/mida-news/miti-working-with-selangor-johor-governments-to-expand-ev-charging-infrastructure/
Ministry of Transport (MOT) Malaysia (2023) National Transport Policy 2019–2030
MPC (Malaysia Productivity Corporation) (2024) Robust EV ecosystem to power up productivity. https://www.mpc.gov.my/robust-ev-ecosystem-to-power-up-productivity
MTE (Malaysia Technology Expo) (2023) Malaysia EV Tech 2023: Paving the Way for Malaysia's Electric Future. https://mtexpo.mte.org.my/2023/11/09/malaysia-ev-tech-mevtech-2023/ [accessed 12 December 2024]
Mulrow J, Grubert E (2023) Greenhouse gas emissions embodied in electric vehicle charging infrastructure: a method and case study of Georgia, US 2021–2050. Environm Res Infrastr Sust 3(1):015013. https://doi.org/10.1088/2634-4505/acc548
PEMANDU (Performance Management and Delivery Unit) (2010) Economic transformation programme: a roadmap for Malaysia. https://pemandu.org/wp-content/uploads/2023/05/Economic-Transformation-Programme-Roadmap.pdf [accessed 15 January 2025]
PLANMalaysia and MGTC (2025) "MEVnet". https://www.planmalaysia.gov.my/mevnet/
Pourrahmani H, Xu C, Van herle J (2022) "Two novel cogeneration charging stations for electric vehicles: energy, exergy, economic, environment, and dynamic characterizations. Energy Convers Manag 271(October):116314. https://www.sciencedirect.com/science/article/pii/S0196890422010925 [accessed 12 December, 2024]. https://doi.org/10.1016/j.enconman.2022.116314

Ravimalar R (2024) Energy: can Malaysia be a hydrogen hub? *The Edge Malaysia*. 18 July. https://theedgemalaysia.com/node/718769 [accessed 15 January 2025]
Robbins J (2025) Road Hazard: evidence mounts on toxic pollution from tires, *Yale Environment 360*. https://e360.yale.edu/features/tire-pollution-toxic-chemicals [accessed 16 January 2025]
Schmidt M, Crawford RH (2018) A framework for the integrated optimisation of the life cycle greenhouse gas emissions and cost of buildings. Energy Build 171:155–167. https://doi.org/10.1016/j.enbuild.2018.04.018
Tang Y et al (2021) Reducing the life cycle environmental impact of electric vehicles through emissions-responsive charging. Iscience 24(12):103499. https://doi.org/10.1016/j.isci.2021.103499
Technode Global Staff (2024) Analysts foresee increased localization investment in Malaysia's EV sector next year, TNGlobal. https://technode.global/2024/12/23/analysts-foresee-increased-localization-investment-in-malaysias-ev-sector-next-year/?utm_source=chatgpt.com
US Environmental Protection Agency (EPA) (2023) Greenhouse gases equivalencies calculator—calculations and references | US EPA, 1–38
Wilson, Lindsay (2023) Shades of green: electric car emissions—2023. Shrink That Footprint. https://shrinkthatfootprint.com/electric-car-emissions/#.UWMjH5xsYH4.email [accessed 22 January 2025]
Wohlschlager D, Haas S, Neitz-Regett A (2022) Comparative environmental impact assessment of ICT for smart charging of electric vehicles in Germany. Procedia CIRP 105(March):583–588. https://doi.org/10.1016/j.procir.2022.02.097. https://www.sciencedirect.com/science/article/pii/S2212827122000981
World Bank Group (n.d) GNI per Capita, Atlas Method (Current US$). https://data.worldbank.org/indicator/NY.GNP.PCAP.CD [accessed 13 January 2025]
World Benchmarking Alliance (2019) Climate and energy benchmark—electric utilities benchmark. Worldbenchmarkingalliance.Org. https://www.worldbenchmarkingalliance.org/publication/electric-utilities/2021/companies/tenaga-nasional-2/ [accessed 6 February 2025]
Yusry M (2024) Mosti: hydrogen-powered car technology ready in Malaysia. Malaymail.Com. 2024. https://www.malaymail.com/news/malaysia/2024/04/01/mosti-hydrogen-powered-car-technology-ready-in-malaysia/126633
Zhang Z et al (2019) Life cycle environmental assessment of charging infrastructure for electric vehicles in China. J Clean Prod 227:932–941. https://doi.org/10.1016/j.jclepro.2019.04.167
Zhong Z, Yu Y, Zhao X (2023) Revisiting electric vehicle life cycle greenhouse gas emissions in china: a marginal emission perspective. IsCience 26(5):106565. https://doi.org/10.1016/j.isci.2023.106565

The Energy Transition in Smart Cities: Practical Insights into Environmental Performance Framework Development

Noor Raida Abd Rahman, Siti Indati Mustapa, and Maslinawati Mohamad

Abstract This chapter reviews the theoretical and empirical literature on smart city performance and its relationship with the energy transition, and explores the challenges associated with assessing environmental performance in smart cities of the Association of Southeast Asian Nations (ASEAN). More specifically, it proposes a framework for evaluating smart city performance in the context of smart cities situated in Malaysia. The study constructed an environmental performance framework (EPF) consisting of eight indicators, comprising a total of 23 items. Our analysis indicates that the mean EPF score for firms in smart cities is 21%, representing a fraction of the total maximum achievable score. The results suggest that concerted efforts are required from both governmental bodies and businesses to facilitate firms' contributions to the energy transition within smart cities.

1 Introduction

As the world continues to use more energy and emit greenhouse gases (GHGs), the global environment becomes an issue of pressing concern. Cities play a significant role in climate change, contributing 75% of worldwide carbon dioxide (CO_2) emissions, with transport and buildings being among the largest contributors (Abubakar and Alshammari 2023). The urgent issue of climate change and the associated GHGs has become more pronounced as cities within the ASEAN region continue to expand (Sandu et al. 2019). The consequences of the intense growth of urbanisation, coupled with the accelerating impact of climate change, underscore the critical need for a transformative energy transition (Horng et al. 2021). The emergence of smart cities offers a potential solution to address these challenges (Nguyen, Nawara and Kashef 2024). Smart cities are expected to form a cornerstone for achieving resource

N. R. Abd Rahman (✉) · S. I. Mustapa
Universiti Tenaga Nasional, Kajang, Malaysia
e-mail: NorRaida@uniten.edu.my

M. Mohamad
Universiti Teknologi MARA, Puncak Alam, Malaysia

H. Phoumin et al. (eds.), *Tackling the Energy Transition: Insights from ASEAN and Beyond*, Climate Change and Energy Transition,
https://doi.org/10.1007/978-981-96-6019-3_8

efficiency, potentially yielding substantial energy savings and heightened resource optimisation, particularly in energy usage (Angelakoglou et al. 2019).

Despite the escalating interest and momentum surrounding smart city projects and initiatives, advancements in the evaluation and measurement of their performance have been comparatively slow, leading to unjustified decisions and unnecessary investments (Angelakoglou et al. 2019). As a result, this deficiency could cause setbacks in achieving the energy transition (Lai and Cole 2023). Given these challenges, there is a clear requirement to expedite thorough performance evaluation measures for smart cities. Appropriate evaluation mechanisms and indicators are required for proper city comparison, setting of requirements during planning phases, and project performance evaluation (Manoharan et al. 2023). This is necessary to ensure that smart cities proactively drive the rapid and effective promotion of sustainable energy practices and help countries achieve their energy transition goals. Despite several studies suggesting frameworks for smart city implementation, there is limited research about smart city assessments in developing economies. In particular, there has been little focus on assessing smart city performance (Mohd Adnan et al. 2016) or whether smart city practices deliver environmental sustainability (Cai et al. 2023). Zhao et al.'s (2021) systematic review of smart city research revealed that only 20 out of 191 publications specifically addressed the measurement and evaluation of smart city performance, which lends support to this observation.

This chapter aims to explore the concept of smart city performance and its relationship with the energy transition. By analysing challenges related to performance evaluation measures specific to smart cities and reviewing existing performance assessment schemes, we propose a framework for measuring smart city performance within the context of a smart environment. In striving to achieve this goal and delivering practical insights, the chapter seeks to add to the ongoing discussions surrounding the notion of the energy transition within the ASEAN region.

The Malaysian government has prioritised addressing environmental concerns at various levels, aiming to decrease carbon footprints and diminish reliance on non-renewable energy (RE) sources. With the robust implementation of the Green Agenda outlined in the 12th Malaysia Plan, smart city initiatives have been strategically integrated into urban planning, placing emphasis on environmental considerations and the well-being of residents to foster sustainable and environmentally conscious development. Hence, the research in this chapter exclusively focuses on smart environments within the context of the Malaysia Smart City Framework (MSCF). The chapter presents a novel research endeavour involving a comprehensive evaluation of smart environment models tailored for firms within smart cities. It introduces an Environmental Performance Framework (EPF) crafted through meticulous adherence to relevant guidelines, standards and reporting schemes, coupled with a systematic literature analysis. The EPF is subsequently assessed across ten Malaysian cities—Kuala Lumpur, Putrajaya, Cyberjaya, Shah Alam, Melaka, Kota Kinabalu, Kuching, Johor Bahru, Georgetown and Kulim—and scrutinises eight key indicators: carbon emissions reduction, energy management, green space and biodiversity preservation, RE sources, namely, smart building technology and management system, environment monitoring applications, water conservation efforts and waste management.

The chapter is structured into five sections. The introduction is followed by a literature review of the theoretical and empirical studies defining the concept of a smart city, with a specific focus on "smart environment" and its relationship with the energy transition. The literature review section also gives a general overview of the issues that ASEAN smart cities are facing in relation to environmental performance measurement. In the third section, we propose an EPF by synthesising insights from relevant guidelines, standards and reporting schemes, as well as a systematic literature analysis. This process allowed us to identify the indicators for the EPF that are anticipated to be implemented by firms in smart cities. In the fourth section, our findings are presented to exemplify the application of the EPF within the ten smart cities mentioned. The last section focuses on discussion and further research.

2 Literature Review and Background

2.1 Smart Cities

The significance of smart cities in advancing sustainability is widely acknowledged in academic literature and practical implementation. The concept of smart cities has evolved into a transformative urban development paradigm, utilising cutting-edge technologies and an intelligent information infrastructure to improve the quality of life, sustainability and efficiency in urban spaces (Söderström et al. 2020). This is achieved through the integration of various dimensions of urban development and investments (Sta 2017). However, there is no universally adopted definition for smart cities (Abu-Rayash and Dincer 2021; Samsudin et al. 2022). A multitude of terms are used interchangeably in this field, including smart sustainable cities, intelligent cities, sustainable cities, eco-cities, future city, green city, resilient cities, low-carbon city and digital city (De Jong et al. 2015). Commonly encountered comprehensive concepts are "intelligent city" and "digital city" (Martins et al. 2021; Zhao et al. 2021). The different terms exist due to the different scopes considered (Lai and Cole 2023).

Numerous scholars have explored various facets of smart cities, encompassing concepts such as the digital city, green city, intelligent city, knowledge city, sustainable city and wired city (Okafor et al. 2023). Through a meticulous analysis of structured literature reviews, Gracias et al. (2023) discern multiple definitions of smart cities and conclude that "smart cities use digital technologies, communication technologies, and data analytics to create an efficient and effective service environment that improves urban quality of life and promotes sustainability". In the ASEAN context, the term smart city is defined as one that strategically employs technological and digital solutions alongside innovative non-technological means to address urban challenges, continuously improving people's lives and creating new opportunities (Centre for Liveable Cities, Singapore 2018).

The idea of a smart city has been around since International Business Machines (IBM) Corporation first introduced the term in 2011, signalling a new era of urbanisation driven mainly by the convergence of emerging technologies such as the Internet of Things (IoT), artificial intelligence and the "cloud" in the urban space. In the view of the company, founded in 1911, much of the idea focused on technical and managerial fixes to increase the efficiency of urban spaces, and the "smarter" label was simply based on their engagement with data and digital technologies. The idea of a smart city, though, has changed over the years. However, while early readings were predominantly technocratic and concerned with state power exercised through data, the notion soon stretched beyond the gates of political philosophy and extended into society and the environment (Abu-Rayash and Dincer 2021; Guo et al. 2022). Still, information and communication technology (ICT) remains central, enabling real-time connectivity and management across key urban systems such as transportation, energy, water and communication. However, contemporary views also emphasise the importance of social inclusion, environmental sustainability and citizen engagement, marking a shift from a purely managerial model to a more holistic approach (Karal and Soyer 2023). The modern concept of a smart city includes a "smart economy, smart mobility, smart environment, smart people, smart living and smart governance" (Wyrwicka et al. 2023). The smart economy encompasses entrepreneurship, income equality and economic development. The smart people dimension involves factors such as qualification levels, social and ethnic diversity, flexibility, creativity and participation in public life. Smart governance is characterised by local smart strategy, participation, access to data and transparent governance. In the realm of smart mobility, considerations include local and international accessibility, smart and green transportation, and sustainable and innovative transport systems. The smart environment dimension encompasses aspects like pollution, natural resource management, waste management and the built environment. Lastly, the smart living dimension encapsulates culture and education, health conditions, smart healthcare and safety (Sotirelis et al. 2022). The hallmark of a smart city lies in its ability to leverage information and communication capabilities that contribute to these six dimensions (Karal and Soyer 2023).

The smart city is perceived as a strategic response to challenges encountered by city governments, such as rapid urbanisation and significant demographic changes, climate and environmental changes, economic restructuring and reforms, and digital technology disruptions (Tompson 2017; Dawood 2023). There is a widespread consensus that the fundamental aim of smart cities is to augment economic growth and foster social development by leveraging technological innovations and promoting increased collaboration (Sarma and Sunny 2017). Smart city implementation may lead to high-quality, more resilient, liveable and sustainable development for a nation (Samsudin et al. 2022). A sound smart city innovation strategy can simultaneously generate benefits for the environment and stakeholders and create long-term competitive advantages for firms (Almihat et al. 2022; Zhao et al. 2021).

2.2 Malaysian Smart Cities

The concept of smart city development is gaining momentum in Malaysia. Smart city initiatives in Malaysia have been included in the Eleventh Malaysia Plan (11MP [2016–2020]), the Twelfth Malaysia Plan (12MP [2021–2025]), the third National Physical Plan (NPP3), and the National Urbanisation Policy 2 (NUP2 [2016]) (Chong et al. 2022). The smart cities initiative in the country also encompasses prominent industrial sectors, including ICT, GreenTech, Smart Grid, Transportation and Infrastructure. It also addresses crucial policy concerns such as 5G, cybersecurity and RE. The advancement of smart cities in Malaysia, in line with the overarching objectives outlined in the MSCF (2018), aligns with the transition towards sustainable energy systems and the mitigation of climate change. These initiatives underscore the pivotal role of smart city development in addressing Malaysia's urbanisation challenges and their implications for sustainability (Horng et al. 2021).

The Association of Southeast Asian Nations (ASEAN) Smart Cities Network (ASCN), initiated during the 32nd ASEAN Summit on 28 April 2018, encompasses 26 pilot cities and has the aim of sharing lessons and resources towards a common goal of smart and sustainable urban environments. Four out of the 26 cited locations are in Malaysia, namely Kuala Lumpur, Kota Kinabalu in Sabah, Kuching in Sarawak and Johor Bahru in Johor. Other smart cities in Malaysia are Shah Alam, Cyberjaya, Putrajaya, Melaka, Georgetown, Kulim and Labuan. The ongoing development of smart cities in Malaysia is characterised by diverse pilot projects and programmes aimed at industrial development. These initiatives align with the overarching vision to transform the Federal Territories, i.e., Putrajaya, Kuala Lumpur and Labuan, into fully realised smart cities by the year 2030.

The MSCF has defined a smart city as one that uses "ICT and technological advancement to address urban issues including to improve quality of life, promote economic growth, develop sustainable and safe environment and encourage efficient urban management practices" (Ministry of Housing and Local Government, Malaysia 2018, p. 7). Smart city Malaysia aims at addressing urban issues and challenges in the drive to achieve the three main pillars: a competitive economy, sustainable environment and enhanced quality of life. According to the Malaysian Industry-Government Group for High Technology (MIGHT), therefore, a smart city is characterised by the use of information and communication technology (ICT) and technological advancements to achieve a better quality of life and smart living (Samsudin et al. 2022, p. 17).

The *Malaysia Smart City Outlook 2021–2022* [*MSCO 2021–2022*] delineates the essential elements of a smart city across seven pillars: smart economy, smart government, smart community, smart digital infrastructure, smart mobility, smart living and smart environment, as presented in Table 8.1.

Table 8.1 Components of Malaysia's smart city conceptualisation

Component	Definition
Smart economy	A "smart economy" is defined by the *MSCO 2021–2022* as "a favourable environment for economic growth, overcoming economic challenges, creating new jobs as well as establishing new and productive technology businesses which are regionally attractive, competitive and innovative. Smart Economy embraces entrepreneurship with market flexibility that respond to and integrate global needs and demands" (p. 8)
Smart government	"Smart Government is defined as the adoption into a city, operations and administration that improve efficiency and performance in the provision of services to citizens" (p. 14)
Smart community	A smart community is defined as one composed of "connected citizens who embrace and deploy technology to enable economic growth, social inclusion and environmental sustainability" (p. 22)
Smart digital infrastructure	"Smart digital infrastructure is the foundation of information technology development for any modern nation. It is fundamental to the economic growth of regions and cities across the world, helping to secure good social, health and environmental standards. A highly advanced infrastructure strengthens a nation's digital capacity and radically improves the quality of life in the long run" (p. 29)
Smart mobility	Smart mobility is defined as "the integration of new and emerging solutions to enhance mobility through the reduction of road congestion. It offers faster, greener and cheaper transportation options for the public. Smart mobility provides alternative modes of travel and puts emphasis on affordable transportation, whilst fostering sustainable lifestyles that are beneficial to the environment" (p. 38)
Smart living	Smart living is "about pursuing lifestyles that are smart, safe, clean, healthy and resilient. Smart living improves the quality of life as well as enriches the aesthetics of daily life in the city" (p. 47)
Smart environment	Smart environment is defined as "the deployment of appropriate technologies increasing more connected and comfortable urban environment, drawn from much-improved climate plans. Smart environment ensures that the built and natural environment provide the physical and mental well-being and all-round happiness of its habitants, as well as help to build a sustainable future" (p. 55)

2.3 *The Performance of Smart Cities and Its Relationship to the Energy Transition*

Smart city environmental performance is crucial for the energy transition due to its significant contribution to reducing energy-related GHG emissions. As cities account for over 70% of global energy consumption and CO_2 emissions, addressing carbon emissions at the urban level is essential for achieving meaningful reductions and mitigating the impacts of climate change (Shen et al. 2023). The transition to sustainable energy systems and the reduction of carbon emissions are key components of the broader energy transition, which aims to shift from fossil-based energy production and consumption to RE sources. The transition towards cleaner energy aligns with the systematic shift towards a low-carbon society, benefitting from the progress in both technological and institutional aspects within smart cities (Lim et al. 2019).

Measuring the comparative performance of smart cities is essential so that their effectiveness, success and ongoing progress can be judged (Tekin Bilbil 2017). Smart city performance can be considered as the city's capability to efficiently deliver core services using advanced technologies (Farmanbar and Rong 2020). It is often evaluated through the use of key performance indicators (KPIs) specific to each dimension (Abu-Rayash and Dincer 2021). The evaluation of a smart city's energy-carbon performance is crucial for understanding the effectiveness of smart city policies and technologies in reducing carbon emissions, increasing energy efficiency and transitioning to sustainable energy systems (Hoang and Nguyen 2021). The imperative to measure the smartness of a city lies in its ability to benchmark it against others (Manoharan et al. 2023). More crucially, it facilitates the identification of those specific smart features in which the city may lag behind others and thus provides a strategic focus for targeted improvements (Mohd Adnan et al. 2016). Additionally, it allows policymakers, researchers and city planners to assess the success and areas for improvement in the implementation of smart city strategies (Saez et al. 2020).

Approaching smart cities through the perspective of the energy transition can help address several development challenges such as human development, pollution and climate change adaptation, biodiversity, the logistics of a circular economy, natural calamity preparedness and energy consumption (Kutty et al. 2020). Smart city initiatives can bolster the energy transition through various means. Firstly, sustainable energy management practices such as utilising advanced metering infrastructures, energy storage systems, intelligent energy management systems and big data analytics, facilitate the real-time optimisation of energy usage and contribute to a more stable energy distribution. Through the implementation of smart metering, energy consumption patterns become monitorable and the data accumulated can significantly improve (Silva et al. 2018).

Secondly, smart city initiatives can bolster the energy transition by seamlessly integrating clean and sustainable energy sources. An effective, efficient approach to integrating, managing and monitoring renewable sources such as solar, wind, geothermal, hydropower, ocean and biofuels as the main energy inputs has been demonstrated to advance energy efficiency, reduce energy use (Konstantinou 2021), and make a significant contribution to reducing pollutant emissions (Hoang and Nguyen 2021). The integration of RE sources to improve efficiency in energy use so that maximum performance can be achieved and emissions can be minimised has been found to be a judicious solution (Kabeyi and Olanrewaju 2022).

Lastly, infrastructure can be enhanced to accommodate and leverage new energy technologies. Smart cities, with the ability to harness ICT for the energy transition, contribute to reduced energy consumption and CO_2 emissions (Lim, Edelenbos and Gianoli 2019; Wyrwicka et al. 2023). Smart city technologies can contribute to each process in the energy system (generation, distribution, storage and consumption) to increase energy efficiency (Calvillo et al. 2016). The use of core technologies in a smart city can increase energy efficiency and contribute to reducing energy consumption and CO_2 emissions (Geels et al. 2018; Shahrokni et al. 2015); these in turn support the energy transition (Lim et al. 2019).

In essence, the evaluation of environmental performance in smart cities plays a vital role in advancing energy transition objectives. This process empowers cities to effectively combat climate change and foster sustainable urban development with low carbon emissions through the methods mentioned above. By scrutinising the effects of smart city initiatives and policies on energy efficiency and carbon emissions reduction, cities can reinforce the theoretical linkage between smart city development and the pursuit of sustainable development goals. This, in turn, contributes significantly to the overall shift towards more sustainable energy systems (Almihat et al. 2022; Xia et al. 2023).

2.4 Challenges in Environmental Performance Assessment

Cities consume a significant amount of energy, mainly for lighting, heating, cooling and transportation, which contributes to greenhouse gas emissions (Le Thiez 2018). As urban populations continue to rapidly expand, the demand for essential resources, including energy, water and transportation, has increased accordingly (Paes et al. 2023). It is within this context that smart cities must proactively confront these challenges. Their aim is to attain ambitious net zero emissions objectives while simultaneously forging a path towards creating sustainable cities for future generations.

Comprehensive discussions on the fundamental elements and performance criteria essential for the success of smart cities are crucial. Additionally, recognising the importance of environmental performance becomes paramount for achieving energy savings and emissions reductions (Juan et al. 2023). These aspects enable cities to identify areas that require improvement and accurately track their progress towards sustainability objectives, allowing for more effective and informed decision-making in urban planning and development.

Nevertheless, as pointed out by Rozman, Azmi and Sukereman (2022), "researchers rarely discuss the specific elements and type of performance needed for smart cities to succeed". Within this context, inadequate sustainability assessment and the lack of environmental and energy indicators emerge as significant shortcomings in existing smart city frameworks (Ahvenniemi et al. 2017). Although specific indicators may be well-defined, the absence of methodologies to guide cities and experts during the deployment of such evaluation frameworks further compounds the issue (Quijano et al. 2022). The absence of a universally recognised and accepted evaluation framework for city assessments deepens the challenge, leading to variations in metrics, evaluation scopes, and the objectives and domains to be measured (Quijano et al. 2022). In particular, there is no standardised method for evaluating environmental performance in smart cities, making it difficult to compare performance across different cities (Martins et al. 2021). Furthermore, while reducing energy consumption remains a crucial objective for smart cities, the incorporation of energy related KPIs is currently constrained within existing smart city frameworks (Angelakoglou et al. 2019). Owing to the lack of standardised methods for evaluating smart cities, prior research often created overly complicated frameworks. The growing complexity of these models is likely to cause measurement errors and endogenous problems (Qian et al. 2023) and poses a challenge for city administrators, smart city implementers, urban planning officers, technology providers, information systems researchers, as well as rural and urban planners (Lacson et al. 2023). As a collective consequence of these issues, the practical applicability of such evaluation frameworks within real-world urban contexts is significantly constrained.

A traditional evaluation of carbon emissions reduction for smart cities requires many different types of high-quality data (Yan et al. 2021). The availability and quality of data on environmental performance, particularly on energy and carbon (Shahrokni et al. 2015), can be a challenge which can hinder the accurate evaluation of smart city performance (Dasgupta et al. 2022), particularly in some ASEAN countries. Most estimates rely on parameters from engineering studies that are applied to survey-based activity measures for transport, energy production and manufacturing. However, the validity of this approach may be particularly questionable when applied to developing countries (Dasgupta et al. 2022).

Past research highlights a significant issue in climate change reporting within ASEAN, with notably low disclosure rates for performance categories. This finding underscores the difficulties that companies encounter when seeking to comprehensively evaluate their environmental performance. Hence, there must be both uniform performance evaluation measures for smart cities and an update of the current literature's perspective on smart city elements and performance. With such a provision, the practical applicability of these evaluation frameworks within real-world urban contexts can be substantially enhanced, thus contributing to more effective and informed decision-making in urban planning and development.

3 Methodology

3.1 The Development of the Environmental Performance Framework (EPF)

This chapter, employing a qualitative analysis methodology, focuses on documents related to performance evaluation schemes. To gain insights into the typology of these selected schemes, guidelines, standards, reporting schemes and literature reviews were included. The initial step involved identifying and selecting items for the EPF, guided by relevant guidelines, standards, reporting schemes and previous literature (Coy and Dixon 2004). The selection process began by aggregating and scrutinising the indicators outlined in these documents and prior studies.

3.1.1 Relevant Guidelines, Standards and Reporting Schemes

In this study, the focus is exclusively on well-established guidelines, standards and reporting schemes, as developing a framework based on these references provides a significantly greater degree of information compared to any scoring system devised without recourse to such references (Morhardt et al. 2002). Moreover, these references are widely adopted due to their structured methodology, ability to measure progress over time, and potential for benchmarking against other cities (Grossi and Trunova 2021; Lacson et al. 2023). The study then concentrates on the guidelines provided by the OECD Smart City Measurement Framework, Global Reporting Initiative (GRI) ASEAN, the Carbon Disclosure Project (CDP) 2022, the WRI *Global Protocol for Community-Scale Greenhouse Gas Emission Inventories (Version 1.1)* 2014, the United Nations' Global Indicator Framework for the Sustainable Development Goals, the United for Smart Sustainable Cities (U4SSC) Initiative, the International Organization for Standardization (ISO)'s standards ISO37122:2019 – Indicators for Smart Cities and ISO37120:2018 – Indicators for City Services and Quality of Life, the ETSI (European Telecommunications Standards Institute) Technical Specification on KPIs for "Sustainable Digital Multiservice Cities" and the Malaysia Smart City Framework (MSCF). Table 8.2 shows the pertinent guidelines, standards and reporting schemes for assessing the performance of smart cities used in this study.

3.1.2 Scientific Publications

As posited by Rozman, Azmi and Sukereman (2022), it is imperative to build upon existing literature by incorporating updates in the evaluation of smart city performance. To collate and synthesise the studies of smart city environmental performance indicators, this study utilised the Scopus database to explore, select and identify studies from the literature. As exhibited in Table 8.3, there were two keywords used in the search string to identify relevant studies; smart city and smart city assessment and tools.

The Scopus search was refined to include conference papers, articles and book chapters, and highly relevant and qualitative literature was emphasised in selecting pertinent items. Within the Scopus database, a total of 445 results were found. To ensure the inclusion of internationally peer-reviewed literature, the search was restricted to English-language publications, resulting in 438 documents.

Smart city indicators vary across geographical regions and countries, with various existing indices differing in themes, measurement levels and scope. To enable meaningful comparisons, this study calls attention to the importance of standardising the scale and scope of smart city indices and of defining measurement scales according to the targeted unit, whether countries, cities or communities (Sharifi 2020). The study now discusses environmental performance indicators within the framework of smart city indices and then moves on to the firms in smart cities as the unit of analysis.

The qualitative analysis conducted in this study identifies key environmental performance indicators for firms in smart cities, as presented in Table 8.4.

Table 8.2 Existing performance assessment guidelines, standards and reporting schemes

Scheme	Definitions used
OECD Smart City Measurement Framework	Energy • Energy consumption per capita (kgoe per person) • Electricity production from renewable sources (%) Climate • CO_2 emissions per unit of electricity produced (in tons of CO_2 equivalent per gigawatt hour) • Level of people's satisfaction with efforts to preserve the environment (%) Biodiversity • Change in tree cover (percentage point) Material footprint • Municipal waste rate (kilos per capita) • Municipal waste that is recycled (%) • Number of road vehicles per 100 people • Change in land consumption per capita (square metres per capita)
GRI ASEAN	Climate • Total emissions (Scope 1, 2 and 3) • GHG emissions reduction as a direct result of reduction initiatives, in metric tons of CO_2 equivalent • Fuel consumption reduction as a direct result of reduction initiatives, in metric tons of CO_2 equivalent • Fuel consumption within the organisation and outside the organisation from renewable sources • The amount of reductions in energy consumption achieved as a direct result of conservation and efficiency initiatives
CDP 2022	Energy • Base year emissions (absolute) target • Fixed-level target • Base year intensity target based on emissions per capita • Base year intensity target based on emissions per unit of GDP • Baseline scenario target **Note: information can be used to measure performance against target*

(continued)

Table 8.2 (continued)

Scheme	Definitions used
WRI *Global Protocol for Community-Scale Greenhouse Gas Emission Inventories (Version 1.1)* 2014	Information on emission changes • "If a city has set a mitigation goal, it shall identify the year chosen as the base year and report base year emissions • If the city is using an inventory to track progress toward a mitigation goal, the city shall identify a significance threshold that triggers base year emissions recalculation (such as acquisition of existing neighboring communities, changes in reporting boundaries or calculation methodologies, etc." (p. 39) Evaluating performance against goal • "Base year emissions goals represent a reduction in emissions relative to an emissions level in a historical base year • Fixed level goals represent a reduction in emissions to an absolute emissions level in a target year" (p. 138) • "Base year intensity goals represent a reduction in emissions intensity relative to an emissions intensity level in a historical base year" (p. 138) • "Baseline scenario goals represent a reduction in emissions relative to a baseline scenario emissions level" (p. 139)
UN Global Indicator Framework for the SDGs (2023)	Goal 7 • Proportion of population with access to electricity • Proportion of population with primary reliance on clean fuels and technology • RE share in total final energy consumption (TFEC) • Energy intensity measured in terms of primary energy and GDP Goal 12 • Material footprint, material footprint per capita, and material footprint per GDP • Domestic material consumption, domestic material consumption per capita, and domestic material consumption per GDP • "Number of parties to international multilateral environmental agreements on hazardous waste and other chemicals that meet reporting obligations (p. 14) • Hazardous waste generated per capita • Proportion of hazardous waste treated, by type of treatment • National recycling rate, by tons of material recycled Goal 13 • Total greenhouse gas emissions per year

(continued)

Table 8.2 (continued)

Scheme	Definitions used
U4SSC initiative	Air Quality • Air pollution • GHG Emissions Water and Sanitation • Drinking Water Quality • Water Consumption • Freshwater Consumption Waste • Wastewater Treatment • Solid Waste Treatment Environmental Quality • EMF (electromagnetic field) Exposure Public Space and Nature • Green Areas Energy • RE consumption • Electricity consumption • Residential thermal energy consumption • Public building energy consumption
ISO37122: 2019	Energy • Percentage of electrical and thermal energy produced from wastewater treatment, solid waste and other liquid waste treatment and other waste heat resources, as a share of the city's total energy mix for a given year • Electrical and thermal energy (GJ) produced from wastewater treatment per capita per year • Electrical and thermal energy (GJ) produced from solid waste or other liquid waste treatment per capita per year • Percentage of the city's electricity that is produced using decentralised electricity production systems • Storage capacity of the city's energy grid per total city energy consumption • Percentage of street lighting managed by a light performance management system • Percentage of street lighting that has been refurbished and newly installed • Percentage of public buildings requiring renovation/refurbishment • Percentage of buildings in the city with smart energy meters • Number of electric vehicles charging stations per registered electric vehicle Environmental and Climate Change • Percentage of buildings built or refurbished within the last five years in conformity with green building principles • Number of real-time remote air quality monitoring stations per square kilometre (km^2) • Percentage of public buildings equipped for monitoring indoor air quality

(continued)

Table 8.2 (continued)

Scheme	Definitions used
ISO37120: 2018	Energy • Total end-use energy consumption per capita (GJ/year) (core indicator) • Percentage of total end-use energy derived from renewable sources (core indicator) • Percentage of city population with authorised electrical service (residential) (core indicator) • Number of gas distribution service connections per 100,000 population (residential) (core indicator) • Final energy consumption of public buildings per year (GJ/m^2) (core indicator) • Electricity consumption of public street lighting per kilometre of lighted street (kWh/year) (supporting indicator) • Average annual hours of electrical service interruptions per household (supporting indicator) • Energy profile indicators (heating degree days and cooling degree days) Environmental and Climate Change • Fine particulate matter (PM2.5) concentration (core indicator) • Particulate matter (PM10) concentration (core indicator) • Greenhouse gas emissions measured in tonnes per capita (core indicator) • Percentage of areas designated for natural protection (supporting indicator) • NO_2 (nitrogen dioxide) concentration (supporting indicator) • SO_2 (sulphur dioxide) concentration (supporting indicator) • O_3 (ozone) concentration (supporting indicator) • Noise pollution (supporting indicator) • Percentage change in number of native species (supporting indicator)

(continued)

Table 8.2 (continued)

Scheme	Definitions used
ETSI Technical Specification	Energy and mitigation • Energy consumption/demand (Annual final energy consumption) • RE production (Renewable energy generated within the city) • CO_2 emissions (in tonnes per capita per year) and local freight transport fuel mix Pollution and waste • Nitrogen dioxide emissions (NO_2) (Annual nitrogen dioxide emissions per capita) • Fine particulate matter emissions (PM 2.5) • Air quality index (Annual concentration of relevant air pollutants) • Noise pollution (Share of the population affected by noise > 55 dB(a) at night) • Recycling rate (Percentage of city's solid waste that is recycled) • Municipal solid waste (The amount of municipal solid waste generated per capita annually)
MSCF	• Percentage of tree canopy covering the land area • Percentage of land cover and land use • Recycling rate per year • Percentage of waste diversion (recycle and recovery) • Total hazardous waste generated in tonnes per year • Number of days recorded as "good" and "medium" measured by the API (air pollution index) in the study area in a year • Reduction in the number of rivers in Class IV (polluted) and Class V (severe polluted) in a year • Number of initiatives for disaster risk management and implementation in a year • Number of deaths by disaster per 100,000 people • Number of missing persons by disaster per 100,000 people • Number persons affected by disaster per 100,000 people • Rate of national Non-Revenue Water (NRW) reduction by 25% in 2025 • Percentage of electricity production from renewable sources • RE share in total final energy consumption (TFEC) • Efficiency of buildings: GDP per unit of energy use • Energy intensity measured in terms of primary energy and GDP

Table 8.3 Keywords for smart city definition and assessment

Keyword	Definition
Smart city	"Smart-Cities" OR "Smart-City" OR "Sustainable And Smart City" OR "ICT-Enabled City " OR "Smart City" OR "Smart Cities" OR "Intelligent City" OR "Intelligent Cities" OR "Digital City" OR "Digital Cities" OR "Smart Sustainable Cities" OR "Sustainable City" OR "Green City" OR "Intelligent City Concept" OR "Knowledge City" OR "Wired City" OR "Internet Of Things For Cities" OR "IoT For Cities" OR "Smart City Planning" OR "Smart City Implementation" OR "Smart City Sustainability" OR "Smart City Research" OR "Smart City Case Studies" OR "Smart Economy" OR "Smart Mobility" OR "Smart Environment" OR "Smart People" OR "Smart Living" OR "Smart Governance" OR "Sustainability City" OR "Sustainable Urban Developments" OR "Eco-City" OR "Livable City" OR "Low-Carbon Cities" OR "Climate-Smart City"
Smart city assessment and tools	"Smart City Assessments" OR "Sustainable City Assessment" OR "Sustainable City Assessments" OR "Urban City Assessment" OR "Urban City Assessments" OR "Emerging City Evaluations" OR "Energy Performance Index" OR "Carbon Performance Index" OR "Energy Performance Indicator" OR "Carbon Performance Indicator" OR "Energy-Carbon Performance" OR "Energy-Carbon Performance Index" OR "Performance Index" OR "Performance Indicator" OR "Performance Framework" OR "Performance Evaluation Index" OR "Performance Evaluation Indicator" OR "City Performance Index" OR "City Performance Indicator" OR "City Performance Framework" OR "City Performance Evaluation Index" OR "City Performance Evaluation Indicator" OR "City Performance Evaluation Framework" OR "City Ranking" OR "City Score" OR "Smart City Energy Efficiency" OR "Smart City Carbon Reduction" OR "City KPI" OR "City Performance Measurement Index" OR "City Performance Measurement Index" OR "City Performance Measurement Indicator" OR "City Performance Measurement Framework" OR "City Performance Roadmap" OR "Smart City Assessment" OR "Energy Transition Index" OR "City Benchmarking" OR "City Performance Criteria" OR "City Key Performance Indicators" OR "City Performance Indices" OR "City Performance Evaluation Indices" OR "City Performance Evaluation Indices" OR "City Performance Measurement Indices" OR "City Performance Assessment Indices" OR "City Key Performance Indicators Indices" OR "Energy Performance Index" OR "Carbon Performance Index"

3.1.3 Selecting the Final List of EPF Indicators

The compilation of the final list for inclusion in the EPF involves synthesising indicators derived from established performance assessment guidelines, standards and reporting schemes (Table 8.2) and previous studies (Table 8.4). Consistent with the methodology outlined by Abd Rahman (2021), the criterion for incorporating a specific item in the EPF is that the item be present in a minimum of two of the reviewed reporting guidelines, standards, reporting schemes or studies. While

Table 8.4 Common environmental performance indicators of smart cities

Indicator	Topic	Representative studies
Carbon emissions reduction	Efforts to minimise carbon emissions through emissions reduction initiatives and sustainable practices within the organisational operations	This category includes 12 articles such as Angelakoglou et al. (2020); Govindarajan et al. (2021); Karal and Soyer (2023); Martins et al. (2021); Mekki et al. (2022); Quijano et al. (2022); Shahrokni, Lazarevic and Brandt (2015); Silva et al. (2018)
Energy management	Monitoring, management and optimisation of energy consumption and efficiency to minimise environmental impact and enhance sustainability within the organisational infrastructure	This category includes 25 articles such as Abu-Rayash and Dincer (2021); Angelakoglou et al. (2020); Faroun et al. (2022); Govindarajan et al. (2021); Juan et al. (2023); Karal and Soyer (2023); Martins et al. (2021); Mekki et al. (2022); Quijano et al. (2022); Rozman et al. (2019); Shahrokni, Lazarevic and Brandt (2015); Shen et al. (2018); Sidani et al. (2022); Silva et al. (2018)
Green space and biodiversity preservation	Implementation of strategies and practices aimed at conserving and enhancing biodiversity within the organisational ecosystem	This category includes 10 articles such as Faroun et al. (2022); Martos et al. (2016); Shen et al. (2018)
Renewable energy sources	Integration of RE sources such as solar, wind or hydroelectric power to meet organisational energy needs and reduce reliance on fossil fuels	This category includes 15 articles such as Faroun et al. (2022); Govindarajan et al. (2021); Karal and Soyer (2023); Mekki et al. (2022); Shahrokni, Lazarevic and Brandt (2015); Shen et al. (2018); Sidani et al. (2022)
Smart building technology and management system	Utilisation of intelligent building systems and technologies to optimise energy usage, enhance occupant comfort and reduce environmental footprint within organisational facilities	This category includes 10 articles such as Al Dakheel et al. (2020); Faroun et al. (2022); Jouili et al. (2017)

(continued)

Table 8.4 (continued)

Indicator	Topic	Representative studies
Smart environment monitoring application	Deployment of smart applications and tools for real-time monitoring of environmental parameters, facilitates proactive environmental management and sustainability initiatives	This category includes 5 articles such as Demertzi et al. (2023); Kaluarachchi (2022); Sharma and Arya (2020)
Water conservation efforts	Implementation of measures to minimise water usage and promote efficient water management practices within the organisational operations	This category includes 9 articles such as Abu-Rayash and Dincer (2021); Faroun et al. (2022); Jouili et al. (2017); Martos et al. (2016); Shen et al. (2018)
Waste management	Adoption of strategies and processes for effective waste reduction, recycling and disposal to minimise environmental impact and promote resource conservation within the organisational framework	This category includes 13 articles such as Abu-Rayash and Dincer (2021); Faroun et al. (2022); Jouili et al. (2017); Martos et al. (2016); Shen et al (2018); Sidani et al. (2022)

adopting a somewhat arbitrary approach, this methodology posits that the authoritative nature of these guidelines lends credence to the importance of an issue when identified by at least two reputable sources, thereby reinforcing its significance in the development of the EPF.

Furthermore, the final list of indicators depends on the unit of analysis and its objectives. This ensures that the selected indicator is relevant, accurate and actionable, facilitating a meaningful comparison of performance and the identification of areas for enhancement.

As indicated in Table 8.5, the final EPF comprises eight indicators, encompassing four items under carbon emissions reduction, three items under energy management, three items under green space and biodiversity preservation, three under RE sources, two under smart building technology and management systems, two under smart environment monitoring applications, three under water conservation efforts, and three under waste management.

Table 8.5 EPF indicators of firms in smart cities

Indicator	Symbol	Items
SE.1 Carbon emissions reduction	SE.1a	Total carbon emissions (in metric tonnes) over a specified period
	SE.1b	Carbon intensity reduction over a specified period
	SE.1c	Percentage reduction in carbon emissions compared to baseline levels
	SE.1d	Adoption of carbon offsetting initiatives or investments in carbon credits
SE.2 Energy management	SE.2a	Total energy consumption (in kWh or equivalent units) over a specified period
	SE.2b	Energy intensity (energy consumption per unit of output or area)
	SE.2c	Percentage improvement in energy efficiency compared to baseline levels
SE.3 Green space and biodiversity preservation	SE.3a	Compliance with biodiversity conservation regulations and standards
	SE.3b	Number of biodiversity enhancement projects implemented
	SE.3c	Percentage increase in green space metrics (integrating parks, gardens and rooftop greenery) over time
SE.4 Renewable energy sources	SE.4a	Percentage of energy sourced from renewable sources (solar, wind, etc.)
	SE.4b	Installed capacity of RE systems
	SE.4c	Investment in RE infrastructure and projects
SE.5 Smart building technology and management systems	SE.5a	Energy savings achieved through smart building technologies (in kWh or equivalent units)
	SE.5b	Reduction in maintenance costs and downtime associated with smart building systems
SE.6 Smart environment monitoring applications	SE.6a	Number of environmental parameters monitored in real-time
	SE.6b	Frequency and severity of environmental incidents. detected and responded to using smart monitoring systems
SE.7 Water conservation efforts	SE.7a	Total water consumption (in cubic metres) over a specified period
	SE.7b	Percentage reduction in water usage compared to baseline levels
	SE.7c	Implementation of water-saving technologies or practices (e.g., low-flow fixtures, rainwater harvesting)
SE.8 Waste management	SE.8a	Total waste generated (in metric tonnes) over a specified period
	SE.8b	Percentage of waste recycled, reused or diverted from landfills
	SE.8c	Implementation of waste reduction initiatives (e.g., source separation, composting)

3.2 EPF Scoring Methodology

The EPF created for this study provides a structured methodology for gathering pertinent data from corporate annual reports through content analysis which serves as a robust framework for investigating communication (Weber 1998).

Both weighted and unweighted index approaches are viable methods for assessing the EPF. This study opts for the unweighted index approach, as empirical evidence suggests that the choice between methodologies yields negligible variations in outcomes (Chithambo 2013). All items are considered equally important, with 1 point awarded for each item identified within the firm's annual report and 0 for non-identification. For each firm, the values against all the items have been summed up to obtain the final score (23 items). The EPF for each firm is then expressed as a percentage, facilitating comparative analysis and benchmarking within the studied sample.

4 Findings

4.1 Applicability of the EPF

We tested the index's applicability on selected companies from Malaysia's smart cities: Kuala Lumpur, Putrajaya, Cyberjaya, Shah Alam, Melaka, Kota Kinabalu, Kuching, Johor Bharu, Georgetown and Kulim. The final sample comprised 45 firms selected through random sampling techniques.

Table 8.6 provides a comprehensive overview of the environmental performance (EPF) scores among the sampled firms. The analysis reveals a mean EPF score of 21.0093, ranging from a minimum of 0 to a maximum of 65.22. Remarkably, the mean EPF score represents only 21% of the total maximum score achievable, underscoring a notable gap in environmental performance. The findings indicate a prevalent trend of low environmental performance among the sampled firms, with a significant portion scoring below 65 per cent of the total possible score.

For carbon emissions reduction (SE.1), the minimum score is zero and the maximum score is 17.39%. The minimum score of zero indicates that some firms do not report any efforts towards carbon emissions reduction. The average SE.1 value of 5.4447 suggests a moderate level of engagement across the sampled firms. Specifically, the breakdown of reporting practices within SE.1 reveals that fewer than half of the firms (46.7%) reported total carbon emissions. A smaller proportion of firms, comprising 20%, reported on carbon intensity. Furthermore, approximately 22.2% of firms reported a percentage reduction in carbon emissions compared to baseline levels, reflecting their progress towards emission reduction targets. Notably, a substantial portion of firms (37.8%) reported on the adoption of carbon offsetting initiatives, indicating efforts to mitigate carbon emissions through compensatory measures.

Table 8.6 Descriptive statistics

Indicator	Minimum	Maximum	Mean	Std. Deviation
SE.1	0.0000	17.3900	5.4447	5.5092
SE.2	0.0000	13.0400	3.5847	4.4757
SE.3	0.0000	13.0400	1.1598	2.5218
SE.4	0.0000	13.0400	1.7398	3.1305
SE.5	0.0000	8.7000	0.9667	2.2506
SE.6	0.0000	8.7000	0.4833	1.6648
SE.7	0.0000	13.0400	4.0589	4.4840
SE.8	0.0000	13.0400	3.5767	3.9656
EPF	0.0000	65.22	21.0093	16.3227

Turning to energy management (SE.2), the minimum score of zero indicates that some entities reported no specific energy management measures within the scope of this indicator. Conversely, the maximum score of 13.04% signifies that some firms are potentially implementing multiple strategies to optimise energy consumption and efficiency. The breakdown of energy management practices highlights the prevalence of certain measures among the sampled firms. Specifically, 56.7% of the companies reported on total energy consumption, indicating a strong emphasis on monitoring and tracking energy usage. Additionally, 20% of the entities reported on energy intensity, reflecting efforts to improve energy efficiency and reduce resource consumption per unit of output. Moreover, 15.6% of the companies reported a percentage improvement in energy efficiency compared to baseline levels, underscoring a commitment to continual improvement and sustainability performance.

The report indicates a relatively low level of engagement and effectiveness in green space and biodiversity preservation (SE.3), with a mean score of 1.16% and a maximum score of 13.04%. In SE.3, specific components include compliance with biodiversity conservation regulations and standards (15.6% of the sample firms), the number of biodiversity enhancement projects implemented (6.7% of the sample firms) and the percentage increase in green space metrics (4.4% of the sample firms). The findings also signal limited progress in expanding green spaces and promoting biodiversity within the studied firms. The low level of firms disclosing this information underscores the need for greater compliance with regulatory frameworks and increased investment in biodiversity enhancement initiatives.

With regard to RE sources (SE.4), the mean score for the indicator stands at 1.74%, suggesting limited implementation of RE strategies across the sampled firms. Specifically, the breakdown of reporting practices within SE.4 revealed that 13.3% of the sampled firms sourced their energy from renewable sources. Furthermore, the installed capacity of RE systems and the investment in RE infrastructure and projects exhibit weaker commitment to expanding these areas among the surveyed firms.

In terms of smart building technology and management systems (SE.5), the descriptive statistics reveal that the adoption of smart building technology varies widely among the sampled firms, with a minimum reported value of zero and a maximum of 8.7%. The mean adoption rate stands at 0.96%, indicating a relatively low overall prevalence of smart building technology implementation among the studied firms. The breakdown of reported benefits associated with the adoption of smart building systems is particularly intriguing. Among the firms that reported on this indicator, 15.6% highlighted energy savings achieved through smart building technologies. Additionally, a smaller percentage (6.7%) reported reductions in maintenance costs and downtime associated with smart building systems.

In terms of the smart environment monitoring application (SE.6), this category has the lowest mean (0.48%) in comparison to other EPF indicators. Only 8.9% of the firms reveal the number of environmental parameters they monitor in real-time, and 2.2% reveal the frequency and severity of environmental incidents they detect and respond to using smart monitoring systems; this highlights the limited use of advanced monitoring technologies in environmental management efforts.

We observe a mean score of 4.06% for water conservation efforts (SE.7), with a maximum score of 13.04%. Of the firms assessed, 44.4% disclose information on total water consumption over a specified period. This indicates a moderate level of transparency regarding water usage practices, allowing stakeholders to gain a better understanding of the firms' water management strategies. Furthermore, 15.6% of the firms disclose the percentage reduction in water usage compared to baseline levels, and 33.3% disclose the implementation of water-saving technologies or practices, demonstrating a commitment to monitoring and improving water efficiency over time.

The report for waste management (SE.8) indicates a mean score of 3.58%, with a maximum score of 13.05%. A closer examination of the data reveals that only 28.9% disclose total waste generated; 8.9% disclose waste recycled, reused or diverted from landfills; and 44.4% report implementation of waste reduction initiatives. These findings underscore a need for enhanced transparency and commitment to sustainable waste management strategies.

Table 8.7 presents the descriptive statistics of EPF scores categorised by cities.

The average EPF scores exhibit substantial diversity among the cities, indicating differences in environmental performance and sustainability practices. Kuala Lumpur stands out with its highest average EPF score of 43.09%, signifying robust environmental performance initiatives and sustainable practices. In contrast, Kuching and Georgetown exhibit the lowest average EPF scores of 7.83%, indicating that firms are facing significant potential shortcomings or challenges in sustainability practices and initiatives there. Shah Alam, Johor Bahru, Melaka, Kulim, Cyberjaya, Putrajaya and Kota Kinabalu are other cities that have moderate mean EPF ratings. These scores range from 16.28 to 30.75%, which shows that these jurisdictions have significantly different levels of environmental performance and sustainability measures. These findings underscore the need for tailored interventions and policies to tackle the distinct environmental challenges and opportunities in each city. This will help improve sustainability outcomes throughout the region.

Table 8.7 Descriptive statistics of EPF scores by cities

City	Minimum	Maximum	Mean	Std. Deviation
Kuala Lumpur	21.7400	65.2200	43.0880	19.26774
Kuching	4.3700	13.0400	7.8280	3.63589
Georgetown	4.3700	13.0400	7.8280	3.63589
Shah Alam	4.3500	52.1700	20.8700	20.24976
Johor Bahru	4.3500	43.4800	23.4790	15.85614
Melaka	0.0000	43.0000	26.1040	17.65215
Kulim	4.3500	24.8900	16.2840	9.13149
Cyberjaya	13.0400	34.7800	21.7367	11.50335
Putrajaya	26.0900	35.4100	30.7500	6.59024
Kota Kinabalu	4.3500	43.4800	18.2620	15.18588

4.2 Comparison of EPF Between Firms in Smart Cities and Non-Smart Cities

In order to facilitate a comparative analysis of EPF among firms situated in smart city and non-smart city contexts, this study selected a sample of 45 firms domiciled in non-smart city areas but operating in the same state as the smart cities. Table 8.8 shows this comparison.

As illustrated in the table, firms situated in smart cities generally demonstrate higher mean scores across most indicators compared to those located in non-smart cities. However, there is no statistically significant difference in EPF scores between firms in smart and non-smart cities. The findings suggest that, despite excelling in various aspects of business operations and market performance, smart cities may not

Table 8.8 Comparison by EPF between firms in smart cities and non-smart cities

Indicator	Firm in smart cities (1)	Firm in non-smart cities (2)	Difference in Mean: (1)- (2)		
	Mean	Mean	Mean Diff	t stat	P-value
SE.1	5.4447	3.5804	1.86422	1.820	0.072
SE.2	3.5847	2.1278	1.45689	1.783	0.078
SE.3	1.1598	1.6429	-0.48311	-0.734	0.465
SE.4	1.7398	1.4498	0.29000	0.454	0.651
SE.5	0.9667	0.2900	0.67667	1.813	0.073
SE.6	0.4833	0.1933	0.29000	0.922	0.359
SE.7	4.0589	3.8660	0.19289	0.211	0.833
SE.8	3.5767	3.5769	-0.00044	-0.001	1.000
EPF	21.0093	16.7213	4.28800	1.291	0.200

necessarily possess a clear advantage in terms of environmental performance. This underscores the need to recognise that the implementation of smart city initiatives by firms, while advantageous for business operations and market performance, may not inherently lead to enhanced environmental sustainability. This finding reveals the critical importance of ensuring that smart city development strategies prioritise environmental considerations to effectively tackle ecological efficiency and sustainability challenges in urban areas. Merely labelling a city as "smart" does not guarantee superior environmental performance at the firm level.

5 Conclusion

This chapter delves into the concept of smart cities, explores smart city performance and examines its relationship with the energy transition. By scrutinising challenges associated with performance evaluation measures unique to smart cities and reviewing existing assessment guidelines, standards, reporting schemes and past studies, this chapter presents a tailored framework for measuring the environmental performance of firms in smart cities within Malaysia.

The assessment of environmental performance in smart cities is instrumental in furthering energy transition goals. Nevertheless, evaluating environmental performance in smart cities presents multifaceted challenges. These challenges include inadequate sustainability assessment tools and a lack of standardised environmental and energy indicators. Additionally, existing smart city frameworks face limitations in integrating energy-related KPIs, and the absence of clear methodologies adds complexity to deploying evaluation frameworks for both cities and experts. Furthermore, the lack of a standardised method for evaluating environmental performance makes it difficult to compare performance across different cities. The growing complexity of these models poses a risk of measurement errors and endogenous problems, highlighting the intricate nature of assessing sustainability in smart urban environments.

This chapter presents a novel research endeavour that evaluates smart environment models specifically designed for firms operating in smart cities. We meticulously developed the EPF in accordance with relevant guidelines, standards and reporting schemes, complemented by a systematic literature analysis. The EPF is subsequently assessed across ten Malaysian smart cities—Kuala Lumpur, Putrajaya, Cyberjaya, Shah Alam, Melaka, Kota Kinabalu, Kuching, Johor Bahru, Georgetown and Kulim. Researching the EPF of firms situated within smart cities holds considerable significance due to their pivotal role in facilitating the transition towards sustainable energy practices (Geels et al. 2018; Shahrokni et al. 2015).

This assessment presents eight key indicators: carbon emissions reduction, energy management, green space and biodiversity preservation, RE sources, smart environment monitoring applications, water conservation efforts and waste management. The findings indicate a prevalent trend of low environmental performance among the sampled firms, with a significant portion scoring below 65% of the total possible score. This indicates that there is significant room for improvement in environmental sustainability practices and suggests the need for targeted interventions to improve overall performance in this critical domain.

The carbon emissions reduction category receives the highest score among EPF indicators, demonstrating a commendable focus on mitigating GHG emissions. This finding underscores the significance of prioritising efforts to reduce carbon emissions, considering their pivotal role in driving climate change. Yet the analysis reveals noteworthy disparities in EPF scores among Malaysian cities. Kuala Lumpur emerges as the frontrunner, boasting the highest average EPF score of 43.09%. This finding suggests that Kuala Lumpur has implemented robust environmental performance initiatives and sustainable policies, positioning it as a leader in environmental stewardship among Malaysian cities. The city's proactive approach to environmental sustainability is commendable and reflects a concerted effort to mitigate the impacts of climate change and foster a greener, more resilient urban environment.

Conversely, Kuching and Georgetown exhibit the lowest average EPF scores, standing at 7.83%. This observation raises concerns regarding the environmental performance and sustainability practices in these cities. The notably low EPF scores indicate potential shortcomings or challenges faced by firms operating in Kuching and Georgetown in adopting and implementing sustainable practices. Addressing these challenges is imperative to enhance environmental sustainability and resilience in these cities, particularly in the face of escalating climate change impacts.

This study presents the EPF as a valuable tool for assessing the environmental performance of firms in smart cities. As noted by Al Dakheel et al. (2020), the EPF serves as a standardised measure, enabling comparison of smart cities' performance against a common set of criteria. This standardised approach is crucial for identifying and understanding the strengths and weaknesses of different smart cities, facilitating informed decision-making and policy development in the context of climate change mitigation and environmental sustainability. This holds particular relevance for ASEAN countries as they strive to achieve their energy transition objectives and fulfill their commitments, including reducing GHG emissions and increasing the proportion of RE in their energy portfolio.

References

Abd Rahman NR (2021) The moderating effect of corporate governance quality on the relationship between voluntary carbon reporting quality and financial performance (Unpublished doctoral dissertation). Universiti Teknologi Malaysia

Abubakar IR, Alshammari MS (2023) Urban planning schemes for developing low-carbon cities in the Gulf cooperation council region. Habitat Int 138:102881

Abu-Rayash A, Dincer I (2021) Development of integrated sustainability performance indicators for better management of smart cities. Sustain Cities Soc 67:102704

Ahvenniemi H et al (2017) What are the differences between sustainable and smart cities? Cities 60:234–245

Al Dakheel J et al (2020) Smart buildings features and key performance indicators: a review. Sustain Cities Soc 61:1–19
Almihat MGM et al (2022) Energy and sustainable development in smart cities: an overview. Smart Cities 5(4):1389–1408
Angelakoglou K et al (2019) Methodological framework for the selection of key performance indicators to assess smart city solutions. Smart Cities 2:269–306
Cai M et al (2023) Are smart cities more sustainable? An exploratory study of 103 US cities. J Clean Prod 416:137986
Calvillo CF, Sánchez-Miralles A, Villar J (2016) Energy management and planning in smart cities. Renew Sustain Energy Rev 55:273–287
Centre for Liveable Cities, Singapore. 2018. *ASEAN Smart Cities Network*. https://www.clc.gov.sg/docs/default-source/books/book-asean-smart-cities-network.pdf
Chithambo L (2013) Firm characteristics and the voluntary disclosure of climate change and greenhouse gas emission information. Intern J Energy Stat 1(03):155–169
Chong KM et al (2022) Sustainability of smart cities in Malaysia and the Philippines using ESG model. Environ Beh Proc J 7(22):145–155
Coy D, Dixon K (2004) The public accountability index: crafting a parametric disclosure index for annual reports. Br Account Rev 36:79–106
Dasgupta S, Lall S, Wheeler D (2022) Cutting global carbon emissions: where do cities stand? World Bank, Washington, DC
Dawood SR (2023) The use of Quadruple Helix model in smart cities development. Theor Emp Res Urban Manag 18(2):78–100
Demertzi V, Demertzis S, Demertzis K (2023) An overview of cyber threats, attacks and countermeasures on the primary domains of smart cities. Appl Sci 13(2):790
De Jong M et al (2015) Sustainable–smart–resilient–low carbon–eco–knowledge cities: making sense of a multitude of concepts promoting sustainable urbanization. J Clean Prod 109:25–38
Farmanbar M, Rong C (2020) Triangulum city dashboard: an interactive data analytic platform for visualizing smart city performance. Processes 8(2):250–272
Faroun NM, El-Badrawy AN, El-Gizawi LS (2022) Transforming old cities into smart cities using environmental key performance indicators to solve environmental problems. Civil Eng Arch 10.5:2075-2088
Garau C, Pavan VM (2018) Evaluating urban quality: indicators and assessment tools for smart sustainable cities. Sustainability 10(3):575
Geels FW et al (2018) Reducing energy demand through low carbon innovation: a sociotechnical transitions perspective and thirteen research debates. Energy Res Soc Sci 40:23–35
Govindarajan HK, Ganesh LS (2021) Renewable energy for electricity use in India: evidence from India's smart cities mission. Renew Energy Focus 38:36–43
Gracias JS et al (2023) Smart cities–a structured literature review. Smart Cities 6(4):1719–1743
Grossi G, Trunova O (2021) Are UN SDGs useful for capturing multiple values of smart city? Cities 114:103193
Guo Q, Wang Y, Dong X (2022) Effects of smart city construction on energy saving and CO_2 emission reduction: evidence from China. Appl Energy 313:118879
Hoang AT, Nguyen XP (2021) Integrating renewable sources into energy system for smart city as a sagacious strategy towards clean and sustainable process. J Clean Prod 305:127161
Horng TT et al (2021) Identifying the determinants for developing smart city initiatives in delivering convenience and safety to local community. Intern J Acad Res Bus Soc Sci 11(17):229–236
ISO-International Organization for Standardization (2019) *ISO 37122:2019; Sustainable Cities and Communities—Indicators for Smart Cities*. Geneva
Jouili K et al (2017) The smart city: how to evaluate performance. International Conference: Responsible Organizations in the Global Context. Georgetown University, Washington DC
Juan AA et al (2023) Promoting energy efficiency and emissions reduction in urban areas with key performance indicators and data analytics. Energies 16(20):7195

Kabeyi MJB, Olanrewaju OA (2022) Sustainable energy transition for renewable and low carbon grid electricity generation and supply. Front Energy Res 9

Kaluarachchi Y (2022) Implementing data-driven smart city applications for future cities. Smart Cities 5(2):455–474

Karal FS, Soyer A (2023) A systematic literature review: setting a basis for smart and sustainable city performance measurement. Sustain Dev 32(1):1–19

Konstantinou C (2021) Toward a secure and resilient all-renewable energy grid for smart cities. IEEE Cons Electr Mag 11(1):33–41

Kutty AA et al (2020) A system thinking approach for harmonizing smart and sustainable city initiatives with united nations sustainable development goals. Sustain Dev 28(5):1347–1365

Lacson JJ et al (2023) Smart city assessment in developing economies: a scoping review. Smart Cities 6(4):1744–1764

Lai CMT, Cole A (2023) Measuring progress of smart cities: indexing the smart city indices. Urban Govern 3(1):45–57

Le Thiez P (2018) Economic outlook smart city: energy challenges facing sustainable cities. IFPEN. https://www.ifpenergiesnouvelles.com/article/smart-city-energy-challenges-facing-sustainable-cities [accessed 26 November, 2024]

Lim Y, Edelenbos J, Gianoli A (2019) Smart energy transition: an evaluation of cities in South Korea. Informatics 6.4:50–70

Manoharan G et al (2023) An investigation into the effectiveness of smart city projects by identifying the framework for measuring performance. *Artificial Intelligence and Machine Learning in Smart City Planning*: 1–84

Martos A et al (2016) Towards successful environmental performance of sustainable cities: intervening sectors. A review. Renew Sustain Energy Rev 57:479–495

Martins F et al (2021) A review of energy modeling tools for energy efficiency in smart cities. Smart Cities 4(4):1420–1436

Mekki Y et al. (2022) Artificial intelligence for smart decision-making in the cities of the future, in *International Conference on Advanced Intelligent Systems for Sustainable Development*, ed. M. Ezziyyani, J. Kacprzyk and V. E. Balas. Cham: Springer Nature Switzerland, pp 168–178

Ministry of Housing and Local Government, Malaysia (2018) *Malaysia Smart City Framework: Executive Summary*. https://www.kpkt.gov.my/kpkt/resources/user_1/GALERI/PDF_PENERBITAN/FRAMEWORK/FRAMEWORK_SMART_CITY_EXECUTIVE_SUMMARY.pdf

Mohd Adnan Y et al. (2016) An initiatives-based framework for assessing smart city. Plan Malaysia 5(V):13–22

Morhardt JE, Baird S, Freeman K (2002) Scoring corporate environmental and sustainability reports using GRI 2000, ISO 14031 and other criteria. Corp Soc Responsib Environ Manag 9(4):215–233

Nguyen H, Nawara H, Kashef R (2024) Connecting the indispensable roles of IoT and artificial intelligence in smart cities: a survey. J Inform Intell 2(3):261–285

Okafor CC, Aigbavboa C, Thwala WD (2023) A bibliometric evaluation and critical review of the smart city concept—making a case for social equity. J Sci Technol Policy Manag 14(3):487–510

Paes VDC et al (2023) Analyzing the challenges for future smart and sustainable cities. Sustainability 15(10):7996

Qian L et al (2023) Carbon emission reduction effects of the smart city pilot policy in China. Sustainability 15(6):5085

Quijano A et al (2022) Towards sustainable and smart cities: replicable and KPI-driven evaluation framework. Buildings 12(2):233

Rozman AT, Azmi NA, Sukereman AS (2022) A review of smart city elements and smart city performances. IOP Conf Series: Earth Environ Sci 1067(1):012027

Saez L, Heras-Saizarbitoria I, Rodriguez-Nunez E (2020) Sustainable city rankings, benchmarking and indexes: looking into the black box. Sustain Cities Soc 53:101938

Samsudin NA et al (2022) A comparative study of smart city initiatives in Malaysia: Putrajaya and Iskandar Puteri. Plan Malaysia 20:14–28

Sandu S et al (2019) Energy-related CO_2 emissions growth in ASEAN countries: trends, drivers and policy implications. Energies 12(24):4650
Sarma S, Sunny SA (2017) Civic entrepreneurial ecosystems: smart city emergence in Kansas city. Bus Horiz 60(6):843–853
Shahrokni H, Lazarevic D, Brandt N (2015) Smart urban metabolism: towards a real-time understanding of the energy and material flows of a city and its citizens. J Urban Technol 22(1):65–86
Sharifi A (2020) A typology of smart city assessment tools and indicator sets. Sustain Cities Soc 53:101936
Sharma R, Arya R (2022) A Secure authentication technique for connecting different IoT devices in the smart city infrastructure. Clust Comput 25(4):2333–2349
Shen L et al (2018) A holistic evaluation of smart city performance in the context of China. J Clean Prod 200:667–679
Shen Y, Yang Z, Zhang X (2023) Impact of digital technology on carbon emissions: evidence from Chinese cities. Front Ecol Evol 11
Sidani D, Veglianti E, Maroufkhani P (2022) Smart cities for a sustainable social inclusion strategy–a comparative study between Italy and Malaysia. Pacific Asia J Assoc Inform Syst 14(2):25–41
Silva BN et al (2018) Urban planning and smart city decision management empowered by real-time data processing using big data analytics. Sensors 18(9):2994
Söderström O, Paasche T, Klauser F (2020) Smart cities as corporate storytelling, in *The Routledge Companion to Smart Cities*, ed. Katharine S. Willis and Alessandro Aurigi. Abingdon, Oxon: Routledge, pp 283–300
Sotirelis P et al (2022) Measuring smart city performance: a multiple criteria decision analysis approach. J Knowl Econ 13:1–29
Sta HB (2017) Quality and the efficiency of data in 'smart-cities.' Futur Gener Comput Syst 74:409–416
Tekin Bilbil E (2017) The operationalizing aspects of smart cities: the case of Turkey's smart strategies. J Knowl Econ 8(3):1032–1048
Tompson T (2017) Understanding the contextual development of smart city initiatives: a pragmatist methodology. She Ji: J des Eco Innov 3(3):210–228
Weber RP (1998) Basic content analysis. Newbury Park, CA[lifornia]: Sage
WRI (World Resources Institute)/ C40 Cities Climate Leadership Group/ ICLEI - Local
Governments for Sustainability (2014) GHG protocol: global protocol for community-scale greenhouse gas emission inventories. https://ghgprotocol.org/sites/default/files/ghgp/standards/GHGP_GPC_0.pdf [11 September 2023]
Wyrwicka MK, Więcek-Janka E, Brzeziński Ł (2023) Transition to sustainable energy system for smart cities-literature review. Energies 16(21):7224
Xia X, Yu R, Zhang S (2023) Evaluating the impact of smart city policy on carbon emission efficiency. Land 12(7):1292
Yan P et al (2021) A stack-based set inversion model for smart water, carbon and ecological assessment in urban agglomerations. J Clean Prod 319:128665
Zhao F et al (2021) Smart city research: a holistic and state-of-the-art literature review. Cities 119:103406

National Case Studies and Energy Transitions

The Energy Transition in Indonesia: The Impact on Women Who Switch to Using Clean Energy for Cooking

Maxensius Tri Sambodo, Felix Wisnu Handoyo, and Han Phoumin

Abstract This study aims to evaluate the impact of the transition from kerosene stoves to 3-kg LPG cylinders on the health status of the community in general, and women in particular. The energy transition will not necessarily improve women's health significantly due to the complex relationship between the transition and women's health. Using panel data from the Indonesian Family Life Survey (IFLS) for 2007 and 2014, the ordered response model and difference-in-differences method were applied. In general, public health conditions have worsened, and women's health is more vulnerable than that of men. This can be seen from the impact of the transition, which has not had a significant impact on women's health. Good and fair transition governance is the key to the success of this process, especially for women.

1 Introduction

Currently, around 2 billion people in the world still depend on polluting fuels and technology to support their cooking needs (UNSD 2024). Globally, of the 17 United Nations Development Programme's Sustainable Development Goals (SDG), SDG number 7 (affordable and clean energy is in the top five in terms of the "on track" category, reaching the target in 2023 (UNSD 2023). Within SDG 7, investment in energy infrastructure is included in the category which shows on-track achievement levels. However, achievements in terms of international energy cooperation are in the red category. This implies that progress in this category is stagnating or even regressing. Achievements related to access to energy, the role of renewable energy (RE) and energy efficiency are included in the reasonable progress category, but acceleration is still needed.

M. T. Sambodo (✉) · F. W. Handoyo
Research Center for Behavioral and Circular Economics, National Research and Innovation Agency (BRIN), Jakarta, Indonesia
e-mail: maxensius.tri.sambodo@brin.go.id

H. Phoumin
Economic Research Institute for ASEAN and East Asia (ERIA), Jakarta Pusat, Indonesia

H. Phoumin et al. (eds.), *Tackling the Energy Transition: Insights from ASEAN and Beyond*, Climate Change and Energy Transition,
https://doi.org/10.1007/978-981-96-6019-3_9

In terms of achieving the SDG 7 target, Indonesia appears to be in a relatively better position in terms of access to clean energy for cooking compared to India and China (Table 9.1). However, in terms of access to electricity, emissions intensity and the role of RE, Indonesia's position lags behind the other two countries.

The provision of clean energy for cooking must continue to be encouraged. A study conducted by Byaro et al. (2024) shows that clean energy and technology for cooking can reduce maternal deaths at the 25th, 50th, 60th and 75th income quantiles. Such improvements will also see a decrease in infant deaths, especially at the 50, 60, 75, and 90 quantiles. Likewise, there was a decrease in the death rate for the group of children under 5 years at the 50, 75 and 90 quantiles. However, the study stated that there would be an increase in the death rate at several other quantiles. This was due to house fires, which caused the deaths of babies and children under 5 years old.

Clean energy policies that aim to ensure energy justice and just transition must focus on marginalised and disadvantaged groups (Rahut et al. 2024). Rahut et al. (2024) emphasised that families with low incomes, female-headed families and disadvantaged groups need to be aware of the benefits of the energy transition, such as better health status; this is especially the case for female family members who are heavily involved in cooking and cooking activities.

Bhakta et al. (2024) are of the view that access to clean energy is very important, and providing better attention to disability groups will also provide benefits to wider groups. They specifically stated that access to clean energy for people with disabilities will reduce malnutrition, poverty, dependency, a lack of reliable energy access and health risks. Regarding health risks, there are two risks that require particular attention: health problems caused by indoor smoke and dangerous conditions resulting from being near an open fire. The World Bank (2023) mentioned that household air pollution is associated with premature deaths—nearly 3.2 million annually—mainly affecting women and children. Improving the quality and reliability of electricity supply can motivate households to invest in more efficient technology to prevent the proportion of income spent on energy from increasing (Akter et al. 2023).

In India, the price factor is the main consideration when women in rural areas rely more on gas and electricity for cooking (Banerjee et al. 2016; Smith and Sagar 2014).

Table 9.1 Comparison of Indonesia, India and China in Achieving SDG 7 in 2023

Indicator	Indonesia	India	China
Population with access to electricity (%)	97.0 (2020)	99.0 (2020)	100 (2020)
Population with access to clean fuels and technology for cooking (%)	84.5 (2020)	67.9 (2020)	79.4 (2020)
CO_2 emissions from fuel combustion per total electricity output (MtCO2/TWh)	2.1 (2019)	1.5 (2019)	1.3 (2019)
RE share in total final energy consumption (%)	9.7 (2019)	15.9 (2019)	10.6 (2019)

Note The number in brackets is the reporting year
Source Sachs, Lafortune and Fuller, 2024

Kapsalyamova et al. (2021) stated that access to clean energy increases the probability of opting for clean fuel; however, free fuel and coal-based heating systems lead to the use of solid fuels. Even though the conversion to clean energy for cooking has many benefits for health and gender equality for women's welfare, it is not directly making households change to clean energy cooking (Banerjee et al. 2016; Rubinstein et al. 2021; Hakam et al. 2022; Nix et al. 2022; Rubinstein et al. 2022; Smith and Sagar 2014; Tachev 2022).

Indonesia transitioned its cooking fuel use by moving from kerosene to 3-kg cylinders of liquid petroleum gas (LPG) in 2007 (Christian and Suryadi 2021; Sambodo 2014). This massive programme succeeded in changing people's behaviour. In 2007, there were around 4,424 households that depended on kerosene as the main source of energy for cooking, followed by firewood (Table 9.2). After the conversion programme, around 70% of households used 3-kg LPG cylinders (known as "gas melons" due to their shape and bright green colour) in 2014. The very high increase indicates that this conversion programme has been very successful. However, around 22.4% of households that year still used firewood as a cooking fuel. This shows that the risk of premature death caused by respiratory infections from firewood smoke is still quite high. There are various reasons for this continued use, such as economic limitations, old habits and limited knowledge of the dangers of firewood smoke. Furthermore, the use of firewood, especially in rural areas, continues because the smoke from firewood can reduce insect attacks that can disturb livestock and also help prevent disease-carrying mosquitoes from biting people.

Conversion programmes from kerosene to LPG have had consequences that drastically increase the demand for LPG. This situation has led Indonesia to import LPG since 2009. In 2020 LPG imports reached 6.4 million metric tonnes, and in 2024 imports reached 6.95 million metric tonnes because domestic production can meet only about 75% of the LPG demand (Christian and Suryadi 2021; Isaac 2024). At the same time, the LPG subsidy also increased; since the majority of people are dependent on the 3-kg cylinders due to the lower price per kilogram, the subsidy was estimated to be more than USD 4.9 billion in 2019 (Hakam et al. 2022; Sambodo

Table 9.2 Types of fuel used for cooking (number of households)

Fuel	2007	2014
Electricity	131	29
LPG/Gas	1,813	7,532
Kerosene	4,424	554
Firewood	4,056	2,404
Charcoal/coal	38	19
Not cooking	271	199
Others	8	4
Total number of households	10,741	10,741

Source Indonesian Family Life Survey (IFLS) 2007 and 2014

2014). Based on the government budget outlook, in 2023, the subsidy for LPG was expected to reach IDR 91.2 trillion, or 49.2% of the total energy subsidy.

In the 1980s, the majority of Indonesia's population was still dependent on firewood, and this led to a shortage of wood supplies and threatened forest sustainability. Meanwhile, the kerosene subsidy policy provided by the government also threatened the sustainability of the state budget. For approximately 25 years, the government was still able to rely on supplies of kerosene for cooking needs, even though Indonesia in 2008 was no longer a member of the (OPEC). In 2007, the government implemented a programme to convert from kerosene to LPG. This programme was quite successful, as stated above. However, after 17 years, the government is again experiencing difficulties because the amount of LPG subsidies continues to increase. Almost the same pattern is occurring because most of the LPG used for cooking has to be imported. Thus, the pressure of energy subsidies and dependence on imports are two important factors that are encouraging the government to carry out an energy transition.

This study argues that the energy transition paradigm cannot be seen narrowly based on the state's financial condition or on the availability of energy sources, such as fossil fuels. The transition process must be able to move towards better goals economically, socially and environmentally. It needs to be an important foundation for the future. At present, for example, health aspects that have a large impact on women do not appear to be an important factor in switching to clean energy sources. On the other hand, the Indonesia Long-Term Strategy for Low Carbon and Climate Resilience (LTS-LCCR) 2050 document states that gender is a strategic issue in the implementation of the strategy (Republic of Indonesia 2021, p. 118). This is, of course, in line with Presidential Instruction No. 9/2000 regarding gender mainstreaming in national development.

Thus, the move to use clean energy for cooking is driven not only by fiscal sustainability issues arising from the burden of subsidies or vulnerability due to dependence on energy imports. It is also very important to improve the health conditions of the community, especially for the women.

In many countries, including Indonesia, household cooking tends to be regarded as the women's responsibility. Women are therefore at greater risk of exposure to indoor air pollution due to their working with cooking fuels. A report from the WHO shows that women and girls are exposed to household fumes from fuel when carrying out one of their gender roles, and in Indonesia, around three in ten households use dirty fuel for cooking (WHO 2020).

A previous study by Imelda (2020) noted that reducing indoor air pollution by replacing kerosene with LPG (from a dirty to cleaner cooking fuel) was beneficial as it led to declining infant mortality rates during the perinatal period and prevalence of low birth weight in Indonesia. Unlike Imelda's, this study looks at a more symmetrical setting between men and women in a family. It seems more natural to see the potential risk of indoor pollution due to cooking activities. This study analyses the impact of the energy transition from kerosene to LPG, paying attention to the female population. Through the 2007 and 2014 data of the Indonesian Family Life Survey (IFLS) (4th and 5th waves) and using the ordered response model analysis technique, an analysis was carried out of the factors that influenced female health status in 2004 and 2014.

To complete the analysis, a difference-in-differences (DiD) equation was built to determine the impact of the conversion programme on health conditions. This study contributes to developing three pillars of the SDGs: affordable and clean energy, good health and wellbeing, and promoting gender equality.

The next section presents the methodology used. This is followed by a discussion of the results. The chapter concludes by synthesising the findings, analysing their implications, offering suggestions for future research and examining the policy implications.

2 Method

This study used the Indonesian Family Life Survey (IFLS) (RAND Corp. 2007, 2014; Strauss et al. 2016; Witoelar et al. 2009). The IFLS is an on-going longitudinal survey in Indonesia. The sample contains over 30,000 individuals living in 13 of the 27 provinces in the country. The first wave of the IFLS (IFLS1) was conducted in 1993/94 by RAND in collaboration with Lembaga Demografi (Demography Agency), University of Indonesia. IFLS2 and IFLS2 + were conducted in 1997 and 1998, respectively, by RAND in collaboration with UCLA and Lembaga Demografi. IFLS2 + covered a 25% sub-sample of the IFLS households. IFLS3, which was fielded in 2000 and covered the full sample, was conducted by RAND in collaboration with the Population Research Center, Universitas Gadjah Mada. The fourth wave of the IFLS (IFLS4), fielded in 2007/2008 and covering the full sample, was conducted by RAND, the Center for Population and Policy Studies (CPPS) of Universitas Gadjah Mada, and the Survey Meter. The fifth wave of the IFLS (IFLS-5) was fielded in 2014–15.

Many studies (such as Munasinghe and Sanghui 1988; Reiche et al. 2000; Peng and Pan 2006; Al Mohtad 2006; and Kanagawa and Nakata 2008) have shown the connection between energy access and people's welfare. To measure the impact of gender access to clean energy on health status, this study used some representative variables that have been used by previous authors. For independent variables, this study absorbed social and economic background information such as type of energy for cooking, age of head of household, years of schooling, urban or rural area, sex, smoking habits and job status. We applied the ordered response model with health status as a dependent variable. Table 9.3 provides details about the variables. Then we also developed interaction gridlines in order to measure the impact of gender on selected variables.

Health Status as a dependent variable has four outcomes as shown; the independent variables are: type of cooking energy source, sex, age, per capita expenditure, chronic diseases, tobacco user, urban and job status, year of observation, treatment variable, and interaction variable (year and treatment variables). The ordered response model can be written as the following equation:

$$y_i^* = x_i' \beta + \varepsilon_i$$

Table 9.3 Description of the variables

No	Variable	Description	Values
1	health status (dependent variable)	current health status of respondents. This variable is a dependent variable	1 = unhealthy 2 = somewhat unhealthy 3 = somewhat healthy 4 = very healthy
2	type of cooking energy source	LPG, kerosene and firewood	We apply a dummy variable for each source
3	years of education	number of years of schooling of respondent	
4	sex	sex of respondent	1 = male 0 = female
5	age	age of respondent	
6	log per capita expenditure	log of per capita expenditure	
7	chronic diseases	respondent with or without chronic diseases	1 = living with chronic diseases 0 = living without chronic diseases
8	tobacco user	respondent consuming tobacco products or not	1 = user of tobacco product 0 = non-user of tobacco product
9	urban	urban–rural area	1 = urban area 0 = rural area
10	job status	employment status	1 = employed 0 = unemployed

$$y_i = j \text{ } if \text{ } \gamma_{j-1} < y_i^* \leq j - 1,$$

in interpreting the ordered logit, authors conducted an additional calculation.[1]

As mentioned above, the analysis was carried out by looking at annual patterns. Alternatively, the authors developed an estimation technique within the DiD. Unobserved heterogeneity (time invariance) in participation is present, but the bias cancels out through differencing. Unobserved heterogeneity is uncorrelated with the treatment over time. The composition of the participant and control groups is fairly stable over time. The treatment and control groups (pre-intervention and after-intervention) were compared. DiD was calculated between the observed mean outcomes for the treatment and control groups before and after the kerosene conversion programme. The DiD is derived as follows:

[1] The formula is as follows: (value of parameter + Uj < = cut point; and value of Uj is obtained from (1 / (1 + 2^(cut point – coefficient value)).

$$DD = E(Y_1^T - Y_0^T \mid T_1 = 1) - E(Y_1^C - Y_0^C \mid T_1 = 0).$$

$$Y_{it} = \alpha + \beta T_{il}t + \rho T_{il} + \gamma t + \varepsilon_{it}.$$

where α is the baseline average, β is difference in changes over time, ρ is differences between two group pre intervention, and γ is time trend in the control group.

$$E(Y_1^T - Y_0^T \mid T_1 = 1) = (\alpha + DD + \rho + \gamma) - (\alpha + \rho)$$

$$E(Y_1^C - Y_0^C \mid T_1 = 0) = (\alpha + \gamma) - \alpha.$$

The DiD model is unbiased only if the potential source of selection bias is additive and time invariant.

3 Results and Discussions

3.1 Data Summary

When comparing health conditions in 2007 and 2014, it appears that public health in general was in decline (Table 9.4). This can be seen in the increasing number of people who changed from unhealthy to somewhat unhealthy status. Important for our study, the sample shows that women are less healthy than men. The number of women and men who were unhealthy or somewhat unhealthy increased between 2007 and 2014. However, the increase in the number of women enjoying very healthy status increased slightly more than that of men. This indicates that women, from a health perspective, are in a much more vulnerable, if dichotomous, situation compared to men. This seems to be confirmed by chronic disease conditions, which are more common in women than men (Table 9.5). For example, in 2007, the absolute number of women experiencing chronic diseases was around 725 more than men, and in 2014, the difference increased to 1,759. This means the women have chronic diseases almost 2.5 times more than the men. This situation certainly needs to be a concern because women have an important role in the family; if the number of women experiencing chronic diseases is increasing, family resilience could be affected in the future.

Women's health, which is generally not as good as men's, can be influenced by five factors (WHO 2020). First, in terms of equality of access, women's position lags behind men in terms of literacy, ownership of agricultural businesses, participation in the workforce and the proportion of doctors. Second, the burden of disease is different between men and women; for example, Alzheimer's disease, hypertension and breast cancer are among the ten main causes of death in women. Third, the daily illnesses that many women suffer are iron deficiency anemia, diarrhea, back and neck pain and asthma. Fourth, the higher prevalence of excess body weight and obesity in

Table 9.4 Cross-tabulation between health status and sex by year

Health status	2007		2014	
	Female	Male	Female	Male
Unhealthy	81	56	269	200
Somewhat unhealthy	2,377	1,681	3,529	2,415
Somewhat healthy	11,381	10,694	9,365	9,165
Very healthy	1,837	2,083	2,513	2,734

Source Indonesian Family Life Survey (IFLS) 2007 and 2014

Table 9.5 Crosstabulation between chronic diseases and sex by year

Chronic diseases	2007		2014	
	Female	Male	Female	Male
Have no chronic disease	11,662	10,931	8,035	8,338
Have chronic disease(s)	1,743	1,018	5,370	3,611

Source Indonesian Family Life Survey (IFLS) 2007 and 2014

women compared to men indicates higher exposure to risks and non-communicable diseases. Fifth, many women report barriers related to gender, for example, travelling alone to seek help, finding money for treatment and distance to health care facilities.

The higher risk of women developing asthma compared to men is also confirmed by Cephus et al. (2017), who say that women are twice as likely to develop asthma than men are, and that this gender difference may be caused by the effect of sex hormones on lung cells. Thus, women who use dirty energy sources for cooking will increasingly develop respiratory problems such as asthma.

3.2 Ordered Logit Modelling

The results of the analysis show that in both 2007 and 2014, all significant variables did not show differences in parameter signs. Even though it is not significant, none of the various types of energy used for cooking has a major effect on health conditions. However, the sign of the kerosene dummy parameter was negative in 2014, indicating that kerosene is more likely to be harmful. Likewise, with the interaction of the dummy variable energy source for cooking with gender, no significant results were found; in 2007, the sign of the interaction parameter dummy and gender was negative. This indicates the possibility that the use of kerosene has a harmful impact on women's health. By looking at the results of 2007 and 2014, it does not appear that there is a strong relationship between the use of energy sources for cooking and women's health. Likewise, no strong evidence was found to conclude that energy source for cooking has a negative impact on women's health.

In both 2007 and 2014, the results of the analysis show that women's health was more likely to be worse than men's. Age has a positive influence on health, but as age increases, the analysis confirms that health status tends to decline. Higher income levels tend to enable people to have better health conditions. Those who have chronic diseases and who are smokers are more likely to have poorer health in general. Likewise, those who work are more likely to be healthier than those who do not work. The length of time in education likely improves health status, though does not significantly affect a person's health. People who live in urban areas are more likely to be less healthy than those who live in rural areas.

The findings presented in Table 9.6 confirm the descriptive statistics as previously described, especially the lower health status of women compared to men. From the results of the ordered response model, it can be seen that gender position has a marginal impact on health conditions. By reference to category 1 (for unhealthy) in Table 9.3: in 2007, women have a probability of unhealthy status of 0.3%, while men have a probability of 0.26%. In 2014, the possibility that a woman was unhealthy was 6.4%, and for a man, it was 4.67%. Thus, health conditions in 2014 decreased compared to 2007, and women's health worsened compared to men.

Although the results in Table 9.7 need to be interpreted carefully because there are no significant interaction variables, it appears in general that after the LPG conversion programme was implemented, the health of women who cooked with LPG was more likely to be better than those who used kerosene and firewood. However, men are more likely to have better health than women, whatever energy source is used in cooking. Referring to the regression results in 2014, it can be concluded that 93.5% of women who use LPG as a fuel source for cooking are somewhat healthy.

The findings from the ordered logit modelling for 2007 and 2014 confirm many studies conducted by WHO that are related to health and gender in Indonesia (WHO 2020). For example, several variables related to education (as a proxy for literacy), economic status (as a proxy for family expenditure) and employment are closely related to health status. Smoking seriously impacts health. Studies show that passive smokers (who are generally women) tend to have poorer health than non-passive smokers (Tim Medis Siloam Hospitals 2023). The health risks associated with indoor pollution are definitely not only caused by smoke from cooking fuels.

3.3 Difference-In-Differences Analysis

Next, we divided the DiD analysis into two sample frames (Table 9.8); the total sample includes men and women, with only women in the sampling frame. The transition from kerosene stoves to LPG has a positive impact on health status. However, in the female sample frame, the results obtained were different from those in the sample aggregation, though the differences are not significant. From the estimated results, households that make the transition from kerosene stoves to LPG are likely to have a 4.48% chance of being unhealthy, while households that continue to use kerosene

Table 9.6 Ordered response model for 2007 and 2014

Variable	2007		2014	
	Estimate	Std. Error	Estimate	Std. Error
dummy kerosene	0.2422933	0.1363559*	-0.0536272	0.1659966
dummy LPG	0.0857907	0.1452332	0.1892422	0.140191
dummy firewood	0.0900219	0.1404505	0.0588461	0.1466278
sex_dummy_kerosene	0.1193652	0.2183059	0.1293324	0.2709607
sex_dummy_lpg	0.0586104	0.2228313	0.1217499	0.2408274
sex_dummy.firewood	0.1796172	0.2186294	0.258284	0.2458168
years_educ	0.0179165	0.0049829***	0.0040624	0.0036357
sex	-0.1536501	0.2195498	-0.3339257	0.2436571
age	0.0063228	0.0069554	0.011749	0.0048456**
age2	-0.0001337	0.00008*	-0.0003206	0.0000557*
sex_age2	-0.0000483	0.0000289*	-0.0000211	0.0000211
log_pce	0.0107157	0.030982	0.1091501	0.0204627*
chronic_dis	-0.8612758	0.0564299***	-0.9169416	0.0302513*
tobacco_user	-0.0938445	0.547539*	-0.1861354	0.0418074*
urban	-0.0583688	0.0400744	-0.0418365	0.0296207
job_status	0.138301	0.0442027***	0.2706799	0.0326253*
/Cut1	-5.94013	0. 4,794,707	-3.014541	0.3296964
/Cut2	-1.694057	0.4532769	-0.0879616	0.3263531
/Cut3	2.458772	0.4531183	2.789832	0.3270443
Observation	18,295		21,677	
Prob > chi2	0.000		0.000	
Pseudo R2	0,0224		0,0438	
Logpseudolikelihood	-12,906.682		-21,345.104	

*** $p < 0.01$, ** $p < 0.05$, * $p < 0.1$

Running under vce (robust)

Table 9.7 Interpretation of the interaction of gender variables and energy for cooking with Table 9.3 category 3 (Somewhat Healthy)

Variable	Gender	2007	2014	Change 2014–2007
Sex.DumCook.kerosene	Female	92,94	93,46	0,520
	Male	92,12	94,21	2,09
Sex.DumCook.lpg	Female	91,68	93,51	1,83
	Male	92,12	94,21	4,415
Sex.DumCook.firewood	Female	90,71	92,63	1,92
	Male	92,12	94,21	4,415

stoves are likely to have a 6.1% chance. These results show that the transition to LPG stoves can reduce the risk that households experience worse health.

Findings from the total sample also show that women are likely to have about a 7.8% chance of being unhealthy, while for men it is about 6.1%. This indicates that women's health is more vulnerable than men's, a finding that is consistent with previous findings. However, a closer look at the female sample group makes it difficult to conclude because the estimation results are not significant and the parameter coefficients are in the opposite direction of the hypothesis. Meanwhile, for other variables, the results of the analysis show the same direction of parameters for both sample frame groups. Thus, converting kerosene stoves to LPG tends to have the same positive impact on all sample groups, both men and women. However, within a sample frame of women who switched from kerosene stoves to LPG and those who continued to use kerosene stoves, there was no strong evidence enabling us to make conclusions about the impact on women's health. An important finding is that certain aspects of household capability need attention in improving health status, namely increasing family income, reducing the risk of chronic diseases, reducing smoking habits and providing employment opportunities.

Table 9.8 Difference-in-Differences (with all household characteristics)

	Total sampling frame		Sampling frame only women	
Variable	Coefficient	Robust Std. error	Coefficient	Robust Std. error
year dummy	-0.1838838	0.1255981	-0.1131836	0.211079
t_kerolpg	-0.0952977	0.0627266	0.279827	0.119841**
y_t_kerolpg	0.3242477	0.1372545**	-0.018496	0.2363779
year edu	0.0144976	0.0057647**	-0.0067232	0.0099147
sex_female	-0.2661002	0.0758941***	-	-
age	0.0357861	0.0104392***	0.0244578	0.0157754
age2	-0.0005576	0.000113***	-0.0004246	0.0001672**
l-pce	0.1343616	0.0338028***	0.0072924	0.053651
chronic_dis	-1.062925	0.0547228***	-1.206472	0.0947109***
tobacco_user	-0.159524	0.0557608***	-0.6680605	0.1914792***
urban	0.071381	0.0471023	0.0510244	0.0837504
marital_stat	0.0530086	0.0703789	0.0818858	0.1012169
job_status	0.4248868	0.0658999***	0.2876362	0.080687***
Cut 1	-2.734158	0.4972745	-4.633699	0.8048205
Cut 2	-0.5215285	0.491786	-1.30062	0.7900072
Cut 3	4.365002	0.4974045	2.447285	0.7889008
Observation	12,104		3,579	
Prob > chi 2	0.000		0.000	
Logpseudolikelihood	-10,546.185		-3236.0775	

*** $p < 0.01$, ** $p < 0.05$, * $p < 0.1$

Our findings differ from several previous studies, such as Imelda (2020), while there are similarities in the direction of parameters such as education level and household expenditure (Andadari et al. 2014). The study findings tend to be in line with the latter study, which stated that the increase in kerosene prices due to the conversion programme not only increased electricity and firewood consumption but also failed to reduce the number of energy-poor people significantly. Overall, public health tended to decline between 2007 and 2014, and this is a factor that strengthens the finding that the kerosene to LPG conversion programme has not succeeded in improving health conditions, especially among women.

To test the robustness of the estimates, an estimation strategy was carried out with and without inclusion of household characteristics. Likewise, estimates were conducted using robust standard errors. The estimated signs show consistent results, especially for statistically significant variables (Table 9.9). Looking at the impact of the transition only on the surveyed group of women, whether using all control variables or not, gives consistent results, namely that although the health status of women who switch to LPG tends to decline, it is not statistically significant. Thus, there is not enough strong evidence to say that the transition from kerosene stoves to LPG has a beneficial impact on the health of women. However, for the total sample frame (men and women), there were indications of improved health status in the group that switched to using LPG. If the health conditions are examined without considering household characteristics, the significance approaches the range of 11%.

It is interesting to develop qualitative answers to the question why the conversion from kerosene stoves to LPG has not significantly improved women's health. As stated by the government, between 2007 and 2010, around 44.6 million 3-kg cylinder LPG stoves were distributed to the public. At the same time, the government also withdrew kerosene supplies from the market (Ministry of Energy and Mineral Resources, Republic of Indonesia 2010). Data from 2018 shows that around

Table 9.9 Difference-in-differences (without household characteristics)

	Total sampling frame		Sampling frame only women	
Variable	Coefficient	Robust Std. error	Coefficient	Robust Std. error
year dummy	-0.3769391	0.1255981***	-0.535388	0.2160732***
t_kerolpg	0.0096033	0.0627266	0.3102875	0.110253***
y_t_kerolpg	0.2195367	0.1372545	-0,102,645	0.2397512
Cut 1	-5.161898	0.098928	-4,809,895	0.1725998
Cut 2	-1.842008	0.044329	-1,444,922	0.0801451
Cut 3	2.219568	0.05093	2,404,918	0.1009736
Observation	14,225		4,053	
Prob > chi 2	0.000		0.000	
Logpseudolikelihood	-12,898.591		-3852.8988	

*** $p < 0.01$, ** $p < 0.05$, * $p < 0.1$

54.9 million households and around 2.29 million microbusinesses used 3-kg LPG cylinders.

The authors consider governance issues to be an important factor behind the lack of a significant impact on women's health. There are at least five problems related to transition governance. First, there is often a shortage of LPG supply due to shipping disruptions caused by weather disturbances. Second, the increasing price parity between subsidised 3- kg LPG cylinders and unsubsidised LPG has made consumers using non-subsidised LPG switch to 3-kg LPG. Third, damage to stove equipment and many accidents in the early stages of the programme prevented people from completely switching to LPG stoves. Fourth, the potential for limited supply is also driven by the government's policy of converting the fuel used by small fishermen from petrol to LPG, such as through Presidential Regulation 126/2015 concerning the Provision, Distribution and Determination of LPG Prices for Fishing Vessels for Small Fishermen (Movanita and Djumena 2018). Fifth, approximately the poorest 30% of the population receives only 25% of the total subsidy; the majority of LPG subsidies are received by the better off (Bangun 2020).

As a result of these issues, LPG supply shortages often become a problem and LPG prices have increased. This causes some people to switch to using firewood because they have difficulty getting 3-kg LPG cylinders (ayobandung.com 2016; Putri 2012; Widodo 2017; Zuhri 2016). The potential of the return to firewood means that the benefits of the transition are not optimal, and data show that many households in Indonesia still use firewood, as mentioned above.

4 Conclusions and Policy Implication

Most Indonesian people use LPG as their main fuel for cooking. The government's efforts to achieve SDG target number 7 need to be encouraged by providing access to clean energy. The government's programme to convert kerosene stoves to LPG in 2007 was expected to have a broad impact on improving overall public health status. However, between 2007 and 2014, general public health showed a decline. IFLS analysis shows that women have higher health vulnerability compared to men. Previously existing chronic pain conditions certainly have an impact on this vulnerability. Although the conversion of kerosene to LPG (3-kg) cylinders can be said to be successful in covering the majority of households, Indonesia has fallen into a new trap of larger energy subsidies. This is not sustainable because it not only will increase the fiscal burden but will also make Indonesia increasingly dependent on LPG imports to meet people's energy needs for cooking.

To further investigate the impact of the energy transition on vulnerable groups, this study examined the effects of transitioning from kerosene to LPG on women's health by using data from the Indonesian Family Life Survey (IFLS) for the years 2007 and 2014. The results of the analysis found that, in general, it appeared that after the LPG conversion programme was implemented, the general health status of people who cook with LPG was more likely to be somewhat better compared to those who used a kerosene stove.

We argue that based on the cross-sectional data set, the health of women who cook with LPG is more likely to be somewhat higher compared to those who use kerosene and firewood. However, in the context of DiD analysis, the transition from kerosene stoves to LPG could not conclude that this programme has had a significant positive impact on women. This is thought to be due to the general public health status which shows a decline in that period, and because of the transitional governance problems that make some people use firewood.

Due to limited of IFLS data, this research project has evaluated only one decade of implementing the conversion of kerosene stoves to 3-kg LPG. Therefore, research encompassing a longer period should be carried out in the near future to analyse its impact on health.

Policy Implication

This study provides five policy implications. First, clean energy transition policies for cooking are key in building on the philosophy of improving human living standards, especially for groups, notably of women, that are vulnerable to the polluting impacts of cooking fuel emissions. It seems unfair that women who prepare food for family members are at risk of worsening health due to using dirty energy sources for cooking. However, the reasons for carrying out an energy transition are mostly explained as economic reasons, such as the burden of fossil fuel subsidies, which are too large, energy subsidies that are not well targeted, dependence on energy imports, and draining foreign exchange reserves. Although these reasons can be justified, the energy transition needs to be based on human interests and preserving human life. If it is clear that energy transitions are geared to supporting human life, potential conflicts of interest between economic, social and environmental goals will not occur. SDG goals can and should be achieved collectively.

Secondly, the amount of funds devoted to LPG subsidies is not much different from the amount devoted to the health sector at around IDR 92.7 trillion. This is, of course, unfair because the health budget, which has a long-term impact on long-term human resource capacity, is not closely related to energy subsidies that are not well targeted and consumptive. LPG subsidies need to be immediately reduced and redirected to increase access and incentives to clean energy-based RE. This is also an important prerequisite for encouraging greater private sector participation in providing environmentally friendly energy.

Third, the government also needs to encourage global cooperation to accelerate the transformation of the use of environmentally friendly energy for cooking, for example in research collaboration in technology development, business models, financing and investment, and in developing areas based on RE.

Fourth, the public health programme indicators in the national medium-term development plan (RPJMN) and the Ministry of Health's strategic plan for 2020–2024 show the importance of adding indicators relating to clean energy for cooking used in households because the existing indicators in the current public health programme cover only the sanitation side and drinking water facilities (Ministry of Health, Republic of Indonesia 2020).

Finally, the government needs to improve the governance and justice dimensions of the energy transition to ensure that people do not return to using firewood due to the supply constraints, price affordability issues and mistargeting of the 3-kg LPG cylinder subsidy policy.

References

Akter S, Mathew NM, Fila ME (2023) The impact of an improvement in the quality and reliability of rural residential electricity supply on clean cooking fuel adoption: evidence from six energy poor Indian states. World Dev 172. https://doi.org/10.1016/j.worlddev.2023.106366

Al Mohtad I (2006) Remote Area Power Supply Systems (RAPSS). Himalayan Small Hydropower Summit (October 12–13), Dehradun, Uttarakhand

Andadari RK, Mulder P, Rietveld P (2014) Energy poverty reduction by fuel switching: impact evaluation of the LPG conversion program in Indonesia. Energy Policy 66:436–449. https://doi.org/10.1016/j.enpol.2013.11.021

ayobandung.com (2016) *Gas 3Kg Langka, Warga Beralih ke Kayu Bakar*. https://www.ayobandung.com/bandung/pr-79615683/gas-3kg-langka-warga-beralih-ke-kayu-bakar [accessed 12 December, 2024]

Banerjee M et al (2016) Induction stoves as an option for clean cooking in rural India. Energy Policy 88:159–167. https://doi.org/10.1016/j.enpol.2015.10.021

Bangun OV (2020) Subsidi Gas LPG Tabung 3 Kg, *Analisis Ringkas Cepat,* no. 7. Pusat Kajian Anggaran Badan Keahlian Sekretariat Jenderal DPR RI. https://berkas.dpr.go.id/pa3kn/analisis-ringkas-cepat/public-file/analisis-ringkas-cepat-public-31.pdf [accessed 12 December, 2024]

Bhakta A, Brown E, Groce NE (2024) Clean cooking for every 'body': including people with disabilities in modern energy cooking services in the global south. Energy Res Soc Sci 108:103399. https://doi.org/10.1016/j.erss.2023.103399

Byaro M, Mmbaga NF, Mafwolo G (2024) Tackling energy poverty: do clean fuels for cooking and access to electricity improve or worsen health outcomes in Sub-Saharan Africa ? World Development Sustainability 4:100125. https://doi.org/10.1016/j.wds.2024.100125

Cephus JY et al (2017) Testosterone Attenuates Group 2 innate lymphoid cell-mediated airway inflammation. Cell Rep 21(9):2487–2499. https://doi.org/10.1016/j.celrep.2017.10.110

Christian J, Suryadi R (2021) Overview of the electric cooking landscape in Indonesia. https://hsi.foundation/assets/2022/06/Electric-Cooking-Landscape-Indonesia-1.pdf

Hakam DF et al (2022) Mega conversion from LPG to induction stove to achieve Indonesia's clean energy transition. Energ Strat Rev 41:100856. https://doi.org/10.1016/j.esr.2022.100856

Imelda (2020) Cooking that kills: cleaner energy access, indoor air pollution, and health. J Devel Econ 147. https://doi.org/10.1016/j.jdeveco.2020.102548

Isaac J (2024) ESDM ministry pushes for domestic LPG production to reduce imports. *Indonesia Business Post*. https://indonesiabusinesspost.com/insider/esdm-ministry-pushes-for-domestic-lpg-production-to-reduce-imports/ [accessed 22 January 2025]

Kanagawa M, Nakata T (2008) Assessment of access to electricity and the socio-economic impacts in rural areas of developing countries. Energy Policy 36(6):2016–2029. https://doi.org/10.1016/j.enpol.2008.01.041

Kapsalyamova Z et al (2021) Why energy access is not enough for choosing clean cooking fuels? Evidence from the multinomial logit model. J Environ Manage 290:112539. https://doi.org/10.1016/j.jenvman.2021.112539

Ministry of Energy and Mineral Resources, Republic of Indonesia (2010) Konversi Minyak Tanah ke LPG : Menggerakkan Perekonomian, Menghemat Energi. https://www.esdm.go.id/id/media-center/arsip-berita/konversi-minyak-tanah-ke-lpg-menggerakkan-perekonomian-menghemat-energi

Ministry of Health, Republic of Indonesia (2020) Indikator Renstra Kemenkes (P2PTM) 2020–2024: Indikator RPJMN Tahun 2020–2024. https://p2ptm.kemkes.go.id/profil-p2ptm/latar-belakang/indikator-renstra-kemenkes-p2ptm-2020-2024
Movanita ANK, Djumena E (2018) *Gunakan Konverter Kit BBM, Nelayan Hemat Hingga Rp 50.000 per Hari*. Kompas.Com. https://ekonomi.kompas.com/read/2018/11/14/200900526/gunakan-konverter-kit-bbm-nelayan-hemat-hingga-rp-50.000-per-hari
Munasinghe M, Sanghui A (1988) Reliability of electricity supply, outage costs and value of service: an overview. Energy J 9.2_suppl:1–18. https://doi.org/10.5547/issn0195-6574-ej-vol9-nosi2-1
Nix E et al. (2022) Complex dynamics in sustaining clean cooking and food access through a pandemic: a COVID-19 impact study in Peri-urban Cameroon. Energy Sust Devel 71:167–175. https://doi.org/10.1016/j.esd.2022.09.017
Peng W, Pan J (2006) Rural electrification in China: history and institution. Chin World Econ 14(1):71–84. https://doi.org/10.1111/j.1749-124X.2006.00007.x
Putri R (2012) Terpaksa Beralih ke Kayu Bakar, Kompas.Com. https://regional.kompas.com/read/2012/02/20/07584492/terpaksa.beralih.ke.kayu.bakar
Rahut DB et al (2024) Examining energy justice: empirical analysis of clean cooking transition across social groups in India, 2004–2018. Renew Sustain Energy Rev 193:114260. https://doi.org/10.1016/j.rser.2023.114260
RAND Corp (2007) *IFLS-4* [Indonesian Family Life Survey 4] *Survey description.* https://www.rand.org/well-being/social-and-behavioral-policy/data/FLS/IFLS/ifls4.html [accessed 12 December, 2024]
RAND Corp (2014) *RAND IFLS-5 Survey Description.* https://www.rand.org/well-being/social-and-behavioral-policy/data/FLS/IFLS/ifls5.html [accessed 12 December, 2024]
Reiche K, Covarrubias A, Martinot E (2000) Expanding electricity access to remote areas : Off-grid rural electrification in developing countries. *World Power 2000*, pp. 52–60. http://www.martinot.info/Reiche_et_al_WP2000.pdf [accessed 12 December, 2024]
Republic of Indonesia (2021) Indonesia: long-term strategy for low carbon and climate resilience 2050 (Indonesia LTS-LCCR 2050). https://unfccc.int/sites/default/files/resource/Indonesia_LTS-LCCR_2021.pdf [accessed 12 December, 2024]
Low Carbon and Climate Resilience 2050 (Indonesia LTS-LCCR 2050). https://unfccc.int/sites/default/files/resource/Indonesia_LTS-LCCR_2021.pdf [accessed 12 December, 2024]
Rubinstein F et al. (2021) Transitioning to modern energy cooking services in cameroon: a policy review of the energy sector. https://mecs.org.uk/wp-content/uploads/2021/10/Transitioning-to-modern-energy-cooking-services-in-Cameroon.pdf [accessed 12 December, 2024]
Rubinstein F et al. (2022) Adoption of electricity for clean cooking in cameroon: a mixed-methods field evaluation of current cooking practices and scale-up potential. Energy Sust Devel 71:118–131. https://doi.org/10.1016/j.esd.2022.09.010
Sachs JD, Lafortune G, Fuller G (2024) The SDGs and the UN summit of the future: sustainable development report 2024. Dublin: Dublin University Press, pp. 20 ff. https://doi.org/10.25546/108572
Sambodo MT (2014) *LPG Price Adjustments in Indonesia: An Unfinished Reform.* ISEAS Perspective, no. 30
Smith KR, Sagar A (2014) Making the clean available: escaping India's Chulha Trap. Energy Policy 75:410–414. https://doi.org/10.1016/j.enpol.2014.09.024
Strauss J, Witoelar F, Sikoki B (2016) The Fifth Wave of the Indonesia Family Life Survey: Overview and Field Report: Volume 1. RAND Labor & Population, WR-1143/1-NIA/NICHD. https://doi.org/10.7249/wr1143.1
Tachev V (2022) The transition to clean cooking: how to replace gas? Energy Tracker Asia. https://energytracker.asia/the-transition-to-clean-cooking/
Tim Medis Siloam Hospitals (2023) *Bahaya Perokok Pasif, Salah Satunya Rentan Terkena Kanker!* https://www.siloamhospitals.com/informasi-siloam/artikel/bahaya-perokok-pasif

UNSD (United Nations Department of Economic and Social Affairs-Statistics Division) (2023) Sustainable development goals progress chart 2023. https://unstats.un.org/sdgs/report/2023/progress-chart/ [accessed 12 December, 2024]

UNSD (United Nations Department of Economic and Social Affairs-Statistics Division) (2024) Affordable and clean energy. https://unstats.un.org/sdgs/report/2023/Goal-07/ [accessed 12 December, 2024]

WHO (World Health Organization) (2020) Indonesia: Gender dan Kesehatan. https://cdn.who.int/media/docs/default-source/searo/indonesia/gender-dan-kesehatan-indonesia.pdf?sfvrsn=a78948fc_5 [accessed 12 December, 2024]

Widodo A (2017) Cari Kemana-mana Gasnya Tidak Ada, Terpaksa Masak Pakai Kayu. Kompas.Com. https://regional.kompas.com/read/2017/09/18/16452051/cari-kemana-mana-gasnya-tidak-ada-terpaksa-masak-pakai-kayu

Witoelar F, Strauss J, Sikoki B (2009) Socioeconomic success and health in later life: evidence from the Indonesia family life survey. RAND Working Paper No. WR- 704. https://doi.org/10.7249/wr704. https://www.rand.org/pubs/working_papers/WR704.html [accessed 12 December, 2024]

World Bank (2023) Moving the needle on clean cooking for all. https://www.worldbank.org/en/results/2023/01/19/moving-the-needle-on-clean-cooking-for-all [accessed 12 December, 2024]

Zuhri A (2016) Gas Elpiji 3 Kg Tembus Rp 35 Ribu di Muaraenim 3 kg [LPG Breached Rp35,000 in Muaraenim], Palembang.Tribunews.Com. https://palembang.tribunnews.com/2016/11/24/gas-elpiji-3-kg-tembus-rp-35-ribu-di-muaraenim

The Potential Economic Impacts on the Lao PDR of CO_2 Emission Reductions Achieved Through the Imposition of a Carbon Tax

Phouphet Kyophilavong, Han Phoumin, Geoffrey Musyoki Kitetu, and Phongsili Soukchalern

Abstract The objective of this chapter is to investigate the potential economic impacts of a carbon tax on energy consumption, GDP, welfare and CO_2 emissions in the Lao People's Democratic Republic. It employs the GTAP-E (Global Trade Analysis Project-Energy/Environment) model and the GTAP database version 11 with a base year of 2017. The simulation results show that the carbon tax reduced both economic growth and welfare; indeed, the greater the increase in the carbon tax, the more GDP and welfare declined. On the other hand, however, the carbon tax does also lead to a significant decline in CO_2 emissions. The more the carbon tax increases, the greater the reduction in CO_2 emissions. Therefore, the government should consider imposing a carbon tax.

1 Introduction

While achieving net zero emission targets presents a severe challenge for developing countries like the Lao People's Democratic Republic (hereafter, Lao PDR) (Handayani et al. 2022), the Government has made a priority of the UNFCCC obligation to reduce CO_2 emissions (Kyophilavong et al. 2021). The government of the Lao PDR "intends to implement policies that support the long-term goal of limiting global GHG emissions in line with the objectives of the United Nations Framework Convention on Climate Change and the findings of the Intergovernmental Panel on Climate Change's Fifth Assessment Report" (Phosalath and Phongpachith 2019).

P. Kyophilavong (✉) · G. M. Kitetu · P. Soukchalern
Faculty of Economics and Business Management, National University of Laos, Vientiane, Laos
e-mail: phouphetkyophilavong@gmail.com

H. Phoumin
Economic Research Institute for ASEAN and East Asia (ERIA), Jakarta Pusat, Indonesia

G. M. Kitetu
Division of International and Area Studies, Pukyong National University, Busan, South Korea

H. Phoumin et al. (eds.), *Tackling the Energy Transition: Insights from ASEAN and Beyond*, Climate Change and Energy Transition,
https://doi.org/10.1007/978-981-96-6019-3_10

The National Strategy on Climate Change (NSCC) was approved in early 2010 (GoL 2010) and was followed by the Climate Change Action Plan 2013–2020 in April 2013. The Lao PDR also submitted its Intended Nationally Determined Contribution (INDC) to the United Nations Framework Convention on Climate Change on 30 September 2015 (GoL 2015) and adopted the Green Growth Strategy to 2030 (GoL 2018).

The Lao PDR's CO_2 emissions are very low compared to other ASEAN members, though industrial development has seen a related increase in emissions. In 2016, the Lao PDR's CO_2 emissions per capita amounted to 0.66 tons. The sectors with the highest CO_2 emissions were transportation, accounting for 36.9% of all CO_2 emissions, followed by non-combustion (23.6%), buildings (18.4%) and other industrial combustion (15.7%) (Kyophilavong et al. 2021). The electricity from hydropower plants is the primary energy source used in the Lao PDR (MoEM 2018) and the country has a high remaining hydropower potential (MoEM 2020). The Lao PDR uses hydroelectric dams to produce electricity, which it then exports to its neighbours. Even though practically all of the electricity used is produced by hydropower, electricity still makes up a very small portion of all energy use (Kyophilavong et al. 2021).

The Lao PDR's total primary energy supply (TPES) increased from 1,618 thousand tonnes of oil equivalent (ktoe) in 2000 to 4,765 ktoe in 2015 at an average annual growth rate of 7.5%. Over the 2000–2015 period, coal saw the largest growth rate at 42.2% per year, while hydropower saw the second highest annual growth rate at 9.8% (Kyophilavong et al. 2021).

The 9th National Socio-Economic Development Plan (NSEDP), which strives for a balance between long-term economic growth, poverty alleviation and GHG reduction, is attuned to the CO_2 emissions reduction plans for the reduction of CO_2 emissions. According to its Nationally Determined Contributions (NDCs), the Lao PDR has six strategic plans to reduce emissions: (1) Forestry Strategy Implementation to 2020; (2) Renewable Energy Development Strategy; (3) Rural Electrification Program; (4) Transport-focused National Appropriate Mitigation Action; (5) Increased use of large-scale hydropower; and (6) Climate Change Action Plans (GoL 2015; Kyophilavong et al. 2021).

While each of the six strategic plans has a set target, only Strategy Plan 3 (Rural Electrification Program) has so far achieved its target (GoL 2021). Electrification in the country is relatively widespread compared to that in some other ASEAN countries, and the Rural Electrification Program not only reduces emissions but also benefits the rural poor. Biomass is still widely used for cooking and creates serious health issues. The rural electrification initiative will continue to reduce GHG emissions and poverty and also promote rural development (Phosalath and Phongpachith 2019).

While achieving net zero emissions by 2050 is possible for the US and certain other developed countries (Deutch 2020), it is not possible for developing countries like the Lao PDR without further policy input. A carbon tax is a powerful instrument for reducing emissions, and both industrialised and developing nations have made use of this policy tool. However, assessing its potential impacts on the Lao PDR is difficult as there have been few studies carried out pertaining to climate change and carbon emissions in this country (Kyophilavong 2011, 2023a, 2023b; Kyophilavong and Takamatsu 2011; Kyophilavong et al. 2021) As far as we are aware, to date there has not yet been any study published on the impact of a carbon tax using the GTAP-E model, the Energy–Environment (E) version of the computable general equilibrium (CGE) model developed by the Center for Global Trade Analysis Project (GTAP) at Purdue University, West Lafayette, IN, USA (GTAP 2025; Widodo et al. 2028). Therefore, the objective of this paper is to employ this model to assess the impacts of a carbon tax on energy consumption, GDP, welfare and CO_2 emissions in the Lao PDR.

The research questions are: (1) Does a carbon tax reduce CO_2 emissions? (2) What are the nation-wide impacts of a carbon tax? (3) How does a carbon tax affect GDP, welfare and industrial output according to sector? (4) How does a carbon tax affect poverty and income inequality?

The next section of this chapter presents the literature review. This is followed by a discussion of the methodology, data and simulation. The fourth section discusses the simulation results and the last section concludes and suggests policy recommendations.

2 Literature Overview

Table 10.1 gives an overview of a selection of research in which the CGE/GTAP has been applied in the ASEAN context. Whalley and Wigle (1991a, 1991b, 1992) are pioneers in the field of carbon taxation in the computable general equilibrium (CGE) framework. Previous studies show that after the introduction of a carbon tax, the financial burden on an economy will rise if the tax territory is changed from the global to the national level and, subsequently, environmental benefits will decline (Hamilton and Cameron 1994; Bruvoll and Faehn 2006). Jaafar, Al-Amin and Siwar (2010) concluded that carbon taxation in the form of an output tax on energy industries would lower Malaysia's CO_2 emissions as well as its GDP and trade performance. Solaymani et al. (2015) assert that a carbon tax would not be beneficial for the Malaysian transportation sector as output and demand would be negatively affected. Nurdianto and Resosudarmo (2016) show that although a carbon tax helps to reduce CO_2 emissions, it would have negative macroeconomic impacts if not accompanied by a recycling mechanism in selected ASEAN member states.

As mentioned, there are very few studies on the impacts of climate change and CO_2 emissions on the economy, poverty and inequality in the Lao PDR. Kyophilavong (2011) and Kyophilavong et al. (2017) used the CGE model to investigate the impact of trade liberalisation on the macroeconomic variables, poverty and income inequality in the country. The results show that trade liberalisation has had a significant impact on emissions. Kyophilavong and Takamatsu (2011) used the GTAP model to investigate the impact of climate change on agricultural productivity, economic growth and poverty in the Lao PDR. Kyophilavong (2023b) also studied the challenges and issues related to the "decarbonisation pathways" in the Lao PDR and argued that "there is a large opportunity for the Lao PDR to refine its goals, modify

Table 10.1 Literature overview

Author(s)	Region/ country	Year(s)	Sector(s)	Simulations	Method	Findings
Guo et al. (2014)	China	2010	Coal, petroleum, natural gas, petroleum processing, coking, thermal power, clean power, and gas	Carbon tax policy simulation	CGE model	The carbon tax has adverse effects on the economy and social wellbeing. It does, however, boost the use of clean energy and reduce the reliance on coal and coke
Sun et al. (2020)	China	2015	Coal, oil, natural gas, fossil-fuel and non-fossil-fuel electricity	Carbon tax	CGE model	Differentiated carbon tax rates across sectors can facilitate further CO_2 reductions without adversely affecting GDP
Timilsina et al. (2018)	China	2015–2030	Energy and electricity sectors	Carbon tax	CGE model	The carbon tax adversely affected GDP. Recycling tax revenues to decrease current taxes would mitigate GDP reduction and enhance welfare distribution
Ayu (2018)	Indonesia	2011	Primary agriculture, forestry and fishing; coal mining; crude oil; natural gas extraction; refined oil products; electricity; energy intensive industries; and other industries	Carbon Tax	CGE model	A carbon tax adversely affects GDP, government and private household consumption, while promoting CO_2 emissions reduction. The effects differ according to the magnitude of the carbon tax imposed

(continued)

Table 10.1 (continued)

Author(s)	Region/ country	Year(s)	Sector(s)	Simulations	Method	Findings
Jaafar, Al-Amin and Siwar (2008)	Malaysia	2000	Ten sectors, including agriculture, mining and quarrying, industry, electricity, gas, etc.	Output-specific carbon tax on domestic production	CGE model based on the 2000 Malaysia Social Accounting Matrix	A carbon tax decreases carbon emissions, but it also decreases GDP, trade, consumption and savings
Nopiah and Widodo (2019)	Asia	2011	Energy sector	Carbon tax	GTAP-E model	A carbon tax is the most effective way for nations to mitigate CO_2 emissions; however, it adversely affects GDP, investment, trade balance, and employment in particular industries
Puttanapong et al. (2015)	Thailand	2010	40 production activities and 49 commodities, including fossil fuels, electricity and manufacturing sectors	Carbon tax	Recursive dynamic CGE model	The carbon tax adversely affects real GDP, employment, consumption and inflation, while positively influencing government revenue and reducing CO_2 emissions

(continued)

Table 10.1 (continued)

Author(s)	Region/ country	Year(s)	Sector(s)	Simulations	Method	Findings
Rajbhandari et al. (2019)	Thailand	2010	Energy and non-energy sectors	Carbon tax	CGE model	The emissions reduction options may lead to a significant decline in GDP. The improvement and implementation of energy-efficient and renewable energy technologies will substantially contribute to decreasing emissions
Tantivasadakarn (2020)	Thailand	2011	18 groups, including coal, oil, gas, electricity and other energy-intensive industries	Carbon tax and ETS scenarios for Thailand and ASEAN5	CGE model with GTAP-E database	A carbon tax generates minimal adverse effects on productivity, consumption, exports, imports, welfare and competitiveness. A unified carbon tax by ASEAN5 is preferable to a unilateral carbon tax imposed by only Thailand

Sources Summarised by the authors

the institutional frameworks within which it operates, and facilitate the financing needed to meet both its climate and economic development goals together".

While these sources investigate a range of related issues, according to our best knowledge, there has yet to be any study on the impact of the carbon tax on the Lao economy. But generally considered, the literature shows that the carbon tax has had negative impacts on the growth and macroeconomic variables in Asia. However, recycling of the carbon tax revenues could mitigate the negative impacts on growth, macroeconomic variables and poverty reduction.

3 Methodology, Data, and Simulation

We employ the GTAP-E, an energy-environment model which extends the global, multisector standard GTAP model (Burniaux and Truong 2002; Hertel and Tsigas 1997; McDougall and Golub 2009) by introducing inter-fuel and energy-capital substitution in production, emissions accounting, taxation and CO_2 emissions trading. The GTAP-E model "captures features missing in [the] standard GTAP model: energy-capital substitution, energy-energy substitution and emissions accounting (i.e. CO_2 by combustion)". It can "model emissions trading, carbon taxes, and carbon leakage" (GTAP 2025).

The GTAP groups together (into what are called "nests") distinct but related inputs in a particular production function. The value-added nest of the GTAP-E model consists of several fundamental factors of production: unskilled labour, skilled labour, land and natural resources, and a capital-energy nest (in which the former can be substituted for the latter). In the standard GTAP model, only capital is in the value-added nest. However, the production structure of the GTAP-E model extends capital into capital-energy. In relation to energy, the electricity nest is divided into electricity and non-electricity; then, the non-electricity nest is divided into coal and non-coal, and the non-coal nest is divided into oil, oil production and gas. The CES (Constant Elasticity of Substitution) function is applied to substitute electricity with non-electricity and coal with non-coal (Burniaux and Truong 2002). This GTAP-E model is widely used to simulate the impact of a carbon tax on CO_2 emission and the national broad economy of many countries (Nijkamp et al. 2005; Ramadhani and Koo 2022; Dissanayake et al. 2020; Kitetu and Ko 2022).

In order to create the GTAP-E dataset, we employed the most recent versions of the GTAP Database (version 11, base year 2017) (Aguiar et al. 2022) and Lee's combustion-based CO_2 emissions data for all GTAP sectors and regions (2008).

The simulation scenarios follow the study of Nurdianto and Resosudarmo (2016) who simulated a uniform carbon tax policy (USD 10 per tonne of CO_2 emissions). Based on this study, we assumed three simulation scenarios at different rates: (1) a carbon tax of USD 10 /tonne of CO_2 emissions; (2) a carbon tax of USD 20/tonne of CO_2 emissions; and (3) a carbon tax of USD 50/tonne of CO_2 emissions.

Table10.2 The impact of the carbon tax on macroeconomic variables and CO_2 emissions

	Carbon tax of USD 10/ tonne of CO_2	Carbon tax of USD 20/ tonne of CO_2	Carbon tax of USD 50/ tonne of CO_2
Real GDP (%)	-0.085	-0.260	-0.915
Equivalent variation (EV) (USD million)	7.001	-3.111	-65.434
Trade balance (%)	0.010	0.018	0.040
CO_2 emission declines (%)	-17.565	-28.510	-46.508

Source Authors' estimations

4 Results

4.1 The Impact on the Macroeconomic Variables and Outputs

The results of the GTAP-E modelling on the impact of a carbon tax on the macroeconomic variables and CO_2 emissions in the Lao PDR are shown in Table 10.2. The first impact of note is that real GDP showed a gradual drop as a consequence of the imposition of the tax. At USD 10 per tonne of CO_2, real GDP experienced a small contraction (0.085%). This small percentage change in GDP increased in line with an increasing carbon tax rate: a decline of 0.260% at the USD 20 rate, and 0.915% at the USD 50 rate.

The carbon tax also reduced welfare (as computed through equivalent variation [EV], as the equivalent change in utility (welfare payments) which would be induced by the change of prices caused by the imposition of the carbon tax).[1] A carbon tax of USD 10 per tonne of CO_2 could lead to an increase in the EV of USD 7 million. However, a carbon tax of USD 20 or USD 50 reduces the EV gradually, by USD 3.11 million and USD 65.43 million, respectively. On the other hand, the introduction of a carbon tax had little effect on the trade balance. The Lao PDR exports electricity, minerals and agriculture, which do not emit carbon. Moreover, electricity is produced by hydropower plants (Kyophilavong 2024) instead of fossil fuels.

After introducing the carbon tax, CO_2 emissions declined by 17.56% at the rate of USD 10 per tonne of CO_2, 28.51% at USD 20 and 46.50% at USD 50. The higher the rate, therefore, the greater the emissions reduction in the Lao PDR.

The impact of the carbon tax on industrial output is shown in Table 10.3. The highest declines were in coal, electricity, gas and Util_Cons (Utilities and Construction). The output of coal declined by 19.66% at USD 10 per tonne of CO_2, 31.41% at USD 20 and 48.98% at USD 50. The output of electricity declined by 3.99% at USD 10, 7.21% at USD 20 and 14.30% at USD 50. The output of gas declined by 2.75% at USD 10, 5.24% at USD 20 and 11.01% at USD 50.

[1] According to Hicks (1939, p. 331), equivalent variation is "the change in income, taking place in the initial price-situation, which induces the same change in utility as is induced by the price-change".

Table 10.3 Impact of the carbon tax on industrial output (%)

		Carbon tax of USD 10/ tonne of CO_2	Carbon tax of USD 20/ tonne of CO_2	Carbon tax of USD 50/ tonne of CO_2
1 GrainsCrops	Grain and crops	0.344	0.585	1.058
2 Coal	Coal mining	-19.669	-31.417	-48.989
3 Oil	Crude oil	0.561	1.090	2.424
4 Gas	Natural gas	-2.758	-5.249	-11.014
5 Oil_pcts	Refined oil products	3.572	6.164	10.409
6 Electricity	Electricity	-3.998	-7.219	-14.302
7 MeatLstk	Meat products	0.501	0.845	1.471
8 Extraction	Extraction	0.893	1.650	3.443
9 ProcFood	Processed food	1.043	1.839	3.527
10 TextWapp	Textiles and clothing	3.374	6.125	12.477
11 LightMnfc	Light manufacturing	2.461	4.396	8.643
12 HeavyMnfc	Heavy manufacturing	2.206	3.918	7.623
13 Util_Cons	Utilities and construction	-2.308	-4.374	-9.642
14 TransComm	Transportation and communication	0.383	0.500	0.166
15 OthServices	Other services	0.573	0.931	1.490

Source Authors' estimation

Surprisingly, the output of TextWapp (textiles and clothing), Oil_pcts (refined oil products), LightMnfc (light manufacturing), and HeavyMnfc (heavy manufacturing) increased following the imposition of the carbon tax. The output of TextWapp increased by 3.37% at USD 10 per tonne of CO_2, 6.12% at USD 20 and 12.47% at USD 50. LightMnfc increased by 2.46% at USD 10, 4.39% at USD 20 and 8.64% at USD 50. HeavyMnfc increased by 2.20% at USD 10, 3.91% at USD 10 and 7.62% at USD 10. There are some reasons for the increase in production output in some sectors. First, electricity is generated from hydropower; it is green energy that does not create CO_2 emissions. Second, the demand for polluting fuels such as coal and natural gas declined, shifting the inputs to the other sectors.

Table10.4 The impact of a carbon tax on CO_2 emissions (%)

		Carbon tax of USD 10/ tonne of CO_2	Carbon tax of USD 20/ tonne of CO_2	Carbon tax of USD 50/ tonne of CO_2
1 Coal	Coal mining	-20.776	-33.432	-53.427
2 Oil	Crude oil	-11.914	-19.360	-29.945
3 Gas	Natural gas	-4.183	-7.964	-17.675
4 Oil_pcts	Refined oil products	-3.919	-7.595	-17.112

Source Authors' estimation

4.2 *Impact on CO_2 Emissions*

As mentioned above, CO_2 emissions declined with the imposition of the carbon tax.

This impact by energy source is given in Table 10.4. The largest impact was on coal, followed by oil and gas. At a rate of USD 10 per tonne of CO_2, the reduction of CO_2 emissions from coal was 20.77%, 33.43% at USD 20 per tonne, and 53.42% at USD 50 per tonne. Regarding the CO_2 emissions reduction from oil, emissions declined 11.91% at the rate of USD 10 per tonne of CO_2, 19.36% at the rate USD 20, and 29.94% at USD 50. Gas and oil products also show the same trend.

5 Conclusion

This study attempts to quantitatively evaluate the potential economic impacts on the Lao PDR of CO_2 emission reductions through the imposition of a carbon tax. From the findings of the simulation carried out using the GTAP-E model, we derived the following conclusions. The carbon tax reduced real GDP and welfare significantly with an increasing carbon tax rate. However, the carbon tax also reduced CO_2 emissions, especially from the coal and gas sectors. It had mixed effects on industrial output. The greatest contractions were seen in coal, electricity, natural gas, and utilities and construction. Surprisingly however, the output of textiles and clothing, refined oil products, and light and heavy manufacturing increased as a result of the carbon tax.

The implementation of a carbon tax to reduce CO_2 emissions should be given careful consideration. While it could hurt the country's growth, recycling of the carbon tax revenues should be the option used to minimise its negative impacts, as Malerba et al. (2021) have argued in relation to Peru. In other relevant research, Sommer et al. (2022) found in the German context that the only carbon tax that received support from more than half those surveyed was the lowest given (€10 / t CO_2) and that there was "disagreement" whether the recycled revenue should be disbursed in the form of a lump sum or in targeted payments to the most affected, poor households. Carbon tax revenues could promote economic growth and help reduce poverty if they were used to fund clean energy projects, create jobs in renewable sectors, subsidise renewable energy, invest in climate adaptation projects, and enhance the access to public goods by lower-income households.

References

Aguiar A et al (2022) The global trade analysis project (GTAP) data base: version 11. J Glob Econ Anal 7:2

Ayu P (2018) The impact of carbon tax application on the economy and environment of Indonesia. Eur J Econ Bus Stud 4(1):110–120

Bruvoll A, Fæhn T (2006) Transboundary effects of environmental policy: markets and emission Leakages. Ecol Econ 59(4):499–510

Burniaux J-M, Truong Truong (2002) GTAP-E: an energy-environmental version of the GTAP model. *GTAP Technical Paper No 16*. https://www.gtap.agecon.purdue.edu/resources/res_display.asp?RecordID=923 [accessed 6 December 2024]

Deutch J (2020) Commentary: is net zero carbon 2050 possible? Joule 4:2237–2243. https://www.sciencedirect.com/science/article/pii/S2542435120304050URL [accessed 5 December 2024]

Dissanayake S, Mahadevan R, Asafu-Adjaye J (2020) Evaluating the efficiency of carbon emissions policies in a large emitting developing country. Energy Policy 136:111080

GoL (Government of the Lao PDR) (2010) Strategy on climate change of the Lao PDR. http://mirror.unhabitat.org/downloads/docs/12679_1_595432.pdf [accessed 7 December 2024]

GoL (Government of the Lao PDR) (2015) Lao PDR's Intended Nationally Determined Contribution (INDC). https://faolex.fao.org/docs/pdf/lao186537.pdf [accessed 6 December 2024]

GoL (Government of the Lao PDR) (2018) National green growth strategy of the Lao PDR till 2030. https://policy.asiapacificenergy.org/sites/default/files/National%20Green%20Growth%20Strategy%20of%20the%20Lao%20PDR%20till%202030.pdf [accessed 7 December 2024]

GoL (Government of the Lao PDR) (2021) Nationally Determined Contribution (NDC). https://unfccc.int/sites/default/files/NDC/2022-06/NDC%202020%20of%20Lao%20PDR%20%28English%29%2C%2009%20April%202021%20%281%29.pdf

GTAP (Global Trade Analysis Project) (2025) About GTAP: global trade analysis project. https://www.gtap.agecon.purdue.edu/about/project.asp [accessed 16 February 2025]

Guo Z et al (2014) Exploring the impacts of a carbon tax on the Chinese economy using a CGE model with a detailed disaggregation of energy sectors. Energy Econ 45:455–462

Handayani K et al (2022) Moving beyond the NDCs: ASEAN pathways to a net-zero emissions power sector in 2050. Appl Energy 311:118580

Hamilton K, Cameron G (1994) Simulating the distributional effects of a Canadian carbon tax. Canad Public Policy/analyse De Politiques 20(4):385–399

Hertel TW, Tsigas ME (1997) Structure of GTAP, in *Global Trade Analysis: Modeling and Applications*. https://www.gtap.agecon.purdue.edu/uploads/resources/download/86.pdf

Hicks JR (1939) Value and capital: an inquiry into some fundamental principles of economic theory. London: The English Language Book Society and Oxford University Press, 2nd. ed. 1941. https://archive.org/details/in.ernet.dli.2015.223876/page/n3/mode/2up?q=equivalent+variation [accessed 16 February 2025]

Jaafar AH, Al-Amin A, Siwar C (2008) A CGE analysis of the economic impact of output-specific carbon tax on the Malaysian economy. Paper presented at 3rd National Conference on Malaysia Economy, Port Dickson, August 20–22. https://www.researchgate.net/publication/24112055_A_CGE_Analysis_of_the_Economic_Impact_of_Output-Specific_Carbon_Tax_on_the_Malaysian_Economy [accessed 7 December 2024]

Kitetu GM, Ko J-H (2022) United states re-enters the 2015 Paris climate agreement: the unexpected twists and the opportunity costs? A CGE Approach Global Trade Analysis Project (GTAP). Paper Presented at the 25th GTAP Annual Conference on Global Economic Analysis Held Virtually on 8–10 June 2022. https://gtap.agecon.purdue.edu/resources/res_display.asp?RecordID=6660 [accessed 7 December 2024]

Kyophilavong P (2011) Trade liberalization, pollution and poverty: evidence from Lao PDR. EEPSEA (Economy and Environment Program for Southeast Asia), IDRC (International Development Research Centre [Ottawa]) Regional Office for Southeast and East Asia, Singapore

Kyophilavong P (2023a) Challenges, opportunities, and recommendations for a just transition in Laos, Climate Strategy (CS) and NUoL (National University of Laos). https://climatestrategies.org/wp-content/uploads/2022/12/Challenges-Opportunities-and-Recommendations-for-a-Just-Transition-in-Laos.pdf [accessed 7 December 2024]

Kyophilavong P (2023b) Decarbonization pathways in Laos: the challenges and solutions. Asian Econ Papers 22(3):46–63

Kyophilavong P (2024) Securing affordable energy for the growing industrial, commercial, and residential sectors in Lao PDR, in H Phoumin and A Phongsavath, eds., *Energy Security White Paper: Policy Directions for Inclusive and Sustainable Development for Lao PDR* (pp 124–139). Ministry of Energy and Mines, and Economic Research Institute for ASEAN and East Asia (ERIA)

Kyophilavong P, Takamatsu S (2011) Impact of climate change on poverty in Laos. Paper prepared for presentation at the Agricultural & Applied Economics Association's 2011 AAEA & NAREA Joint Annual Meeting, Pittsburgh, PA, USA

Kyophilavong P et al. (2021) ASEAN green future project phase 1 report decarbonization in Lao PDR: the options and challenges. https://www.climateworkscentre.org/wp-content/uploads/2022/02/Lao-PDR-Report-Phase-1_Sept-21.pdf [accessed 5 December 2024]

Kyophilavong P, Takamatsu S, Oh JS (2017) Impact of trade liberalization on pollution and poverty: evidence from Lao PDR. In: Kobayashi K et al (eds) Economic integration and regional development economic integration and regional development: the ASEAN economic community. Routledge, Abingdon, pp 232–243

Lee H-L (2008) An emissions data base for integrated assessment of climate change policy using GTAP. Available at https://www.gtap.agecon.purdue.edu/resources/res_display.asp?RecordID=1143

Malerba D, Gaentzsch A, Ward H (2021) Mitigating poverty: the patterns of multiple carbon tax and recycling regimes for Peru. Energy Policy 149:111961

McDougall R, Golub A (2007) GTAP-E: a revised energy-environmental version of the GTAP model. GTAP Research Memorandum, 15

MoEM (Lao PDR Ministry of Energy and Mines) (2018) Lao PDR energy statistics 2018. https://www.eria.org/uploads/media/0_Lao_PDR_Energy_Statistics_2018_complete_book.pdf [accessed 6 December 2024]

MoEM (Lao PDR Ministry of Energy and Mines) (2020) Lao PDR energy outlook 2020. Jakarta: ERIA. https://www.eria.org/uploads/media/Research-Project-Report/Lao-Energy-Outlook-2020/Lao-PDR-Energy-Outlook-2020.pdf

Nijkamp P, Wang S, Kremers H (2005) Modeling the impacts of international climate change policies in a CGE context: the use of the GTAP-E model. Econ Model 22(6):955–974

Nopiah R, Widodo T (2019) Climate change mitigation through market-based instruments in large Asian emitters. Yogyakarta: Master and Doctoral Program, Economics Department, FEB, Gadjah Mada University. https://mpra.ub.uni-muenchen.de/91230/1/MPRA_paper_91230.pdf [accessed 7 December 2024]

Nurdianto DA, Resosudarmo BP (2016) The economy-wide impact of a uniform carbon tax in ASEAN. J Southeast Asian Econ 33,1:1–22. https://people.anu.edu.au/budy.resosudarmo/2016to2020/Nurdianto_Reso_2016.pdf

Phosalath S, Phongpachith C (2019) Climate change adaptation roadmap of the Lao people's democratic republic, in *Towards a Resilient ASEAN Volume 2: Advancing Disaster Resilience and*

Climate Change Adaptation: Roadmaps and Options for Implementation, ed. V. Anbumozhi, J. Gross and S. Wesiak. Jakarta: ERIA (Economic Research Institute for ASEAN and East Asia), pp 197–219

Puttanapong N et al (2015) A Monte-Carlo dynamic CGE model for the impact analysis of Thailand's carbon tax policies. J Sust Energy Environ 6:43–53

Rajbhandari S, Limmeechokchai B, Masui T (2019) The impact of different GHG reduction scenarios on the economy and social welfare of Thailand using a computable general equilibrium (CGE) model. Energy Sust Soc 9:1–21

Ramadhani DP, Koo Y (2022) Comparative analysis of carbon border tax adjustment and domestic carbon tax under general equilibrium model: focusing on the Indonesian economy. J Clean Prod 377:134288

Sommer S, Mattauch L, Pahle M (2022) Supporting Carbon Taxes: the role of fairness. Ecol Econ 195:107359

Sun Y et al (2020) Greener economic development via carbon taxation scheme optimization. J Clean Prod 275:124100

Tantivasadakarn C (2020) Carbon pricing and international competitiveness for Thailand and ASEAN. Thammasat Review of Economic and Social Policy 6(2):34–76

Whalley J, Wigle R (1991a) Cutting CO_2 emissions: the effects of alternative policy approaches. Energy J 12(1):109–124

Whalley J, Wigle R (1991b) The international incidence of carbon taxes, in *Global Warming: Economic Policy Responses*, ed. R. Dornbusch and J. Poterba. Cambridge, MA: MIT Press

Whalley J, Wigle R (1992) Results for the OECD comparative modelling project from the Whalley–Wigle model, OECD Economics Department Working Papers, No 121

Widodo T et al. (2018) A long-run estimation of natural gas demand in Indonesian manufacturing sector: computable general equilibrium model approach, MPRA Munich Personal RePEc Archive Paper No. 86887. https://mpra.ub.uni-muenchen.de/86887/

Zhang M (2011) CGE simulation for levying carbon tax in China and international experience of levying carbon tax. Chinese J Popul Resour Environ 9(2):84–89

Energy Transition in Vietnam: Paving the Way for Sustainable Development

Thai-Ha Le and Lam Truong Phuong Do

Abstract This chapter delves into Vietnam's energy transition from a coal-based system to increased adoption of renewable resources like wind and solar. We explore historical trends, development barriers and financing mechanisms, pinpointing specific challenges, including ancillary and transmission limits and a non-competitive market, that constrain the use of these abundant resources to generate electricity. This study also innovatively applies dynamic principal component analysis (PCA) to measure the energy transition index in Vietnam and its evolution between 2003 and 2020. The advantages of dynamic PCA are the ability to capture both the cross-sectional and time dimensions of the input factors. Using dynamic PCA, we create an energy transition index revealing a positive, albeit complex, progression towards a greener energy mix. The increasing capacity of renewables and the policy reforms and enhanced investments, both local and international, affirm Vietnam's ongoing journey to balance energy security, economic growth and environmental sustainability. Despite notable challenges, the collective endeavours of various stakeholders promise a sustainable trajectory in Vietnam's energy landscape.

JEL classification C1 · Q4

Keywords Energy transition index · Dynamic principal component analysis · Vietnam

---

T.-H. Le (✉)
VinUniversity & VinFuture Foundation, Hanoi, Vietnam
e-mail: v.md@vinfutureprize.org

L. T. P. Do
Fulbright School of Public Policy and Management, Fulbright University Vietnam, Ho Chi Minh City, Vietnam

Monash University, Melbourne, Australia

H. Phoumin et al. (eds.), *Tackling the Energy Transition: Insights from ASEAN and Beyond*, Climate Change and Energy Transition,
https://doi.org/10.1007/978-981-96-6019-3_11

1 Introduction

Vietnam is a rapidly developing nation in Southeast Asia. Since the introduction of the Doi Moi economic reform in 1986 with the objective of creating a socialist-oriented market economy, Vietnam has been experiencing spectacular development. Starting at only USD 598.9 in 1986, Vietnam's GDP per capita multiplied in just 33 years, 5.49 times to USD 3,288.4 in 2019, at an average growth rate per annum of 5.31%. Despite slowing down during 2020–21 due to the COVID-19 pandemic, Vietnam was one of a few countries that kept growth in positive territory. This country has also shown high resistance and quick recovery capability, as seen in the annual growth rate reaching 8.02% in 2022 (see Fig. 11.1).

The energy sector, especially the electricity sector, has supported Vietnam's magnificent progress as the government maintains low electricity tariffs to attract foreign direct investment. In addition, low tariffs serve as a subsidy to the residential sector so that most citizens can access electricity at an affordable cost. Consequently, from 1990 to 2019, electricity consumption rose significantly, with an annual growth rate higher than the GDP growth rate (Do and Le 2024; EREA and DEA 2022; Le and Pitts 2019).

Vietnam's rising economic development has led to an increase over time of per capita CO_2 emissions. While its emissions were still lower than those of Brunei Darussalam, Singapore, Malaysia and Thailand, its rapid growth should be a concern since Vietnam is expected to pass Thailand in the near future (see Fig. 11.2). The Vietnamese government recognises the urgent need to reduce the country's carbon footprint and contribute to global efforts to combat climate change. Vietnam submitted its intended nationally determined contribution (NDC) in September 2015 and submitted the update in 2022. According to the most recent version, Vietnam

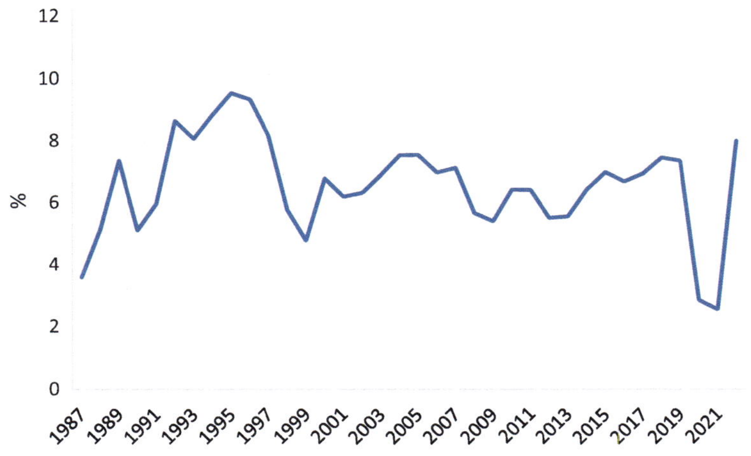

Fig. 11.1 Vietnam annual GDP growth, 1985–2021. *Source* World Bank

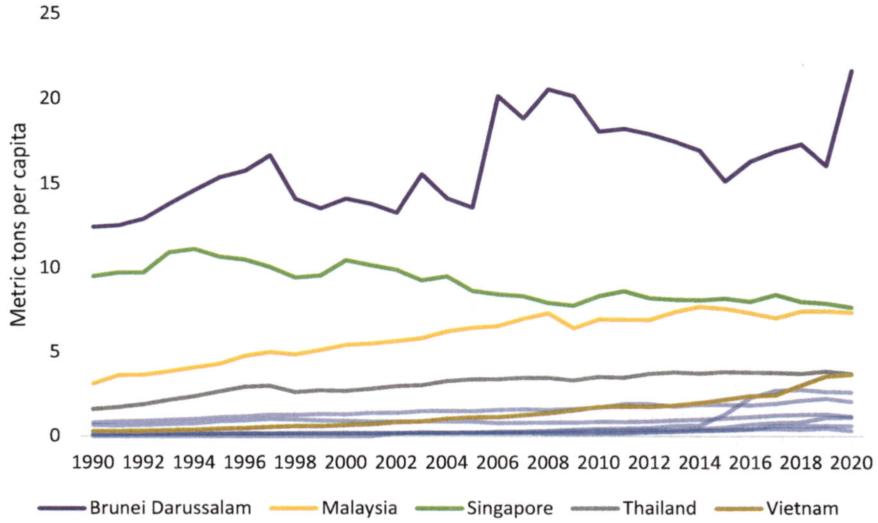

Fig. 11.2 Per capita CO_2 emissions of Southeast Asian countries, 1990–2020. *Note* Blue lines show the remaining countries. *Source* World Bank

aims to reduce 9% of the total greenhouse gas emissions by 2030, compared to the business-as-usual scenario. In addition, at the 2021 United Nations Climate Change Conference (COP26) in Glasgow, Prime Minister Pham Minh Chinh made a solid commitment to the net zero target by 2050.

An effective energy transition is crucial as the core strategy to reduce emissions and achieve the net zero target. Additionally, a successful energy transition ensures energy security, reduces dependence on imported fuels and fosters economic growth by unlocking the potential of renewable energy (RE) resources. This chapter critically examines the energy transition in Vietnam, delving into its significance, progress achieved, challenges encountered and the trajectory towards a sustainable energy future. Moreover, to quantify the energy transition in Vietnam, it constructs an energy transition index from 2003–20, following the framework of Neofytou et al. (2020). By analysing these aspects, this study aims to provide valuable insights and policy recommendations to support Vietnam's efforts in paving the way for sustainable development through its energy transition journey.

The remainder of this chapter is constructed as follows. Section 2 reviews the energy transition in Vietnam, focusing on the historical trend in the power sector, the challenge to expand RE, and the availability of financing support from both domestic and international bodies. Section 3 provides a brief literature review on the energy transition in Vietnam and the composition of the energy transition index. This section also introduces the methodology for building the index for Vietnam and presents results from the analysis. Section 4 concludes this chapter with some policy recommendations.

2 Review of the Energy Transition in Vietnam

2.1 Overview of the Power Sector

The energy transition is achieved through electrification in sectors such as transport, industry and agriculture; therefore, the power sector should be prioritised in the energy transition (EREA and DEA 2022). To encourage RE development in the power system, the Vietnamese government introduced multiple policies for a wide range of sources, including small hydropower, biomass, solid waste, solar and wind (see Fig. 11.3).

One of the noteworthy incentives is the feed-in-tariff (FiT). For projects using solid waste, the FiT is US 10.05 cents/kWh (direct burning), and US 7.28 cents/kWh (gas burning from landfills). The FiT for biomass co-generation heat power projects is US 7.03 cents/kWh, and US 8.47 cents/kWh for the remaining biomass plants. If the commercial operation date of a solar project was 21 December 2020 at the latest, the project would enjoy a FiT of US 7.09 cents/kWh. The FiT for wind power plants which were in operation on or before 1 November 2021, is US 9.8 cents/kWh (offshore wind), and US 8.5 cents/kWh (onshore wind).

Under the FiT scheme, solar and wind projects were rapidly constructed and began to operate, while the expansion of biomass and solid waste was relatively modest. There are several reasons for this. First, in recent years, the solar and wind energy technologies have been intensively developed, which results in lower investment costs. Second, the inputs for solar and wind energy are free, unlike biomass and solid waste for which the inputs can be costly due to price volatility. As a result, over the five-year period 2018 to 2022, the installed capacity of RE (excluding hydropower) increased from only 329 MW to 20,671 MW. In 2022, wind and solar accounted for 26.4% of the total capacity (see Fig. 11.4). On the other hand, the capacity of biomass and solid waste is extremely low.

With the great increase in wind and solar projects, the power generation from these sources, as a share of the total generation, rose significantly from less than 1% in 2015 to 12.8% in 2022. However, solar and wind are not effectively used, as the generation from these two sources is still less than half of their installed capacity. In addition, solar and wind power may not help reduce the use of coal. From 2015 to 2020, coal generation grew from 34.4% to 50.01% of the total generation. It decreased to 46% in 2021 and continued to fall to 39.09% in 2022 (see Fig. 11.5).

The downward trend of coal usage in 2021 and 2022 can probably be explained by the increase in hydropower generation thanks to favourable climate conditions. In May and June 2023, when there were extremely hot days, the operation of hydropower was severely affected. As a result, rolling blackouts and power disruptions occurred throughout the cities and provinces in the North. While the significant rise in the energy demand in the North may explain this situation (see Fig. 11.6), the major reasons lie in the structure and mechanism of the power system in Vietnam.

First, given that RE like solar or wind is highly dependent on weather conditions, a high penetration of RE may negatively affect the stability of the power system.

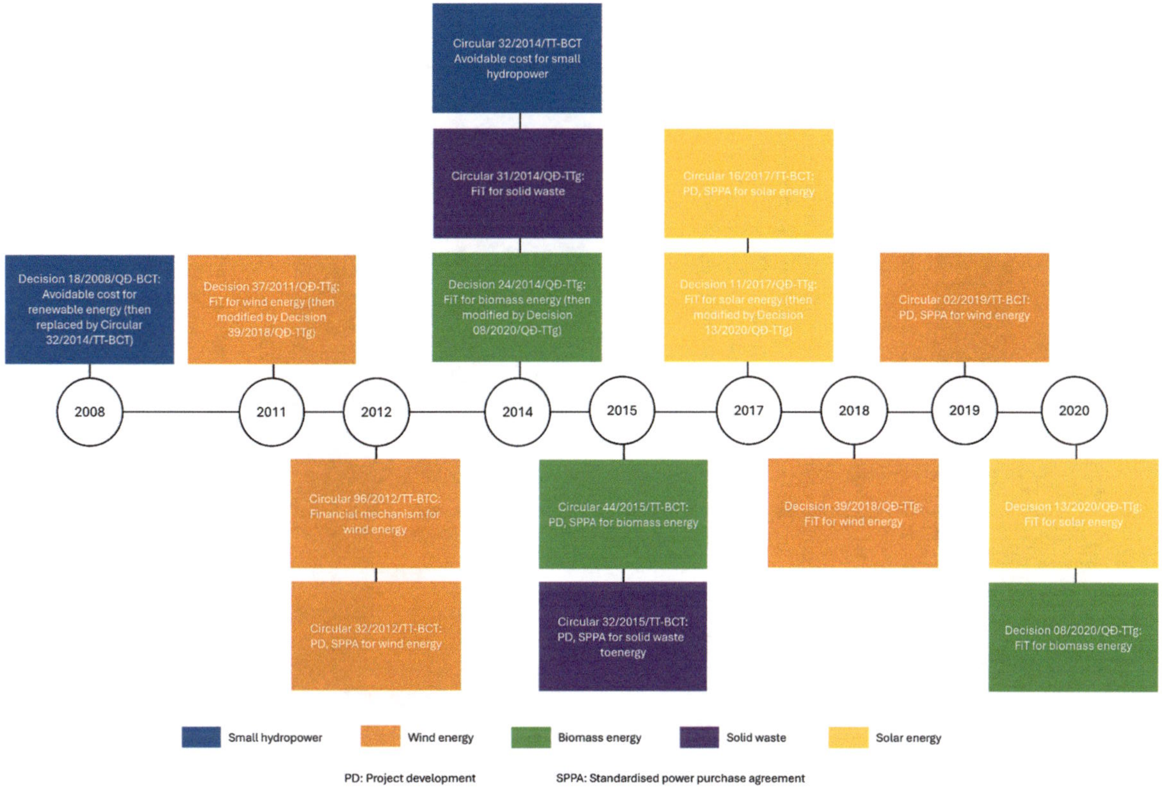

Fig. 11.3 Policies to encourage renewable energy development in Vietnam, 2008–2020. *Source* Authors' translation from Institute of Energy (2021)

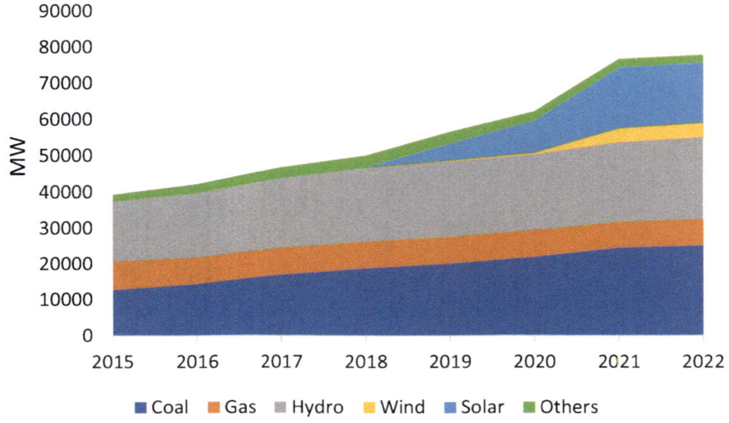

Fig. 11.4 Installed capacity of the power system by source, 2015–2022. *Sources* For 2015 to 2020, Vietnam Energy Statistics 2020. For 2021, see https://nangluongvietnam.vn/tap-doan-dien-luc-viet-nam-nam-2021-ket-qua-qua-nhung-thu-thach-28161.html and https://vietnamnet.vn/bung-no-dien-gio-dien-mat-troi-viet-nam-top-dau-dong-nam-a-811431.html. For 2022, see https://kinhtevadubao.vn/nang-luong-tai-tao-dang-chiem-162-trong-toan-he-thong-25288.html

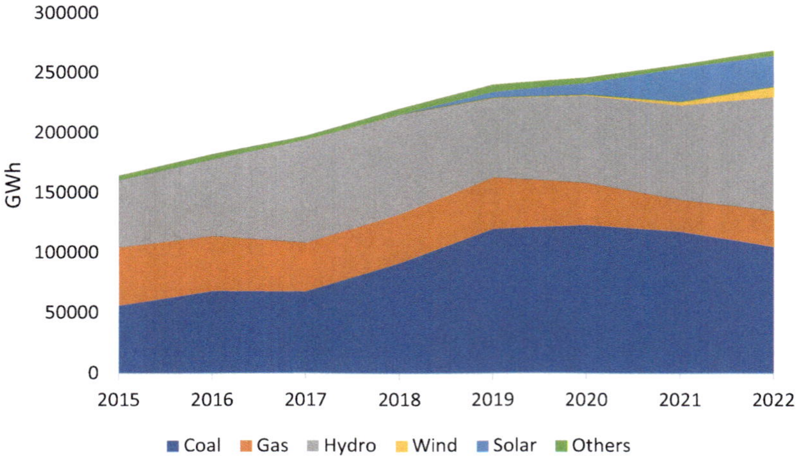

Fig. 11.5 Power generation by source, 2015–2022. *Sources* For 2015 to 2020, Vietnam Energy Statistics 2020. For 2021, see https://nangluongvietnam.vn/tap-doan-dien-luc-viet-nam-nam-2021-ket-qua-qua-nhung-thu-thach-28161.html. For 2022, see https://nangluongvietnam.vn/tap-doan-dien-luc-viet-nam-nam-2022-thu-thach-huong-phat-trien-30102.html

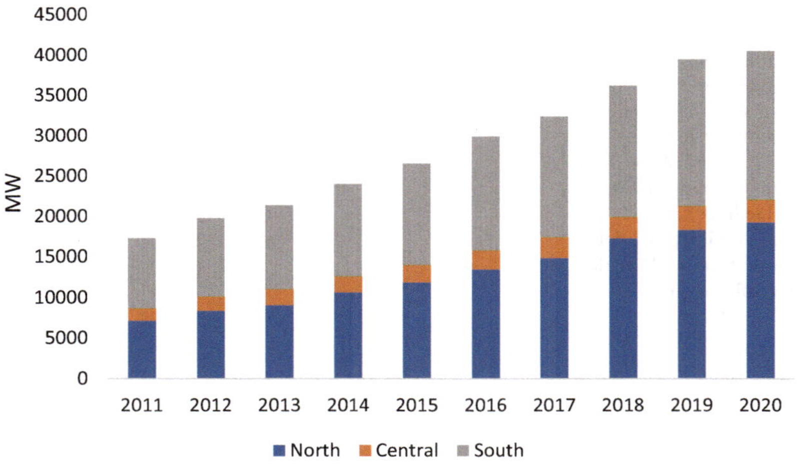

Fig. 11.6 Peak demand by region, 2011–2020. *Source* Institute of Energy (2021)

This downside of RE can be mitigated through ancillary services, such as frequency regulation and spinning and non-spinning reserves. Unfortunately, there is not yet a market for ancillary services in Vietnam, making RE less preferred than traditional generation sources.

Second, most RE projects are situated from the central coast to the south of Vietnam, as the climate conditions in this part of the country support wind and solar. Consequently, electricity is abundant with no risk of power disruption. Surplus electricity can be transferred to the north, but at the current stage, due to the limitation in the 550 kV transmission lines, the electricity delivered from the south and the central is not adequate for this region (see Fig. 11.7). Hence, the government still relies on coal generation as well as large hydropower and imports to meet the demand in the north.

Third, since the competitive electricity market is under construction, and the authorities impose heavy regulations on the sector, the market operates inefficiently. Although the Vietnam Competitive Generation Market was established in 2012, Vietnam Electricity (EVN), a state-owned enterprise, is still a dominant actor in this market. The positioning of EVN allows it to enjoy bargaining power and give preference to its partners (Nguyen-Trinh and Rizopoulos 2018). Hence, EVN does not have strong incentives to develop RE. In addition, the electricity price in Vietnam is strictly governed by the authorities. The industrial tariff is kept low to attract foreign direct investment, while the low residential tariff ensures that all citizens can access electricity affordably. Compared to other Southeast Asia countries, the residential tariff in Vietnam is low (see Fig. 11.8), and raising it is extremely challenging. According to the 30 June 2017 Decision 24/2017/QĐ-TTg on the mechanism for the adjustment of the average retail electricity price, this price would be modified only if the input parameters, including generation, transmission, distribution and operation, increase

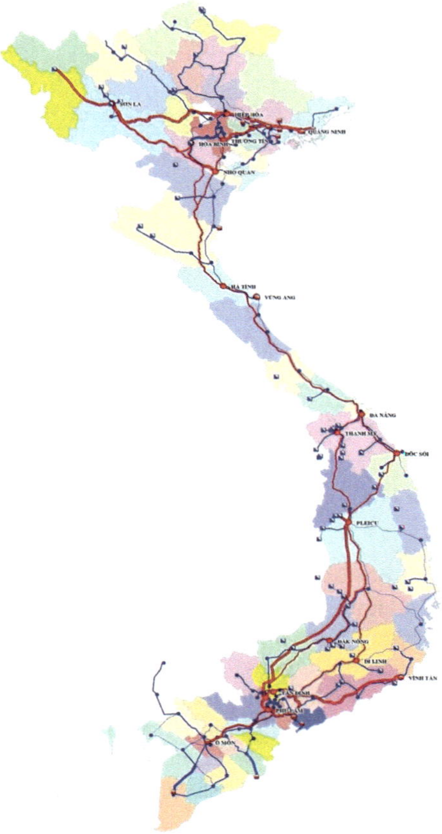

Fig. 11.7 Transmission lines in mainland Vietnam, 2019. *Source* https://nangluongvietnam.vn/duong-day-500kv-mach-3-ky-1-tong-quan-he-thong-dien-viet-nam-22731.html. *Notes* Red line: 500 kV transmission line; Blue line: 220 kV transmission line; Red dot: 500 kV substation; Blue dot: 220 kV substation

by at least 3%. In the 2020–22 period, the price remained unchanged to support the economy during and post-COVID-19. As the cost is not reflected in the tariff, sources which have high marginal costs have a lower potential of being integrated into the system.

2.2 *Release of the Power Development Plan 8 (PDP8) (Socialist Republic of Viet Nam, 2023)*

The Power Development Plan for the 2021–30 period with the vision to 2050 (PDP8) is the official and most comprehensive power plan for Vietnam. Released in April 2023, this plan outlines future power production and distribution in the country. One of the noteworthy strategies for the next years is to achieve supply and demand balance within regions while restricting inter-regional transmission. Self-generation

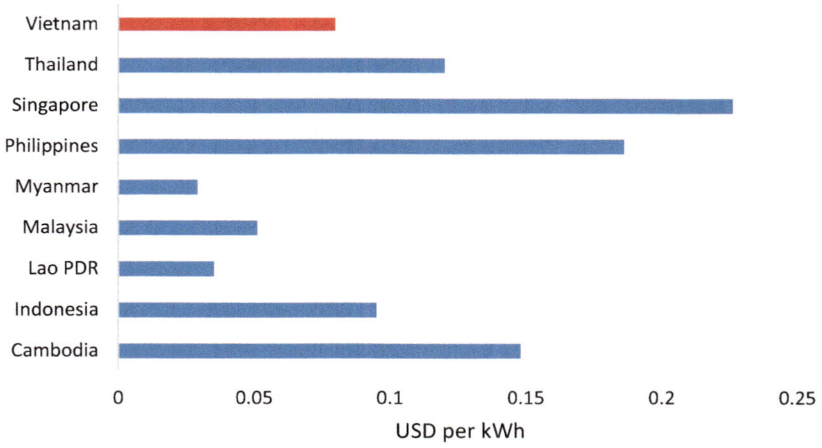

Fig. 11.8 Residential tariff of Southeast Asian countries (except Brunei Darussalam and Timor Leste), Q3/2023. *Source* Global Petrol Prices

and self-dissipation in power sources are encouraged, as the government does not impose any limits on the installed capacity of solar and wind energy. Besides these two strategies, PDP8 determines other priorities to improve the power system, among which are:

- an improvement in the transmission and distribution networks, smart grid technologies, and energy storage systems to enhance system reliability and flexibility;
- a promotion of energy efficiency, demand-side management and distributed generation to optimise energy use and reduce losses;
- encouraging the private sector to participate in the power system, including generation, transmission and distribution. The importance of competitive electricity retail market development is also reconfirmed.

PDP8 also outlines the optimal generation mix to achieve the commitment to net zero. Under this pathway, Vietnam must explore liquefied natural gas (LNG), offshore wind and pumped storage hydropower/battery energy storage systems (PHS/BESS), besides existing sources. The details are shown in Table 11.1. Some highlights are:

- no coal thermal power by 2050;
- the share of solar and wind power in the total installed capacity will reach 27.05% by 2030, and 26.5 – 29.4% by 2050. In particular, the potential of offshore wind power will be rigorously explored, with 6,000 MW installed capacity by 2030 and 70,000 – 91,500 MW by 2050;
- an increase in LNG as a transition fuel, which will rise to 22,400 MW by 2030, and to 29,900 MW by 2050;

Table 11.1 Installed capacity (MW) by source over 2021–2030 with the vision to 2050

	2030	2050
Coal (only)	About 30,000	0
LNG	22,400	20,900 – 29,900
Hydro	29,346	36,016
Wind	27,880	130,050 – 168,550
+ *Offshore wind*	6,000	70,000 – 91,500
Solar	12,836	168,594 – 189,294
Other RE	2,270	6,015
PSH/BESS	2,700	30,650 – 45,550

Source Authors' calculations from Decision 500/QD-TTG (Socialist Republic of Viet Nam, 2023)

- a wide range of RE is used, including hydropower, thermal power from biomass and ammonia, etc.

2.3 Financing the Energy Transition in Vietnam

Vietnam's energy transition is expected to bring multiple benefits, such as lower carbon emissions, air pollution and dependence on imported fuels, higher energy security and new opportunities for green growth and job creation. However, this progress faces many challenges, such as financing, regulation, market design, grid integration, social and environmental impacts and regional cooperation. Therefore, the energy transition requires proactive and continued reforms, strong political commitment and effective collaboration among all stakeholders.

The main sources of financing for the energy transition are a combination of domestic and international public and private funds. Some of the examples are:

- The Vietnam Energy Partnership Group (VEPG), a platform for policy dialogue and cooperation between the Vietnamese government and development partners in the energy sector. The VEPG supports the implementation of the energy transition through policy advice, technical assistance and financing.
- The World Bank Group, which provides loans, guarantees and technical assistance to support Vietnam's energy transition, especially in RE, energy efficiency and grid modernisation.
- The Asian Development Bank (ADB), which supports Vietnam's energy transition through policy-based lending, project financing, technical assistance and knowledge sharing. The ADB also helps mobilise private sector investment through co-financing and risk-sharing mechanisms.
- The Green Climate Fund (GCF), established under the UNFCCC and headquartered in the Republic of Korea, which provides grants and concessional loans to

support low-carbon and climate-resilient projects in Vietnam, such as solar power plants, energy-efficient buildings and green transport systems.
- The Just Energy Transition Partnership (JETP), a major international deal between Canada, France, Germany, Italy, Japan, the United Kingdom and the United States (the G7 countries) and Denmark, Norway and Vietnam, which was established on 14 December, 2022. This partnership aims to mobilise USD 15.5 billion of public and private finance "over the next three to five years" from that date to accelerate Vietnam's transition away from coal. According to the European Commission (2022), the objectives of the JETP are:
  - moving the peak greenhouse gas emissions in Vietnam forward from 2035 to 2030;
  - reducing the peak annual emissions of the power sector by a maximum 30%, from 240 to 170 megatons;
  - reducing Vietnam's peak coal capacity from the current quantity (37 GW) to 30.2 GW;
  - Encouraging the share of RE so that it will account for at least 47% of total electricity generation by 2030.

To unlock more financing for the energy transition in Vietnam, several key measures are needed. *First*, a comprehensive and coherent policy and regulatory framework should be established. This framework should provide clear signals and incentives for RE development and integration while also outlining a roadmap for phasing out coal and fossil fuel subsidies. Such a framework would provide a stable and predictable environment for investors and encourage the growth of RE generation (Wanniachchi et al. 2016). *Second*, implementing a market-based and competitive mechanism for RE procurement is crucial (Dapice et al. 2022). Options such as auctions or feed-in-premiums should be considered, ensuring that the costs and benefits of different energy sources are accurately reflected. This approach would enable fair competition among RE projects and help drive down costs over time. *Third*, there is a need to strengthen and expand the transmission and distribution networks, as well as to invest in smart grid technologies and energy storage systems. These infrastructure improvements would enhance the reliability and flexibility of the energy system, facilitating the integration of RE sources and reducing reliance on conventional power generation (Wanniachchi et al. 2016). *Fourth*, diversifying and mobilising financing sources, instruments and mechanisms is essential. This can involve using green bonds, blended finance approaches, public–private partnerships, and risk-sharing facilities to leverage public funds and attract private investment (Ha-Duong 2022). By tapping into different financial resources and mechanisms, Vietnam can mobilise the necessary capital to support its energy transition. Furthermore, facilitating access to finance, particularly for small and medium enterprises, local developers and communities, is vital. This can be achieved through capacity building initiatives, technical assistance programmes and financial intermediation. By empowering these stakeholders and providing them with the necessary tools and support, Vietnam can foster a more inclusive and sustainable energy transition.

In summary, unlocking more financing for the energy transition in Vietnam requires a comprehensive policy framework, competitive procurement mechanisms, infrastructure improvements, energy efficiency measures, diversified financing sources and improved access to finance. By implementing these measures, Vietnam can accelerate its transition towards a greener and more sustainable energy future.

3 Constructing an Energy Transition Index for Vietnam

3.1 Brief Literature Review

Studies on the energy transition in Vietnam are scant since this topic has only just begun to emerge recently. Most studies discuss the historical, current and forward situation of the energy sector. Nong et al. (2020) present a range of perspectives including resources, markets and policies. They conclude that the main barriers for Vietnam to achieve cleaner energy in the short and medium terms are the lack of financing and advanced technology. Hence, to overcome these challenges, the government should improve policies, boost human resources and research, and attract financial support from international bodies. Shem et al. (2019) analyse policies in the energy markets, dividing these policies into four categories: climate change, efficiency, electrification and renewables. Their findings showed that while Vietnam has a wide range of policies, they are not as effective as desired. Ideally, all of the policies should be aligned, and for each one there should be a governing body that is mainly responsible for its implementation. Currently, there are many policies for which the governing body is not clear. Other papers consider the drivers, barriers and potential strategies for specific sources. Do and Burke (2023) argue that attracting international support is the key driver of a coal phase-out. However, the efforts to mitigate coal usage are threatened by concerns about energy shortages and insufficient regulations. Strategies to resolve these issues include reforming regulations, maintaining prioritisation of relevant policies and building support from stakeholders. Do et al. (2020) examined the case of solar photovoltaic (PV) energy. Incentives from the government, including FiT and other policies like tax exemptions, are the main reasons for the surge in solar installation. However, stakeholders are still worried about the capacity of the transmission grid and complicated administration procedures. Market-based mechanisms must play a key role in tackling these problems.

An evaluation of the energy transition should be quantified through an appropriate index. Previous papers have proposed various approaches to determine the measures of such an index. Neofytou et al. (2020) constructed the index across four pillars: social, political-regulatory, economic and technological; they used the Preference Ranking Organisation Method for Enriching Evaluation II (PROMETHEE II) and Analytical Hierarchy Process (AHP) methods. Hu et al. (2022) believe that an energy transition follows the energy ladder hypothesis, in which the transition aims for (i) cleaner energy solutions, and (ii) more efficient energy solutions. They apply the two-step system GMM (generalised method of moments) to study the energy transition in OECD countries. The World Economic Forum has constructed the energy transition index for 120 countries. This index evaluates the energy transition in two aspects: system performance and transition readiness. In relation to system performance, it measures security, equity and sustainability, while in transition readiness, it considers regulations and political commitment, finance and investment, education and human capital, infrastructure and innovation. Each sub-component contains a list of indicators for measurement. The energy transition index was first published in 2014 and has been updated annually.

While the energy transition index from the World Economic Forum provides a comprehensive overview of the energy transition in each country, it may not fully reflect the energy transition of Vietnam. In addition, the extensive use of 40 indicators in the index can sometimes make it challenging to isolate the key factors driving the energy transition in Vietnam specifically. Therefore, in this study, we construct an energy transition index for Vietnam from 2003 to 2020, following the framework of Neofytou et al. (2020). Subject to the situation and data availability, our index is based on seven criteria which allow us to focus on the unique aspects of Vietnam's energy transition. Table 11.2 explains our criteria.

The data outlined in Table 11.3 provide a comprehensive summary of our variables, revealing noteworthy insights. The average mean for years of schooling is 7.6, which correlates with a fairly moderate human development index (HDI) of 0.667, confirming the significant link between educational attainment and developmental indices. Environmental taxes, averaging at 48.5%, point to a balanced incorporation of environmental concerns within the tax framework. However, a notable carbon lock-in value of 5.216 features a prevailing reliance on fossil fuels or similar non-renewable resources. Energy access is marked by a dichotomy: while access to electricity is pervasive at 97%, access to clean cooking is markedly constrained, averaging at 59.8%. This disparity highlights a challenge in ensuring equitable and diverse energy access. Governance is spotlighted by a negative World Governance Index, indicating existent challenges and offering an avenue for targeted governance reforms. Concurrently, development investment expenditure is moderately set at 17.2%, signifying an intermediary level of developmental investment. The RE variable, standing at an average of 17.3%, underscores an evident gap and presents an opportunity for enhanced integration of green energy sources to diversify the energy portfolio and enhance sustainability. In sum, these preliminary observations offer not only an overview of the interplay between development, environmental stewardship and governance efficacy within the examined demographic, but also a foundation for targeted policy enhancements and strategic investments.

3.2 Methodology

Principal Component Analysis (PCA) is a popular method to construct an aggregate index because it can reduce the dimensions without losing important information

Table 11.2 Criteria of the energy transition index

No	Criterion	Variable	Data source
1	**Public awareness and acceptance**		
1.1	Level of education	Mean years of schooling	World Bank
2	**Human capital**	Human development index	World Bank
3	**Political will**		
3.1	Actions by the government to tackle climate change	Environmental taxes (% taxes on energy [incl. transportation] relative to GDP)	World Bank
3.2	Potential to tackle climate change, based on quality of governance	As by World governance indicator	World Bank
4	**Indicators of sustainable energy regulation**		
4.1	Access to electricity	% of total population	World Bank
4.2	Access to clean cooking	% of total population	World Bank
4.3	Renewable energy	% of renewables in total installed capacity	U.S. Energy Information Administration
5	**Financial sector sustainability**	Financial development index	International Monetary Fund
6	**Carbon lock-in**	$Carbonlockin = \sqrt{Age \times FFshare}$ Where Age is the age of all coal plants, assuming operated for 40 years, relative to current year, and is calculated as: $Age = \frac{\sum_{i=1}^{n} Cap_i[(Operyear_i + 40) - 2023]}{\sum_{i=1}^{n} Cap_i}$ Where Cap_i is the installed capacity of plant i; and $Operyear_i$ is the year that plant i started to operate $FFshare$ is the share of fossil fuel in the total installed capacity	PDP8 (draft) U.S. Energy Information Administration
7	**Infrastructure and innovation**	% of development investment expenditure in total expenditure	Budget allocation from the Ministry of Finance

from the inputs (Carlson 2017; Le et al. 2019). By taking a linear combination of variables that accounts for the greatest possible variance in the data, PCA reveals a set of components, in which the first contains the largest data variance, the second contains the second largest, and so on (Gandhi 2015; Peterson et al. 2010). PCA has been employed to investigate various topics in the energy sector, such as by Le et al. (2023) who modelled electricity supply security for ASEAN countries plus Australia, China, India, Japan, Korea and New Zealand; by Doukas et al. (2012) on energy sustainability; by Hayat et al. (2018) on the finance-growth-energy nexus; and Zhang et al. (2015) on energy market integration in East Asia. However, PCA,

Table 11.3 Summary of descriptive statistics

Variable	Obs	Mean	SD	Min	Max
Mean years of schooling	18	7.597	0.655	6.279	8.370
Human development index	18	0.667	0.027	0.617	0.710
Environmental taxes	18	0.485	0.187	0.250	0.820
World governance index	18	–0.479	0.093	–0.600	–0.328
Access to electricity	18	0.970	0.031	0.903	1.000
Access to clean cooking	18	0.598	0.250	0.221	0.947
Renewable energy	18	0.173	0.071	0.090	0.292
Financial development index	18	0.225	0.049	0.153	0.326
Carbon lock-in	18	5.216	0.169	4.879	5.458
Development investment expenditure	18	0.172	0.067	0.060	0.309

Source Authors' work

or more precisely, static PCA does not consider the dynamic of the inputs (Ku et al. 1995; Mancino and Renò 2005; Pan et al. 2017). Therefore, in this chapter, we employ the dynamic PCA to capture both the cross-sectional and time dimensions of the input factors. We follow the two-step procedure from Zhang et al. (2015) and Wang et al. (2020) to retrieve economic implications. In the first stage, we apply PCA to determine the most important factors for each indicator from its criteria. In the second stage, we establish our index of interest by employing the PCA to the aggregated indicators that we have computed in the first stage.

Since our variables have different scales, we must normalise our variables before conducting our analysis. We examine four different normalisation methods: z-score, min–max, softmax and sigmoid.

z-score measures the distance between a value and its mean. A z-score always has zero mean and 1 standard deviation. The formula of this method is as follows:

$$z = \frac{x_i - \overline{X}}{\sigma} \tag{1}$$

where z is the z-score, x_i is a value, $\overline{X}$ is the group mean, and σ is the standard deviation.

Min–max normalisation is the linear transformation of the data. One benefit of this method is that it conserves the linear relationship of the original data:

$$mm = \frac{x_i - X_{min}}{X_{max} - X_{min}} \tag{2}$$

where X_{min}, X_{max} are the minimum and maximum value of the data, respectively.

Softmax normalisation applies the exponential function to measure the normalisation, using the formula as follows:

Table 11.4 Results from the Barlett test of sphericity and Kaiser–Meyer–Olkin Measure of Sampling Adequacy

	Barlett test of sphericity			Kaiser–Meyer–Olkin measure of sampling adequacy
	Chi-square	Degrees of freedom	p-value	
Z-score	292.284	45	0.000***	0.544
Min–max	292.284	45	0.000***	0.544
Softmax	298.968	45	0.000***	0.607
Sigmoid	298.968	45	0.000***	0.607

Source Authors' work
Note *** $p < 0.01$; **; $p < 0.05$; *; $p < 0.1$

$$softmax = \frac{1}{1 + exp^{-v}} \tag{3}$$

where $v = \frac{x_i - \overline{X}}{\sigma}$

Sigmoid normalisation implies the use of a logistic sigmoid function to normalise variables, which is as:

$$sigmoid = \frac{1 - exp^{-v}}{1 + exp^{-v}} \tag{4}$$

where $v = \frac{x_i - \overline{X}}{\sigma}$

Next, we conduct the Barlett test of sphericity and Kaiser–Meyer–Olkin Measure of Sampling Adequacy to assess the feasibility of PCA. The Barlett test of sphericity examines whether a correlation matrix is different from the identity matrix (Bartlett 1951), while the Kaiser–Meyer–Olkin Measure of Sampling Adequacy confirms the appropriation of the data to run PCA. The threshold of the Kaiser–Meyer–Olkin Measure of Sampling Adequacy varies and depends on the authors; it should however be at least 0.5 (Kaiser 1974). Table 11.4 shows that in four normalisation methods, the p-values of the Barlett test of sphericity indicate that the correlation matrix is different from the identity matrix. In addition, the Kaiser–Meyer–Olkin Measure of Sampling Adequacy is greater than 0.5, implying that our data is suitable to conduct PCA. The results are shown in Table 11.4.

3.3 Results and Discussion

Table 11.5 shows the first stage results of our dynamic PCA model for the indicators that have multiple criteria. Since the proportion of cumulative variance of the first component in the four normalisation methods is approximately 90%, the majority of the information for each indicator can be represented by this component.

Table 11.5 First-stage results of dynamic PCA according to the respective indicators

		Component	Eigenvalue	Difference	% of variance	Cumulative variance %
Z-score	Political will	1	1.760	1.520	0.880	0.880
		2	0.240		0.120	1.000
	Regulatory indicator for sustainable energy	1	2.735	2.505	0.912	0.912
		2	0.230	0.195	0.077	0.988
		3	0.035		0.012	1.000
Min–max	Political will	1	1.760	1.520	0.880	0.880
		2	0.240		0.120	1.000
	Regulatory indicator for sustainable energy	1	2.735	2.505	0.912	0.912
		2	0.230	0.195	0.077	0.988
		3	0.035		0.012	1.000
Softmax	Political will	1	1.760	1.519	0.880	0.880
		2	0.240		0.120	1.000
	Regulatory indicator for sustainable energy	1	2.735	2.505	0.912	0.912
		2	0.230	0.195	0.077	0.988
		3	0.035		0.012	1.000
Sigmoid	Political will	1	1.760	1.519	0.880	0.880
		2	0.240		0.120	1.000
	Regulatory indicator for sustainable energy	1	2.735	2.505	0.912	0.912
		2	0.230	0.195	0.077	0.988
		3	0.035		0.012	1.000

Source Authors' work

Table 11.6 highlights the second stage of the PCA results from our aggregated indicators. The first three components collectively explain over 93% of the variation, indicating their sufficiency in representing the majority of the information in the dataset. Subsequent components contribute minimally to the explained variance, with the sixth and later components each explaining less than 1% of the variance. This minimal contribution supports our decision to focus on the first three components in our continued analysis.

Table 11.7 outlines the relationship between normalised variables and principal components, providing insights into the significant contributors to each component. It is important to note that, using a cut-off value of 0.5, none of the variables is strongly and directly associated with the first component across all four methods. However, there are still key variables worth examining, namely human capital, regulatory indicators for sustainable energy, and public awareness and acceptance.

Human capital is the most important indicator to promote energy transition. Alvarado et al. (2021) distinguished human capital as a more influential factor in

Table 11.6 Second-stage results of dynamic PCA according to the four normalisation methods

	Component	Eigenvalue	Difference	% of variance	Cumulative variance %
Z-score	1	5.247	4.483	0.750	0.750
	2	0.764	0.264	0.109	0.859
	3	0.499	0.201	0.071	0.930
	4	0.299	0.122	0.043	0.973
	5	0.176	0.166	0.025	0.998
	6	0.010	0.006	0.002	0.999
	7	0.005		0.001	1.000
Min–max	1	5.247	4.483	0.750	0.750
	2	0.764	0.264	0.109	0.859
	3	0.499	0.201	0.071	0.930
	4	0.299	0.122	0.043	0.973
	5	0.176	0.166	0.025	0.998
	6	0.010	0.006	0.002	0.999
	7	0.005		0.001	1.000
Softmax	1	5.227	4.461	0.747	0.747
	2	0.767	0.230	0.110	0.856
	3	0.537	0.260	0.077	0.933
	4	0.276	0.097	0.040	0.972
	5	0.179	0.169	0.026	0.998
	6	0.010	0.006	0.001	1.000
	7	0.004		0.001	1.000
Sigmoid	1	5.227	4.461	0.747	0.747
	2	0.767	0.230	0.110	0.856
	3	0.537	0.260	0.077	0.933
	4	0.276	0.097	0.040	0.972
	5	0.179	0.169	0.026	0.998
	6	0.010	0.006	0.001	1.000
	7	0.004		0.001	1.000

Source Authors' work

reducing fossil fuel consumption than economic development, a conclusion drawn from a study spanning 35 years across 27 OECD countries. Zhang et al. (2022) concurred, positioning human capital as an instrumental resource in the pursuit of sustainable energy objectives. This principle is not restricted to developed nations; it has proven applicable in developing countries as well, illustrated by studies conducted in China and several African nations by Wiredu et al. (2023).

The role of regulatory indicators for sustainable energy is undeniable. While Vietnam has made progress towards universal access to electricity and the percentage

Table 11.7 Eigenvectors of the first three components in four methods in the second-stage dynamic PCA

	Indicator	Component 1	Component 2	Component 3
Z-score	Public awareness and acceptance	0.415	–0.210	–0.050
	Human capital	0.428	–0.132	–0.022
	Political will	0.349	0.376	0.602
	Regulatory indicator for sustainable energy	0.418	-0.069	0.009
	Financial sector sustainability	0.398	0.171	0.256
	Carbon lock-in	–0.296	–0.597	0.719
	Infrastructure and innovation	–0.319	0.638	0.229
Min–max	Public awareness and acceptance	0.415	–0.210	–0.050
	Human capital	0.428	–0.132	–0.022
	Political will	0.398	0.171	0.256
	Regulatory indicator for sustainable energy	–0.296	–0.597	0.719
	Financial sector sustainability	-0.319	0.638	0.229
	Carbon lock-in	0.349	0.376	0.602
	Infrastructure and innovation	0.418	-0.069	0.009
Softmax	Public awareness and acceptance	0.419	–0.187	–0.059
	Human capital	0.429	–0.128	–0.030
	Political will	0.393	0.182	0.309
	Regulatory indicator for sustainable energy	–0.290	–0.596	0.720
	Financial sector sustainability	–0.320	0.648	0.223
	Carbon lock-in	0.350	0.368	0.576
	Infrastructure and innovation	0.421	–0.078	–0.013
Sigmoid	Public awareness and acceptance	0.419	–0.187	–0.059
	Human capital	0.429	–0.128	–0.030
	Political will	0.393	0.182	0.309
	Regulatory indicator for sustainable energy	–0.290	–0.596	0.720
	Financial sector sustainability	–0.320	0.648	0.223
	Carbon lock-in	0.350	0.368	0.576
	Infrastructure and innovation	0.421	–0.078	–0.013

Source Authors' work

of RE in its total installed capacity, sustainable energy can be enormously improved through encouraging access to clean cooking. According to the Vietnam Population and Housing Survey 2019, around 15% of the population relies on coal or biomass for cooking. This phenomenon underscores the urgent need to transition to more sustainable cooking energy sources.

Public awareness and acceptance also play an important role. As Perlaviciute et al. (2018) underscore, securing public support is a foundational step for the success of energy transition projects. Bayulgen (2020) echoes this sentiment, emphasising the centrality of public engagement in the energy transition discourse, given that public resistance can substantially undermine energy reform initiatives.

In sum, while no single variable demonstrates a dominant correlation with the first component, a combination of human capital, regulatory indicators for sustainable energy, and public awareness and acceptance are essential considerations for the success of a sustainable energy transition. Each factor plays a unique and synergistic role in shaping the trajectory towards more sustainable and green energy practices. The incorporation of these variables offers a comprehensive insight into the multi-dimensional aspects of energy sustainability, underscoring the complexity and integrative nature of the transition.

Figure 11.9 provides a visual representation of the evolution of Vietnam's energy transition index over the period 2003–20, employing four distinct calculation methods. It is noteworthy that the indices derived from the z-score and min–max methods are consistent, as are those from the softmax and sigmoid methods.

A close examination reveals a generally upward trajectory in the index over the observed period, indicative of Vietnam's progress towards a more sustainable energy landscape despite intermittent declines. These fluctuations underscore the complex

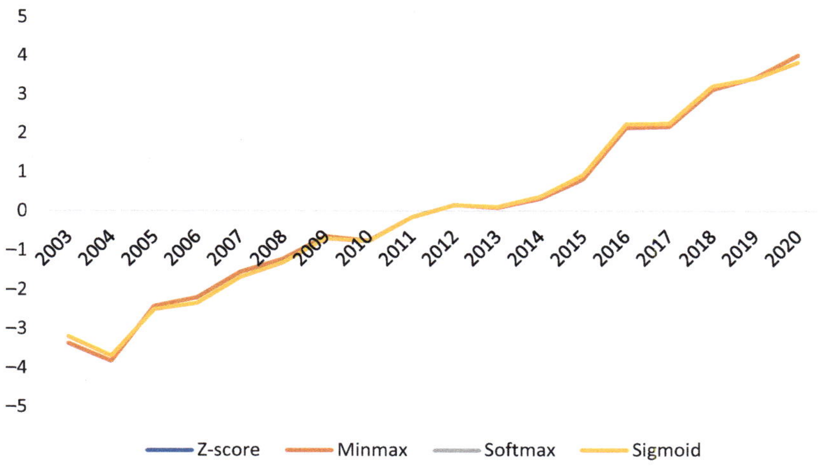

Fig. 11.9 The energy transition index of Vietnam according to the four methods, 2003–2020

and multifaceted nature of energy transition, influenced by a myriad of variables including policy shifts, technological innovations and global energy trends.

The underpinning data and trends illuminated in Fig. 11.9 can be contextualised and enriched by the insights gleaned from Tables 11.3, 11.6 and 11.7. The primary component from Table 11.6, accounting for approximately 74% of the total variance across all methods, plays a crucial role in influencing the trajectory of the energy transition index depicted in Fig. 11.9. It is indicative of a predominant underlying factor that significantly sways the index's direction.

The eigenvectors in Table 11.7 provide insights into the variables contributing to these principal components. Human capital and sustainable energy regulation, alongside public awareness and acceptance are the three most important indicators contributing to the energy transition in Vietnam. These variables not only elucidate the fluctuations in the energy transition index but also underline the multifaceted nature of the energy transition shaped by societal, educational and developmental factors.

The period 2016–20 is of particular interest, marked by a pronounced upswing in the energy transition index. This surge can be attributed to Vietnam's intensified efforts to pivot towards sustainable energy sources and practices, in alignment with global energy trends and environmental imperatives. The upward spike is indicative of Vietnam's concerted efforts to bolster sustainable energy, mirrored in the improved scores in human capital and to promote public awareness and acceptance.

Overall, Fig. 11.9, when interpreted in conjunction with the data in Tables 11.3, 11.6 and 11.7, offers a holistic view of the energy transition landscape in Vietnam. It reflects the intertwined influence of education, human development and environmental policy on the nation's journey towards enhanced energy sustainability and paints a comprehensive picture of both the challenges and achievements along this path.

4 Conclusion

Vietnam is undergoing a rapid shift from a predominantly coal-based power system to a more diversified and cleaner energy mix with a higher share of RE. The country has made ambitious commitments to reduce greenhouse gas emissions and achieve net zero emissions by 2050, while also phasing out coal-based power by the 2040s. The government has implemented supportive policies, such as the introduction of a feed-in tariff system, to incentivise RE investment. As a result, Vietnam has emerged as a regional leader in RE, with solar and wind power experiencing exponential growth in recent years. Vietnam has also witnessed a surge in foreign direct investment in RE projects, showcasing its attractiveness as an investment destination. These advancements have not only diversified the energy mix but have also created jobs in RE and stimulated economic growth.

Our study, anchored in principal component analysis, underscores the indirect yet significant roles of access to clean cooking, public awareness and human capital in the energy transition narrative. The increasing trend in the energy transition index signals Vietnam's steady progress in fulfilling its net zero commitment.

The findings of this study probe more deeply into this transition. In particular, the country's push towards cleaner energy is proved to be not just about government policies or investments but also about people. Since the energy transition is so important, and given that the role of human capital in promoting it is significant, policymakers in this field should prioritise investments in related education and skills development. Initiatives aimed at enhancing the technical expertise and knowledge base of the workforce, particularly in the RE sector, are crucial. Additionally, programmes focusing on raising awareness and promoting sustainable energy practices among the general population should be implemented. To foster greater public support, policymakers should prioritise communication and outreach efforts. Engaging with communities and stakeholders through education campaigns and participatory decision-making processes can help build consensus and overcome resistance to energy reform initiatives. Furthermore, regulatory indicators for sustainable energy are found to play a vital role in shaping the transition to cleaner energy sources. Vietnam should strengthen its regulatory frameworks to encourage the adoption of sustainable energy practices, particularly in areas such as access to clean cooking. This may involve the implementation of policies and incentives to promote the use of clean cooking technologies and phase out reliance on coal and biomass.

There has been a recent uptick in the energy transition index, a sign that Vietnam is making progress. Yet, there are bumps along the way. Despite some occasional drops in the index over the years, they are more like temporary setbacks rather than full stops. The upward general trend marks a period of accelerated efforts and achievements in sustainable energy. However, the energy generated from renewable sources has not yet met its full potential. The reasons are multifaceted. First, renewable forms of energy such as solar or wind are highly variable as they depend on weather conditions. Without ancillary services, integrating RE into the system is risky and challenging. Secondly, most RE projects are located from the central coast to the south of the country. The limitations of the transmission network make it challenging to transmit abundant electricity from the south to the north. Hence, the government must continue to use coal and import electricity from neighbouring countries, namely Lao PDR and China, to meet the demand. Thirdly, the energy market mechanism is not competitive. EVN is a dominant buyer in the market, and the price is still heavily regulated without fully reflecting the cost. As a result, EVN is discouraged from buying electricity from renewable sources, whose price is higher due to the FiT.

The introduction of PDP8 outlines a comprehensive strategy to reach the 2050 net zero target. It emphasises balancing supply and demand within regions, transitioning to a more competitive market structure, and fostering RE development. However, to turn these plans into reality, substantial financial backing is essential. Initiatives like JETP, bolstered with a USD 15.5 billion fund, are expected to fast-track Vietnam's shift away from coal.

In summary, Vietnam's journey to a sustainable and resilient future, marked by an energy transition, is both challenging and essential. A decreased dependency on fossil fuels and increased capacity in RE, aided by the adoption of innovative technologies, will put Vietnam in a position to confront climate change, assure energy security and unveil new economic opportunities. Challenges tied to financing, developing infrastructure and implementing policies are significant and demand the united efforts of the government, private sector and civil society. Armed with a strong commitment, willingness to collaborate and ability to sustain needful actions, Vietnam is on a path not only to navigate its energy transition successfully but also to emerge as a regional leader in RE, contributing to a greener and more sustainable planet.

As for future research directions, our study lays a foundation for more detailed exploration into Vietnam's energy transition landscape. One potential avenue for expansion is the extension of our energy transition index to subnational levels, allowing for a more specific understanding of regional dynamics and disparities within the country. By delving deeper into specific geographical areas or sectors, such as rural electrification or industrial energy efficiency, we can tailor interventions to address localised challenges and opportunities. Furthermore, drawing insights from methodologies employed in assessing energy transition vulnerability in other contexts offers valuable conceptual frameworks for refining our approach. Incorporating these considerations into future research endeavours will not only enhance the robustness of our analysis but also provide actionable insights to policymakers and stakeholders navigating Vietnam's evolving energy landscape.

References

Alvarado R et al (2021) Do economic development and human capital decrease non-renewable energy consumption? Evidence for OECD countries. Energy 215:119147. https://doi.org/10.1016/j.energy.2020.119147

Bartlett MS (1951) The effect of standardization on a $\chi 2$ approximation in factor analysis. Biometrika 38(3/4):337–344. https://doi.org/10.2307/2332580

Bayulgen O (2020) Localizing the energy transition: town-level political and socio-economic drivers of clean energy in the United States. Energy Res Soc Sci 62:101376. https://doi.org/10.1016/j.erss.2019.101376

Carlson DL (2017) Principal component analysis. In: Carson DL (ed) Quantitative methods in archaeology using R. Cambridge University Press, Cambridge, pp 265–278

Dapice D, Le PV, Le TH (2022) Phase change: getting to a sustainable energy future in Vietnam. In: Asif M (ed) Handbook of energy and environmental security. Academic, London, pp 109–125

Do L, Le VP (2024) Residential electricity efficiency and implications for Vietnam's clean energy transition. Electr J 37:107428. https://doi.org/10.1016/j.tej.2024.107428

Do TN, Burke PJ (2023) Phasing out coal power in a developing country context: insights from Vietnam. Energy Policy 176:113512. https://doi.org/10.1016/j.enpol.2023.113512

Do TN et al (2020) Underlying drivers and barriers for solar photovoltaics diffusion: the case of Vietnam. Energy Policy 144:111561. https://doi.org/10.1016/j.enpol.2020.111561

Doukas H et al (2012) Assessing energy sustainability of rural communities using principal component analysis. Renew Sustain Energy Rev 16(4):1949–1957. https://doi.org/10.1016/j.rser.2012.01.018

EREA (Electricity and Renewable Energy Authority, Vietnam) and DEA (Danish Energy Agency) (2022) Vietnam energy outlook report 2021. http://vepg.vn/wp-content/uploads/2022/06/Vietnam-Energy-Outlook-Report-2021-English.pdf [accessed 4 December 2024]

European Commission (2022) Political declaration on establishing the just energy transition partnership with Viet Nam. https://ec.europa.eu/commission/presscorner/detail/en/statement_22_7724 [accessed 11 January 2025]
Gandhi V (2015) Interfacing brain and machine. In: Gandhi V (ed) Brain-computer interfacing for assistive robotics. Academic Press, San Diego, pp 7–63
Ha-Duong M (2022) A study on financial mechanisms to develop the power system in Vietnam. Petrovietnam J 10:59–69. https://www.pvn.vn/DataStore/Documents/2022/T%E1%BA%A0P%20CHI%20DK/T10/p.59-69%20-%20HA%20DUONG%20MINH.pdf [accessed 4 December, 2024]
Hayat F, Pirzada MDS, Khan AA (2018) The validation of granger causality through formulation and use of finance-growth-energy indexes. Renew Sustain Energy Rev 81:1859–1867. https://doi.org/10.1016/j.rser.2017.05.282
Hu K et al (2022) Achieving energy transition in OECD economies: discovering the moderating roles of environmental governance. Renew Sustain Energy Rev 168:112808. https://doi.org/10.1016/j.rser.2022.112808
Institute of Energy [Vietnam] (2021) National Power Development Plan (draft)
Kaiser HF (1974) An index of factorial simplicity. Psychometrika 39(1):31–36. https://doi.org/10.1007/BF02291575
Ku W, Storer RH, Georgakis C (1995) Disturbance detection and isolation by dynamic principal component analysis. Chemom Intell Lab Syst 30(1):179–196. https://doi.org/10.1016/0169-7439(95)00076-3
Le T-H, Chuc AT, Taghizadeh-Hesary F (2019) Financial inclusion and its impact on financial efficiency and sustainability: empirical evidence from Asia. Borsa Istanbul Rev 19(4):310–322. https://doi.org/10.1016/j.bir.2019.07.002
Le T-H et al (2023) Electricity market development in Vietnam: historical trends and future outlooks. Utilities Policy 81:101510. https://doi.org/10.1016/j.jup.2023.101510
Le VT, Pitts A (2019) A survey on electrical appliance use and energy consumption in Vietnamese households: case study of Tuy Hoa city. Energy Build 197:229–241. https://doi.org/10.1016/j.enbuild.2019.05.051
Mancino ME, Renò R (2005) Dynamic principal component analysis of multivariate volatility via Fourier analysis. Appl Mathem Fin 12(2):187–199. https://doi.org/10.1080/1350486042000255861
Neofytou H, Nikas A, Doukas H (2020) Sustainable energy transition readiness: a multicriteria assessment index. Renew Sustain Energy Rev 131:109988. https://doi.org/10.1016/j.rser.2020.109988
Nguyen-Trinh HA, Rizopoulos Y (2018) Market conditions and change for low-carbon electricity transition in Vietnam. J Energy Devel 43(1–2):1–26
Nong D, Wang C, Al-Amin AQ (2020) A critical review of energy resources, policies and scientific studies towards a cleaner and more sustainable economy in Vietnam. Renew Sustain Energy Rev 134:110117. https://doi.org/10.1016/j.rser.2020.110117
Pan A, Bosch D, Ma H (2017) Assessing water poverty in china using holistic and dynamic principal component analysis. Soc Indic Res 130(2):537–561. https://doi.org/10.1007/s11205-015-1191-3
Perlaviciute G et al (2018) At the heart of a sustainable energy transition: the public acceptability of energy projects. IEEE Power Energ Mag 16(1):49–55. https://doi.org/10.1109/MPE.2017.2759918
Peterson P, Baker EL, McGaw B (2010) International encyclopedia of education, 3rd edn. Elsevier/AP, Amsterdam
Shem C et al (2019) Potentials and opportunities for low carbon energy transition in Vietnam: a policy analysis. Energy Policy 134:110818. https://doi.org/10.1016/j.enpol.2019.06.026
Socialist Republic of Viet Nam (2023) Gov't Approves 8th National Power Development Plan. https://en.baochinhphu.vn/decision-approving-national-power-development-plan-8-111230614195813455.htm [accessed 4 December 2024]

Wang Y et al (2020) Regional renewable energy development in China: a multidimensional assessment. Renew Sustain Energy Rev 124:109797. https://doi.org/10.1016/j.rser.2020.109797
Wanniachchi AK et al. (2016) Viet Nam energy sector assessment, strategy, and road map. Manila: Asian Development Bank and Asian Development Bank Institute. https://www.adb.org/sites/default/files/institutional-document/178616/vie-energy-road-map.pdf [accessed 5 December 2024]
Wiredu J et al (2023) Energy transition in Africa: the role of human capital, financial development, economic development, and carbon emissions. Environ Sci Policy 146:24–36. https://doi.org/10.1016/j.envsci.2023.04.021
Zhang D, Shi X, Sheng Y (2015) Comprehensive measurement of energy market integration in East Asia: an application of dynamic principal component analysis. Energy Econ 52:299–305. https://doi.org/10.1016/j.eneco.2015.11.006
Zhang Y et al (2022) The eco-innovative technologies, human capital, and energy pricing: evidence of sustainable energy transition in developed economies. Appl Energy 325:119729. https://doi.org/10.1016/j.apenergy.2022.119729

An Analysis of India's Quest for a Clean and Just Energy Transition

Sangeeta V. Sharma and Vinod K. Sharma

Abstract The clean and just energy transition (CJET) poses a huge challenge globally and, if not managed properly, it may adversely affect many developing economies. This study critically reviews the present situation and prospects of India's quest for a CJET. It compares various forms of clean energy currently being promoted in the country through a comprehensive analysis of their strengths, weaknesses, opportunities and challenges. It is observed that India is working in multifarious directions to enhance its non-fossil fuel energy and presently ranks fourth in the world in terms of renewable energy production. However, the country may face multiple financial, technological and socio-economic challenges during its clean energy transition from about 44% at present to the target (about 80%) by 2070. With pan India implementation of policies, application of technologies and strict monitoring, the clean energy targets seem achievable. However, in terms of energy justice, the progress may be sluggish and will require additional efforts towards providing clean and affordable energy to all and creating alternatives for the lost businesses and employment in the traditional energy sectors. India can seize the opportunity in meeting its CJET goals, even before 2070, by building just energy transition partnerships to augment its technological infrastructure and attract investments in clean energy.

1 Introduction

Globally, almost 32 million people are employed in the fossil fuel sector. A large-scale transition to clean energy, albeit required, will discard the existing fossil-fuel energy systems, rendering their huge workforce unemployed. Therefore, creation of

S. V. Sharma
SIES, Indian Institute of Environment Management (SIES IIEM), Navi Mumbai, India
e-mail: sangeetavs@sies.edu.in

V. K. Sharma (✉)
Indira Gandhi Institute of Development Research (IGIDR), Mumbai, India
e-mail: vks@igidr.ac.in

H. Phoumin et al. (eds.), *Tackling the Energy Transition: Insights from ASEAN and Beyond*, Climate Change and Energy Transition,
https://doi.org/10.1007/978-981-96-6019-3_12

jobs in clean energy systems, particularly in the emerging economies, is critical for a clean and just energy transition (CJET) to be sustainable.

India is one of the largest and fastest-growing economies in the world and the country may face multiple challenges during its quest for the transition. India's Nationally Determined Contributions (NDCs) propose to reduce by 2030 the emission intensity of country's GDP by 45% from the 2005 level and to install 50% of power capacity from non-fossil energy sources to achieve net zero emissions by 2070. In India, about half a million workers are employed in coal mines alone, which are expected to be decommissioned by 2035. Around 3.6 million people are estimated to be employed (in direct and indirect jobs) in the fossil fuel sector (Birol and Kant 2022; Hingne and Swami 2023). Therefore, India's clean energy transition must address multiple challenges: making clean energy affordable to all; reducing greenhouse gas (GHG) emissions; regenerating the profile of employment; rehabilitating and resettling those presently associated with the fossil-fuel sector and upskilling and training them for jobs in the clean and renewable energy (RE) sector.

Yang et al. (2022) suggested some important policy options to accelerate the energy transition: reducing fossil-fuel energy; reconfiguring the energy systems in terms of technology, operations and planning; addressing the negative impact on coal mining regions; and facilitating a learning-based transition governance. More than 30 countries, including the UK, US and EU member states, signed the "Just Transition Declaration" at COP26 in 2021, which aims at ensuring a just transition to a cleaner and sustainable economy (ORF 2022). Since the costs and benefits of clean transition are often unequally distributed, the vulnerable communities may be adversely affected (Haldar et al. 2023). Therefore, for an equitable just energy transition (JET) to be practical and sustainable, partnerships within and outside national boundaries are essential. But only a handful of developing economies like South Africa, Indonesia and Vietnam have framed just energy transition partnerships (JET-Ps) with developed countries (Bhushan and Banerjee 2023).

India currently imports over 40% of its primary energy requirements, costing over USD 90 billion annually as estimated by the Ministry of New and Renewable Energy (MNRE 2025). Major sectors like mobility and industrial production are significantly dependent upon imported fossil fuels. This necessitates a shift towards technologies that enable an enhanced share of domestic renewable sources in the energy mix, and therefore a progressive reduction of the reliance on fossil fuels. Sharma et al. (2019, 2023) highlight that availability of round-the-clock electricity at an affordable price is still a luxury in many parts of the country, especially in rural areas. Many Indian cities are plagued with severe air pollution affecting the health and welfare of people. Therefore, a multipronged approach, encompassing substantial reduction in fossil-fuel imports, increasing share of RE, technological up-grading and cross border energy trade, etc. is required for the promotion of a CJET in India.

There are several studies on India's striving for clean energy but very few highlight the importance of a just energy transition. Since the focus on a large-scale transition to REs has become clear only in the last few years, an equitable distribution of the benefits of clean energy is required. A Strengths, Weaknesses, Opportunities and Threats (SWOT) analysis has been used to identify three factors affecting India's

CJET: the cost-competitiveness of RE, the inadequacy of skilled manpower for RE and 100% electrification of the household and transportation sectors (Indrajayanthan et al. 2022). A recent empirical analysis (Rahut et al. 2024) focusing on the use of clean fuels by various social groups indicates some improvement in energy justice but there is still a large gap between rural and urban groups and among economically weaker sections throughout the country.

This chapter critically reviews the present situation and prospects of India's targets on CJET. It compares various clean energy forms using a comprehensive Strengths, Weaknesses, Opportunities and Challenges (SWOC) analysis. The objective is to explore the opportunities and challenges associated with CJET and identify the policy measures that could accelerate the just energy transition. The study observes that while progress on the provision of clean energy is achievable, an equitable distribution of the transition benefits will require additional efforts. It is emphasised that in addition to implementing appropriate policies on the financial and technological fronts, addressing the issue of socioeconomic equity is of paramount importance in India's transition to a clean and sustainable economy. While India may find it difficult to meet its targeted reduction in GHG emissions in the short-term, i.e. by 2030, the country should be able to achieve its ultimate goal of near net zero emissions committed by 2070 or earlier. Findings of the study may provide insights for policymakers and other stakeholders involved in India's quest for the CJET.

This chapter is arranged into five sections. The first section or introduction has identified the issues associated with India's CJET; section two sets the background and reviews the literature; section three describes methodology and data sources used in the study; section four describes the results of a SWOC analysis of some major non-fossil fuel energy forms being promoted in India; and the last section concludes the study and highlights its policy relevance.

2 Background

Inadequate measures to mitigate GHG emissions over the past several decades have resulted in an urgent need for a transition to clean energy to protect the planet from the catastrophic impacts of global warming. Ever-increasing GHG emissions along with geopolitical insecurities, economic instabilities and pandemic risks have aggravated the problem of global energy security. Clean energy systems require decommissioning of the existing thermal power plants and creating non-fossil fuel-based energy installations ensuring lower GHG emissions. Although measures for a CJET are essential for sustainable economic growth and improving the quality of life, they pose a huge challenge globally, particularly to developing economies. To address these challenges, nations have manoeuvred their efforts towards promoting non-fossil fuel-based energy systems. With the help of innovative and green technologies, clean energy can be produced on a large scale; however, its equitable availability, affordability and inclusiveness, especially in the developing countries, will require effective planning and implementation.

2.1 Urgency of Clean Energy

The carbon budget refers to the total limit set for further carbon dioxide (CO_2) emissions to keep global warming within 1.5 °C. The IPCC Sixth Assessment report (2021) states that the residual global carbon budget to maintain this limit is only 400 billion tonnes of CO_2 from the start of 2020, which on an average, translates to each country's share of global CO_2 budget remaining for the next seven years only. Since the present global CO_2 emissions are about 36 billion tonnes per year, under a no-reduction scenario, the above CO_2 budget may last for only about 11 years (Carbon Independent 2024; IPCC 2021). Therefore, for the survival of humankind, not only the present and future global GHG emissions should be near zero, but also those emissions, which are historically accumulated in the atmosphere, need to be removed on an urgent basis.

"The energy sector employed over 65 million people in 2019, equivalent to around 2% of global employment, which includes about 21 million in fuel supply, 20 million in the power sector and in end uses (24 million) such as energy efficiency and vehicle manufacturing" (IEA 2022c, p. 6). In general, the CJET involves a high cost globally, and attracting investments in this sector is crucial for the emerging economies. A study of the Asia–Pacific region (McCauley and Pettigrew 2023) describes four essential elements of a just transition strategy that can help raise investments in clean energy and decrease the reliance on fossil fuels: boosting sustainable energy investments; giving priority to equity when making decisions; creating all-encompassing finance plans; and giving priority to restorative justice techniques.

The objective of the CJET should be to ensure that negatively affected communities receive fair compensation for their losses, have access to employment programmes, and are trained to change over to new jobs in clean energy systems or other sectors of the economy. IRENA (2019) reports that changes in geopolitics during the global energy transition are inevitable as there will be an increase in RE sources and a decrease in fossil fuels. The growth of global trade in RE may cause significant structural changes in economies and societies. Policies and strategies for the CJET should be designed and implemented to benefit the poorest, most vulnerable and marginalised people of the countries which are already committed to the energy transition and can easily afford to adopt new technologies. Thus, the CJET requires an active, bottom-up, participatory and socially inclusive approach (Long 2021).

A cost–benefit analysis by the World Bank indicates that there is a net benefit for investing in more resilient infrastructure in low and middle-income countries, amounting to about USD 4.2 trillion and, thus, the cost of climate-proofing infrastructure can be offset by the economic benefits of avoiding damage from extreme climate-change related weather events (UNESCAP 2023). The Asian Development Bank estimates that the Asia–Pacific region requires approximately USD 1.7 trillion per year in infrastructure investment until 2030 to meet its development needs, of which USD 200 billion accounts for climate change mitigation and adaptation costs. If managed properly, the transition to low-carbon energy could create 30 million jobs globally and deliver clean energy to nearly 800 million people. However, if the CJET is mismanaged, it could be costly and create inequities for the world's most vulnerable populations (Lakic et al. 2023). The cost of India's fossil-fuel imports increased fourfold from about INR 4.8 trillion in 2011 to INR 16.8 in 2023 (Statista 2024) and it may rise further with increased demand for energy.

2.2 *State of India's Clean Energy*

The Twentieth Electric Power Survey (EPS) report of the Central Electricity Authority (CEA 2022) forecasts India's electricity demand. By 2030–31, the present peak electricity demand of 243 GW is expected to rise to 350 GW, which may require an additional capacity of about 464 GW, including a thermal capacity addition of about 88 GW and an RE addition of about 52 GW. Thus, in the short term, India needs to increase its fossil-based power along with its energy from renewable sources. However, the intensification of the phase-down in coal demand of the developed countries may jeopardise India's energy transition. India can address these challenges by: adopting technological innovations; accelerating production of various RE forms; attracting domestic and international investors towards green finance; and applying technological and economic instruments for reducing pollution.

In April 2024, the U.S. Environmental Protection Agency (USEPA) outlined regulations requiring operators of coal-fired and new gas-fired power plants to reduce greenhouse gas (GHG) emissions by 90% by 2032 (Cronkite News 2025). However, if the United States were to repeal these regulations and promote the construction of additional coal and gas plants, it could set a troubling precedent for countries like India and China, potentially leading them to increase their coal power production. Such a shift could undermine global efforts to meet GHG reduction targets, jeopardising progress in addressing climate change.

As of 30 November 2024, India's installed power generation capacity was about 456 GW, consisting of about 53.2% fossil-fuel based and about 46.8% non-fossil-fuel based energy including hydro and nuclear energy (MoP 2025). India has set ambitious targets to reduce its carbon emissions by decreasing its dependency on fossil fuels and increasing its share of RE. As is evident from Fig. 12.1, from 2015 to 2023, the share of fossil-fuel energy was continuously decreasing, and that of non-fossil-fuel energy was increasing. As shown in Fig. 12.2, among non-fossil-fuel energy types, hydro, solar and wind are dominating; the percentage distribution of various RE forms is also shown. MNRE's vision on RE generation during 2022–2047 is ambitious: from a 22% share of RE in total generation in 2022 to about a 67% share in 2047. To achieve these targets and its ultimate goal of about 80% energy generation from non-fossil sources by 2070, India needs to make exceptional efforts in its quest for CJET.

India's National Energy Policy proposes several reforms, including energy pricing reforms; provision of affordable and "round the clock" electricity for all; and the increased contribution of RE in India's energy basket. These reforms may open up

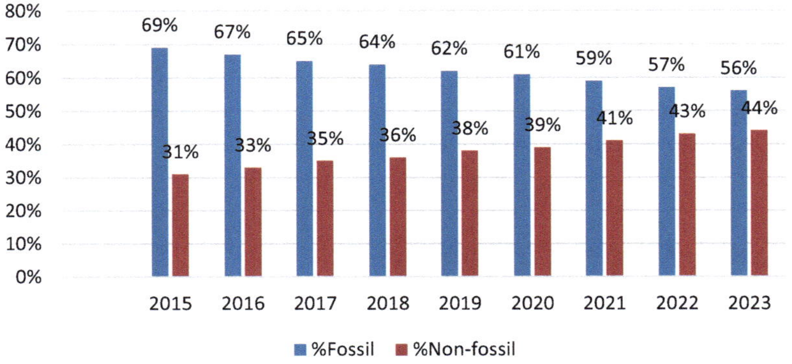

Data Source: MNRE (2025).

Fig. 12.1 Share of fossil and non-fossil energy in India (2015–2023). *Data Source* MNRE (2025)

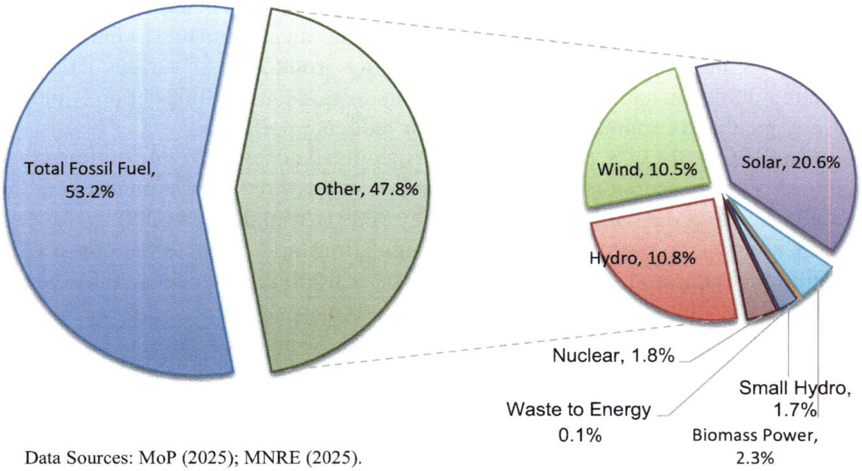

Data Sources: MoP (2025); MNRE (2025).

Fig. 12.2 Share of various forms of non-fossil energy in India in 2024. *Data Sources* MoP (2025), MNRE (2025)

the energy markets and accelerate the production and consumption of electricity from renewables, which, in turn, will translate into several social, economic and environmental benefits, including reduction in GHG emissions and overall social welfare in India. By promoting cross border clean energy trade with its neighbouring countries, India could play a major role in developing sustainable energy systems in the South Asian region. However, Climate Action Tracker rates India's climate policies and targets as "highly insufficient", and inconsistent with the Paris Agreement's 1.5 °C temperature limit (CAT 2023).

2.3 India's Quest for a CJET

India's commitment to achieve net zero CO_2 emissions by 2070 is reflected in its policies and strategies. The country is the third largest contributor to global GHGs emissions, after China and the USA, with 7% of global CO_2 emissions, but it had very low per capita emissions of 1.9 metric tons in 2021 (European Commission 2023). India ranks fourth globally in RE capacity. It increased its RE capacity by 250% from 2014 to 2021 and is determined to replace fossil fuel use with RE in energy production and the industrial sector (ADB 2023). Its RE capacity is growing at a faster rate than any other major economy and is expected to double by 2026. The country is accelerating the use of emerging technologies such as green hydrogen, green ammonia, EV battery storage, and the production of low-carbon steel, cement and fertilisers. India intends to generate 50% of its electricity requirements from renewable sources by installing 500 gigawatts of RE capacity and reducing the emissions intensity of its economy by 45% by 2030. There is a commitment "to grow, industrialise and provide a better quality of life to [India's] citizens without the need to carbonize" (Birol and Kant 2022).

The probability of India accomplishing a Just Energy Transition (JET) with the integration of clean energy is high, but it may face challenges related to monetary and legislative constraints (Anjanappa 2023). There are several factors such as social equity and inclusiveness that are looming large in the energy transition scenario in India. A recent report (iFOREST 2024), focusing on Maharashtra, one of the most industrialised states in India and which accounts for about 10% of the country's total GHG emissions, highlights several opportunities for creating green jobs as progress towards a CJET is made. The unequal power dynamics is linked to the implementation of RE in certain parts of India; for example, provision of RE in the state of Kerala shows social inequality (Bedi 2021). For example, middle and upper class consumers are given priority in the solar projects of the Kerala government, including rooftop solar promotion programmes. Clean energy is not provided to the historically marginalised communities, such as those living below the poverty line and indigenous people, because they are not given priority by the governmental agencies that are implementing the RE project in Kerala. This is contrary to the principles of social equity in a CJET and, thus, inclusiveness should be prioritised while building low carbon emission strategies to maintain social and environmental equities.

Many consumers in India still face unreliable electricity supply. Continued dependence on traditional fuels for cooking, heating and other household needs not only poses significant health risks but also contributes to high levels of pollution, leading to poor air quality in Indian cities. This reliance exacerbates environmental and public health challenges, affecting the well-being of millions. Therefore, India's CJET needs to prioritise multiple benefits including clean air, resilience and socioeconomic equity (NITI Aayog and Rocky Mountain Institute 2020).

Due to increased energy demand, India's coal-fired power generation reached an all-time high in 2021, jumping 13% above the 2020 level (IEA 2022a, 2022b). The

Reserve Bank of India (RBI) is actively involved in India's climate defence policies and research initiatives. The RBI reports that, under the business-as-usual (BAU) scenario, the country's carbon emissions could increase from 2.7 gigatonnes (GT) in 2021 to 3.9 GT in 2030, but with balanced policy interventions they would decline to 0.9 GT. Accordingly, India requires accelerated reduction in the energy intensity of its GDP to about 5% annually and enhance its RE to about 80% of its total energy by 2070–71 (RBI 2023).

One important issue for the expansion of RE programmes in India is the acquisition of large areas of land for solar and wind farms. Another daunting task is the equitable distribution and application of clean energy technologies at the household level. Studies on the uptake of solar photovoltaic by individual families in India show that adoption of RE technologies is still expensive for them (Koshy 2023). One inclusive approach could be the advent of smart grids, wherein homes are not only consumers of energy; they can also become solar energy producers. Sharma et al. (2024) have projected that India could achieve its targets for net zero emissions well ahead of 2070. By focusing on large scale electrification, promoting emerging technologies, tackling hard-to-abate sectors and increasing energy efficiency, the country has a unique opportunity to become a net zero economy by 2050.

India's energy transition needs to benefit its citizens, and well-designed policies can limit the potential trade-offs between affordability, security and sustainability. While the country has worked in multifarious dimensions in the march towards net zero emissions, a sharp increase in global prices has made energy less affordable and has increased energy security risks. However, India needs to prioritise the implementation of CJET policies and investments so that its non-fossil-fuel capacity is almost tripled and its target of reducing CO_2 emissions by 1 billion tonnes by 2030 is met. Ensuring sustainable investments is critical for the CJET as the poor financial health of the existing electricity distribution companies is impeding the transition process. India's green financing requirement is estimated to be 2.5% of GDP annually until 2030 (RBI 2023). The Union Budget of 2024 estimated that India requires an investment support of USD 1.4 trillion, an average of USD 28 billion per year, to become a net-zero economy by 2070. It also stated that mobilising finance as well as investment on competitive terms and resolution of land acquisition issues are necessary for realising the INR 30.5 lakh crore (one USD = 86.5 INR at current rates) investment required for meeting the target 500GW of RE capacity in India by 2030 (Reddy 2025).

3 Methodology

This chapter offers a critical review of existing literature focusing on the provision of a CJET in India. The Ministry of New and Renewable Energy (MNRE) is the nodal agency of the Government of India (GoI) for all related matters. India aims to enhance its energy security by increasing the share of clean energy, enhancing energy availability and affordability and ensuring energy equity (MNRE 2025). The study focuses on India's policies and their effectiveness in ensuring a clean and equitable energy transition, the financing of the energy transition and pathways for achieving the country's net zero goals. A comprehensive Strengths, Weaknesses, Opportunities and Challenges (SWOC) analysis framework as suggested by Kenton (2024) is used. While the strengths and weaknesses depend on internal factors, opportunities and challenges are external and are identified and tabulated accordingly. Based on these factors, the analysis includes the present status and future prospects of some major RE forms, viz., solar, wind, biomass energy and biofuels and green hydrogen. Such analysis may suggest feasible pathways to overcome the weaknesses and address the challenges in achieving clean energy targets.

The analysis is conducted not only for the clean energy transition but also for the just energy transition (JET). Due to the lack of secondary data on JET and constraints of time and other resources, collecting primary data and application of detailed statistical or mathematical tools was not possible. Therefore, this study uses a theoretical SWOC framework by focusing on the existing policies, technological innovations, financial status and social conditions. It takes into account the policies that will help India foster international just energy transition partnerships (JET-Ps) for attracting stable foreign investments. The analysis also focuses on green financing and other measures that will boost public–private partnerships within the country. Thus, the study tries to integrate clean and just energy transitions and to assess India's potential for achieving its goals of net zero emissions by 2070 and, during this journey, simultaneously adapt just energy transitions to ensure social inclusion.

4 Results and Discussion

An analysis of the existing framework of policies on technological innovations, financial status and social conditions was conducted. In general, the internal factors in India's quest for a CJET are strong and offer several opportunities for switching from a fossil-fuel-based to an RE-based economy. In addressing the challenges in terms of socio-economic equity, the country should take into account the weaknesses related to the financial and technological aspects. The results of the SWOC analysis of the major RE forms and JET are discussed below.

4.1 SWOC Analysis of Major REs

Solar Energy. India's National Solar Mission was launched on 11 January 2010 and its cumulative solar power installed capacity reached around 97.86 GW as of 31 December 2024 (MNRE 2025). Policies supporting major solar schemes in India include the Grid Connected Solar Rooftop Programme; Solar Parks and Ultra Mega Solar Power Projects; Production Linked Incentive (PLI) Scheme; National Programme on High Efficiency Solar PV Modules; and off-grid programmes like

Pradhan Mantri Kisan Urja Suraksha evam Utthaan Mahabhiyaan (PM KUSUM) (the "Prime Minister's Farmers Energy Security and Enhancement Campaign"). The GoI provides subsidies on capital expenditure (CAPEX) and operating expenditure (OPEX) to solar project developers.

Various government and institutional initiatives are fostering the adoption of rooftop solar solutions to tackle issues like inefficient energy conversion and strained grid capacities. Recent policies on Roof-Top Solar Power in the budget for FY 2024–2025 aim at solar power generation in 10 million Indian households. These households can supply the surplus electricity generated to the grid in exchange for 300 free units of electricity per month (MNRE 2025). Developments in solar technology, energy storage and grid integration will improve efficiency and the capacity factor of solar energy. Advancements in bifacial PV modules and tracking systems hold promise for boosting energy generation efficiency.

Rooftop solar offers compelling benefits, including reduced upfront and operating costs, as well as the ability to provide electricity to remote areas. Moreover, it represents a significant opportunity for generating clean energy and curbing GHG emissions, aligning with broader sustainability goals. Nevertheless, concerns persist around its economic feasibility, despite policy support. Challenges remain with respect to intermittency, managing end-of-life modules and developing effective energy storage solutions. Overcoming these hurdles is crucial for fully unlocking the potential of rooftop solar and integrating it into comprehensive sustainable energy plans. The SWOC analysis of solar energy is summarised in Table 12.1.

Wind Energy. As of 31 December 2024, with about 48.1 GW, India has the fourth highest wind energy installed capacity in the world (MNRE 2025). The GoI

Table 12.1 SWOC analysis of solar energy

Internal strengths (S)	Internal weaknesses (W)	External opportunities (O)	External challenges (C)
Various policies supporting rooftop solar	Poor efficiency (below 23%; average of only 18–19%)	Development of bi-facial PV modules to improve capacity factor, tracking, etc.	Lack of policies in the commercial and residential sectors
Requires relatively less CAPEX and OPEX	Poor capacity factor of only 15–21%	Development of solar thermal for heating application and energy generation	Lack of grid capacity leading to grid overload
Easily available and can be installed anywhere	Not available through -out the day (24 × 7)	Ability to power remote and isolated locations	End of lifecycle disposal of PV modules
High energy potential capacity and reduction of GHGs	Economic viability is a problem despite several policies to address it	Space- and satellite-based power and ground solar farms	Lack of efficient and cheap storage technologies

is promoting wind power projects in the entire country through private sector investments by providing various fiscal and financial incentives such as accelerated depreciation tax benefit and concessional custom duty exemption on certain components of wind electric generators.

Internally, wind energy presents cost efficiencies compared to fossil fuels and requires less land for power generation. It also has greater relative continuous availability and higher efficiency relative to solar power. However, there are challenges such as suitability in low wind speed regions. Also, the initial investment and operational costs per megawatt remain comparatively high as do the transmission expenses for distant energy utilisation. Externally, several opportunities are available, including innovative turbine designs, use of airborne or kite turbines for high wind areas and job creation potentials across the wind energy supply chain. Offshore wind power, in particular, offers cost-saving benefits by circumventing land acquisition needs.

Despite various advantages, challenges like landscape alterations, threats to wildlife and turbine failures necessitate attention. Nearby inhabitants may be affected by the noise and aesthetic pollution (turbines as "eyesores" across the landscape) and, in the event of mechanical failure of the installations, there could be large-scale damage to property and life. Overcoming these obstacles while maximising opportunities is crucial for the sustainable advancement of wind energy. The SWOC analysis of Wind Energy is summarised in Table 12.2.

Hydro Energy. India generates hydroelectric power by harnessing energy not only from flowing or falling water from rivers and rivulets, but also from artificially created storage dams or canal drops.

Hydroelectric power offers significant internal strengths, including being the largest source of RE currently available and providing a reliable, flexible option to meet both base and peak loads. Additionally, hydroelectric power is considered

Table 12.2 SWOC analysis of wind energy

Internal strengths (S)	Internal weaknesses (W)	External opportunities (O)	External challenges (C)
Cheaper than fossil fuel-based energy	Not suitable in the event of low wind speeds	Use of airborne/kite turbines for high wind	Landscape blemish
Lower land usage than solar per TWh	May become an intermittent source of energy	Land use could be mitigated by onshore turbines	Threat to wildlife and birds
Generally available 24 × 7 in selected locations	Higher CAPEX and OPEX per MW compared to solar	Job creation potential in manufacturing, installation, operation and maintenance of wind turbines/farms	Noise and aesthetic pollution in the area
Greater efficiency than solar	High energy transmission cost if utilised at distant locations	Offshore wind power reduces the cost by avoiding land acquisition	Mechanical failures may lead to catastrophes

the cheapest form of energy and has greater capacity and load factors, and efficiency compared to other RE forms. However, there are internal weaknesses, such as its location-specific nature, making it unsuitable for areas with high land costs, and the permanent alteration of the environment. Furthermore, large projects can disrupt local ecosystems, impact fauna and flora, and may suffer from climatic changes like droughts and floods, potentially affecting their reliability.

Externally, there are opportunities to integrate storage solutions such as pumped hydro energy sources, providing flexibility and the ability to act as backup for other intermittent RE sources. Hydroelectric projects also create water storage for various purposes like drinking, irrigation and recreation. However, external challenges include landscape distortion caused by large hydro projects and the significant costs associated with the rehabilitation and resettlement of project-affected people. Moreover, there are concerns about mechanical failures in large dams, leading to catastrophic consequences. Balancing internal strengths and weaknesses; capitalising on external opportunities and addressing challenges are vital for the sustainability of hydro-electric power. The SWOC analysis of hydro energy is summarised in Table 12.3.

Biomass Energy. India's National Biofuel Policy 2018, amended in 2022, has aggressively revised targets for the blending of biofuels in fossil fuels. The earlier targets of 20% blending of ethanol in petrol and 5% blending of biodiesel in fossil-diesel by 2030 are now revised and to be achieved by 2025–26. The GoI policies are supporting biogas programmes for farms and households. The main objective of these programmes is to establish biogas plants for clean cooking fuel, lighting, and meeting consumers' small thermal and power demands. These programmes are resulting in GHG reduction, improved sanitation, female empowerment, rural job creation and the facilitation of biogas-based decentralised RE sources from off-grid electricity generation. Internally, biomass energy offers ready availability and eliminates the

Table 12.3 SWOC analysis of hydro energy

Internal strengths (S)	Internal weaknesses (W)	External opportunities (O)	External challenges (C)
Largest source of RE at present	Location specific, not suitable in areas with high cost of land	Can be started and stopped at any time	Large hydro projects lead to landscape distortion
Cheapest form of energy	Permanently alters land topography	Provides opportunities to integrate storage in the form of pumped hydro energy sources	Rehabilitation and resettlement of project-affected persons can be costly
Reliable and flexible form of RE to meet base and peak loads	Disrupts local fauna and flora	Creates water storage for drinking, irrigation and recreation	Mechanical failures of large dams can lead to catastrophes
Greater capacity factor, load factor and efficiency	May suffer from weather/ climate changes such as droughts and floods	Can work as backup for intermittent RE sources	May alter food, water quality and agriculture systems

need for energy storage systems, boasting superior energy efficiency and capacity factors compared to other RE sources. It can cater to both base load and peak load demands, ensuring flexibility in energy generation. India generates about 750 million tonnes of biomass annually, which can be utilised for bioenergy in the residential, industrial and transport sectors thereby reducing air pollution from stubble burning (Sharma et al. 2024).

The internal limitations of biomass energy include competition with food and fodder crops, as in the use of corn and sorghum for ethanol production, significant water requirements for irrigation, and the necessity for large land areas for biomass cultivation. Thus, biomass for energy may inadvertently trigger food and fodder crises for small-scale farmers. Rising demand for non-agricultural use of land for residential and other purposes may also derail efforts for balancing the use of agriculture land for biofuels and food crops.

Externally, numerous opportunities exist for exploring diverse energy pathways and conducting research and development in biomass utilisation, with potential by-products adding further value. Economic benefits of biofuel crops accruing to farmers and reduced reliance on fossil fuel imports to the country are appealing prospects. However, external challenges, such as the potential lack of locally sourced raw materials, could inflate transportation costs and create a risk of water scarcity or drought affecting energy security. Effectively navigating these internal strengths and weaknesses while capitalising on external opportunities and addressing challenges is essential for the sustainable progress of biomass-derived RE. The SWOC analysis of the Biomass Energy is summarised in Table 12.4.

Green Hydrogen. India's National Green Hydrogen Mission 2023 aims to produce hydrogen by electrolysing water and splitting it into hydrogen and oxygen

Table 12.4 SWOC analysis of biomass energy

Internal strengths (S)	Internal weaknesses (W)	External opportunities (O)	External challenges (C)
Readily available	Competition with food crops such as corn for ethanol	Can provide other valued by-products	Raw materials may not be locally sourced
Eliminate need for energy storage systems	High water demand for irrigation	Variety of energy pathways and high opportunities in research and development	Some biomass requires treatment plant
Better energy efficiency and capacity factor than other RE systems	Large land requirement for biofuel crops	Economically beneficial for farmers and agricultural labourers	Water scarcity or drought could challenge energy security
Can provide base load and peak load	Can create food and fodder crises for small farmers	Saving in foreign exchange due to less need to import fossil fuels	High transportation costs in case of distant biofuel plants

using electricity generated from RE sources. Another method planned for producing green hydrogen is from biomass, which involves its gasification to produce hydrogen (MNRE 2025). Both of these methods are clean and sustainable, making green hydrogen an attractive option for India's transition to clean energy and to represent internal strengths in driving forward hydrogen technology. The Nuclear Business Platform estimates that "by 2050, green hydrogen could satisfy nearly 94% of hydrogen demand, a significant increase from [the estimate of] 16% in 2030". India's green hydrogen market has the "potential to reach USD 8 billion by 2030 and USD 340 billion by 2050" (NBP 2024). India intends to build capabilities to produce at least 5 million metric tonnes (MMT) of green hydrogen per annum by 2030, with the potential to reach 10 MMT per annum with the growth of export markets (MNRE 2025). To produce 5 MMT of green hydrogen by 2030, India will require a continuous supply of about 125 GW of clean power from RE (Sharma et al. 2024). However, internal weaknesses, such as the lack of infrastructure and the necessity for safe storage systems of the hydrogen because of its highly inflammable nature, still persist. Externally, there are opportunities for significant advancements in high-efficiency technology and the potential for lucrative business ventures in infrastructure development and associated green hydrogen products. Nonetheless, challenges remain, including the substantial capital expenditure for infrastructure and the ambiguous market dynamics. Despite its clean energy credentials and the potential to obviate the need for energy storage systems, hydrogen technology also encounters obstacles in terms of economic viability and technological maturity. Nevertheless, its superior capacity factor, high energy, and power density make it an appealing option for both base load and peak load applications. With opportunities for the technology's seamless integration into existing structures, India could emerge as a global leader in the field. The SWOC analysis of green hydrogen in India is summarised in Table 12.5.

4.2 SWOC Analysis of the Just Energy Transition

Along with the transition to clean energy, a just energy transition (JET) is essential to ensure the equitable distribution of the benefits of clean energy to all. The clean energy transition will transform most fossil-fuel related businesses and occupations and may render fossil-fuel units inoperable and their workforce unemployed. India should prioritise developing alternative uses for these units and creating jobs for their employees. However, rapidly growing non-fossil and RE systems will require different skill sets. Therefore, national policies should invest in training programmes for creating those skills among the unemployed. Worldometer (2024) estimates that the current population of India is over 1.45 billion. Obviously, meeting the energy demand of its huge population is the biggest challenge for India. Most vulnerable communities, informal workers, senior citizens and persons with disabilities, etc., will require that particular attention be given to their compensation and rehabilitation. It may also become necessary to curb possible corruption in providing facilities to affected persons. Addressing these challenges is crucial for managing the

Table 12.5 SWOC analysis of green hydrogen

Internal strengths (S)	Internal weaknesses (W)	External opportunities (O)	External challenges (C)
Policies like the National Green Hydrogen Mission	Lack of infrastructure	Scope for high efficiency technical advancement	Economic viability still to be ascertained
Clean energy source with no toxic emissions; eliminates need for energy storage systems	Need for safe storage system for the hydrogen	Business opportunities in infrastructure development and in associated green hydrogen products	Safety concerns due to highly inflammable nature
Better capacity factor; high energy and power density	Lack of maturity in high efficiency processes such as SOEC	Opportunities in integration with existing structure	High CAPEX infrastructure
Can provide base load and peak load	Economics is lacking for the proficient RE technology	India can emerge as a global leader	Dynamics of market still not clear

clean energy transition effectively and minimising the economic impact on affected workers and businesses.

An earlier survey of ASEAN (Han et al. 2021) has implications for India in that the energy transition will entail issues of higher energy costs, energy affordability, accessibility and security risks along with people's willingness to pay these costs. Another study suggested that economic poverty was a dominant correlative to energy poverty in millions of households in India (Sharma et al. 2019). Increasing per capita income, resulting in high energy consumption, may undermine India's efforts towards sustainable production and consumption of energy (UNDESA 2023). Therefore, providing sustainable energy to all households, improving access, availability and affordability of clean energy is crucial. Presently, India is doing better than other developing countries but several deficiencies in the system of the CJET still exist that may hinder the country's set targets for clean energy for all.

Steps in the right direction include India's efforts for global CJET partnerships like the international solar alliance in collaboration with France. The Indian Ministry of Skills Development and Entrepreneurship, along with the ADB, is developing support facilities for workers in the coal-mining sector. India's CJET should prioritise a substantial reduction in its fossil fuel imports to achieve energy security and sustainable economic growth. The country should also consider developing mechanisms to buffer against the geopolitical risks and trade disputes associated with the production and distribution of RE technologies, minerals, materials, etc., which could affect global energy security and supply chains.

The EU's Carbon Border Adjustment Mechanism (CBAM), effective from 2026, will impose charges on imported goods based on the CO_2 emissions embedded in their production. While such carbon tariffs will reduce global carbon emissions only by less than 0.2% (relative to an emissions trading scheme with a carbon price of USD 108 per metric tonne and no carbon tariff), it may reduce global exports to the EU by around 0.4% and Asia's exports to the EU by around 1.1% (ADB 2024). Therefore, India's quest for a CJET should take into account such international policies as they may increase the cost of its exports and reduce competitiveness in the global markets.

On the positive side, India has a huge opportunity to forge JET partnerships at regional and global levels. Although India's share of contributions to global GHG emissions is large in absolute terms, its per capita emissions are still very low, which weighs in the country's favour in attracting foreign investment in the clean energy sector. While clean energy targets are important for meeting global norms, the JET and creation of jobs in green energy sectors are required to fulfill the needs of the country's huge population. Thus, India should simultaneously focus on creating a robust clean energy system with more jobs, ensuring inclusive growth, provision of sustainable energy for all and socioeconomic development.

The Skill Council for Green Jobs (SCGJ) of the Ministry of Skill Development and Entrepreneurship along with several other ministries and industries is promoting green businesses and jobs for the present and future requirements in various sectors. SCGJ's vision for 2047 in RE, construction, transport, green hydrogen, solid waste management, water management and e-waste management, aims to have a huge pan-India impact. By 2030, the SCGJ targets establishing several programmes in clean and green technologies. These include about one million training programmes and about two million up-skilling and re-skilling programmes through 20 pan-India centres of excellence having 750 affiliated training centres and 7,500 certified trainers. The SCGJ's long-term plans include creation of about 30 to 35 million green jobs and over one million skill training and job facilitation centres. It is proposed to include green energy as a part of every household and industry. All traditional job roles in the fossil fuel sector will be up-skilled to work in green energy sectors and technological advances may further create job opportunities (SCJG 2022).

The SWOC analysis of the JET is summarised in Table 12.6.

5 Conclusions and Policy Relevance

In its quest for a clean and just energy transition (CJET), India's approach is multi-faceted and includes formulating and implementing policies and launching nation-wide schemes to promote various forms of clean energy. Increasing the share of RE will help in ensuring energy security and socio-economic development. Based on a comprehensive review of the literature and a qualitative SWOC analysis, summarised in Tables 12.1, 12.2, 12.3, 12.4, 12.5 and 12.6, the following conclusions are drawn, and policy recommendations are suggested for an effective and sustainable CJET.

Table 12.6 SWOC analysis of the just energy transition

Internal strengths (S)	Internal weaknesses (W)	External opportunities (O)	External challenges (C)
Favourable policies and strategies for growth and job creation in the clean energy sector	Lost businesses and jobs due to transition to non-fossil fuel sectors	Forging global CJET partnerships for attracting investments	International pressure to phase out coal and scale up the RE systems
Environmental benefits of clean energy utilisation	Public resistance, and social conflicts related to the siting of RE projects may delay CJET efforts	Acceleration of support for skills development in fossil-fuel sector workforce	Large number of unemployable workers available for employment in green jobs
Rising per capita income may increase affordability of energy	High cost of RE infrastructure and energy efficiency for small businesses and low-income households	Improving the quality of life	Attractive policies and strategies for green investments

5.1 Conclusions

To accelerate solar energy programmes, extending CAPEX schemes for the industrial sector, at least for small and medium size businesses, could be effective. Although production-linked incentive (PLI) schemes support high efficiency solar PV manufacturers, there is a gap in solar thermal. Since heating consumes about 18% of India's energy consumption, research and development of new products for solar thermal is necessary. Schemes to support residential rooftop power projects and technical upgrading will be required to support hybrid solar panel PV and low-cost maintenance tracking systems. Financial support for roof-top solar programmes in the budget for FY 2024–2025 and the related proposed generation in 10 million Indian households are welcome. These households can supply the surplus electricity generated to the grid in exchange for 300 free units of electricity per month. Such schemes can go a long way in accelerating India's efforts towards accomplishing the CJET.

To promote wind energy, there are policies to provide loans and interest rebates for replacing the old systems with the latest wind turbines. The national policy on wind-solar hybrid provides a framework for promotion of large grid connected systems for the optimal and efficient use of land and transmission infrastructure. Financial and technological support will be required for installation of vertical axis wind turbines (VAWT) in residential areas, small-scale industries and remote locations. The use of flying (airborne kite type) turbines at high wind speeds and offshore wind power projects with storage systems could eliminate the risk of intermittency, lower the capacity factor and avoid socio-economic issues involved in land acquisition.

Although hydropower is a clean energy source that could be used as a base load, it could potentially disrupt the topography and wildlife that may be dependent on the water streams. While commissioning large dams, particularly in areas where high land cost may be a hindrance, pumped hydro energy could potentially lead to more solar and wind power plant installations for efficient use of clean energy.

Enhanced production of biofuels can provide multiple benefits such as increasing farmers' income, savings on foreign currency expenditure and reducing dependence on fossil fuel imports, and thus develop rural infrastructure, generate rural employment, etc. Also, the judicious and considerate location of biofuel crops can enrich the green cover, which might be helpful in earning carbon credits and, therefore, their promotion could immensely benefit India. It is of course necessary to take a priori measures, such as growing biofuel crops, as far as possible on non-crops lands such as waste lands, so that fuel crops do not adversely affect supplies of food and fodder crops.

The National Hydrogen Mission 2023 may have a significant effect on the decarbonisation of the economy, may reduce reliance on fossil fuel imports, and may position India as a leader in the technology and market aspects of green hydrogen. The Mission is expected to facilitate deployment of this ecosystem and create opportunities for innovation and investments across the related value chain, translating into investments, jobs and economic growth.

Along with the targeted and increased share of various clean energy forms, it is very important that the benefits of the energy transition are inclusive and encompass economically weaker households and vulnerable communities. The objective of a clean and just energy transition should be integrated and include not only provision of clean energy to all but also the creation of large-scale employment including for those rendered unemployed due to the closing of fossil fuel plants.

5.2 Policy Relevance

- India's policies for increasing the share of various forms of clean energy have set quite ambitious targets, which, under the business-as-usual scenario, seem achievable. However, their pan-India implementation is necessary and, therefore all state governments should follow the GoI central planning policies. Conflicts between the GoI and state policies may obstruct or delay the country's CJET targets. Therefore, close coordination of Central and State governments, irrespective of their political orientation, is of vital importance.
- Timely implementation of policies for the promotion of various forms of RE and strict monitoring of the process are essential. Bureaucratic hurdles and the possibility of corruption in providing licences, incentives, loans and tax relaxations should be avoided. Financial incentives and technological upgrading will help pumped and other hydro projects with solar and wind. Extreme care is needed to avoid fuel-food-fodder conflict; the use of waste lands for fuel crops, solar and wind energy maximise the benefits of RE development. By overcoming financial and technological challenges in production, storage and transportation of green hydrogen, India could become a sustainable low-carbon economy.

- The possibility of India achieving its clean energy targets, both short-term by 2030 and long-term by 2070, is high. However, as regards the just energy transition, India may face multiple challenges such as growing demand for energy, employment and quality of life. Provision of clean and affordable energy is still a dream to a large section of the population. Due to heightened unemployment from discarded fossil fuel units, sluggish progress in the JET is expected in the short term. With careful planning and building JET-Ps at the national and international levels, the country can address financial and socioeconomic challenges and achieve JET targets too.
- India aims to be the world's third largest economy by the end of this decade, and an energy independent and developed country by 2047. These targets seem difficult without increasing the country's industrial output, which would result in higher energy demand and GHG emissions without RE. It is the right time for India to seize this opportunity by increasing the share of clean energy in its energy mix. By balancing its economic progress with social achievements, India can set an example for other developing economies of the world and meet its CJET goals well ahead of 2070.

Acknowledgements The authors sincerely acknowledge the valuable comments and suggestions of the referees—Prof. Muyi Yang of AIT, Thailand and Prof. Xunpeng Shi of UTS Australia, who helped in improving this study.

References

ADB (Asian Development Bank) (2023) Ensuring a just transition is key to India's energy transition goals. https://www.adb.org/- news/features/ensuring-just-transition-key-india-energy-transition-goals [accessed 6 June 2023]

ADB (Asian Development Bank) (2024) EU carbon tariff likely to have limited impact on emissions without global efforts. https://www.adb.org/news/eu-carbon-tariff-likely-have-limited-impact-emissions-without-global-efforts [accessed on 4 March 2024]

Anjanappa J (2023) Just transition in India: urgency to address challenges for sustainable and equitable development. SSRN Electr J. https://papers.ssrn.com/sol3/papers.cfm?abstract_id=4503101 [accessed 17 January 2025]

Bedi HP (2021) Solar power for some? Energy transition injustices in Kerala, India. Environ Plan E Nat Space 5(3):1146–1163

Bhushan C, Banerjee S (2023) Just energy transition for India: policies, plans and institutional mechanism. New Delhi: International Forum for Environment, Sustainability and Technology (iFOREST)

Birol F, Kant A (2022) India's clean energy transition is rapidly underway, benefiting the entire world. Paris: IEA (first published by *The Times of India*). https://www.iea.org/commentaries/india-s-clean-energy-transition-is-rapidly-underway-benefiting-the-entire-world [accessed 15 January 2024]

Carbon Independent (2024) The global CO_2 budget runs out in 7 Years. https://www.carbonindependent.org/54.html [accessed 24 February 2024]

CAT (Climate Action Tracker) (2023) India data. https://climateactiontracker.org/countries/india/ [accessed 30 May 2023]

CEA (Central Electricity Authority, India) (2022) Report on twentieth electric power survey of India. https://cea.nic.in/wp-content/uploads/ps_lf/2023/02/Volume_I_Report_of_20th_Electric_Power_Survey.pdf [accessed 2 December 2024]

Cronkite News (2025) Trump's vow to repeal Biden regulations on carbon from coal-fired power plants will hamper fight against climate change, critics warn. https://cronkitenews.azpbs.org/2024/12/18/donald-trump-end-carbon-caps-coal-fired-power-plants/ [accessed 15 January 2025]

European Commission (2023) EDGAR - emissions database for global atmospheric research, country fact sheet, India. https://edgar.jrc.ec.europa.eu/country_profile/IND [accessed 5 June, 2023]

Haldar S, Peddibhotla A, Bazaz A (2023) Analysing intersections of justice with energy transitions in India - a systematic literature review. Energy Res Soc Sci 98:103010

Han P, Kimura F, Arima J (2021) ASEAN's energy transition towards cleaner energy system: energy modelling scenarios and policy implications. Sustainability 13(5):2819

Hingne A, Swami D (2023) Contextualizing just transitions: contours of a just low carbon pathway for India. WRI (Word Resources Institute). https://wri-india.org/blog/contextualizing-just-transitions-contours-just-low-carbon-pathway-india#:~:text=Almost%203.6%20million%20people%20in,sector-%20(Pai%2C%202021) [accessed 29 March 2024]

IEA (2022a) CO_2 emissions in 2022. Paris. https://www.iea.org/reports/co2-emissions-in-2022 [accessed 25 May 2023]

IEA (2022b) Global energy review: CO_2 emissions in 2021. Paris. Available at https://www.iea.org/reports/global-energy-review-co2-emissions-in-2021-2 [accessed 21 May 2023]

IEA (2022c) World energy employment. Paris. https://www.iea.org/reports/world-energy-employment [accessed 4 February 2024]

IEA Bioenergy (2021) India biofuel economy roadmap – challenges and prospects. *IEA Bioenergy Task 39 Newsletter Issue #56*. https://www.ieabioenergy.com/blog/publications/india-biofuel-economy-roadmap-challenges-prospects [accessed 25 January 2024]

iFOREST (International Forum for Environment, Sustainability and Technology) (2024) Just energy transition in Maharashtra, an opportunity for green growth and green jobs, Report of the International Forum for Environment, Sustainability and Technology (iFOREST), New Delhi, released 2 February 2024. https://iforest.global/events/just-energy-transition-in-maharashtra-to-support-green-growth-and-green-jobs-meeting-report-release/ [accessed 3 December 2024]

Indrajayanthan V et al. (2022). Investigation on current and prospective energy transition scenarios in Indian landscape using integrated SWOT-MCDA methodology. Sustainability 14.9:4940. https://www.mdpi.com/2071-1050/14/9/4940 [accessed 3 December 2024]

IPCC (2021) IPCC sixth assessment report, the physical science basis. https://www.ipcc.ch/report/ar6/wg1/ [accessed 26 January 2024]

IREDA (Indian Renewable Energy Agency) (2024) Hydro Energy. https://www.ireda.in/hydro-energy [accessed 26 January 2024]

IRENA (International Renewable Energy Agency) (2019) A new world: the geopolitics of the energy transformation. https://www.irena.org/publications/2019/Jan/ [accessed 15 January 2024]

Kenton W (2024) How to perform a SWOT analysis. Investopedia. https://www.investopedia.com/terms/s/swot.asp [accessed 3 December 2024]

Koshy Jacob (2023) Despite subsidies, rooftop solar still too expensive. *The Hindu*, 17 November 2023. https://www.thehindu.com/news/-national/despite-subsidies-rooftop-solar-still-too-expensive-study/article67541086.ece [accessed 2 December, 2024]

Lakic I et al. (2023) A just energy transition takes an ecosystem. BCG (Boston Consulting Group). https://www.bcg.com/publications/2023/exploring-challenges-of-just-transition [accessed 2 December 2024]

Long WJ (2021) A Buddhist approach to international relations: radical interdependence. Cham: Palgrave MacMillian-Springer Nature. Download from https://link.springer.com/book/https://doi.org/10.1007/978-3-030-68042-8

McCauley D, Pettigrew K (2023) Building a just transition in Asia-pacific: four strategies for reducing fossil fuel dependence and investing in clean energy. Energy Policy 183:113808. https://doi.org/10.1016/j.enpol.2023.113808
MNRE (Ministry of New and Renewable Energy, Government of India) (2025) Physical achievements. https://mnre.gov.in/en/physical-progress/ [accessed 13 January 2025]
MoC (2024) Ministry of coal, government of India. https://coal.gov.in/en/public-information/reports/annual-reports/annual-report-2022-23 [accessed 25 February 2024]
MoP (Ministry of Power, India) (2025) Power sector at a glance "ALL INDIA". https://powermin.gov.in/sites/default/files/uploads/power_sector_at_glance_Nov_2024.pdf [accessed 14 January 2025]
NBP (Nuclear Business Platform) (2024) High growth prospects for clean hydrogen in India. https://www.nuclearbusiness-platform.com/media/insights/high-growth-prospects-for-clean-hydrogen-in-india [accessed 19 March 2024]
Neefjes K, Ngo Thi To Nhien (2021) Prospects for a socially just energy transition in Viet Nam: 2021 and beyond. https://library.fes.de/pdf-files/bueros/vietnam/18201-20210907.pdf [accessed 4 February 2024]
NITI Aayog and Rocky Mountain Institute (RMI) (2020) Towards a clean energy economy: post COVID-19 opportunities for India's energy and mobility sectors. https://www.niti.gov.in/sites/default/files/2023-02/India_Green_Stimulus_Report_NITI_VF_June_29.pdf [accessed 4 December, 2024]
ORF (Observer Research Foundation) (2022) Just transition declaration: can it be the way towards achieving universal access to clean cooking fuels and technologies? https://www.orfonline.org/expert-speak/just-transition-declaration-can-it-be-the-way-towards-achieving-universal-access-to-clean-cooking-fuels-and-technologies [accessed 3 December 2024]
Rahut DB et al. (2024) Examining energy justice: empirical analysis of clean cooking transition across social groups in India, 2004–2018. Renew Sust Energy Rev 193(C). https://doi.org/10.1016/j.rser.2023.114260 [accessed 24 March 2024]
RBI (2023) Report on currency and finance 2022–23: towards a greener cleaner India. https://rbidocs.rbi.org.in/rdocs/Publications/PDFs/RCF03052023395FAF37181E40188BAD3AFA59BF3907.PDF [accessed 15 January 2025]
Reddy A (2025) Union budget 2024 | India needs $1.4 trillion to turn net-zero economy by 2070. *Deccan Herald*, 22 July. https://www.deccanherald.com/business/union-budget/india-needs-1-4-trillion-to-turn-net-zero-economy-by-2070-3116580 [15 January 2025]
SCGJ (Skill Council for Green Jobs) (2022) Green jobs handbook. https://sscgj.in/wp-content/uploads/2024/02/Green-Jobs-Handbook-SCGJ.pdf [accessed 17 March 2024]
Sharma P et al. (2024) Chance of a lifetime: can India show the developing world a unique path to net zero? https://www.woodmac.com/horizons/india-net-zero-path [accessed 26 November 2024]
Sharma SV et al. (2024) India's cross border electricity trade with BIMSTEC countries, in *Large-Scale Development of Renewables in the ASEAN. Economics, Law, and Institutions in Asia Pacific,* ed. Han Phoumin et al. Singapore: Springer
Sharma SV, Han P, Sharma VK (2019) Socio-economic determinants of energy poverty amongst Indian households: a case study of Mumbai. Energy Policy 132:1184–1190
Sharma SV, Han P, Sharma VK (2023) The effect of energy sector reforms on promotion of renewable electricity and social welfare in India, in *Energy Market Reforms in the ASEAN, China, India and Japan*, ed. Han Phoumin et al. Singapore: World Scientific
Statista (2024) Value of petroleum products imported into India from financial year 2011 to 2023. https://www.statista.com/statistics/625218/import-value-of-petroleum-india/ [accessed 2 March 2024]
Uhunamure SE, Shale K (2021) A SWOT analysis approach for a sustainable transition to renewable energy in South Africa. Sustainability 13:3933. https://doi.org/10.3390/su13073933
UNESCAP (United Nations Economic and Social Commission for Asia and the Pacific) (2023) Forging the right partnerships for climate-resilient infrastructure development

in Asia and the pacific. https://www.unescap.org/blog/forging-right-partnerships-climate-resilient-infrastructure-development-asia-and-pacific [accessed 3 December 2024]
UNDESA (United Nations Department of Economic and Social Affairs) (2023) India to Overtake China as world's most populous country in April 2023, United Nations Projects. https://www.un.org/en/desa/india-overtake-china-world-most-populous-country-april-2023-united-nations-projects [accessed 31 May 2023]
Worldometer (2024) India's Population (Live). https://www.worldometers.info/world-population/india-population/ [accessed 27 February 2024]
Yang M, Sharma D, Shi X (2022) Policy entry points for facilitating a transition towards a low-carbon electricity future. Front Eng Manag 9:462–472. https://doi.org/10.1007/s42524-022-0214-4

GPSR Compliance

The European Union's (EU) General Product Safety Regulation (GPSR) is a set of rules that requires consumer products to be safe and our obligations to ensure this.

If you have any concerns about our products, you can contact us on ProductSafety@springernature.com

In case Publisher is established outside the EU, the EU authorized representative is:

Springer Nature Customer Service Center GmbH
Europaplatz 3
69115 Heidelberg, Germany

Batch number: 10725825

Printed by Printforce, the Netherlands